CW00693640

WOODWORK
PATTERN BOOK

WOODWORK PATTERN BOOK

80 PROJECTS TO MAKE BY HAND

A W P Kettless

BATSFORD

To my wife Rose-Mary
who has cheerfully endured considerable inconvenience
in the cause of craftsmanship

First published in the United Kingdom in 1963

Revised and updated edition published in 2007 by
Batsford
10 Southcombe Street
London W14 0RA

An imprint of Anova Books Company Ltd

ISBN-10: 0 7134 9020 9
ISBN-13: 978 0 7134 9020 6

A CIP catalogue record for this book is available from the British Library.

15 14 13 12 10 09 08 07
10 9 8 7 6 5 4 3 2 1

Typeset by SX Composing DTP, England
Printed in China

This book can be ordered direct from the publisher at the website:
www.anovabooks.com
Or try your local bookshop

Note: This book was originally published in 1963 and therefore some of the working methods described are more traditional than modern.

Preface to the 1963 edition

This book has been written with the hope that it will be of some assistance to craft teachers, craftsmen, students and all others interested in the craft of woodworking; to encourage a good standard of design and craftsmanship and inculcate a love for that unique and satisfying material – wood.

The designs have been arranged, as far as possible, progressively. They cater for the development of fundamental tool operations and woodworking techniques, and where it is felt to be necessary full constructional details are given. In the early stages the actual making of something tangible and knowledge of the materials and processes involved in its production is of great value to the development of the student. The drawings are intended to give adequate information for use in design and drawing classes.

The designs should be used as the basis from which an infinite variety of work can be produced, and students should be encouraged to adopt their own innovations. The book contains information on a wide variety of woodworking subjects, including cabinet and chair making, carpentry and joinery, pattern making and boatbuilding. Carving, veneering, laminating, steam bending, and the use of recently developed materials are dealt with where the need arises.

If this book helps all those concerned with woodwork, whether as established craftsmen, or learners in schools and colleges, to use wood to its fullest capacity, the work which has gone into its preparation will have been well worth while.

My sincere thanks are due to Mr E. F. Marshall, Principal of Shoreditch Training College, for facilities made available. To Mr R. A. Williams, Deputy Principal and Head of the Craft Department, for advice kindly given. I am also indebted to my colleague Mr W. E. Sawdy, Principal Lecturer, who gave generously of his time and experience in the reading of the manuscript, for which I am most grateful.

Alonzo Wm Kettless
Surrey, 1963

Contents

Basic Kit of Tools

Saws

Cross-cut saw, 660mm (26in), 8–9 points
Tenon saw, 350mm (14in), 14 points
Dovetail saw, 200mm (8in), 18–22 points
Coping saw

Planes

Jack plane (wood), 57mm (2¼in) cutter
Smoothing plane (metal), 60mm (2⅜in) cutter
Jack plane (metal), 375mm (15in), 60mm (2⅜in) cutter
Rebate plane (metal, with adjustable fence)
Spokeshave, flat 54mm (2⅛in)
Spokeshave, round 54mm (2⅛in)
Wood file, 200mm (8in)
Wood rasp, 200mm (8in)
2 Cabinet scrapers 125mm (5in), one for shaped work
Cork rubber

Marking and Testing Tools

Folding rule, 600mm (24in)
Steel rule, 300mm (12in)
Marking knife
Marking gauge
Mortise gauge
Cutting gauge
Try square, 150mm (6in)
Combination square, 300mm (12in)
Winding strips
Sliding bevel

Tools for Boring

Brace 200mm (8in) sweep
Twist bits, 6.5mm (¼in), 8.0mm (5/16in), 9.5mm (⅜in), 12.5mm (½in), 16.0mm (⅝in)
Shell bits, 3mm (⅛in), 4mm/5mm (3/16in)
Drills, twist, 1.6mm–6.5mm (1/16in–¼in)
Countersinks, rosehead and snailhead, 13mm (½in)
Bradawl
Wheelbrace

Chisels

Firmer, 3mm (⅛in), 6mm (¼in), 13mm (½in), 25mm (1in)
Bevelled edge firmer, 6mm (¼in), 10mm (⅜in), 20mm (¾in), 32mm (1¼in)
Sash mortise chisels, 6mm (¼in), 8mm (5/16in)
Gouge, 13mm (½in) firmer
Gouge, 6mm (¼in) scribing

Sharpening Accessories

Oilstone, fine, 200mm × 50mm × 25mm (8in × 2in × 1in) in box
Oilstone, medium, 200mm × 50mm × 25mm (8in × 2in × 1in) in box
Oilstone slip, 100mm (4in)
Oilcan
1 piece of leather, 200mm × 50mm (8in × 2in)

Miscellaneous

Mallet
Hammer, Warrington, 225g (8 oz)
Hammer, pattern makers, 75g (3 oz)
Pincers, 200mm (8in)
Screwdriver, cabinet pattern, 200mm (8in)
Screwdriver, ratchet, 125mm (5in)
Nail punches, 1 small
Nail punches, 1 medium
'G' cramps, 2
Thumb screws, 6
Raw linseed oil
White polish

Tools not included in Basic Kit are specified after the cutting list in each job.

Note: sizes given in designs on pages 10–64 are for timber as sawn, with an allowance of 3mm (⅛in) in width and thickness for planing. From page 66 onwards, all sizes given in the cutting lists, unless otherwise stated, are finished sizes.

Pencil Holder

This gives practice in planing, use of testing and marking out tools, sawing, chiselling, and the boring of holes to a given depth; making and using a thumb gauge; working of a simple chamfer. It encourages an appreciation of the properties of wood and the problems involved in its working, and aids familiarity with important and fundamental terms such as *face side* and *face edge.*

Method

1. Planing face side. Select best side of material, and plane flat, using a jack plane for this operation. Make frequent tests with a straight edge and parallel or winding strips. Apply face side mark when true.
2. Select best edge, place wood in vice and plane edges square with face side. Make frequent tests with straight edge and try square, apply face edge mark when true.
3. *Gauging width:* set marking gauge to 40mm (1½in) and gauge the width from the face edge. Remove waste with jack plane.
4. *Gauging thickness:* set marking gauge to thickness 20mm (¾in) and gauge the thickness all round from the face side. Remove the waste with jack plane. A sharp pencil run down the gauge line often makes it easier to see.
5. *Marking out:* using a marking knife and try square, mark out length of stand leaving about 13mm (½in) waste at each end. The diagram shows method of marking out and finding centres of holes. With brace and an 8mm (5⁄16in) twist bit bore the holes, maintaining the bit in an upright position. Cut material to length. Make thumb gauge and mark out chamfer as shown in isometric view. Work chamfer on sides with a smoothing plane. With a 25mm (1in) chisel and using a shearing action make end chamfers.
6. Clean up with a smoothing plane.
7. *Finish:* white polish, lightly applied with a rag.

Material

Selected pine, 300mm × 50mm × 25mm (12in × 2in × 1in). These sizes allow for practice in planing techniques.

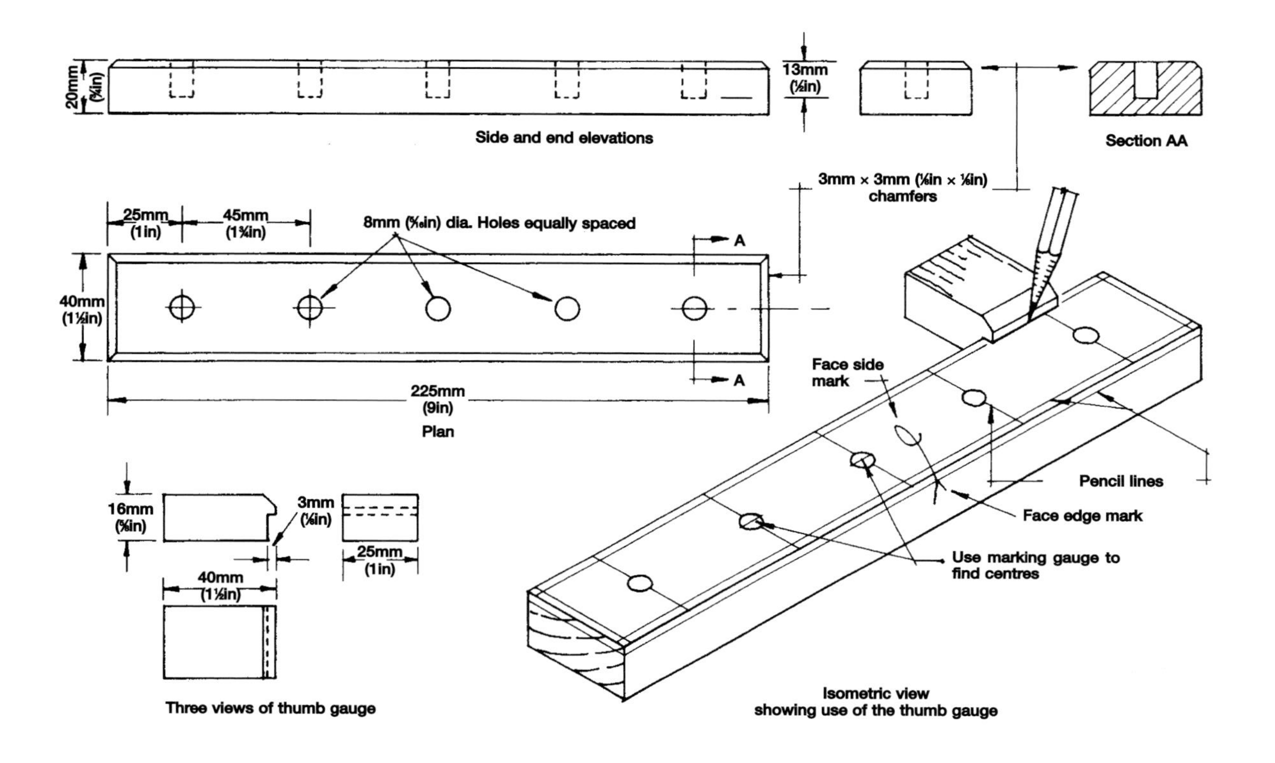

20mm (¾in)
13mm (½in)
Side and end elevations
Section AA
3mm × 3mm (⅛in × ⅛in) chamfers
25mm (1in)
45mm (1¾in)
8mm (5⁄16in) dia. Holes equally spaced
A
A
40mm (1½in)
225mm (9in)
Plan
Face side mark
Pencil lines
Face edge mark
Use marking gauge to find centres
16mm (⅝in)
3mm (⅛in)
25mm (1in)
40mm (1½in)
Three views of thumb gauge
Isometric view showing use of the thumb gauge

Chisel Rack

This is a further planing, marking out, sawing and grooving exercise; also an introduction to plywood, glue, panel pins and wood finishing, and the use of wood drills and countersink. The rack is designed to hold a 6mm (¼in) sash mortise chisel and 6mm, 13mm, 20mm and 25mm (¼in, ½in, ¾in and 1in) bevelled edge firmer chisels.

Method

1. Plane material to dimensions as given in drawing.
2. Mark out length of rack and position of grooves with a marking knife, and use a pencil on the edges of the work. Gauge depth of grooves marking only the spaces to be removed. With thumb gauge and pencil mark the chamfers.
3. Cut grooves with dovetail saw, making sure the saw kerf is in the waste, and stops at the gauge line. Place work in vice and remove waste, making the bottom of the grooves flat and taking care not to chisel below the line.
4. Work chamfers as in previous job.
5. Mark out plywood back and cut to size with a dovetail saw. Plane the edges with a smoothing plane, shape corners with coping saw and finish with a wood file. Drill and countersink for holes as shown. Using a cork rubber and a piece of No 1½ glasspaper clean up plywood back. Clean up rack with smoothing plane.
6. Carefully apply glue to back and rack, and fix with eight 16mm (⅝in) panel pins. Clean off surplus glue with a clean damp cloth. When dry, glasspaper lightly.
7. *Finish:* brush on a thin coat of white polish.

Material

Selected pine, 250mm × 50mm × 25mm (10in × 2in × 1in),
plywood, 290mm × 63mm × 4mm (11½in × 2½in × 3/16in).

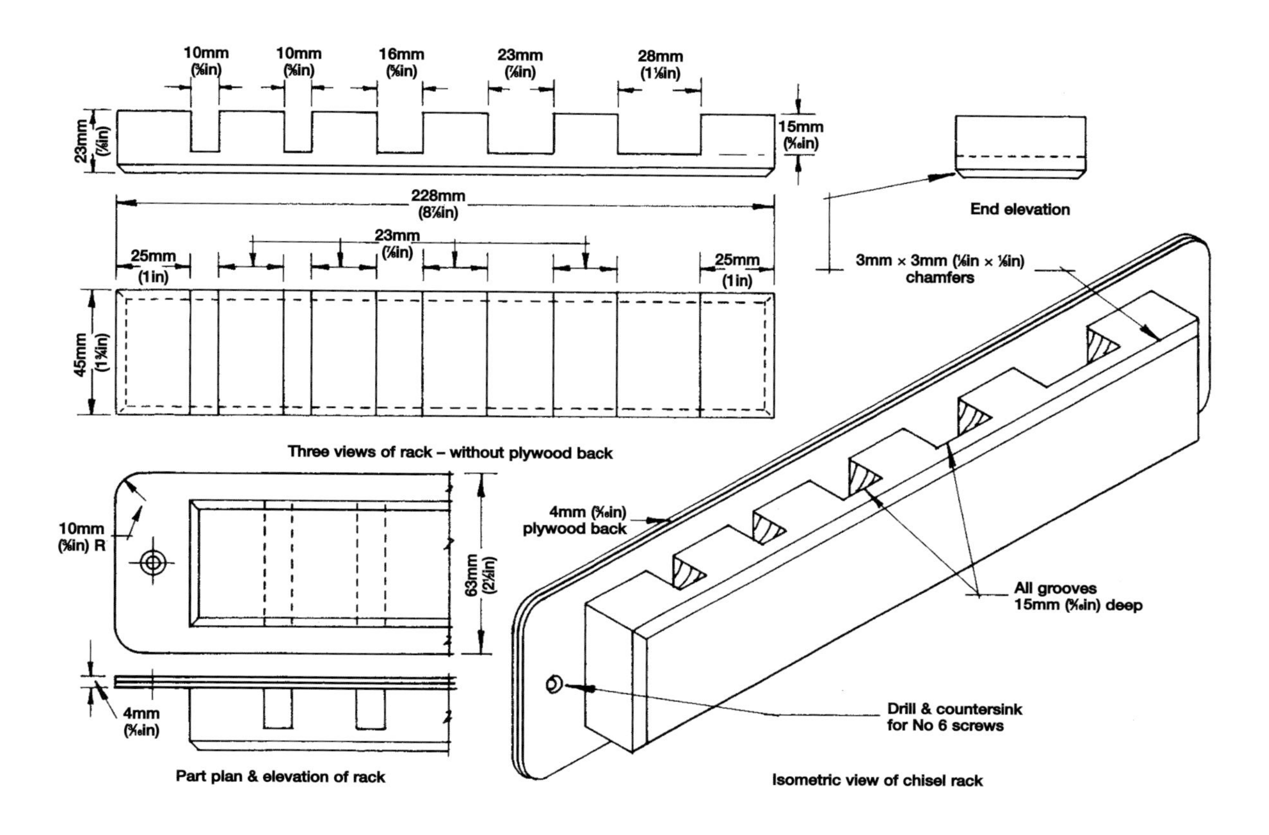

10mm (⅜in)
10mm (⅜in)
16mm (⅝in)
23mm (⅞in)
28mm (1⅛in)
23mm (⅞in)
15mm (9/16in)
228mm (8⅞in)
23mm (⅞in)
25mm (1in)
25mm (1in)
45mm (1¾in)
End elevation
3mm × 3mm (⅛in × ⅛in) chamfers
Three views of rack – without plywood back
10mm (⅜in) R
63mm (2½in)
4mm (3/16in)
Part plan & elevation of rack
4mm (3/16in) plywood back
All grooves 15mm (9/16in) deep
Drill & countersink for No 6 screws
Isometric view of chisel rack

Spade Cleaner

This article will give further practice in planing techniques, marking out, boring holes, and an introduction to horizontal and vertical paring.

Method

1. Plane material to width and thickness as given in drawing.
2. Mark out length with marking knife and using, preferably, an 'H' pencil mark out on the face side all the lines and centres as shown in the plan. Mark edge as shown in the elevation, thus completing the marking out except for the 4mm (3/16in) at bevelled end. This is marked out with thumb gauge after sawing off to cut line.
3. Place width of material in the vice, and using a large chisel with a shearing action, make the end bevel.
4. Place the thickness of the material in the vice, and make a saw kerf nearly 10mm (3/8in) deep to locate the intersecting surfaces (see plan) for horizontal paring: chisel from each side until the bottom of the saw kerf is reached, repeat on the other side.
5. Bore hole.
6. Saw off waste at end. Vertical paring: chisel the semicircular end.
7. Clean up with smoothing plane.
8. *Finish:* brush on a thin coat of clear varnish.

Material

Selected pine, 200mm × 50mm × 20mm (8in × 2in × 3/4in).

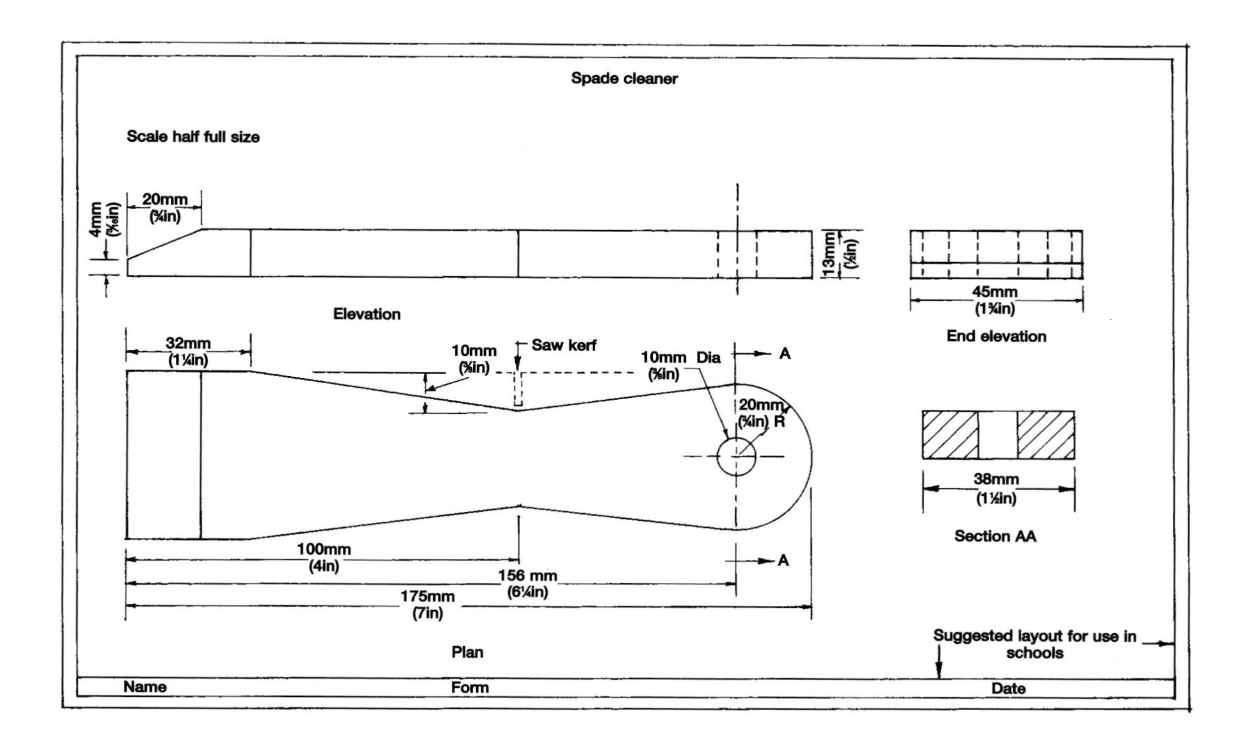
Spade cleaner
Scale half full size
20mm
(¾in)
4mm
(3/16in)
13mm
(½in)
45mm
(1¾in)
Elevation
End elevation
32mm
(1¼in)
10mm
(⅜in)
Saw kerf
10mm Dia
(⅜in)
A
20mm
(¾in) R
38mm
(1½in)
Section AA
100mm
(4in)
156 mm
(6¼in)
175mm
(7in)
A
Plan
Suggested layout for use in schools
Name
Form
Date

Pen Rest

This pen rest involves further exercises in planing techniques, marking out, boring of holes, vertical paring. It gives an introduction to the housing joint, and use of the shooting board when planing end grain.

Method

1. Prepare material to given sizes.
2. Using a marking knife set out length of base and position of rests, and gauge 3mm (⅛in) for depth of housing. A pictorial view of a housing joint is shown on page 19.
3. Cut grooves keeping saw kerfs in the waste, and remove waste with a 10mm (⅜in) chisel; make bottom of grooves flat and saw base to length.
4. Chisel quadrant shape at ends and with the aid of a shooting board plane ends to cut lines. Work chamfers, using a flat-bottom spokeshave for shaped ends.
5. Mark out rests, bore holes and shape ends.
6. Fit, clean up and assemble rests.
7. Clean up base and glue rests in position.
8. *Finish:* one coat of brush polish, when dry, lightly rub down with fine glasspaper, and wax.

Material

Selected pine or abura.

Cutting list

Description	Length	Width	Thickness
base	200mm (8in)	82mm (3¼in)	20mm (¾in)
rests	175mm (7in)	23mm (⅞in)	20mm (¾in)

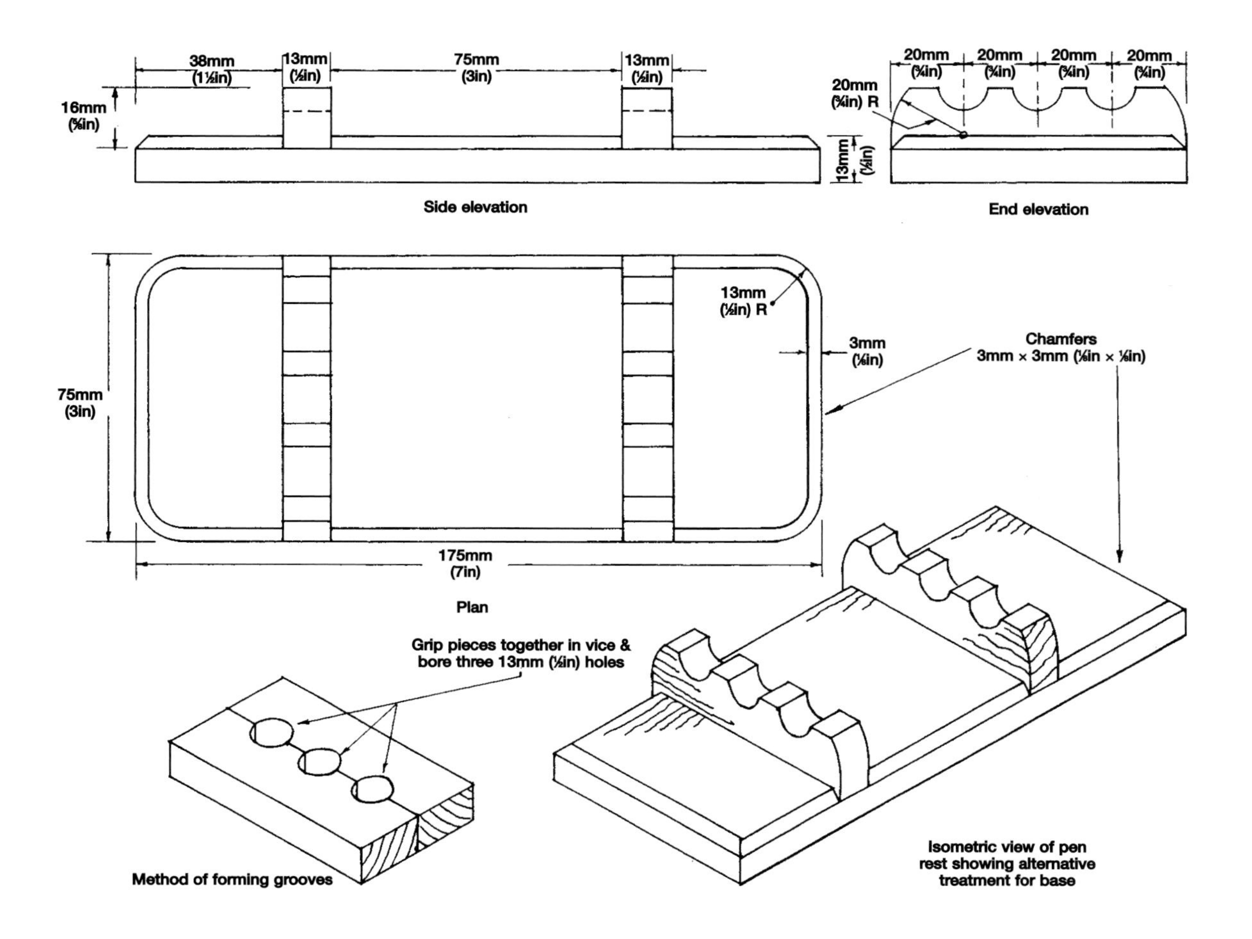
38mm
(1½in)
13mm
(½in)
75mm
(3in)
13mm
(½in)
16mm
(⅝in)
Side elevation
20mm
(¾in)
20mm
(¾in)
20mm
(¾in)
20mm
(¾in)
20mm
(¾in) R
13mm
(½in)
End elevation
13mm
(½in) R
3mm
(⅛in)
Chamfers
3mm × 3mm (⅛in × ⅛in)
75mm
(3in)
175mm
(7in)
Plan
Grip pieces together in vice &
bore three 13mm (½in) holes
Method of forming grooves
Isometric view of pen
rest showing alternative
treatment for base

Plant Stand

The plant stand gives further practice in planing techniques – including use of the shooting board – sawing, chiselling, use of the round and flat bottom spokeshaves, router, and coping saw. The design incorporates a simple through housing joint (see pictorial view) and gives an opportunity for accurate marking out and working to given dimensions.

Method

1. Prepare material to given sizes.
2. Mark out ends in pairs, in one length, and cut grooves, finishing to gauge lines with router.
3. Complete as much as possible of the shaping before separating ends.
4. Mark out shelf, cut and shoot ends, bevel the sides, and fit shelf. Round the corners as shown in drawing.
5. Cut plywood edgings to length and shape.
6. Clean up and chamfer finger grip with round bottom spokeshave and prepare ends, shelf and edging for gluing up.
7. Fix ply edging to shelf using glue and 16mm (⅝in) panel pins, punch heads below the surface.
8. Fix shelf to ends with glue and 25mm (1in) panel pins. Test to ensure that the ends are square with shelf.
9. *Finish:* hard gloss paint, to suit colour scheme. Give stand one priming coat, stop up all holes, rub down and finish with hard gloss paint.

Material

Selected pine.

Cutting list

Description	Length	Width	Thickness
base	325mm (1ft 1in)	140mm (5½in)	16mm (⅝in)
ends	300mm (1ft)	120mm (4¾in)	16mm (⅝in)
2 plywood edgings	275mm (11in)	35mm (1⅜in)	5mm (3/16in)

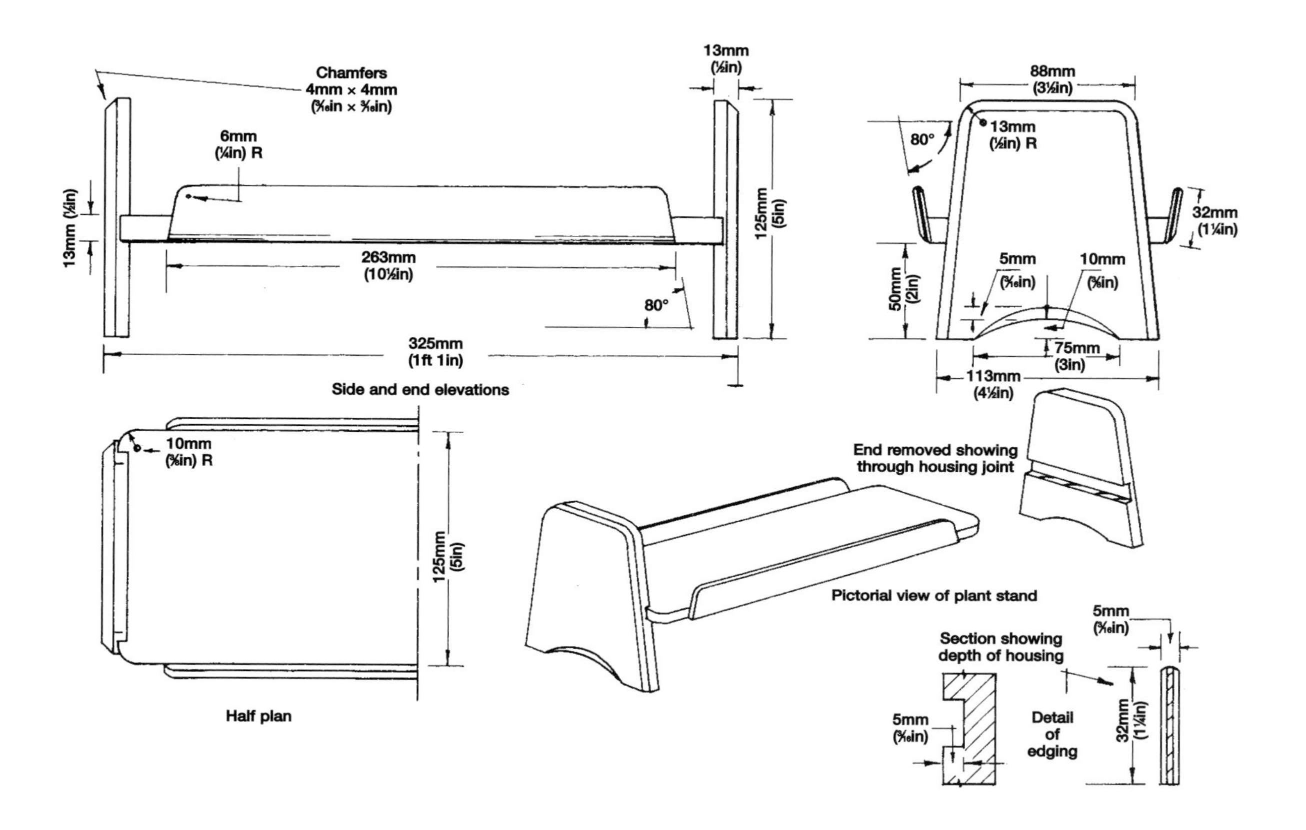

Side and end elevations

Half plan

Toast Rack

This toast rack gives further experience in the use of plywood and its working qualities; also an introduction to the stopped housing joint and the technique of polishing surfaces before gluing up.

Method

1. Prepare material.
2. Mark out base and cut grooves, finish to depth with router.
3. Mark out divisions and handle, as given in drawing. Use a 20mm (¾in) centre-bit to bore hole in handle. With a dovetail saw carefully cut to size. Finish radius with wood file, and soften all edges with glasspaper.
4. Fit all parts into position testing for upright.
5. Bevel and chamfer base and clean up for polishing.
6. Mask all joints to protect gluing surfaces, and lightly polish base and divisions.
7. Glue up, taking care to remove surplus glue.
8. When dry lightly rub down with flour glasspaper, to give a matt finish.

Material

Sycamore with mahogany plywood divisions.

Cutting list

Description	Length	Width	Thickness
base	163mm (6½in)	82mm (3¼in)	16mm (⅝in)
divisions	350mm (1ft 2in)	75mm (3in)	6mm (¼in)

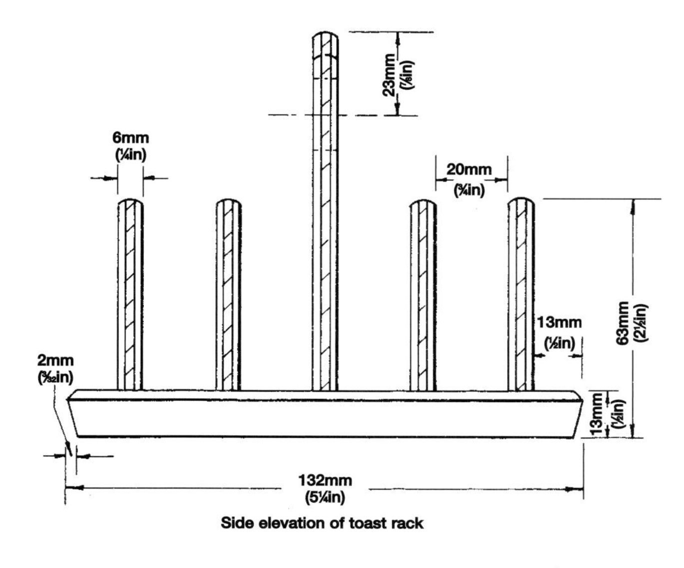

Side elevation of toast rack

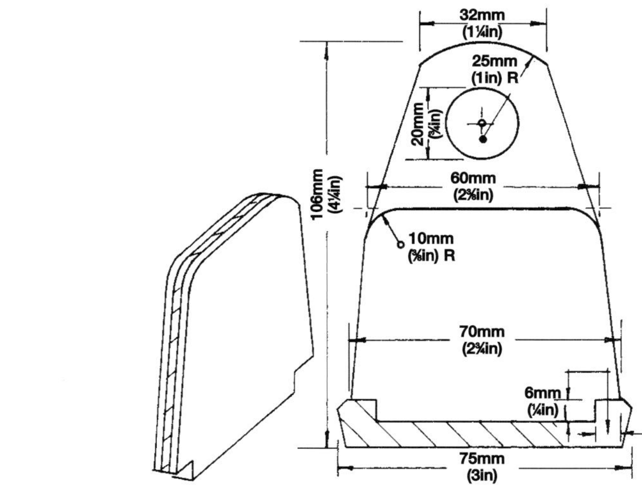

Half full-size details of divisions

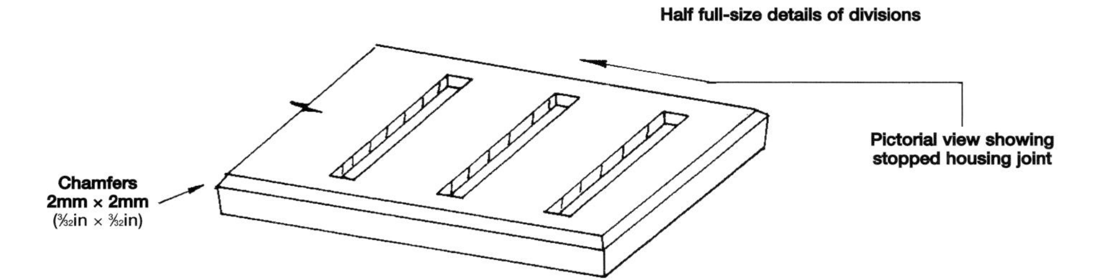

Table Mat Stand

The making of this stand gives an opportunity for individual design, the development of a sense of proportion and form and the use of new materials and contrasting woods.

Method

1. Prepare material.
2. Mark out base and spokeshave to given shape. For alternative base with 6mm (¼in) radius at corners, remove waste – saw kerf down to a gauge line – with a 25mm (1in) chisel and clean up ends of recess with a 6mm (¼in) scribing gouge.
3. Cut base to length and bevel ends.
4. Mark out plywood, using the base to give shape at bottom, cut to shape with coping and dovetail saws. Plane edges and soften with glasspaper wrapped round a cork rubber. Use a flat-bottom spokeshave for shaped top, and a wood file for bottom shaping.
5. Screw on sides to base and test for alignment. Remove screws, clean up all surfaces, and prepare for polishing, masking all joints as necessary.
6. Polish base and inner surfaces of sides.
7. Glue up and replace screws, file to clean flush surface, and complete polishing.

Material

Abura or sycamore, with mahogany plywood side pieces.

Cutting list

Description	Length	Width	Thickness
1 base	150mm (6in)	45mm (1¾in)	20mm (¾in)
2 side pieces	125mm (5in)	90mm (3½in)	4mm (3/16in)

Table-mat sizes to suit own requirements.

Suggested Material

Plywood or plastic-faced hardboard.

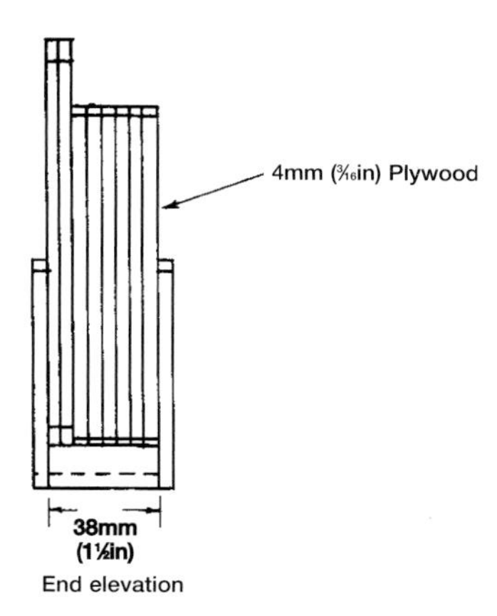

End elevation

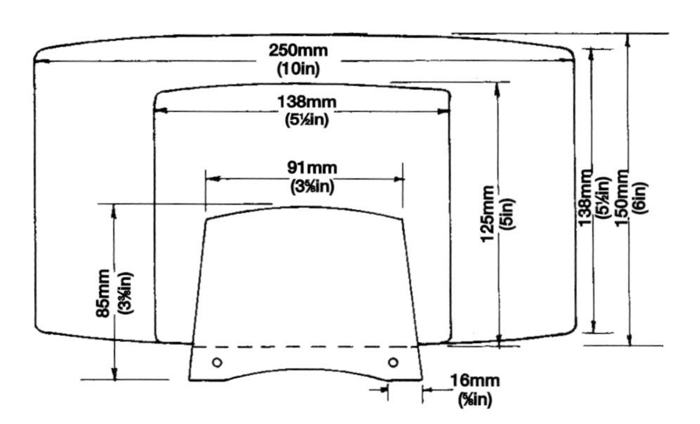

Front elevation

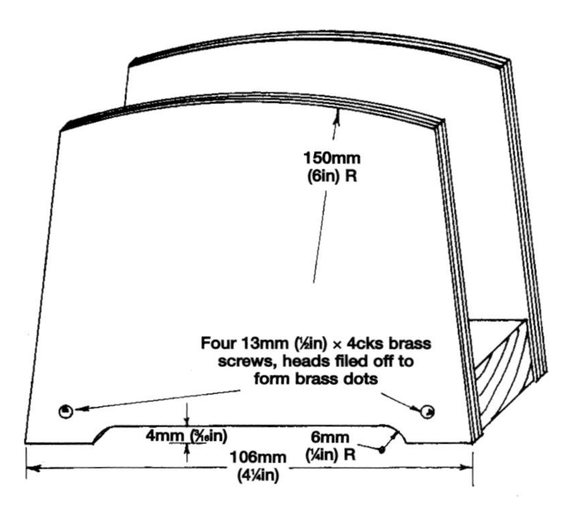

Oblique projection of stand

Letter Rack

This letter rack gives scope for individual design, and an introduction to the use of the plough.

Procedure

1 Prepare base, and mark out length and position of plough grooves. Note alternative treatment at base – stopped grooves.
2 To plough grooves, fix base in sash cramp, place in vice, and plough grooves 6mm (¼in) deep, check with divisions for correct size.
3 Cut plywood divisions to shape, clean up and fit into base.
4 Work chamfers on base and clean up.
5 Mask all joints, and complete polishing.
6 Carefully glue in divisions.

Material

Sycamore, 150mm × 70mm × 20mm (6in × 2¾in × ¾in), for base; divisions of 4mm (3⁄16in) plywood to given dimensions or to suit individual requirements.

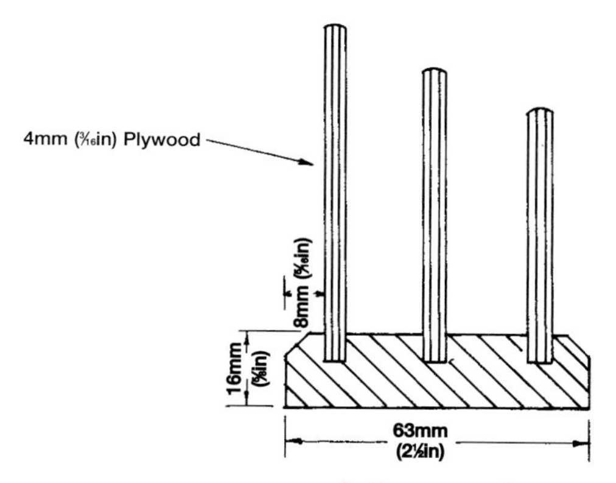

Section on centre line

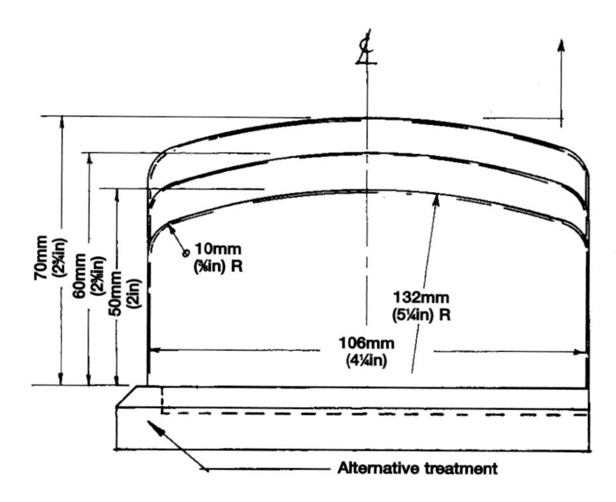

Elevation of letter rack

Teapot Stand

The main feature of this teapot stand could well be a decorated or plain tile, with a suitable contrasting wood. It incorporates the angle halving joint, and gives excellent practice in setting out.

Method

1. Prepare material.
2. Set out angle halving joints as shown in drawing, noting position of face side and face edge marks. All the gauging for this joint is done from the face side.
3. With a dovetail saw cut all the joints, leaving the shoulders until last.
4. Assemble frame, adjust as necessary, and screw together dry with 13mm (½in/No 4) countersunk screws. Remove screws, apply glue to joints and reassemble.
5. Flush all joints with smoothing plane. Pin and glue on plywood base.
6. Flush plywood with edge of frame, and check size with tile.
7. Work chamfer on moulding, cramp and glue to frame as shown in drawing. Note alternative moulding.
8. Round the corners with flat-bottom spokeshave.
9. Clean up job and polish.
10. Cement or glue tile in place.
11. Cut out four baize discs 20mm (¾in) diameter and glue to bottom.

Material

Selected pine, with sycamore or African walnut moulding.

Cutting list

Description	Length	Width	Thickness
2 for frame	225mm (9in)	23mm (⅞in)	20mm (¾in)
1 base plywood	106mm (4¼in)	106mm (4¼in)	3mm (⅛in)
2 base mouldings	275mm (11in)	25mm (1in)	13mm (½in)
tile	100mm (4in)	100mm (4in)	4mm–6mm (3/16in–¼in)

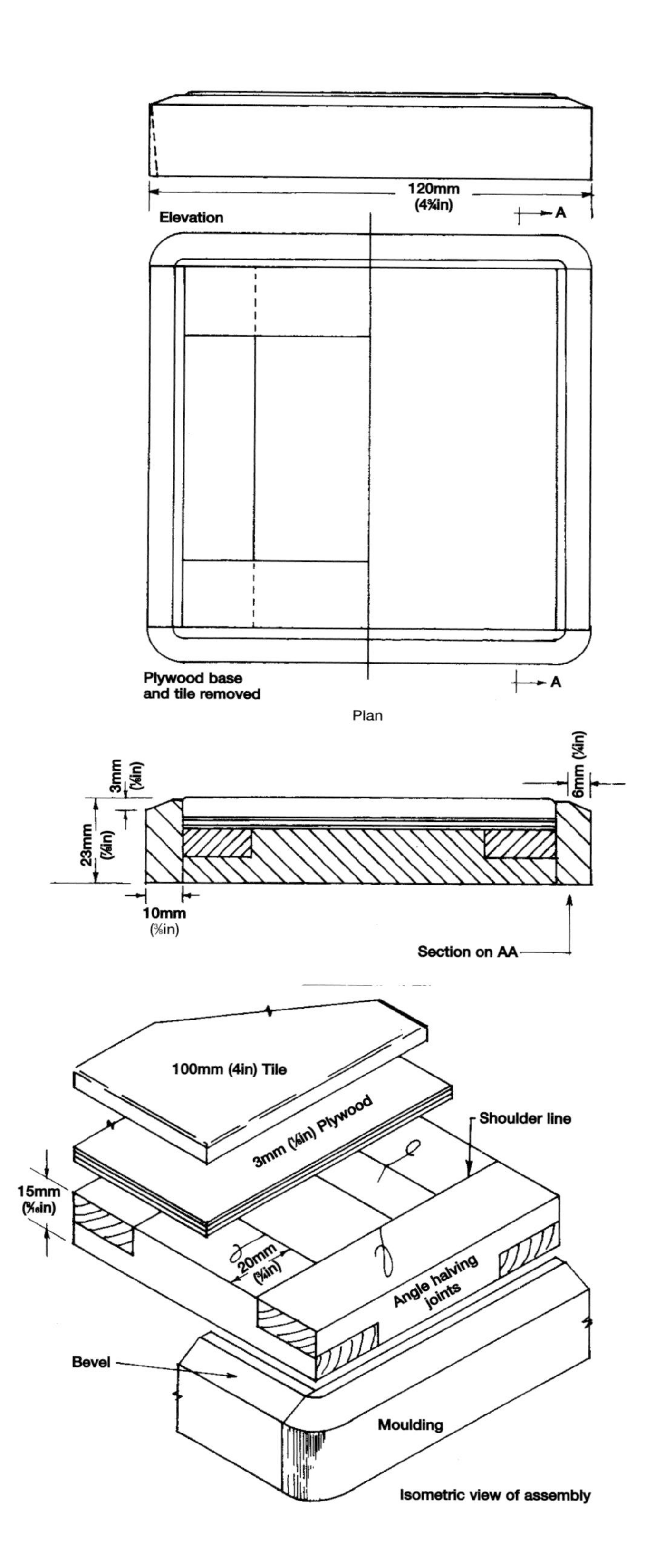
120mm
(4¾in)
A
Elevation
Plywood base
and tile removed
A
Plan
3mm
(⅛in)
23mm
(⅞in)
10mm
(⅜in)
6mm (¼in)
Section on AA
100mm (4in) Tile
3mm (⅛in) Plywood
Shoulder line
15mm
(⁹⁄₁₆in)
20mm
(¾in)
Angle halving
joints
Bevel
Moulding
Isometric view of assembly

Display Shelves

A useful and simple form of shelving, incorporating the cross halving, tee halving, and mortise-and-tenon joints. It gives further opportunity for practice in setting out, shaping and finishing. It provides an introduction to tenon proportions, use of the mortise gauge and mortise chisel. The shelving could easily be extended in length, width and depth, by increasing the number of shelf supports, and re-positioning as required. It should be fixed to the wall with mirror plates, or screw-through uprights.

Method

1. Prepare material to dimensions shown.
2. Set out for halving joints on back frame and mark out position of mortises to take supports (see diagrams) and set mortise gauge to 8mm (5/16in), gauge mortises in rails and tenons at end of supports.
3. Cut and fit all halving joints, and cut mortises in rails.
4. Clean all inner edges of frame, glue the joints, screwing from the back, and flush all surfaces.
5. Shape supports, fit and glue into position. Test for squareness.
6. Fit plywood shelves to framing, cut to length, round corners, clean up.
7. Arrange for two 16mm (5/8in/No 6) countersunk screws in supports and four 16mm (5/8in/No 6) countersunk screws along back edging. Glue and screw into place.
8. *Finish:* painted, colour as required.

Material

Selected pine.

Cutting list

Description	Length	Width	Thickness
2 top and bottom rails	400mm (1ft 4in)	28mm (1 1/8in)	23mm (7/8in)
1 upright (to cut 2)	375mm (1ft 3in)	28mm (1 1/8in)	23mm (7/8in)
1 support (to cut 2)	200mm (8in)	28mm (1 1/8in)	28mm (1 1/8in)
2 shelves plywood	390mm (1ft 3 1/2in)	103mm (4 1/8in)	6mm (1/4in)

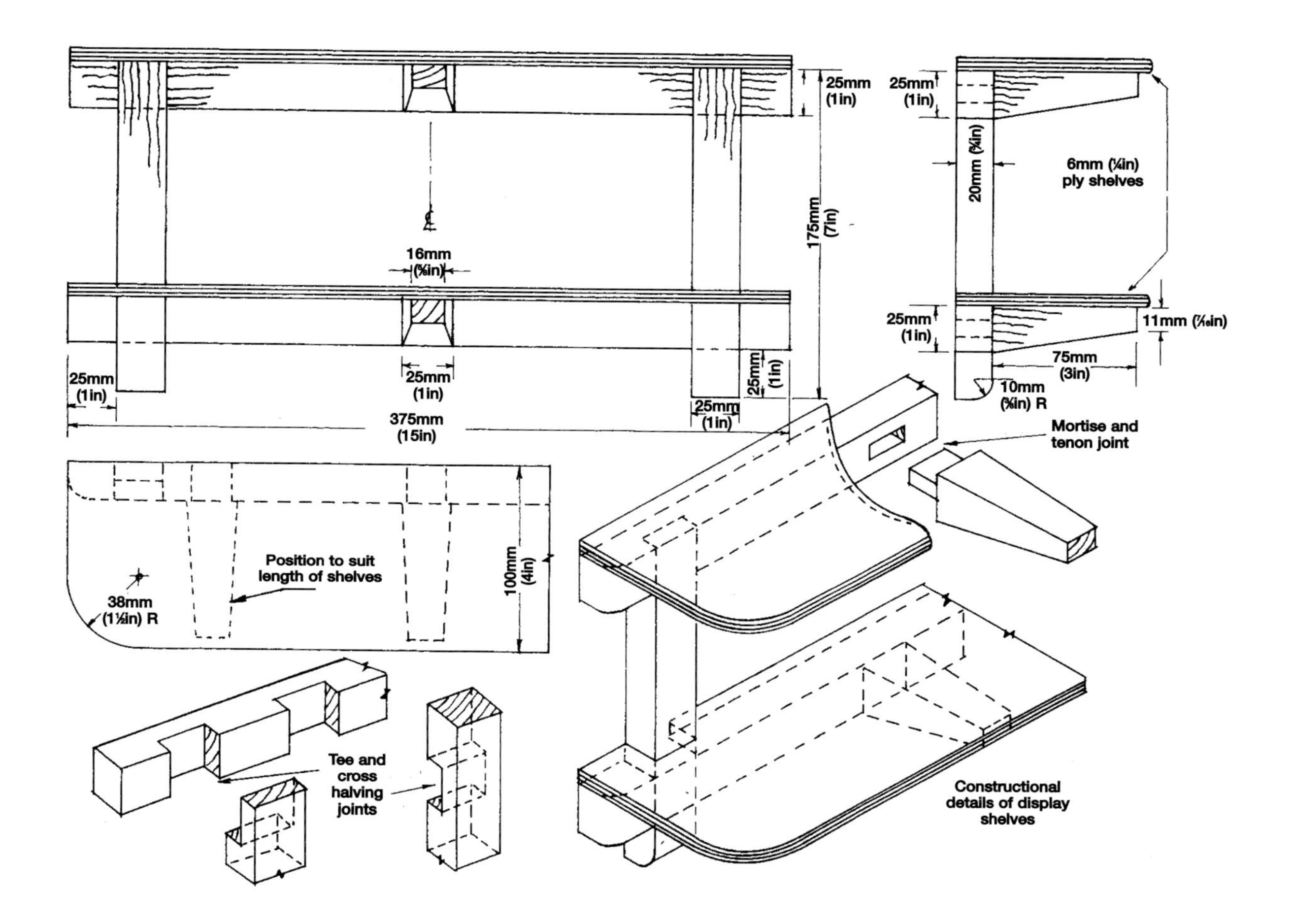
25mm (1in)
25mm (1in)
175mm (7in)
20mm (¾in)
6mm (¼in) ply shelves
16mm (⅝in)
25mm (1in)
11mm (7⁄16in)
75mm (3in)
10mm (⅜in) R
25mm (1in)
25mm (1in)
25mm (1in)
375mm (15in)
Mortise and tenon joint
Position to suit length of shelves
38mm (1½in) R
100mm (4in)
Tee and cross halving joints
Constructional details of display shelves

Individual Supper Tray

This tray is specially suitable for serving light refreshments.

Contrasting woods are suggested, oak for the tray bottom, walnut for the sides and handles. As an alternative, decorated plastic surfaced plywood 6mm (¼in) thick would add a distinctive touch. The tray gives further practice in shaping, use of screws, cleaning up and using a cabinet scraper, use of cramps and gluing up.

Method

1. Prepare material.
2. Mark out bottom, shoot ends and round corners.
3. Bevel handles as shown in detail, keeping material in one length for this operation, cut to size, cleaning up end grain with a block plane. To facilitate construction the handle could be partly shaped, glued and screwed into position, then by cramping the tray to bench, remove the waste as shown by dotted lines in detail drawing.
4. Bevel sides and shape ends.
5. Prepare work for polishing, masking all joints. Complete polishing except for outer surfaces of the sides.
6. Cramp and glue sides to bottom, leave to dry.
7. Make 4mm (3⁄16in) diameter pins, drill 4mm (3⁄16in) diameter holes in sides, glue and drive pins in, flush off and complete polishing.

Material

Quartered oak for bottom (or 6mm [¼in] plastic-faced ply or hardboard); sides and handles in walnut.

Cutting list

Description	Length	Width	Thickness
1 bottom	400mm (1ft 4in)	182mm (7¼in)	13mm (½in)
2 sides	300mm (1ft)	25mm (1in)	10mm (⅜in)
handles (to cut 2)	250mm (10in)	40mm (1½in)	23mm (⅞in)

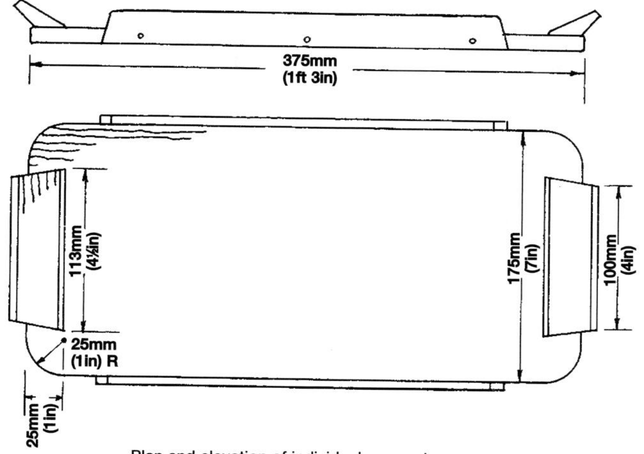

Plan and elevation of individual supper tray

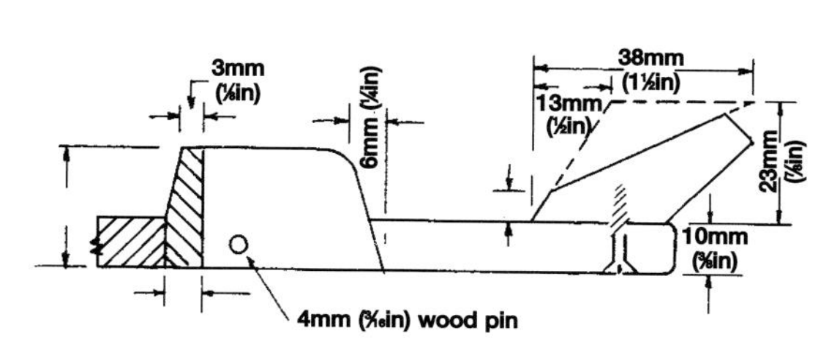

Half full-size details of handles and sides

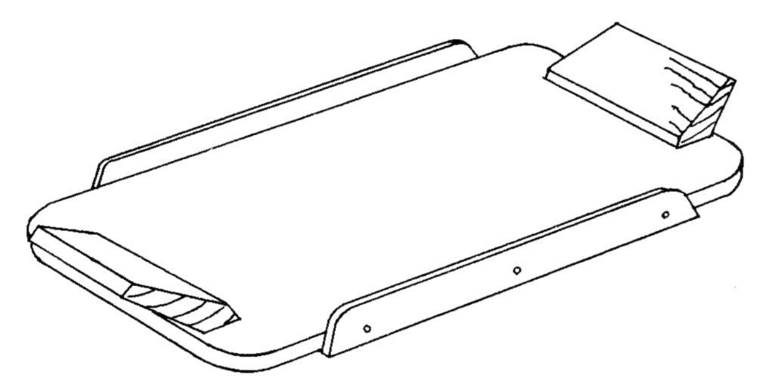

Pictorial sketch of tray

Cheese Platter

A useful article for the host or hostess, this platter gives additional practice in planing, marking out, shaping, and working in hardwood.

Method

1. Prepare material.
2. Mark out platter, cut to shape and clean up.
3. Mark out side view of handle and cut to shape using coping or bow saws, finish to line with flat- and round-bottom spokeshaves.
4. Taper handle as shown in plan, and clean up for polishing.
5. Bore holes in platter, countersink, and screw on handle.
6. Remove handle and polish same.
7. Work chamfers on platter, clean up, glue and screw handle in position.
8. Wipe platter over with olive oil and rub well in.

Material

Sycamore or beech, 325mm × 156mm × 13mm (1ft 1in × 6¼in × ½in); handle in sycamore, 150mm × 40mm × 28mm (6in × 1½in × 1⅛in).

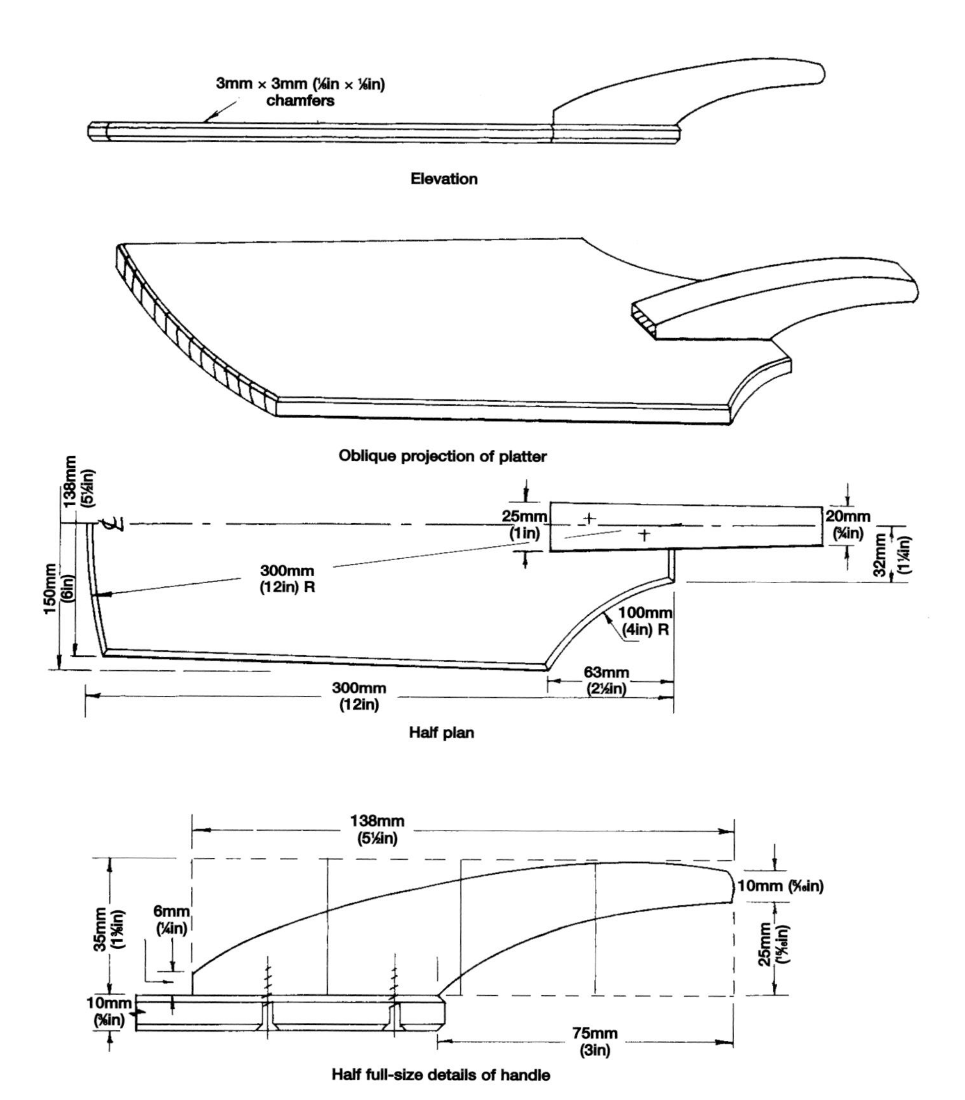

Elevation

Oblique projection of platter

Half plan

Half full-size details of handle

Candle Holder

Designed to hold tall candles, this elegant-looking holder provides good practice in accurate marking out and plane control.

Method

1 Prepare material.
2 Mark out on face side and fix centres for holes.
3 Bore holes with a 11mm (7⁄16in) twist bit (use a gauge to control depth), taking care to keep the bit upright.
4 Cut to length and plane to shape as given in plan.
5 Mark out slope on edges and plane to shape.
6 Using a thumb gauge mark out, and work chamfers.
7 Clean up and prepare for polishing.
8 Glue baize on bottom.

Material

Oak, 200mm × 53mm × 25mm (8in × 2⅛in × 1in).

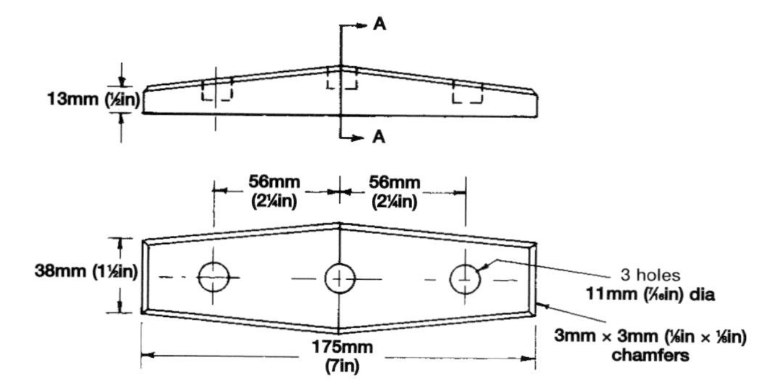

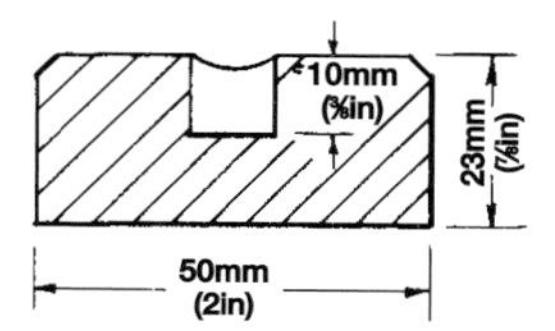

Enlarged section AA

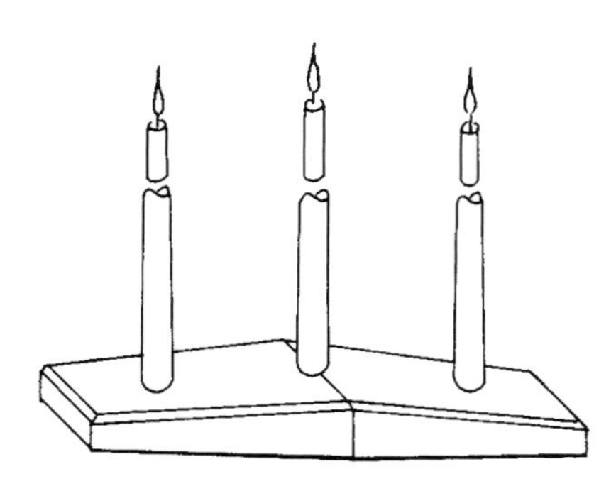

Oblique projection of holder

Circular Candle Holders

The three shaped, single-candle holders can be arranged in a variety of ways, one of which is shown in diagram A, and afford excellent table decoration. The exercise introduces the marking out and making of a template, and gives further practice in shaped work.

Method

1. Prepare material.
2. Make a cardboard template of one section to dimensions as given in drawings, and locate hole.
3. Using template mark out three sections on the material and bore holes.
4. Bow saw to shape and clean up.
5. Cut to length and plane end grain. Round corners using a wood file for this operation.
6. Work chamfers, clean up for polishing, and polish.
7. Glue baize on bottom.

Material

Mild working mahogany, 375mm × 56mm × 23mm (1ft 3in × 2¼in × ⅞in).

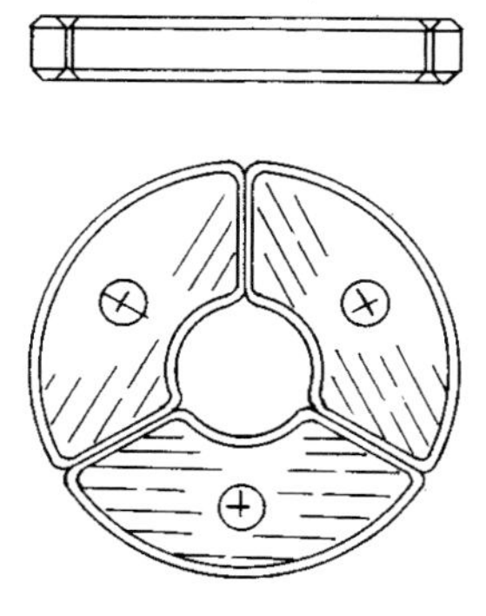

Diagram A

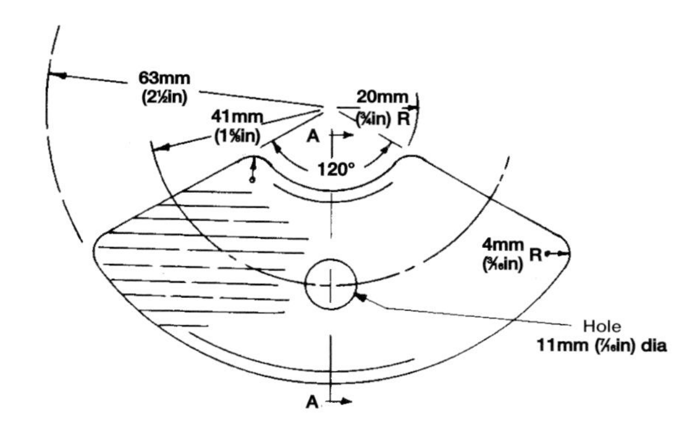

Plan of candle holder

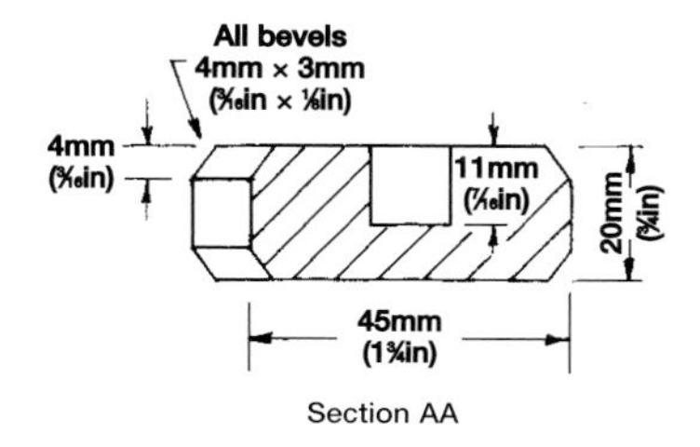

Section AA

Book Ends

The making of these book ends will help beginners to develop a sense of shape, encourage free expression, and give further experience in the use of wood rasps, files, and glasspaper, and the working qualities of various woods.

Method

For design as shown in isometric view

1 Prepare material.
2 Mark out, cut ends to length and plane end grain.
3 Cut metal base to shape and form dovetail, drill holes, and clean up.
4 Place metal base on end and mark out dovetail, set gauge to thickness of metal and remove waste (see drawing).
5 Mark out on edge, the tapering as shown in drawing, and remove waste with a smoothing plane.
6 Complete marking out, including chamfers, and round corners.
7 Work chamfers, and clean up for polishing.
8 Lightly polish, cut down with flour glasspaper and finish with wax.

For free shaping of ends in beech or elm

1 Prepare material.
2 Mark out, cut and shoot base of end only.
3 Cut and fit metal base.
4 Mark out free shape on end, cut aperture, and work shape, using spokeshaves, wood rasps, files and glasspaper.
5 *Finish:* as above.

Note: in shaped work difficulty is often experienced with the holding or fixing of this type of work to the bench or in the vice. This can be overcome by allowing about 50mm (2in) extra in length for cramping or holding in vice – see dotted outline in drawing.

Material

Oak for a pair, 275mm × 103mm × 25mm (11in × 4⅛in × 1in); beech or elm for free-shape designs, 275mm × 110mm × 25mm (11in × 4⅜in × 1in) and 280mm × 103mm × 25mm (11in × 4⅛in × 1in); metal base, 18 s.w.g. aluminium to cut two pieces, 200mm × 95mm (8in × 3¾in).

Pictorial sketch of stand

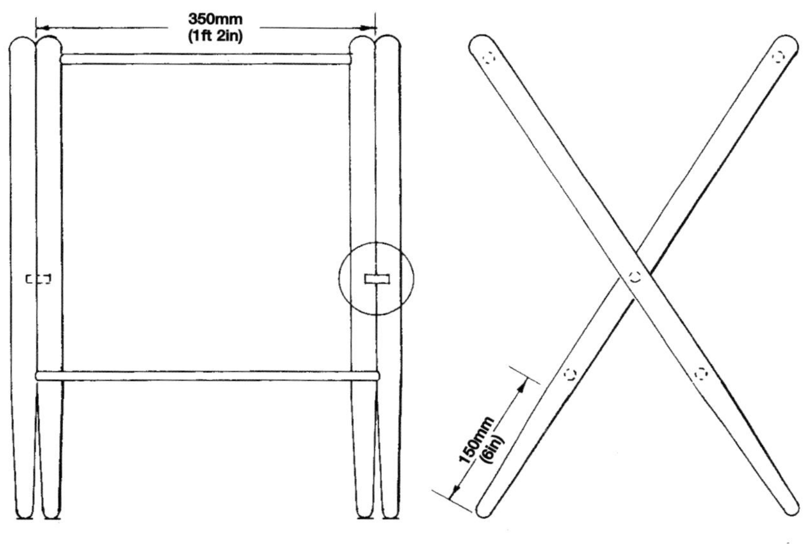

Elevations

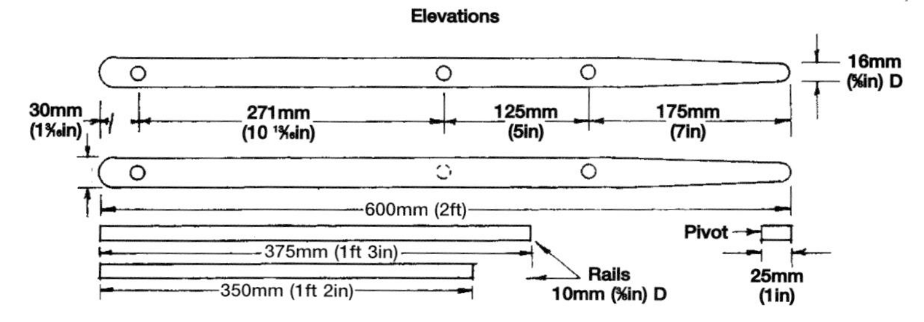

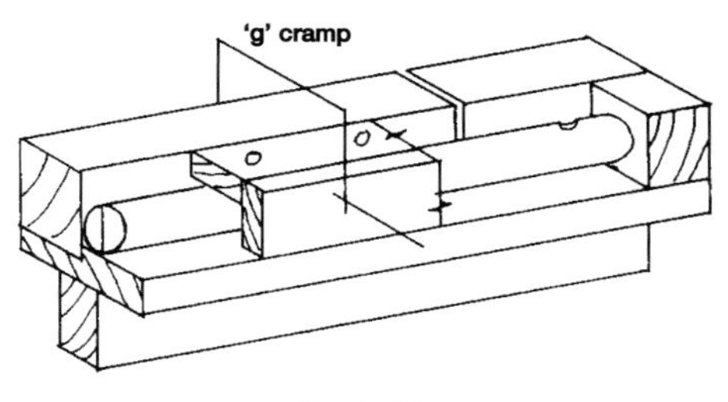

Sketch of jig

Tray

This tray has been designed to introduce the application of a simple dovetail joint, the method of marking out and the general sequence of operations for making this joint; to give practice in making stopped chamfers, and the working of a mason's mitre. The student has an opportunity to try out various treatments in the contrasting woods.

Method

1 Prepare material.
2 Mark out length of sides and ends (square all round with a marking knife), saw off waste, leaving cut lines showing. Using a shooting board and steel jack plane carefully plane ends of material down to cut lines. Lay out sides and ends in their respective positions and number, making sure that all face marks are outside, and face edge marks are on the same plane (see drawing).
3 Set a cutting gauge to the thickness of the material and lightly gauge round the ends.
4 Mark out dovetails on side pieces and saw down the lines, do not remove waste (see saw kerf in isometric view).
5 Place side piece on to the end grain of end piece – held in vice – and check numbers before marking. Holding side piece firmly in the correct position, draw end of dovetail saw through the cuts previously made. This will leave marks for the pins.
6 Saw down on the waste side of saw kerf mark.
7 Complete marking out, and remove waste between half pins (see drawing) with coping saw, finishing carefully to the gauge lines with a paring chisel. Remove waste on side pieces with a dovetail saw.
8 Complete all the cutting and try joints, fitting where necessary. Note the alternative method as shown in drawing, when the waste is removed to allow an awl to be used for marking out.
9 Mark out handles, cut dovetails, and shape.
10 Position handles on tray ends, mark round dovetail with an awl, and gauge depth. Remove waste and fit handles.
11 Mark out and work chamfers. The chamfers on inside of ends stop short of joints, and are finished as a mason's mitre on completion of gluing up. Run out chamfers at handle cut-out on outside of ends, as indicated in drawing.
12 Clean up and glue in handles.
13 Clean up, mask all joints and polish inside surfaces. Glue up, test for squareness and leave to dry.
14 Complete mason's mitre on chamfers, flush all joints and complete polishing.
15 The bottom can be prepared while waiting for frame to dry. Prepare bottom to size and chamfer edges, drill and countersink for screws, and screw together dry.
16 Remove bottom, complete polishing, and reassemble. Cover with baize (use thin glue for this), keeping edges about 3mm (⅛in) in.

Material

Quartered oak

Cutting list

Description	Length	Width	Thickness
1 bottom	475mm (1ft 7in)	325mm (13in)	10mm (⅜in)
2 sides	475mm (1ft 7in)	32mm (1¼in)	13mm (½in)
2 ends	325mm (1ft 1in)	32mm (1¼in)	13mm (½in)
Teak or walnut handles (to make two)	100mm (4in)	78mm (3⅛in)	16mm (⅝in)

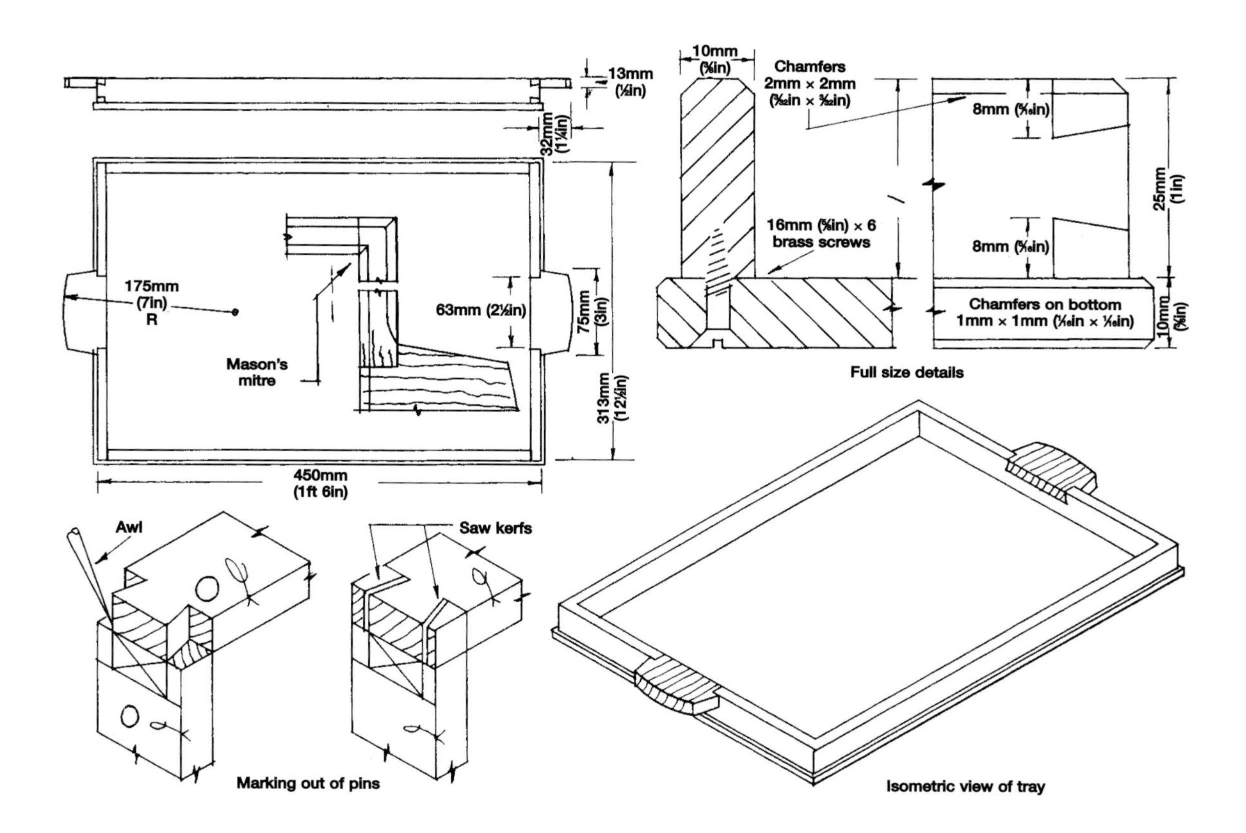

Nail and Screw Box

A useful item for the busy craft worker, this box provides further practice in planing material to given dimensions, shaping, use of the keyhole or pad saw, stopped housing, cross halving and simple lap joints, gluing up, nailing and screwing technique.

Method

1. Prepare material.
2. Mark out sides in pairs, cut grooves and make laps (note larger groove for handle).
3. Mark out ends in pairs, deducting thickness of laps from overall length, and cut grooves.
4. Mark out division forming handle, bore holes as shown in sectional elevation AA and remove remainder of waste with keyhole or pad saw, finish with a wood file and glasspaper. Work chamfers on aperture, complete shaping and chamfering of handle.
5. Mark out divisions, cut to length, make cross halving joints and fit; assemble box.
6. Clean off inner surfaces; glue up, nailing at corners and centre division (see dovetail nailing on page 63).
7. Plane bottom to size and carefully mark positions of screw-holes in bottom. Drill and countersink for 20mm (¾in/No 6) screws, and fix. Remove all sharp edges with glasspaper.
   Note: to ensure the bottom lies flat the under edges of the work should first be carefully cleaned off with a smoothing plane, and tested with a straight edge to ensure that all edges are flat and in the same plane.
8. *Finish:* stop up nail holes, paint or varnish.

Cutting list

Description	Length	Width	Thickness
2 sides	275mm (11in)	53mm (2⅛in)	13mm (½in)
2 ends	225mm (9in)	53mm (2⅛in)	13mm (½in)
handle	225mm (9in)	100mm (4in)	16mm (⅝in)
2 divisions	200mm (8in)	47mm (1⅞in)	10mm (⅜in)
2 divisions	125mm (5in)	47mm (1⅞in)	10mm (⅜in)
bottom plywood	263mm (10½in)	213mm (8½in)	4mm (3⁄16in)

Material

Selected pine.

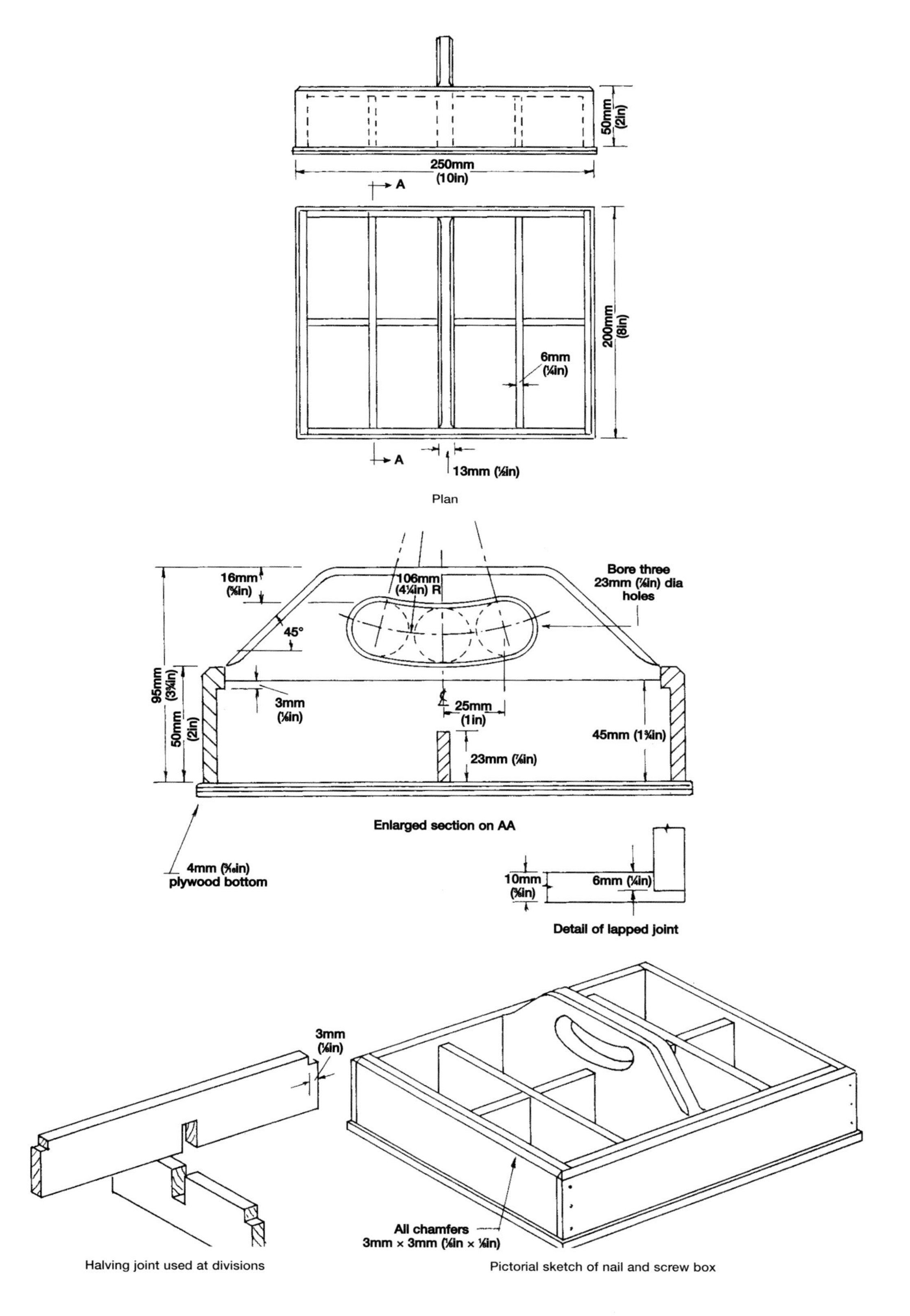

Halving joint used at divisions

Pictorial sketch of nail and screw box

Box for Fishing Tackle

This neat box is indispensable for the fisherman, and also gives good practice in many woodworking techniques, including marking out, housing, fitting butt hinges and gluing up, and it also introduces the technique of sawing off a lid.

Method

1 Prepare all material.
2 Mark out sides and ends, and cut all grooves and laps.
3 Mark out divisions, cut grooves and fit up box.
4 Clean up inner surfaces, using a waterproof glue, then glue up and nail, carefully arranging nails to clear cutting line of lid. Test for squareness. Glue in hinging fillet.
5 Flush edges of box and test for winding (see page 63).
6 Cut plywood for top and bottom. Clean up inside surfaces and glue to box. To prevent plywood sliding when pressure is applied, fix with two brass pins and place cramping blocks on top and bottom and apply pressure using several small 'G' cramps or thumb screws.
7 *Note:* clearly mark top of the box to prevent the catastrophe of cutting through the divisions when sawing off the lid.
8 Clean up sides of box and round edges of plywood.
9 Set marking gauge to depth of lid and gauge all round, cut on gauge line with a tenon saw and remove lid: it is helpful to slide a piece of thick veneer in saw kerf when changing position of box in vice.
10 Carefully plane joint surfaces of box and lid taking off the minimum of shavings to make a good joint.
11 Prepare lining for inside of lid, mitre and glue in.
12 *Hinging:* set out position of butt hinges on lid, gauge and cut recesses, fit and screw butts to lid. Place lid in correct position, mark off position of butts on box, gauge and cut recesses, fit and screw up. Test lid.
13 Fit plywood for inner lid, screw on butts as shown, and fit lifting dowel.
14 Screw on metal fittings.
15 Remove fittings, clean up with fine glasspaper.
16 *Finish:* give three coats of yacht varnish. When dry replace fittings.

Material

Selected pine or spruce; marine or exterior grade plywood for top, bottom and inner lid.

Cutting list

Description	Length	Width	Thickness
2 sides	240mm (9½in)	47mm (1⅞in)	13mm (½in)
2 ends	163mm (6½in)	47mm (1⅞in)	13mm (½in)
2 divisions	200mm (8in)	25mm (1in)	6mm (¼in)
1 division	150mm (6in)	25mm (1in)	6mm (¼in)
1 hinging fillet	225mm (9in)	16mm (⅝in)	13mm (½in)
2 lid linings	375mm (1ft 3in)	23mm (⅞in)	4mm (3/16in)
top	228mm (9⅛in)	153mm (6⅛in)	3mm (⅛in)
bottom	228mm (9⅛in)	153mm (6⅛in)	3mm (⅛in)
inner lid	225mm (9in)	150mm (6in)	4mm (3/16in)

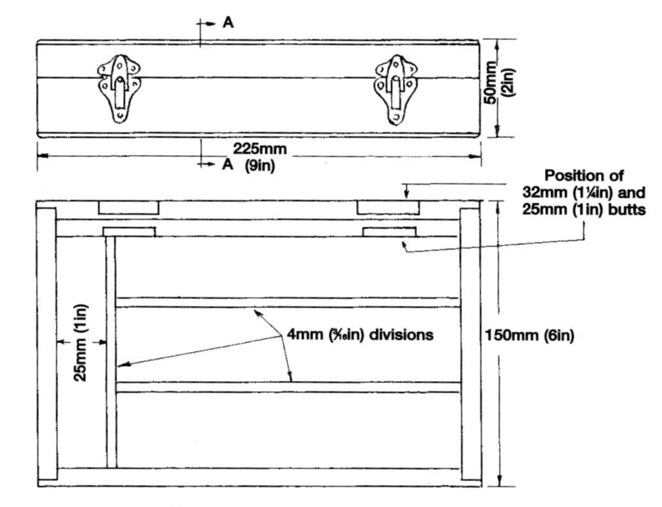

Plan with lids removed

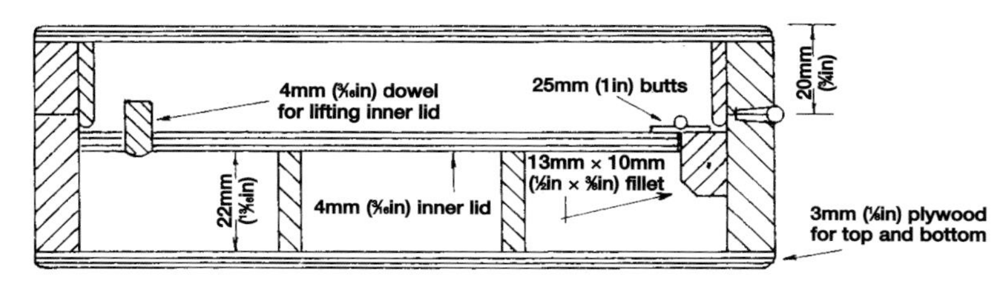

Half full-size details on section AA

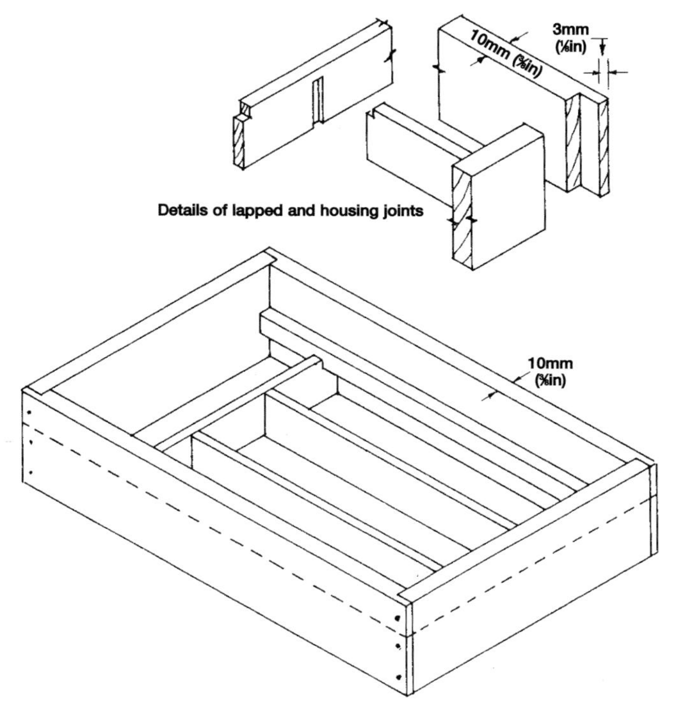

Details of lapped and housing joints

Isometric projection showing construction of box for fishing tackle

Book Trough

This is a simple, well-proportioned book trough, designed to give practice in setting out, shaping, making a shouldered housing joint, bevelling, gluing up and the use of sash cramps. It gives ample scope for alternative simple end treatments, mouldings and shaping of the shelf.

Method

1. Prepare all material.
2. Set out ends (handed). Note that these are not alike but are right hand and left hand to form a pair.
3. Cut grooves for the shelf and back rail.
4. Shape ends.
5. Mark out shelf and back rail, cut to length; cut shoulders and fit to ends.
6. Mark out and work all bevels on ends, shelf, and back rail.
7. Clean up, mask all joints and polish inside surfaces.

   Note: it is essential to be fully prepared for any gluing up job. Always have sufficient cramping blocks close at hand, and adjust all sash cramps to the correct length, and try the job together dry. Plan to have sufficient glue and make sure it is fresh.
8. Glue up, test for squareness and wind.
9. Complete polishing.

Material

Oak.

Cutting list

Description	Length	Width	Thickness
ends (to cut two)	500mm (1ft 8in)	178mm (7⅛in)	23mm (⅞in)
shelf	500mm (1ft 8in)	153mm (6⅛in)	20mm (¾in)
back rail	500mm (1ft 8in)	78mm (3⅛in)	20mm (¾in)

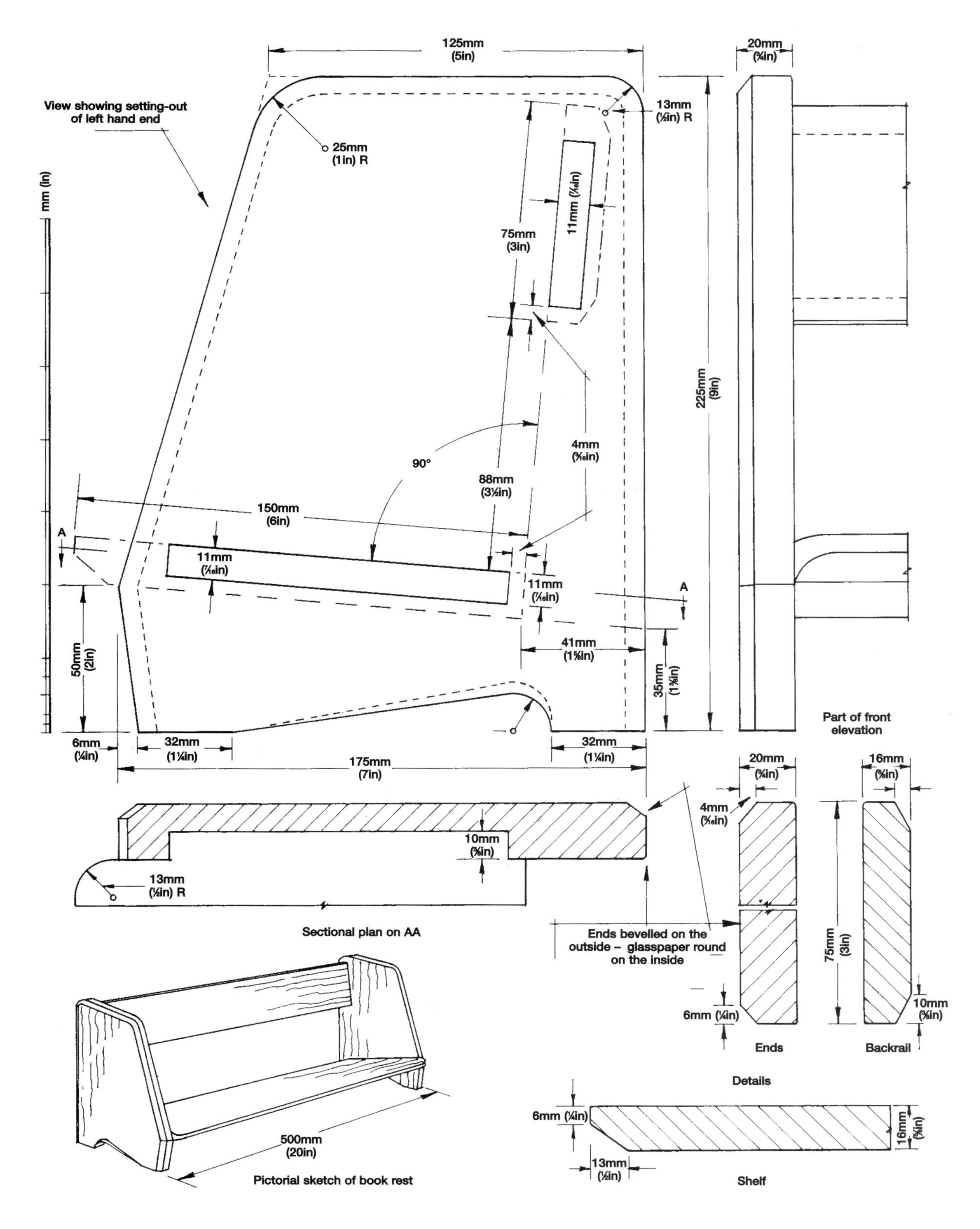

View showing setting-out of left hand end
mm (in)
125mm (5in)
20mm (¾in)
13mm (½in) R
25mm (1in) R
11mm (7/16in)
75mm (3in)
225mm (9in)
4mm (3/16in)
90°
88mm (3½in)
150mm (6in)
A
11mm (7/16in)
11mm (7/16in)
A
41mm (1⅝in)
50mm (2in)
35mm (1⅜in)
6mm (¼in)
32mm (1¼in)
32mm (1¼in)
175mm (7in)
Part of front elevation
20mm (¾in)
16mm (⅝in)
4mm (3/16in)
10mm (⅜in)
13mm (½in) R
Sectional plan on AA
Ends bevelled on the outside – glasspaper round on the inside
75mm (3in)
6mm (¼in)
10mm (⅜in)
Ends
Backrail
Details
6mm (¼in)
16mm (⅝in)
13mm (½in)
Shelf
500mm (20in)
Pictorial sketch of book rest

Sharpening

When purchasing tools, buy only those made by a reputable manufacturer, and pay a little extra for the best. Tools are an investment and should be taken care of. The grinding and sharpening of tools is of paramount importance to the craftsman. Sharp tools are a necessity in the production of good handcraft work.

Grinding and sharpening techniques for plane irons and chisels

Make a careful study of the illustrations opposite. Grinding should be done on a wet grindstone, which will not overheat the tool and thus 'draw the temper' of the steel. The use of the dry emery wheel for quick results should be strictly avoided.

Sharpening

Two oilstones are an advantage, a medium grade India (an artificial stone) for general work, and a fine grade Washita (a natural stone) for really fine work. Lubricate the stone with olive oil or a light-grade machine oil (never linseed oil, which forms a skin) and commence sharpening by placing the grinding angle on the stone. Lift up until oil is squeezed out in front of plane iron or chisel. This gives the sharpening angle which should be about 30 degrees. Maintain this angle and work back and forth several times. This action forms a burr or wire edge, which is removed by rubbing the back of the plane iron or chisel on the oilstone – it must be kept flat. To produce a really keen edge, strop on a piece of supple leather.

Useful Hints

Never hold an oilstone in the vice. It is better to make a box for it. When sharpening, use the full length of stone. Small wood blocks at each end of the stone enable this to be done. When sharpening small chisels do not stay in the centre of the stone; use the full width. Two small pins at the end of the box prevent it slipping on the bench. Never leave the lid off the box.

Sharpening Gouges

The firmer gouge is sharpened on the oilstone with a rocking movement so that every part of the bevel is rubbed evenly. Remove the burr with an oilstone slip. The scribing gouge is sharpened with the oilstone slip and the burr taken off by rocking the outer surface flat on the oilstone. Scraper sharpening, see illustrations.

Saws

Craftsmen should learn to sharpen their own; if unable to do this satisfactorily, send them to a good ironmongers for attention.

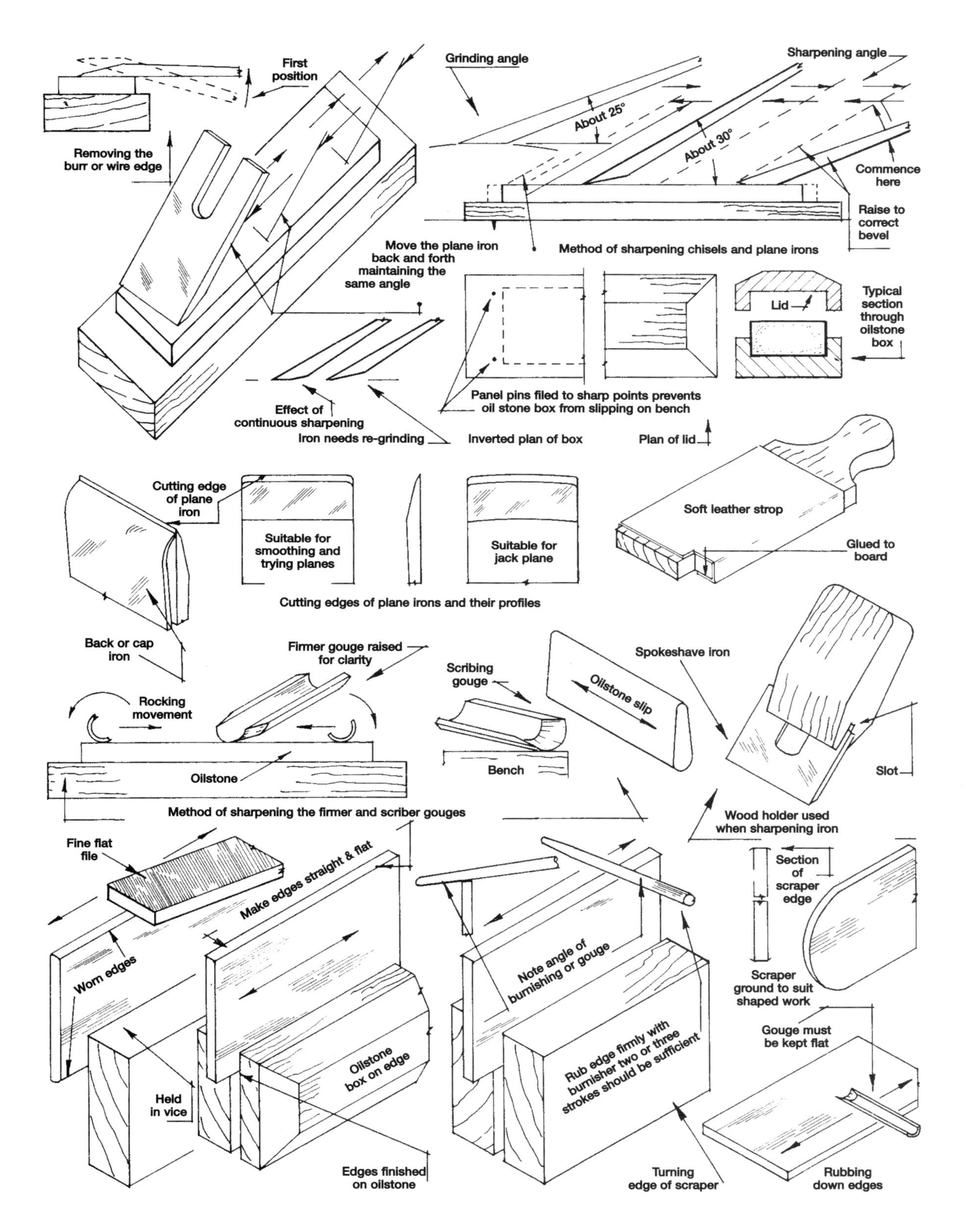

First position
Removing the burr or wire edge
Grinding angle
Sharpening angle
About 25°
About 30°
Commence here
Raise to correct bevel
Move the plane iron back and forth maintaining the same angle
Method of sharpening chisels and plane irons
Lid
Typical section through oilstone box
Effect of continuous sharpening
Iron needs re-grinding
Panel pins filed to sharp points prevents oil stone box from slipping on bench
Inverted plan of box
Plan of lid
Cutting edge of plane iron
Suitable for smoothing and trying planes
Suitable for jack plane
Soft leather strop
Glued to board
Cutting edges of plane irons and their profiles
Back or cap iron
Firmer gouge raised for clarity
Rocking movement
Scribing gouge
Oilstone slip
Spokeshave iron
Oilstone
Bench
Slot
Method of sharpening the firmer and scriber gouges
Wood holder used when sharpening iron
Fine flat file
Make edges straight & flat
Worn edges
Held in vice
Oilstone box on edge
Edges finished on oilstone
Note angle of burnishing or gouge
Rub edge firmly with burnisher two or three strokes should be sufficient
Turning edge of scraper
Section of scraper edge
Scraper ground to suit shaped work
Gouge must be kept flat
Rubbing down edges

Wood Finishing

The technique used for most designs in this book is to clean up all inner surfaces and mask the joints and polish before gluing up. This method saves time and eliminates the difficulty of polishing internal angles. The preparation of wood for polishing is basically the same, no matter what kind of polish is used. As an example, the preparation of a piece of mahogany to receive white french polish is described.

Use a smoothing plane for finishing (note the separate drawing on page 53 showing the profile of a smoothing plane iron, as compared with a jack plane iron). Set the cap iron fairly close to the cutting edge of the plane iron – about 1mm (1⁄32in) or even closer – and adjust the plane iron to take off a fine shaving. A sharp and correctly set plane should remove a silk-like shaving from most woods. Difficult and interlocking grain which cannot be planed in the direction of the grain without plucking up, can often be finished by planing at right angles or across the grain. This is generally described as traversing. After using the smoothing plane the surfaces should be flat. Test with a straight edge. A cabinet scraper is used to remove plane marks or other blemishes left by the smoothing plane.

Glasspaper should be used with care – wrapped round a cork rubber – and rubbed in the direction of the grain, commencing with No 1½ and working through the grades to fine. To prevent the initial coat of polish 'raising the grain' the surface should be damped with clean water, allowed to dry, and lightly rubbed down with flour grade glasspaper. Apply the polish sparingly with a pad or brush, using two or three thin coats rather than one heavy one. When dry, lightly rub down with a fine grade of wire wool or worn flour grade glasspaper. This provides a good base for a wax polish finish, and wood finished in this way retains a natural quality which can rarely be excelled.

A Small Table

This small table, specially designed for the beginner, incorporates many important features basically necessary for sound construction and gives the student an opportunity to study joint proportions and their application to a particular job.

The solid top is fixed with wood or metal buttons to allow for shrinkage and angle blocks have been used to strengthen the joints at end rails. A diminished or secret haunch is shown in the drawing, and a square haunch can be seen in the next job.

Note the setting-out details, such as position of face and face edge marks. The 'horn' strengthens the job during mortising and protects the end from being damaged. A simple decorative treatment – the waggon bevel – is worked on the rails. This can be made with a flat-bottom spokeshave. Dowels have been used to increase the strength of the housing joint at end rails (see drawing) and they make a pleasing decorative feature.

Method

Spend a few minutes looking at the drawing.

1 Prepare material.
2 Set out legs in pairs, mark length (cut lines), position of mortises and sight lines in pencil.
Note: carefully mortise and tenon proportions. These are designed to produce a good joint without weakening the material.
Note: face and face edge marks and their relative positions.
3 Set out side rails, make a cut line for the shoulders.
4 Set mortise gauge to a 6mm (¼in) mortise chisel and gauge mortise and tenons.
5 Set out end rails and cut to size.
6 Cut mortises to a depth of 32mm (1¼in) and make diminished or secret haunchings.
7 Cut tenons and fit together. See page 59 for method of aligning rails and note position of rails in relation to sight lines.
8 Taper legs (note alternative treatment) and cut mortises for buttons.
9 Work waggon bevels, clean up, mask all joints and polish inner edges.
10 Glue up the two side frames and test legs for wind.
11 Flush joint surfaces, mark out and cut housings for end rails and fit.
12 Clean up, mask joints, polish all inner surfaces, glue and cramp up end rails. Test for squareness diagonally, and rub in glue blocks.
13 Cut off horns and legs to length, and work a small chamfer round the floor line to protect the base of leg. Bore holes, fit dowels and glue.
14 Carefully flush top edges of table, testing with a straight edge.
15 Shape and bevel top, clean up all parts and polish.
16 Button top in place.
17 *Finish:* as for wax.

Material

Oak or walnut

Cutting list

Description	Length	Width	Thickness
4 legs	425mm (1ft 5in)	47mm (1⅞in)	25mm (1in)
2 side rails	475mm (1ft 7in)	66mm (2⅝in)	25mm (1in)
2 end rails	300mm (1ft)	66mm (2⅝in)	25mm (1in)
1 top	600mm (2ft)	356mm (14¼in)	23mm (⅞in)
buttons	450mm (1ft 6in)	28mm (1⅛in)	20mm (¾in)
angle blocks (cut down diagonally)	100mm (4in)	28mm (1⅛in)	28mm (1⅛in)
beech or birch dowels	250mm (10in)	8mm (5/16in) diameter	

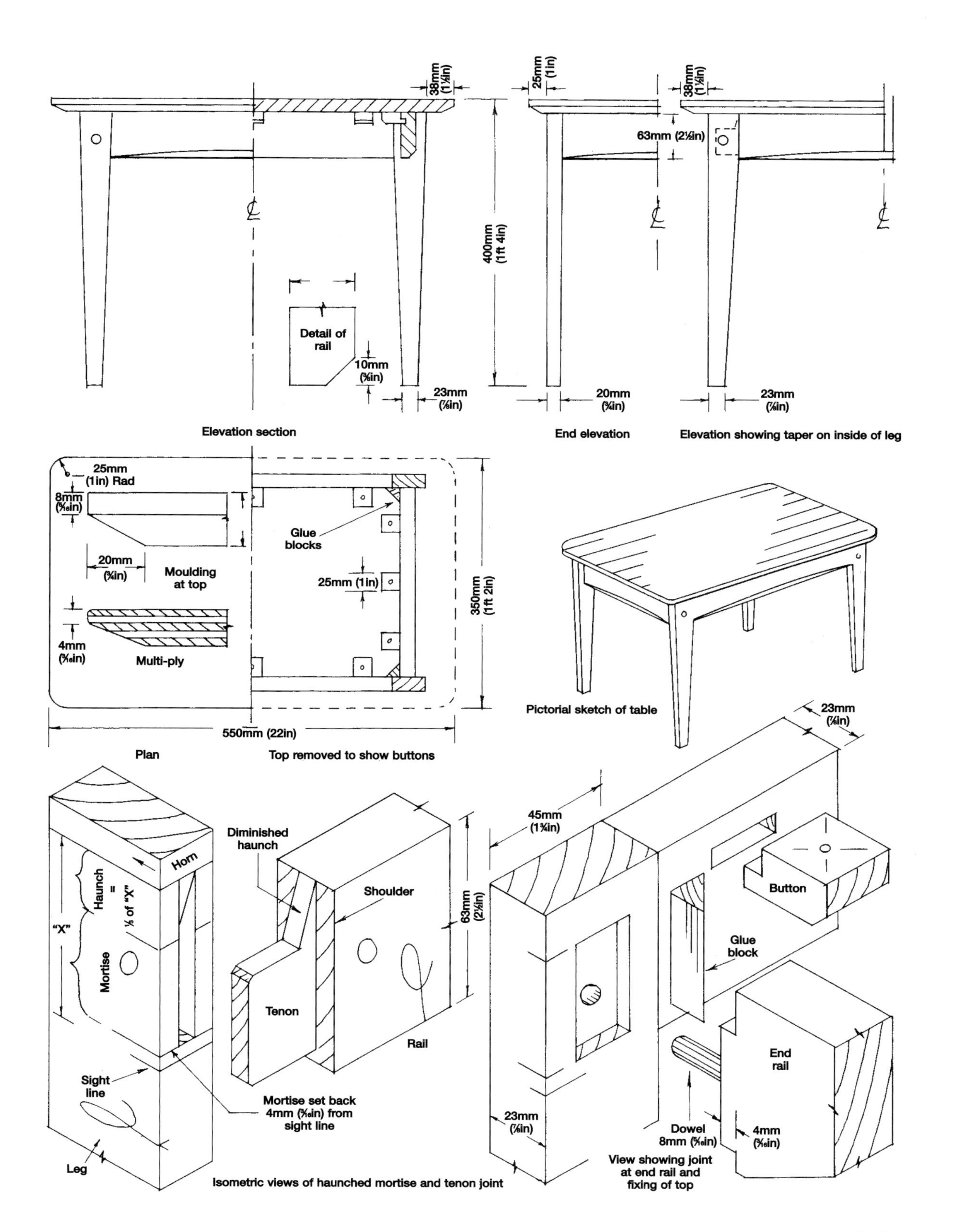
38mm (1½in)
25mm (1in)
38mm (1½in)
63mm (2½in)
400mm (1ft 4in)
Detail of rail
10mm (⅜in)
23mm (⅞in)
20mm (¾in)
23mm (⅞in)
Elevation section
End elevation
Elevation showing taper on inside of leg
25mm (1in) Rad
8mm (5⁄16in)
20mm (¾in)
Moulding at top
4mm (3⁄16in)
Multi-ply
Glue blocks
25mm (1in)
350mm (1ft 2in)
550mm (22in)
Plan
Top removed to show buttons
Pictorial sketch of table
23mm (⅞in)
Horn
Haunch = ⅓ of "X"
"X"
Mortise
Sight line
Leg
Diminished haunch
Shoulder
Tenon
Rail
63mm (2½in)
Mortise set back 4mm (3⁄16in) from sight line
Isometric views of haunched mortise and tenon joint
45mm (1¾in)
Button
Glue block
End rail
23mm (⅞in)
Dowel 8mm (5⁄16in)
4mm (3⁄16in)
View showing joint at end rail and fixing of top

A Bathroom Stool

This is a simple job in soft wood, incorporating many interesting features of joint design and construction. The drawing explains such terms as square haunch, tenon cheeks, shoulder lines and sight lines. The isometric view of joints used in stool construction shows clearly the application of the face side and face edge marks and their relative position. Note tenon proportions, setting out and pairing of legs, and the numbering of the job for ease of assembly and to avoid confusion. The job gives further practice in the use of the plough and introduces the making of a square edged joint for the top.

Method

1. Prepare all material.
2. Set out legs in pairs (see diagram). Note mortise and tenon proportions, the proper use of pencil and cut lines.
3. Set out long and short rails in pairs, note cut lines at shoulders, and position of face marks.
4. Set mortise gauge to an 8mm (5⁄16in) mortise chisel and gauge all mortises and tenons.
5. Cut mortises and haunchings.
6. Saw down the tenons, make plough grooves for the buttons and bevel rail before removing tenon cheeks.
7. Saw down the shoulders, mark and cut haunchings.
8. Mark length of tenons and cut mitres (see drawing).
9. Carefully fit all joints. For method of testing for alignment, see drawing.
10. Cut legs at floor line, mark out and taper legs on the inside.
11. Work round on legs – inside round is run out at bevel.
12. Clean up all inner surfaces.
13. Prepare cramps and cramping blocks, and glue up the two long sides. Carefully wipe off surplus glue and leave to dry.
14. Glue in short rails. Test for square and alignment. Wipe off surplus glue and leave to dry.
15. Flush all joints, remove horns and fit top, glue on cork.
16. *Finish:* painted, colour optional.

Material

Selected pine.

Cutting list

Description	Length	Width	Thickness
4 legs	400mm (1ft 4in)	38mm (1½in)	38mm (1½in)
2 rails	300mm (1ft)	78mm (3⅛in)	25mm (1in)
2 rails	250mm (10in)	78mm (3⅛in)	25mm (1in)
2 tops	375mm (1ft 3in)	156mm (6¼in)	20mm (¾in)
(or plywood)	375mm (1ft 3in)	306mm (12¼in)	13mm (½in)
cork sheeting	350mm (1ft 2in)	300mm (12in)	6mm (¼in)

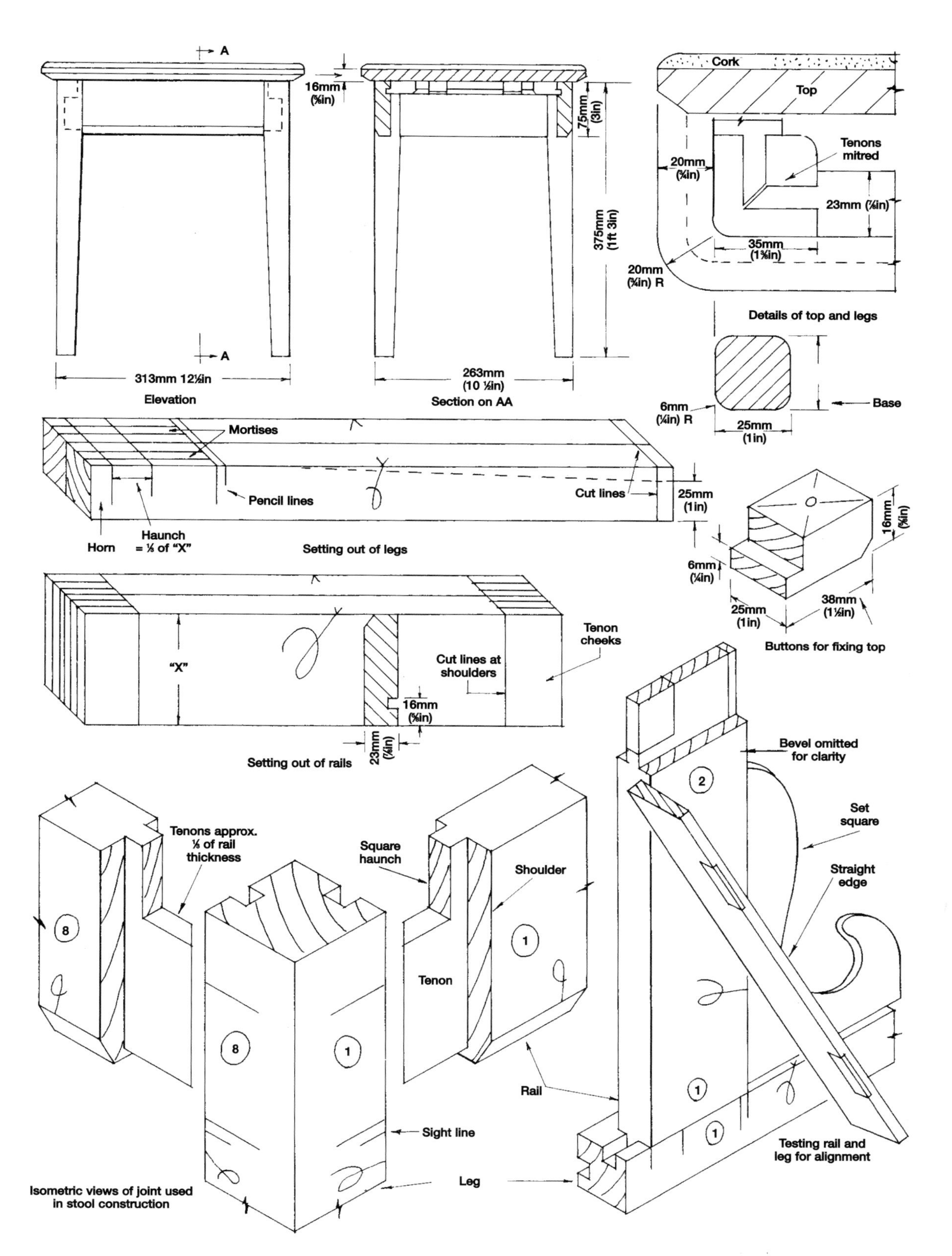
A
16mm
(⅝in)
75mm
(3in)
375mm
(1ft 3in)
A
313mm 12½in
Elevation
263mm
(10 ½in)
Section on AA
Cork
Top
Tenons
mitred
20mm
(¾in)
23mm (⅞in)
35mm
(1⅜in)
20mm
(¾in) R
Details of top and legs
Base
6mm
(¼in) R
25mm
(1in)
Mortises
Pencil lines
Cut lines
25mm
(1in)
Horn
Haunch
= ⅙ of "X"
Setting out of legs
16mm
(⅝in)
6mm
(¼in)
25mm
(1in)
38mm
(1½in)
Buttons for fixing top
"X"
Tenon
cheeks
Cut lines at
shoulders
16mm
(⅝in)
23mm
(⅞in)
Setting out of rails
Bevel omitted
for clarity
Tenons approx.
⅓ of rail
thickness
Square
haunch
Shoulder
Set
square
Straight
edge
Tenon
Rail
Sight line
Leg
Isometric views of joint used
in stool construction
Testing rail and
leg for alignment

Book Ends

In making the book ends the student should be encouraged to design an alternative form for the shaped block, and to devise a suitably carved or inlaid motif for the same. The book ends have been designed to give further practice in through dovetailing, and to introduce the Continental method of marking out this joint; this can be clearly followed in the illustration, which shows the method of marking out tails when pins are cut first. Students who are prepared to make a lap dovetailed joint, with the tails on the base, should see pages 135 and 145.

Method

1 Prepare all material.
2 Joint and glue up the three pieces to make the centre blocks.
3 Mark out base and upright to length, square ends, and gauge thickness of material all round and mark out and cut pins.
4 Position work and mark out dovetails with an awl as shown in diagram, and cut tails taking care to cut in the waste.
5 Clean out waste, and assemble.
6 Shape bases and uprights.
7 Make a template for shape of blocks and mark out.
Note: in the shaping of small pieces of work one of the problems is how to hold the job satisfactorily. The drawing shows one of the book end blocks mounted on a small piece of wood, with a piece of paper glued between the two. Use animal glue for this work.
8 Square ends of blocks, cut to length, make template for dowels, bore holes in block, base and upright, and assemble with dowels in position.
9 Partly cut block to shape and glue to piece of wood. Do not forget the paper between the joint.
10 Complete shaping, using round and flat bottom spokeshaves, and carving tools. Mask base and polish it.
11 Gently tap end of block with chisel to break the paper joint, clean off paper and glue up book ends.
12 Flush off joints, complete polishing and glue baize to bottom.

Material

Oak with walnut centre strip for block.

Cutting list

Description	Length	Width	Thickness
2 pieces	275mm (11in)	103mm (4⅛in)	23mm (⅞in)
2 centre blocks	250mm (10in)	88mm (3½in)	32mm (1¼in)
walnut inserts	250mm (10in)	88mm (3½in)	10mm (⅜in)

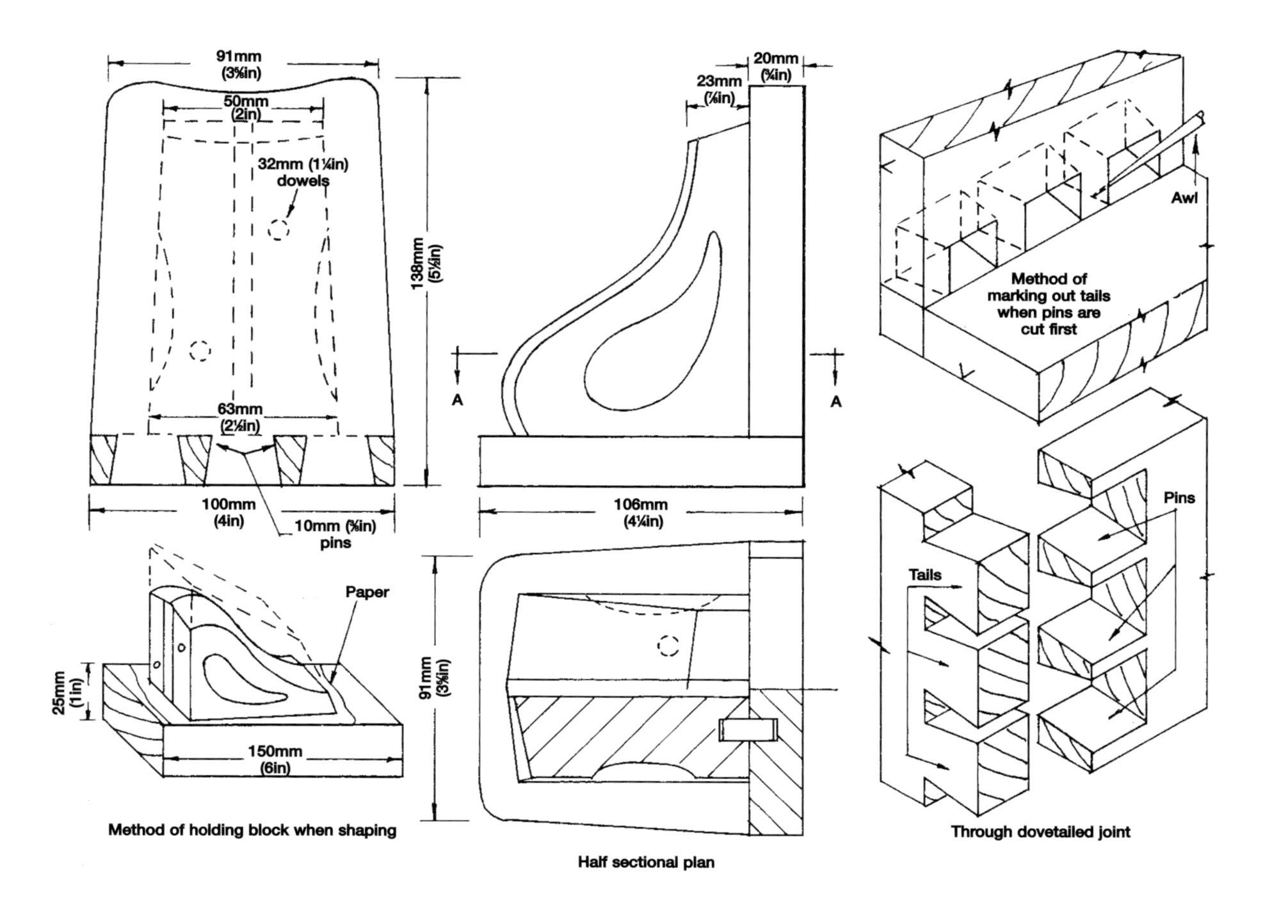

Method of holding block when shaping

Half sectional plan

Through dovetailed joint

Shoe Brush Box

This neat and compact container for shoe brushes, polish and dusters incorporates a sloping surface for use as a footrest. It is designed to give further practice in working accurately to given dimensions, and in the use of manufactured boards such as laminboard and multi-ply; and to give the student an opportunity to appreciate the qualities and uses of wood in this form. The laminboard top is shown lipped, and introduces a technique which is widely used in the woodworking industry. Other interesting features include nailing and screwing techniques, the fitting of butts and the rebating in of the bottom.

Method

1 Prepare material.
2 Mark out sides, cut rebate forming lap, and shape.
3 Mark out ends, cut grooves, saw and shoot ends to length.
4 Rebate sides and ends for plywood bottom.
5 Cut plywood division to shape and assemble job.
6 Clean up all surfaces, round top edge of division, glue up and nail joints.
7 Cut plywood bottom to fit, glue and pin in position. Punch all pins slightly below surface of wood.
8 Bevel back and front to suit sides, flush joints and round corners, as shown in detail of lapped joint.
9 Cut laminboard or multi-ply top to size and plough for lipping.
10 Work tongue on lipping, mitre and fit round top, make allowance for thickness of rubber matting or lino, and glue up.
11 Shape lipping on lid and round corners, fit and glue in rubber or lino top.
12 Fit butts and locating strip on lid as shown in drawing – note, nearly the full knuckle thickness of the hinge is let into the box. See page 175 for method of hinging.
13 Locate lid and mark hinge position on box, cut recesses, fit hinges and test.
14 Shape and cut feet to length, and screw to bottom, as shown in detail.
15 *Finish:* painted, inside and outside to harmonize with colour scheme.

Material

Selected pine, multi-ply or laminboard with suitable hardwood for lipping and feet; sufficient lino or rubber to cover top.

Cutting list

Description	Length	Width	Thickness
2 sides	250mm (10in)	120mm (4¾in)	16mm (⅝in)
1 end	188mm (7½in)	120mm (4¾in)	16mm (⅝in)
1 end	188mm (7½in)	82mm (3¼in)	16mm (⅝in)
feet (to cut 2)	350mm (1ft 2in)	20mm (¾in)	16mm (⅝in)
1 top plywood	250mm (10in)	182mm (7¼in)	13mm (½in)
1 bottom plywood	238mm (9½in)	175mm (7in)	6mm (¼in)
1 division plywood	225mm (9in)	66mm (2⅝in)	6mm (¼in)
1 locating strip	163mm (6½in)	13mm (½in)	6mm (¼in)
1 lipping (to cut 2)	600mm (24in)	20mm (¾in)	16mm (⅝in)
1 lipping (to cut 2)	400mm (16in)	20mm (¾in)	20mm (¾in)

1 pair of 32mm (1¼in) solid brass butts

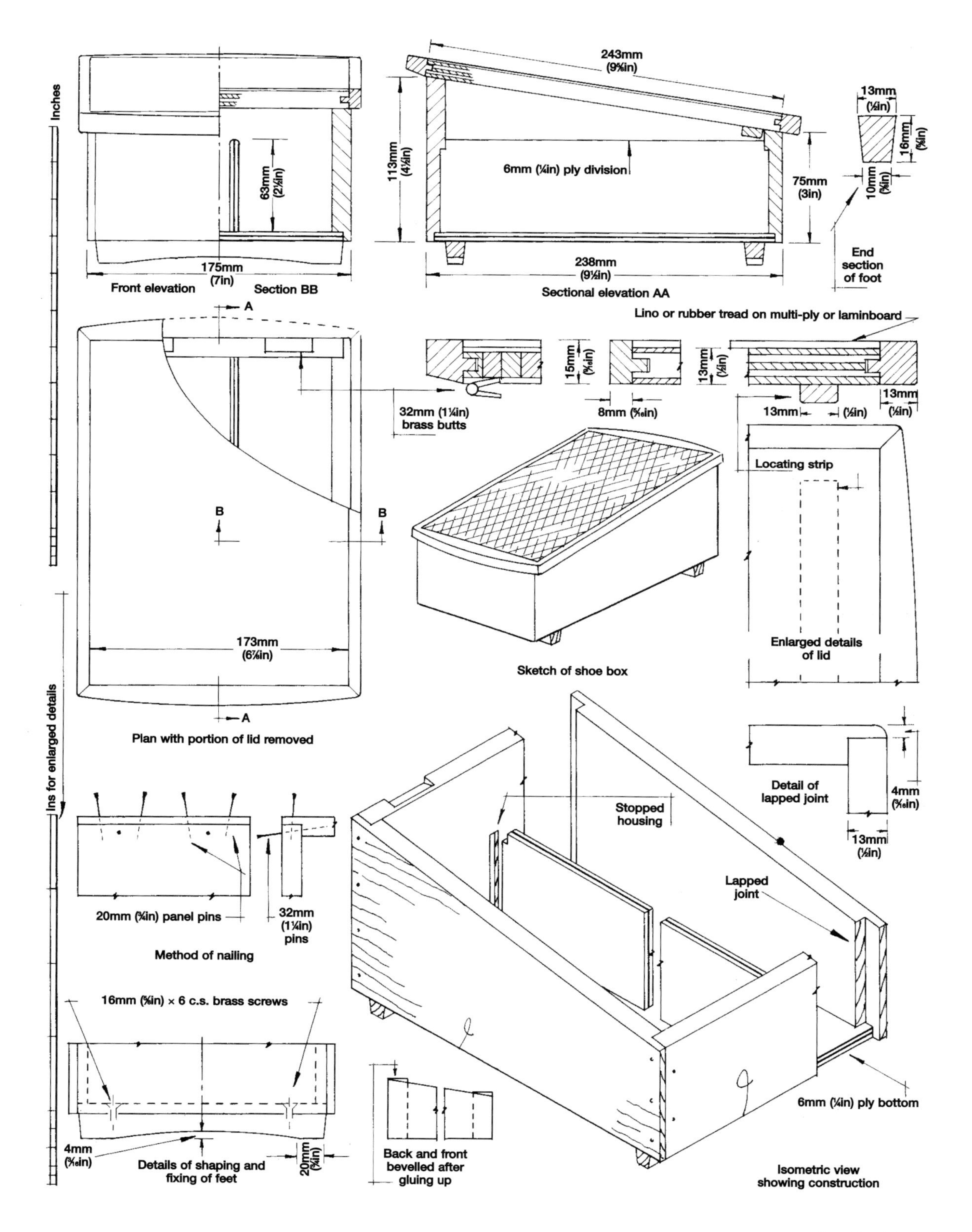
Inches
Ins for enlarged details
175mm
(7in)
Front elevation
Section BB
63mm
(2½in)
243mm
(9⅝in)
113mm
(4½in)
6mm (¼in) ply division
75mm
(3in)
238mm
(9½in)
Sectional elevation AA
13mm
(½in)
16mm
(⅝in)
10mm
(⅜in)
End
section
of foot
A
B
B
A
173mm
(6⅞in)
Plan with portion of lid removed
Lino or rubber tread on multi-ply or laminboard
15mm
(⅝in)
13mm
(½in)
32mm (1¼in)
brass butts
8mm (⁵⁄₁₆in)
13mm
(½in)
13mm
(½in)
Sketch of shoe box
Locating strip
Enlarged details
of lid
Detail of
lapped joint
4mm
(⁵⁄₃₂in)
13mm
(½in)
Stopped
housing
Lapped
joint
6mm (¼in) ply bottom
Isometric view
showing construction
20mm (¾in) panel pins
32mm
(1¼in)
pins
Method of nailing
16mm (⅝in) × 6 c.s. brass screws
4mm
(⁵⁄₃₂in)
Details of shaping and
fixing of feet
20mm
(¾in)
Back and front
bevelled after
gluing up

Folding Table

This compact table is useful both in the home and the garden. Its special features include the table rim which completely contains the legs when folded, and the leg frames, which are of equal size. It also incorporates a simple locking device for the legs. The design incorporates some good examples of joint construction. It provides further practice in dovetailing and introduces the mitred edge to the through dovetail joint. An alternative design which gives a tray-like finish to the top is shown in a separate diagram.

Method

1. Prepare material.
2. Set out rails. Set mortise gauge to a 6mm (¼in) mortise chisel, gauge and cut the tenons.
3. Set out legs, taking dimensions from centre line of bolt (note rails are set in from the face edge), adjust gauge accordingly, gauge and cut the mortises.
4. Shape legs, diminish in two elevations as shown in drawing, and bore hole for bolts before rounding top.
5. Make saw kerfs in tenons, fit and assemble legs and rails and test for wind. Work waggon bevels on rails and clean up. Mask joint surfaces and polish rails and inner surfaces of legs.
6. Glue up and wedge leg frames, and test for square and wind.
7. Set out dovetails for table frame, gauge rebate for top and cut out dovetails – note the through dovetail is mitred on one edge (see detail of corner joint). This arrangement leaves a mitred edge on the top surface. Work rebate on edge and check depth with top.
8. Clean and glue up frame, check for square. Mark out centres and bore holes for bolts.
9. Glue Formica on plywood (see page 98 for gluing technique).
10. Fit top into rebate and glue in.
11. Bevel bottom and top edge of frame.
12. Make brass locking levers and cut out slots in frame to receive them.
13. Fix legs temporarily and fit in corner blocks (these can be seen in section AA), bevel blocks to suit splay of legs, screw and glue in position.
14. Complete all polishing.
15. Assemble table complete with bolts and washers. Fit brass locking device.

Material

Any suitable hardwood.

Cutting list

Description	Length	Width	Thickness
4 legs	450mm (1ft 6in)	41mm (1⅝in)	23mm (⅞in)
2 top rails	400mm (1ft 4in)	35mm (1⅜in)	20mm (¾in)
2 bottom rails	400mm (1ft 4in)	25mm (1in)	20mm (¾in)
2 side rails	700mm (2ft 4in)	66mm (2⅝in)	22mm (1³⁄₁₆in)
2 end rails	450mm (1ft 6in)	66mm (2⅝in)	22mm (1³⁄₁₆in)

top 10mm (⅜in) plywood with Formica or plastic-faced hardboard

4 corner blocks 63mm × 23mm × 16mm (2½in × ⅞in × ⅝in)

2 pieces of 12-gauge brass, for locking levers

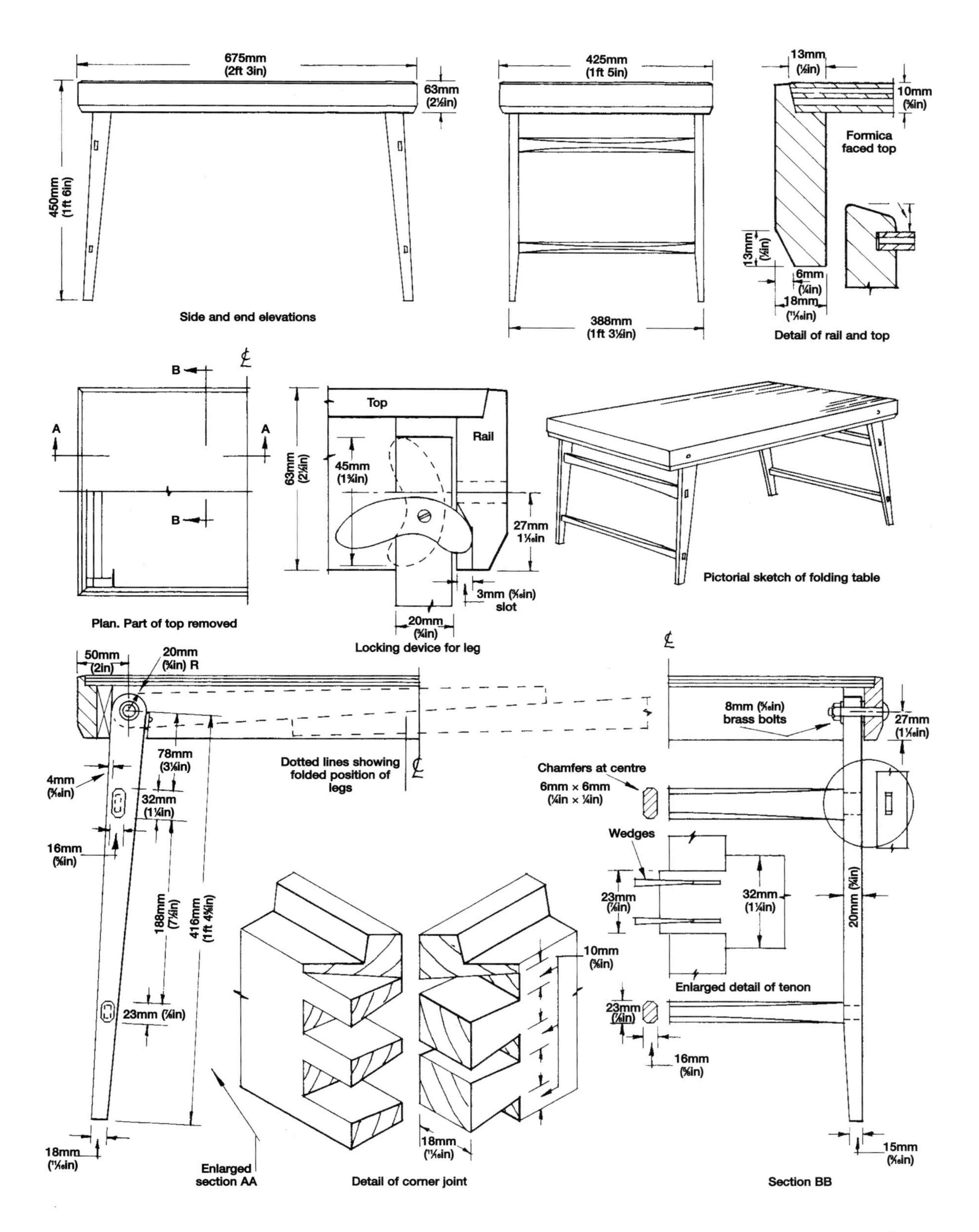
675mm
(2ft 3in)
63mm
(2½in)
450mm
(1ft 6in)
Side and end elevations
425mm
(1ft 5in)
388mm
(1ft 3½in)
13mm
(½in)
10mm
(⅜in)
Formica
faced top
13mm
(½in)
6mm
(¼in)
18mm
(¹¹⁄₁₆in)
Detail of rail and top
B
A
A
B
Plan. Part of top removed
Top
Rail
63mm
(2½in)
45mm
(1¾in)
27mm
1¹⁄₁₆in
3mm (⅛in)
slot
20mm
(¾in)
Locking device for leg
Pictorial sketch of folding table
50mm
(2in)
20mm
(¾in) R
78mm
(3⅛in)
4mm
(³⁄₁₆in)
32mm
(1¼in)
16mm
(⅝in)
188mm
(7½in)
416mm
(1ft 4⅜in)
23mm (⅞in)
18mm
(¹¹⁄₁₆in)
Dotted lines showing
folded position of
legs
Enlarged
section AA
18mm
(¹¹⁄₁₆in)
Detail of corner joint
8mm (⁵⁄₁₆in)
brass bolts
27mm
(1¹⁄₁₆in)
Chamfers at centre
6mm × 6mm
(¼in × ¼in)
Wedges
23mm
(⅞in)
32mm
(1¼in)
Enlarged detail of tenon
23mm
(⅞in)
16mm
(⅝in)
20mm (¾in)
15mm
(⅝in)
Section BB

Small Box

The making of this small box necessitates neat and accurate work. The through dovetailing and strings or lines make decorative features and they must be carefully fitted. It introduces the scratch stock, and gives further practice in the shaping of work to a template, and in sawing off a box lid. The student should have the opportunity to design an alternative shape for the box and lid, and be made aware of design possibilities.

Method

1 Prepare all material, and inspect wood carefully for matching of grain.
2 Mark out sides and cut tails: for method of marking out dovetails, see enlarged details. The large pin allows for the sawing off and fitting of the lid.
3 Mark out ends and cut pins.
4 Clean up inner surfaces, fit together and glue up.
5 Flush top and bottom edges of box.
6 Rebate top and bottom and fit to box, clean up inner surfaces and polish.
7 Shape base to form plinth, and bevel only the outer edge of top. Glue and cramp up base and top.
8 Gauge depth of lid all round. Before shaping outside of box, mark out for strings with cutting gauge, removing waste with scratch stock.
Note: the strings could be cut in before fixing top.
9 Make a template to radius shown, and shape box, testing frequently with template.
10 Glue in strings, and prepare linings.
11 Saw off and fit lid and glue on baize for bottom.
12 Mitre and fit linings, see illustration of scribed and mitred joint for linings for second small box on page 69.
Note: a lining mitred the full depth, usually shows a gap when shrinkage takes place.
13 Fit hinges to box and chamfer as shown – see page 175 for hinging.
14 Complete polishing.

Suggested Material

Oak with rosewood strings or walnut with box strings and sycamore linings.

Cutting list

Description	Length	Width	Thickness
2 sides	238mm (9½in)	66mm (2⅝in)	13mm (½in)
2 ends	125mm (5in)	66mm (2⅝in)	13mm (½in)
1 base	225mm (9in)	100mm (4in)	10mm (⅜in)
1 top	225mm (9in)	100mm (4in)	11mm (7⁄16in)
2 linings	313mm (1ft ½in)	45mm (1¾in)	3mm (⅛in)
2 strings	238mm (9½in)	2mm (3⁄32in)	2mm (3⁄32in)

baize for base
1 pair of 32mm (1¼in) solid brass butts and screws

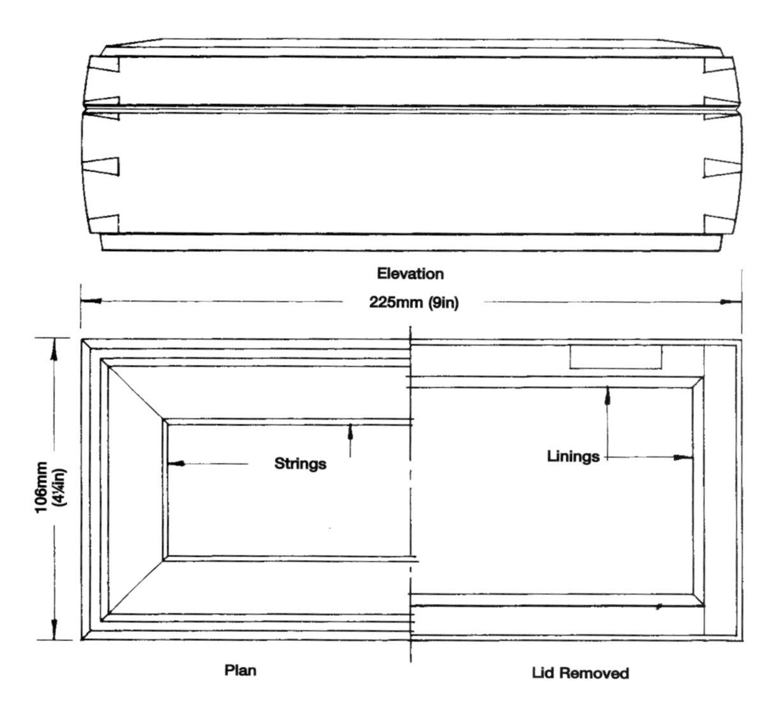

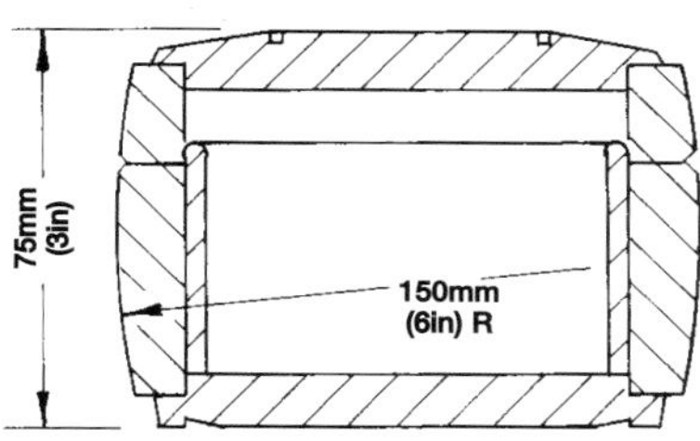

Sectional elevation

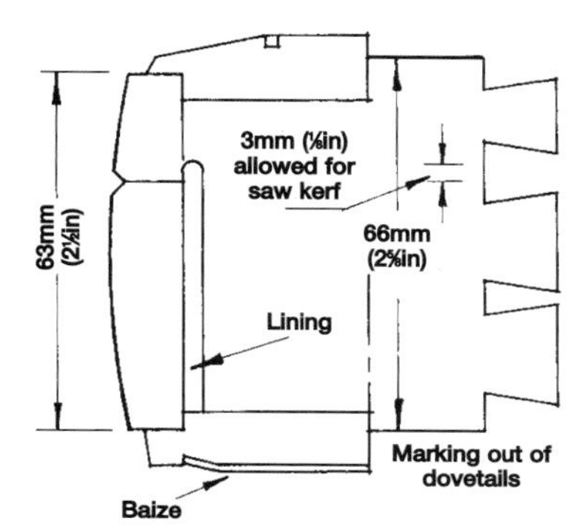

Enlarged details

Second Small Box

This design is for a small box with an elegant line, suitable for experimenting with different kinds of woods, in the solid and in veneer form. It introduces simple veneering as a decorative feature; and the use of veneer keys in the simple lap joint obviates the use of nails. A neat finger-grip sunk in and fixed with a dowel gives a distinctive finish.

Note: when gluing strings or lines on outer edges, hold firmly by winding tape or string round the box.

Method

1. Prepare all material.
2. Mark out sides and cut lap.
3. Cut ends to length.
4. Rebate sides and ends for top and bottom. The detail drawing shows the rebate as 6mm (¼in) and 4mm (3/16in) deep respectively. They can be reduced to allow for strings.
5. Clean up inner surfaces and glue up, use suitable cramping blocks and small 'G' cramps for this operation.
6. Veneer plywood top (see page 161 for information on veneering).
7. Fit top and bottom and glue in.
8. Mark out for decorative keys, make saw kerfs and glue in.
9. Clean up keys, fit mitres and glue in rosewood lines.
10. Clean up – taking care not to plane the veneer – gauge the lid and saw off.
11. Fit the lid, sink and glue in the finger-grip.
12. Mitre and scribe linings and glue in.
13. Fit butts and glue on baize at base.
14. Finish as for wax.

Note: see figure 1 at bottom of diagram for alternative treatments to top.

Suggested Material

Mahogany with rosewood lines and finger-grip.

Cutting list

Description	Length	Width	Thickness
2 for sides and ends	275mm (11in)	47mm (1⅞in)	10mm (⅜in)
1 plywood top	163mm (6½in)	95mm (3¾in)	6mm (¼in)
1 plywood bottom	163mm (6½in)	95mm (3¾in)	4mm (3/16in)
1 rosewood string	1050mm (3ft 6in)	3mm (⅛in)	3mm (⅛in)
1 lining	500mm (1ft 8in)	28mm (1⅛in)	3mm (⅛in)
1 finger-grip	40mm (1½in)	20mm (¾in)	3mm (⅛in)

oddments for veneer keys

1 pair of 25mm (1in) solid brass butts

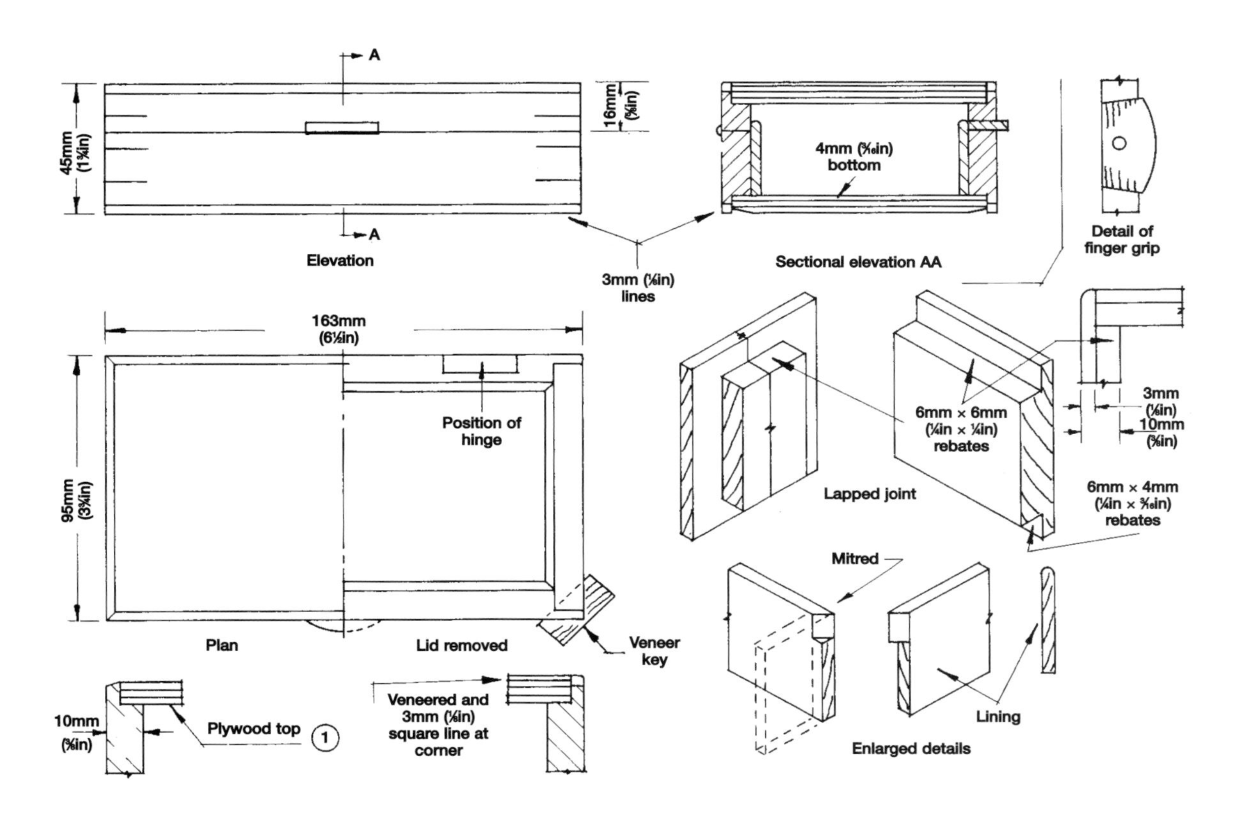
A
A
45mm (1¾in)
16mm (⅝in)
Elevation
4mm (³⁄₁₆in) bottom
Sectional elevation AA
Detail of finger grip
3mm (⅛in) lines
163mm (6½in)
95mm (3¾in)
Position of hinge
Plan
Lid removed
Veneer key
6mm × 6mm (¼in × ¼in) rebates
Lapped joint
3mm (⅛in)
10mm (⅜in)
6mm × 4mm (¼in × ³⁄₁₆in) rebates
Mitred
Lining
Enlarged details
10mm (⅜in)
Plywood top
1
Veneered and 3mm (⅛in) square line at corner

Coffee Table

Designed to be made in solid wood, this small, well-proportioned table embodies some interesting examples of joints, their construction and application. The bridle joint is often used in tables, stands and mirror frames. It is interesting to note that the dovetailing at end rails runs parallel to the grain and not square off the bevelled end; this avoids weakening the joint with cross grain. (For further reference to splayed dovetailing see page 181.) The table provides a good exercise in setting out. It makes use of the bevel for splayed work, and necessitates neat and accurate workmanship.

Method

1. Prepare material.
2. Set out legs and side rails, use a bevel for marking out bridle joints.
3. Set mortise gauge to 10mm (⅜in) and gauge legs and rails for bridle joint (see joint details in isometric view).
4. Cut joints and fit.
5. Shape ends of top rail and mark out dovetails.
6. Bevel end rails, mark out and cut pins.
7. Cut legs at floor line, and taper in two elevations as shown in drawing.
8. Cut mortises for buttons.
9. Make waggon bevels on side and end rails, and try table together.
10. Clean up all inner surfaces, mask joints and polish.
11. Glue up side frames, place a piece of paper and a cramping block on either side of bridle joint, and cramp up with 'G' cramps. Check legs for alignment.
12. Flush joints on face side and clean up sides.
13. Glue up end rails and test table for square.
14. Flush dovetails and clean up for polishing.
15. Cut top to size, shape, chamfer and clean up.
16. Complete all polishing.
17. Fix top with buttons.

    Note: a separate detail shows alternative construction with dovetail housing joint at end rails.

Suggested Material

Guarea, African walnut, Columbian pine, oak.

Cutting list

Description	Length	Width	Thickness
4 legs	425mm (1ft 5in)	45mm (1¾in)	23mm (⅞in)
2 side rails	600mm (2ft)	50mm (2in)	20mm (¾in)
2 end rails	350mm (1ft 2in)	47mm (1⅞in)	20mm (¾in)
1 top	675mm (2ft 3in)	390mm (15½in)	20mm (¾in)
10 buttons	40mm (1½in)	25mm (1in)	20mm (¾in)

10 32mm (1¼in) × 8 countersunk screws

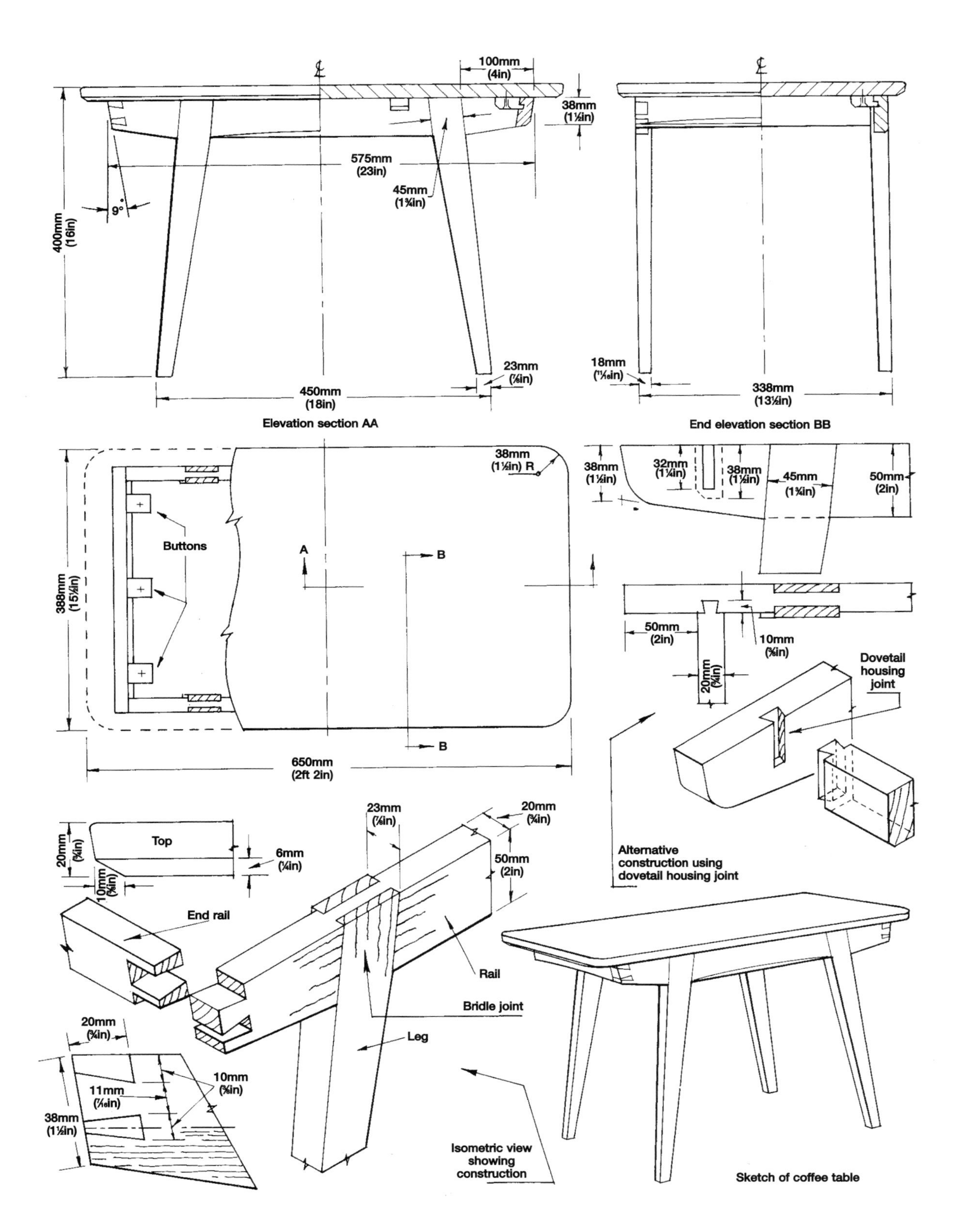
100mm
(4in)
38mm
(1½in)
575mm
(23in)
45mm
(1¾in)
9°
400mm
(16in)
23mm
(⅞in)
450mm
(18in)
Elevation section AA
18mm
(11/16in)
338mm
(13½in)
End elevation section BB
38mm
(1½in) R
Buttons
A
B
388mm
(15½in)
650mm
(2ft 2in)
38mm
(1½in)
32mm
(1¼in)
38mm
(1½in)
45mm
(1¾in)
50mm
(2in)
50mm
(2in)
10mm
(⅜in)
20mm
(¾in)
Dovetail
housing
joint
Alternative
construction using
dovetail housing joint
20mm
(¾in)
Top
6mm
(¼in)
10mm
(⅜in)
23mm
(⅞in)
20mm
(¾in)
50mm
(2in)
End rail
Rail
Bridle joint
Leg
20mm
(¾in)
10mm
(⅜in)
11mm
(7/16in)
38mm
(1½in)
Isometric view
showing
construction
Sketch of coffee table

Bedside Table

This table is a clean, well-proportioned design, with unusual features. It has no back, and both sides are similarly finished, and if required it can be used as an occasional table. The shaped ends and chamfering makes an attractive finish. Note the running out of chamfers at bottom of legs and the top corner treatment; the dovetails are arranged to accentuate the corner. The student should be aware of design possibilities and encouraged to make neat sketches of alternative designs, within the dimensional limits of the table.

Suggestions

1 A back, and a door fitted.
2 Back and drawer only.

It introduces the circular tenon and wedge as a decorative feature and gives further chamfering and dovetailing practice.

Method

1 Prepare all material, arrange and match the grain.
2 Mark out top for dovetailing, and cut tails.
3 Mark out ends in pairs, cut pins and fit dovetails.
4 Mark out positions of circular tenons on sides and bore the 16mm (5/8in) diameter holes: bore from each side to prevent splitting, keeping the bit at right angles to the wood.
5 Cut stopped housings at bottom and shelf, finishing to correct depth with a router.
6 Cut and fit shelf.
7 Fit bottom shelf into housing, and with an awl, mark round inside of holes to give positions of circular tenons. Bevel bottom edges of both shelves.
8 Cut tenons square, remove waste between with a bow saw, and round tenons with a wood file. Fit tenons, and test for square. Make saw kerf for wedges – note direction of saw kerf.
9 Bow saw legs, clean up and work all chamfers.
10 Clean up inside surfaces for polishing and mask all joints.
11 Cut rosewood wedges, prepare cramping pieces, adjust sufficient cramps and glue up. Make diagonal test for squareness. Glue and carefully drive in wedges.
12 Flush all joints, make chamfers at end of dovetails, and finish top corners with a flat-bottom spokeshave – see constructional views.
13 *Finish:* polish or wax.

Suggested Material

African walnut or oak.

Cutting list

Description	Length	Width	Thickness
2 sides	625mm (2ft 1in)	225mm (9in)	18mm (11/16in)
1 top	400mm (1ft 4in)	225mm (9in)	18mm (11/16in)
1 bottom	400mm (1ft 4in)	225mm (9in)	18mm (11/16in)
1 shelf	375mm (1ft 3in)	225mm (9in)	18mm (11/16in)

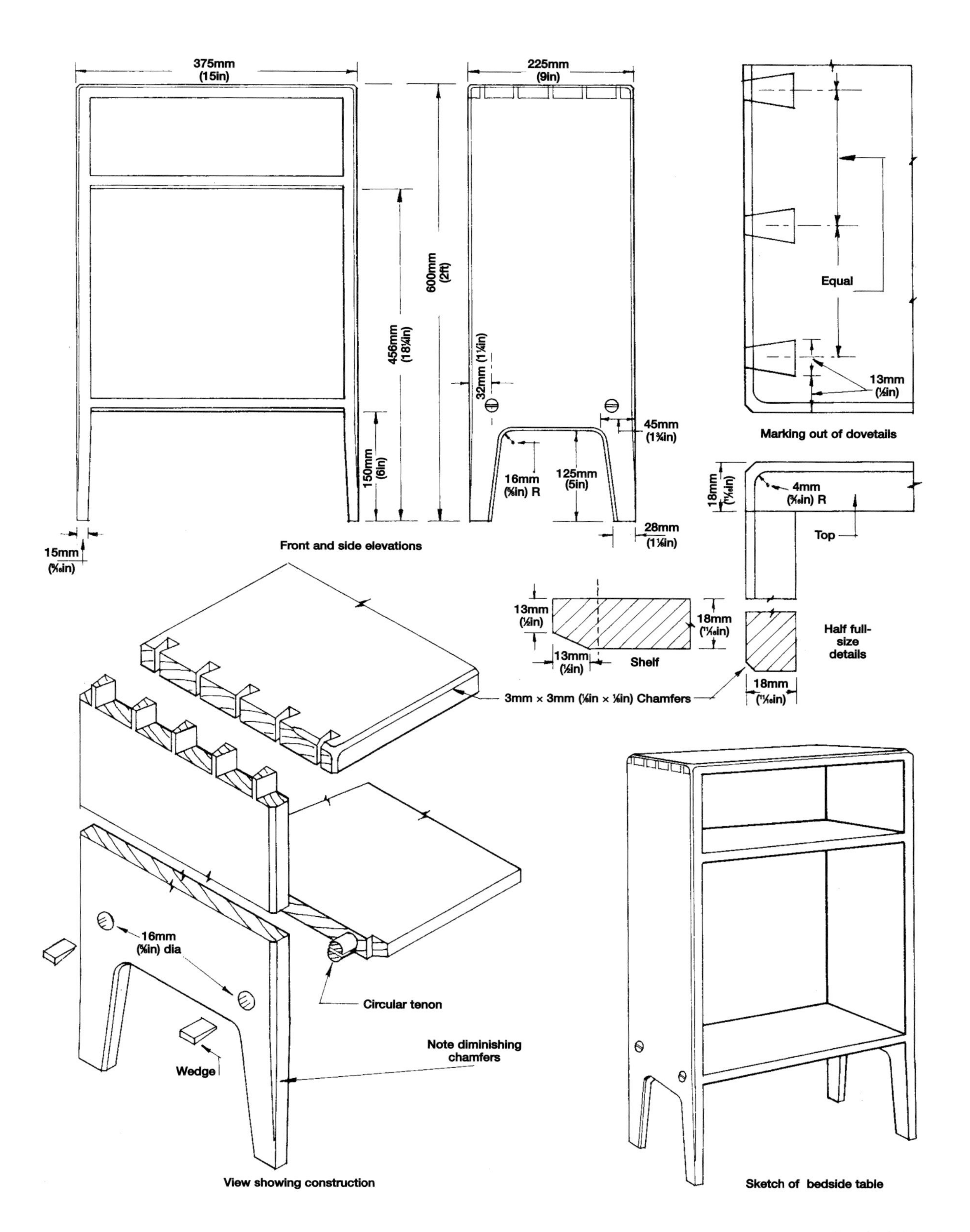
375mm
(15in)
225mm
(9in)
600mm
(2ft)
456mm
(18¼in)
32mm (1¼in)
45mm
(1¾in)
16mm
(⅝in) R
125mm
(5in)
150mm
(6in)
28mm
(1⅛in)
15mm
(⅝in)
Front and side elevations
Equal
13mm
(½in)
Marking out of dovetails
18mm
(11⁄16in)
4mm
(3⁄16in) R
Top
13mm
(½in)
18mm
(11⁄16in)
13mm
(½in)
Shelf
Half full-size details
18mm
(11⁄16in)
3mm × 3mm (⅛in × ⅛in) Chamfers
16mm
(⅝in) dia
Circular tenon
Note diminishing chamfers
Wedge
View showing construction
Sketch of bedside table

Bookcase

This could be an invaluable small bookcase for the home, simple in design and construction. The shelves are set in slightly from the sides; this treatment gives an individual touch and facilitates cleaning up. Diminished sides remove that heavy look, and cater for books of various sizes. The main constructional feature is the housing joint, strengthened with through and wedged tenons, which resists the outward thrust of the books upon the sides. A good alternative joint designed to resist this type of thrust is the dovetail housing joint (see page 135). It is particularly good for carcase work. The plinth and bottom shelf are strengthened with glue blocks. Wedge up with a contrasting wood. With slight modifications a panelled back could be incorporated.

Method

1. Prepare material, arrange and match the grain.
2. Mark out sides in pairs (handed).
3. *Sides:* mark out position of circular tenons and bore the 16mm ($\frac{5}{8}$in) diameter holes.
4. *Sides:* cut stopped housings and finish to correct depth with a router.
5. *Sides:* work rebates for plywood back and cut grooves for plinth (see details), shape sides and work chamfers.
6. Mark out shelves, and circular tenons as described in previous plate.
7. Fit shelves and bevel front edges, make saw kerfs in circular tenons.
8. Work tongues and fit plinth.
9. Clean up all inner surfaces and mask joints for polishing.
10. Prepare for gluing up, glue blocks made, sash cramps adjusted and cramping blocks ready.
11. Glue up and wedge, test for square, rub glue blocks into position and remove all surplus glue.
12. Fit plywood back and clean up for polishing, fix and screw at 100mm (4in) centres with 16mm ($\frac{5}{8}$in) × 6 countersunk screws.
13. Fit, glue and screw up back rail.

    Note: alternative square tenon at bottom shelf.

Suggested Material

African walnut, mahogany, oak or parana pine.

Cutting list

Description	Length	Width	Thickness
2 sides	975mm (3ft 3in)	213mm (8$\frac{1}{2}$in)	18mm (1$\frac{1}{16}$in)
1 bottom shelf	613mm (2ft $\frac{1}{2}$in)	200mm (8in)	18mm (1$\frac{1}{16}$in)
1 shelf	613mm (2ft $\frac{1}{2}$in)	188mm (7$\frac{1}{2}$in)	18mm (1$\frac{1}{16}$in)
1 shelf	600mm (2ft)	175mm (7in)	18mm (1$\frac{1}{16}$in)
1 top shelf	613mm (2ft $\frac{1}{2}$in)	163mm (6$\frac{1}{2}$in)	18mm (1$\frac{1}{16}$in)
1 plinth	600mm (2ft)	82mm (3$\frac{1}{4}$in)	13mm ($\frac{1}{2}$in)
1 back rail	600mm (2ft)	73mm (2$\frac{7}{8}$in)	13mm ($\frac{1}{2}$in)
1 plywood back	825mm (2ft 9in)	600mm (24in)	4mm ($\frac{3}{16}$in)
glue blocks out of	200mm (8in)	32mm (1$\frac{1}{4}$in)	32mm (1$\frac{1}{4}$in)

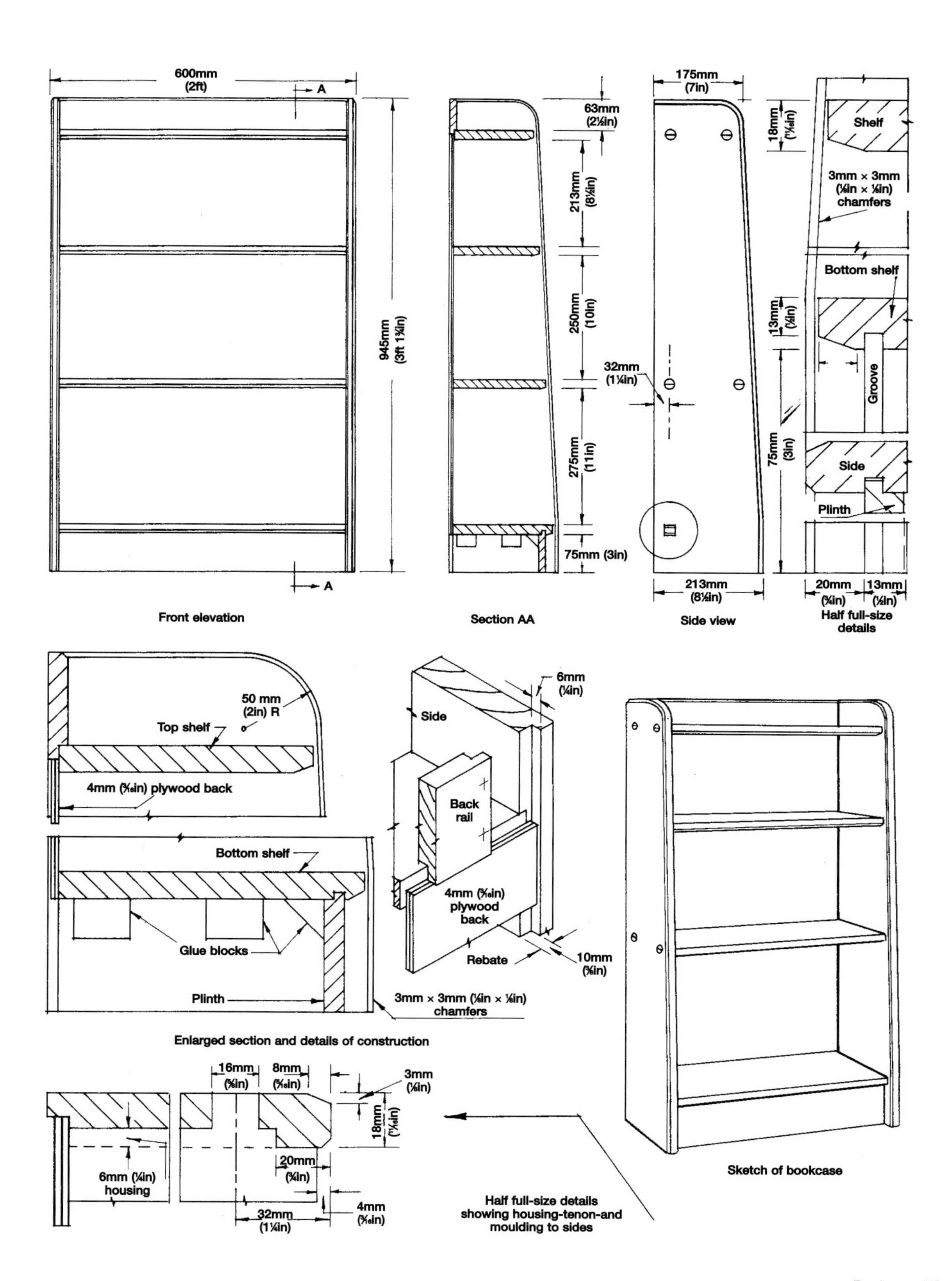
600mm
(2ft)
A
945mm
(3ft 1¼in)
A
Front elevation
63mm
(2½in)
213mm
(8½in)
250mm
(10in)
275mm
(11in)
75mm (3in)
Section AA
175mm
(7in)
32mm
(1¼in)
213mm
(8½in)
Side view
18mm
(11/16in)
Shelf
3mm × 3mm
(⅛in × ⅛in)
chamfers
Bottom shelf
13mm
(½in)
Groove
75mm
(3in)
Side
Plinth
20mm
(¾in)
13mm
(½in)
Half full-size
details
50 mm
(2in) R
Top shelf
4mm (3/16in) plywood back
Bottom shelf
Glue blocks
Plinth
3mm × 3mm (⅛in × ⅛in)
chamfers
Enlarged section and details of construction
6mm
(¼in)
Side
Back
rail
4mm (3/16in)
plywood
back
Rebate
10mm
(⅜in)
Sketch of bookcase
16mm
(⅝in)
8mm
(5/16in)
3mm
(⅛in)
18mm
(11/16in)
20mm
(¾in)
6mm (¼in)
housing
32mm
(1¼in)
4mm
(3/16in)
Half full-size details
showing housing-tenon-and
moulding to sides

Workbox

This is a compact yet commodious workbox, designed to be made in oak with walnut mouldings and dowels. By giving some thought to colour harmony other suitable woods might be used. Design features to be noted: diminished bevels at outside of legs, applied mouldings and dowels of a contrasting wood and the use of multi-ply for the top, which is not lipped as the plies make an attractive texture. However, for more advanced work the top could be veneered both sides and lipped (see page 163). The sliding tray is dovetailed and mitred on top and bottom edges, to take moulding and rebate. (See pages 65 and 137 for further application of this joint.) The front and back are ploughed to receive the fillets on which the tray slides. Note the proportions of the mortise-and-tenon joints at legs, and that the secret haunch is preferable to a square haunch in this situation. The ends are tongued and dowelled to the legs.

Method

1 Prepare the material, arrange and match the grain to the best advantage.
2 Set out legs in pairs, and gauge mortises.
3 Set out sides, adjust mortise gauge and gauge the tenons.
4 Mark out and make grooves on legs to receive ends, stop grooves 25mm (1in) from top and bottom edges of rails.
5 Cut mortises and tenons.
Note: as an alternative to sawing tenons on a wide rail, try using a metal rebate or fillister plane, fitted with a spur for cross grain work. Fit sides together.
6 Set out ends, cut tongues and try together.
7 Work rebates for bottom, and plough sides for tray fillets.
8 Diminish legs, and work inside bevels, clean up all inner surfaces; as sides and ends are set in from the legs they must be cleaned up before gluing. Mask all joints and polish.
9 Glue up front and back, allow to dry and work outer bevels. Glue in tray fillets.
10 Fit and screw plywood bottom (see enlarged details for method of fitting corners).
11 Glue up ends and fix bottom.
12 Bore holes, and glue in dowels.
13 Flush legs at top and clean off dowels.
14 Prepare applied mouldings, glue and screw to bottom edge of box.
15 Prepare and shape top, fit butts and stay, and complete polishing.
16 *Tray:* mark out ends, cut dovetails and make grooves for divisions. Mark out sides and cut pins. Fit divisions and try together. Work moulding on top edge and rebate for bottom. See drawing for dovetail proportions. Note the top and bottom edges are mitred to receive the rebated and moulded edges of tray.
17 Glue up. Fit and glue bottom in place.
18 Polish tray.

Suggested Material

Oak with walnut mouldings and dowels.

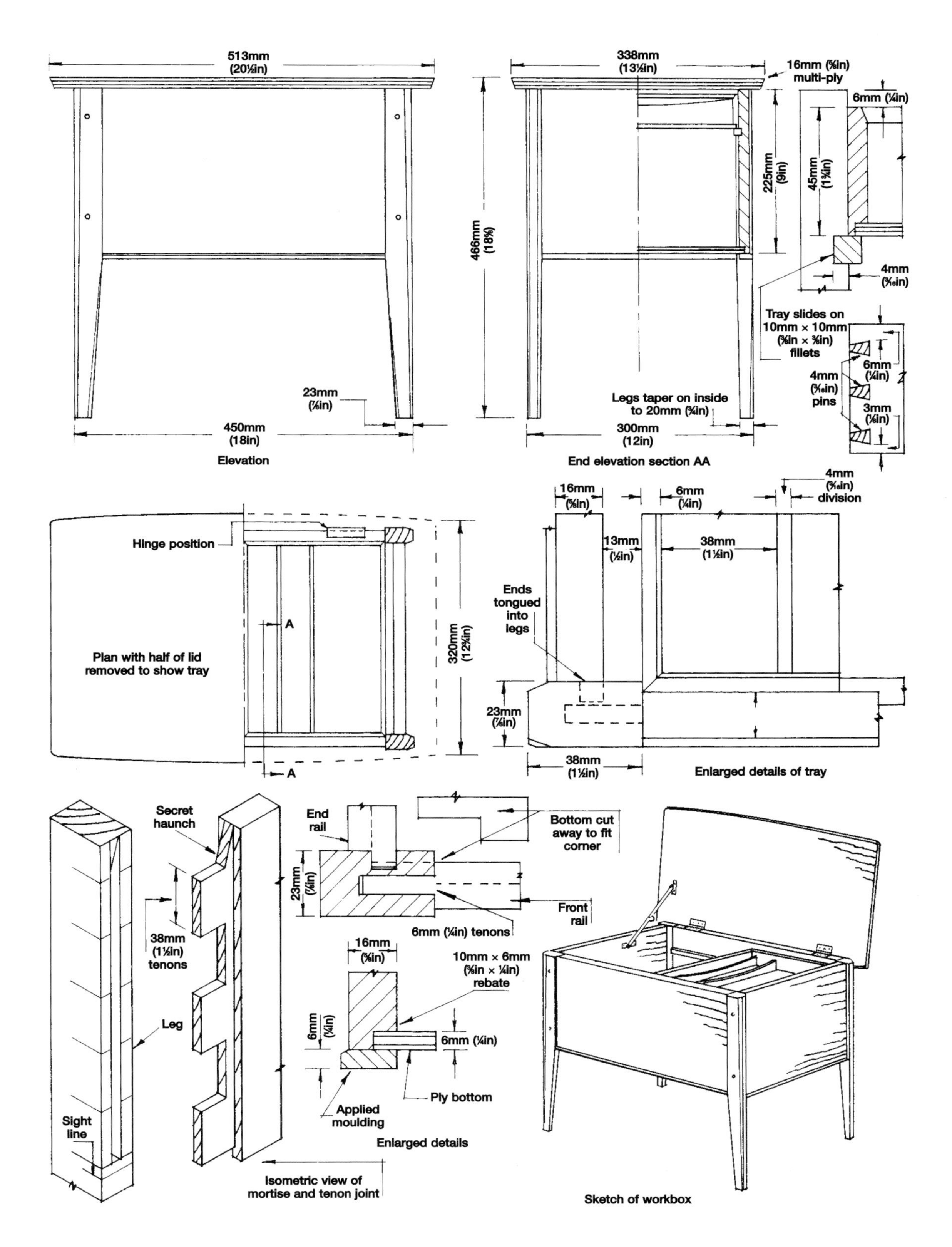

513mm
(20½in)
450mm
(18in)
23mm
(⅞in)
Elevation
338mm
(13¼in)
16mm (⅝in)
multi-ply
466mm
(18⅝)
225mm
(9in)
Legs taper on inside
to 20mm (¾in)
300mm
(12in)
End elevation section AA
6mm (¼in)
45mm
(1¾in)
4mm
(3/16in)
Tray slides on
10mm × 10mm
(⅜in × ⅜in)
fillets
4mm
(3/16in)
pins
6mm
(¼in)
3mm
(⅛in)
Hinge position
Plan with half of lid
removed to show tray
A
A
320mm
(12⅝in)
16mm
(⅝in)
6mm
(¼in)
4mm
(3/16in)
division
13mm
(½in)
38mm
(1½in)
Ends
tongued
into
legs
23mm
(⅞in)
38mm
(1½in)
Enlarged details of tray
Secret
haunch
38mm
(1½in)
tenons
Leg
Sight
line
Isometric view of
mortise and tenon joint
End
rail
23mm
(⅞in)
Bottom cut
away to fit
corner
Front
rail
6mm (¼in) tenons
16mm
(⅝in)
10mm × 6mm
(⅜in × ¼in)
rebate
6mm
(¼in)
6mm (¼in)
Applied
moulding
Ply bottom
Enlarged details
Sketch of workbox

Cutting list

Description	Length	Width	Thickness
4 legs	475mm (1ft 7in)	38mm (1½in)	23mm (⅞in)
2 sides	450mm (1ft 6in)	225mm (9in)	16mm (⅝in)
2 ends	300mm (1ft)	225mm (9in)	16mm (⅝in)
2 tray sides	300mm (1ft)	45mm (1¾in)	6mm (¼in)
2 tray ends	200mm (8in)	45mm (1¾in)	6mm (¼in)
2 partitions	200mm (8in)	36mm (1⁷⁄₁₆in)	4mm (³⁄₁₆in)
2 fillets	450mm (1ft 6in)	10mm (⅜in)	10mm (⅜in)
2 side mouldings	400mm (1ft 4in)	20mm (¾in)	6mm (¼in)
2 end mouldings	275mm (11in)	20mm (¾in)	6mm (¼in)
1 multi-ply top	525mm (1ft 9in)	338mm (13½in)	16mm (⅝in)
1 plywood bottom	425mm (1ft 5in)	300mm (1ft)	6mm (¼in)
1 tray bottom	275mm (11in)	188mm (7½in)	3mm (⅛in)
8 dowels	50mm (2in)	6mm (¼in) diameter	
1 pair 38mm (1½in) solid brass butts			
1 rule joint stay, brass 100mm (4in)			

Tools not in Basic Kit

Shoulder plane – for finishing rail shoulders. Plough – to make grooves for tray fillets.

Occasional Table

This design would be suitable for a television or hall table. A distinctive feature of this well-proportioned and elegant table are the tapered legs; the rails have been set back to accentuate the taper and line of the legs. The alternative rail treatments suggested give scope for individual work. A cock bead or string in a contrasting wood adds a distinctive touch. The drawing clearly shows setting-out procedure, joint proportions, and the use of the mortise-and-tenon joint for table construction. As an alternative to solid wood for the top, the drawing shows the use of lamin-board or multi-ply which can be veneered or faced with Formica, and lipped. The rails, alternatively, could be veneered as shown in one of the detail drawings. The table provides good practice in setting out, mortise-and-tenon work, use of the plough and rebate planes, cleaning up, preparing work for polishing and gluing up.

Method

1. Prepare material, arrange and match the grain.
2. Set out legs in pairs. The drawing gives full details of tenon proportions, method of setting out, use of marking knife, pencil and application of face marks.
3. Set out in pairs the long and short rails. Set mortise gauge to an 8mm (5/16in) mortise chisel and gauge the tenons.
4. Owing to the rails being set back, re-adjust the mortise gauge, gauge and cut the mortises.
5. Saw down the tenons, plough the groove for buttons, and make rebates for beads.
6. Saw down the shoulders to remove the tenon cheeks, mark size of tenon, and cut mitres and secret haunch.
7. Carefully fit all joints, testing for square and alignment (see page 59).
8. Cut legs at floor line and taper to dimensions as shown in drawing.
9. Clean up all surfaces including face side of rails, mask joints and polish.
10. Glue up the two long sides, and check for wind (see page 176), making sure all surplus glue has been removed. Leave to dry.
11. Check fitting of short rails. Complete gluing up and test for square.
12. *Top:* sometimes it is necessary to join two pieces together to obtain the required width. In these circumstances carefully match the grain. Shoot the edges and glue up as a straight joint. Shape and work mouldings, clean up and polish.
13. Make cock bead, polish, glue and panel pin to rebate.
14. Button top, and complete polishing as required.

    Note: alternative laminated and lipped top as shown in separate detail, may, owing to its non-shrinkage properties, be pocket screwed to table frame.

Suggested Material

African walnut, guarea or mahogany, with suitable contrasting beads.

Cutting list

Description	Length	Width	Thickness
4 legs	625mm (2ft 1in)	35mm (1⅜in)	35mm (1⅜in)
2 rails	500mm (1ft 8in)	75mm (3in)	20mm (¾in)
2 rails	375mm (1ft 3in)	75mm (3in)	20mm (¾in)
1 top	625mm (2ft 1in)	450mm (18in)	20mm (¾in)
2 cock beads	450mm (1ft 6in)	13mm (½in)	4mm (3/16in)
2 cock beads	325mm (1ft 1in)	13mm (½in)	4mm (3/16in)
12 buttons	45mm (1¾in)	32mm (1¼in)	20mm (¾in)

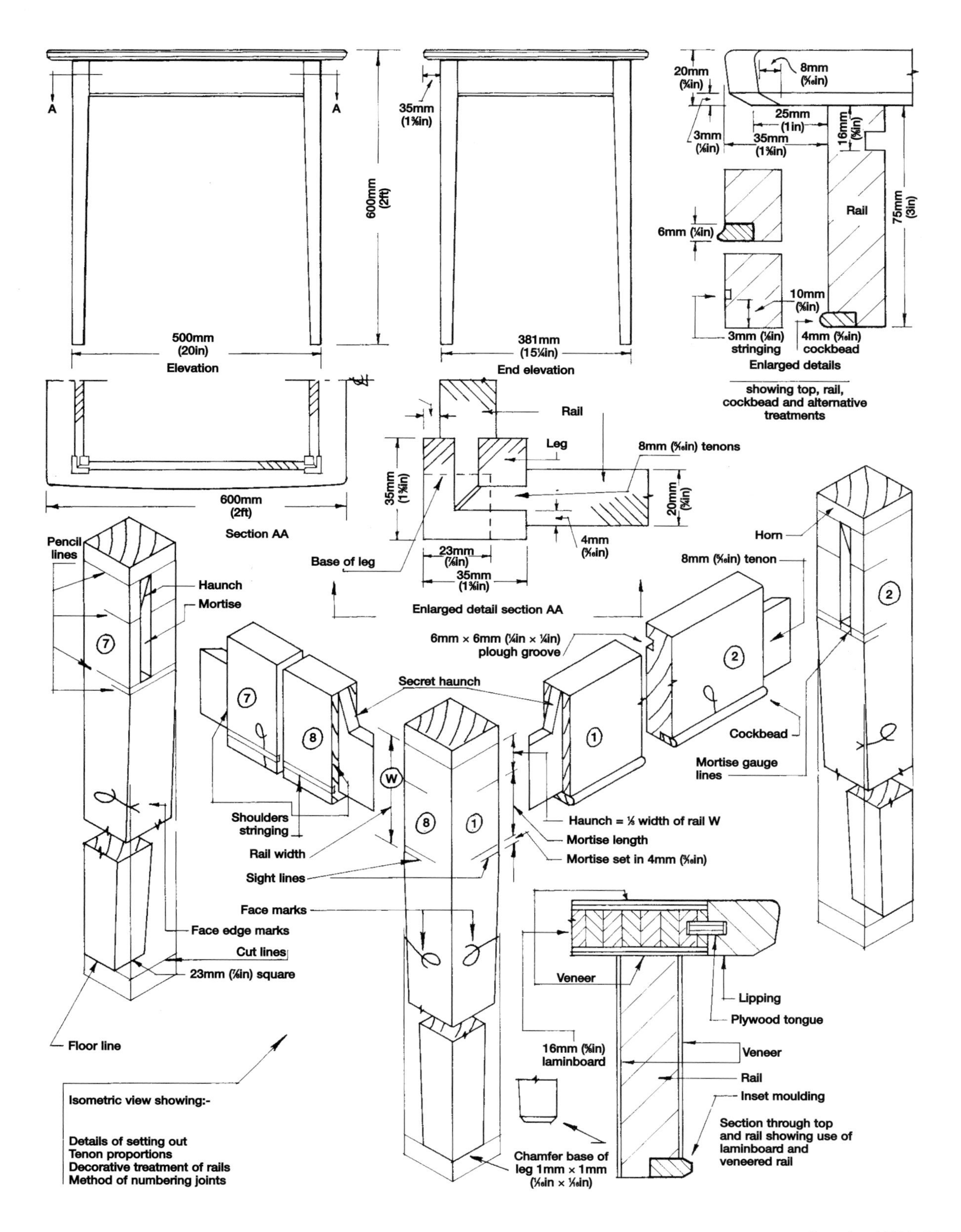
A
A
35mm
(1⅜in)
600mm
(2ft)
500mm
(20in)
Elevation
381mm
(15¼in)
End elevation
20mm
(¾in)
3mm
(⅛in)
8mm
(5⁄16in)
25mm
(1in)
35mm
(1⅜in)
16mm
(⅝in)
Rail
75mm
(3in)
6mm (¼in)
10mm
(⅜in)
3mm (⅛in)
stringing
4mm (3⁄16in)
cockbead
Enlarged details
showing top, rail,
cockbead and alternative
treatments
600mm
(2ft)
Section AA
Rail
Leg
8mm (5⁄16in) tenons
35mm
(1⅜in)
20mm
(¾in)
4mm
(3⁄16in)
23mm
(⅞in)
35mm
(1⅜in)
Base of leg
Enlarged detail section AA
Pencil
lines
Haunch
Mortise
Horn
8mm (5⁄16in) tenon
6mm × 6mm (¼in × ¼in)
plough groove
Secret haunch
Cockbead
Mortise gauge
lines
Shoulders
stringing
Rail width
Sight lines
Haunch = ⅙ width of rail W
Mortise length
Mortise set in 4mm (3⁄16in)
Face marks
Face edge marks
Cut lines
23mm (⅞in) square
Floor line
Veneer
Lipping
Plywood tongue
16mm (⅝in)
laminboard
Veneer
Rail
Inset moulding
Section through top
and rail showing use of
laminboard and
veneered rail
Chamfer base of
leg 1mm × 1mm
(1⁄16in × 1⁄16in)
Isometric view showing:-
Details of setting out
Tenon proportions
Decorative treatment of rails
Method of numbering joints

Small Workbox Table

This small workbox has somewhat similar features to the workbox on page 76, mainly because the ends have tongued-and-dowelled joints. The workbox consists of a simple tongued-and-grooved carcase, strengthened with dowels, which also make a design feature. The solid wood lid is clamped to keep it flat, and the hinging arrangements allow it to swing through an angle of 180 degrees, and form a useful extended table. Various methods of clamping are shown in the detail drawings and any one of them could be used quite successfully for this job. One detail shows the use of multi-ply and this would look well if veneered or faced with Formica, and lipped. The stand has slightly splayed legs and the through joints form a decorative treatment. The small tray is bevelled to suit the carcase and dovetailed (for angle dovetailing see page 183) and the divisions are designed to hold cotton-reels.

Method

1 Prepare material for carcase, select and match the grain.
2 It is important to make a full-size drawing of section BB, from which all bevels for carcase and stand can be taken.
3 Mark out sides, and cut grooves for ends, the grooves must stop just below the lid. At the bottom the grooves are contained within the rebate. Make grooves on top edges to take the hinging rail. Finish all grooves to depth with a router.
4 Mark out ends, cut tongues and fit together. Work rebates for the bottom on ends and sides. Stop the side rebates at the grooves. Round the corners and edges as shown in drawing. Fit and chamfer hinging rail and top of ends.
5 Clean up inner surfaces, mask all joints and polish.
6 Prepare cramps and blocks, and glue up. Test for square. Bore holes for dowels and glue in.
7 Fit bottom, glue and screw in.
8 Prepare material for stand.
9 Taper the legs full length and set out in pairs for the bridle joint and the mortise-and-tenon joints. Set mortise gauge to a 6mm (¼in) mortise chisel and gauge the bridle joint.
10 Set out long rails (note bevelled shoulders) and gauge the tenons.
11 Set out the short rails, adjust mortise gauge, gauge the tenons and mortises in the legs.
12 Cut all mortises and tenons. The bridle joint is sometimes called a slot mortise and tenon joint. Saw down the slot, keeping saw kerf in the waste, and remove centre with a mortise chisel.
13 Make waggon bevels on side rails; shape end rails and make saw kerfs in tenons for wedges.
14 Fit up side frames, fit end rails, and assemble.
15 Check for length and cut dovetails on top rails, mark round the tails to give socket positions on side rails, remove waste. Fit dovetails.
16 Clean up all inner surfaces, mask joints and polish.
17 Glue up side frames and when dry, flush the joints.
18 Glue up stand complete with end rails, and top dovetailed rails. Flush all joints.

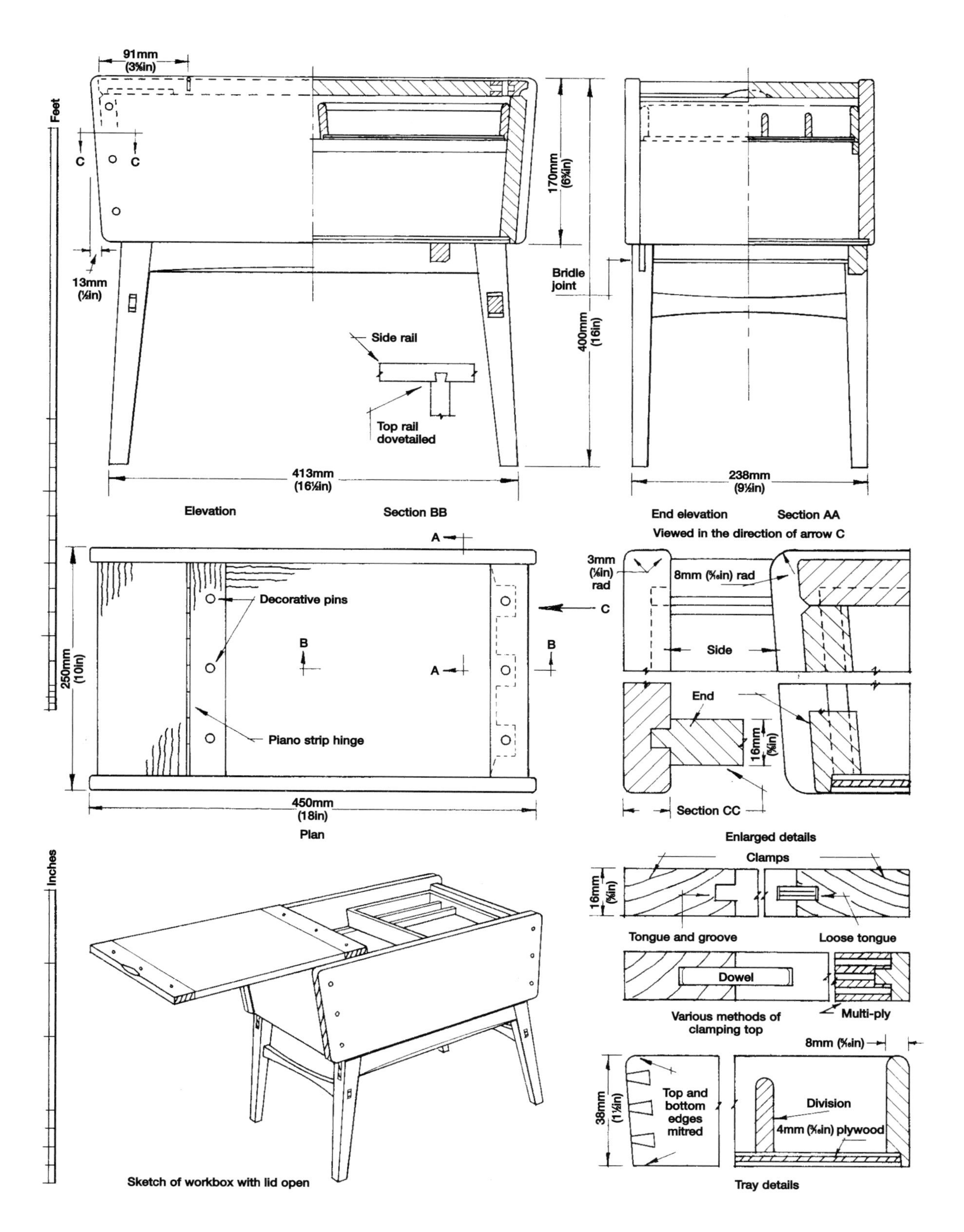

Feet
Inches
91mm
(3⅝in)
C
C
13mm
(½in)
170mm
(6¾in)
Bridle
joint
400mm
(16in)
Side rail
Top rail
dovetailed
413mm
(16½in)
238mm
(9½in)
Elevation
Section BB
End elevation
Section AA
Viewed in the direction of arrow C
A
Decorative pins
B
B
A
C
250mm
(10in)
Piano strip hinge
450mm
(18in)
Plan
3mm
(⅛in)
rad
8mm (5/16in) rad
Side
End
16mm
(⅝in)
Section CC
Enlarged details
Clamps
16mm
(⅝in)
Tongue and groove
Loose tongue
Dowel
Various methods of
clamping top
Multi-ply
8mm (5/16in)
38mm
(1½in)
Top and
bottom
edges
mitred
Division
4mm (3/16in) plywood
Tray details
Sketch of workbox with lid open

19 Flush top of stand and fix carcase through bottom into dovetailed rails.
20 Prepare material for lid and tray.
21 Cut top to length, mark out clamps and gauge mortises and tenons.
22 Cut mortises and tenons and fit together. Glue up, bore holes for decorative pins and glue in.
23 Flush all surfaces of lid, fit to carcase. Hinge lid and make recess for lifting.
24 Set out dovetails for tray, cut grooves for divisions (note bevelled ends and mitred edges of tray), make dovetail joints and rebate for bottom.
25 Fit tray divisions and bottom, clean up all surfaces and glue up.
26 Screw fillets inside to take the tray.
27 Finish polishing.

Suggested Material

Guarea, African walnut, abura, sapele, or any suitable hardwood, with sycamore for tray.

Cutting list

Description	Length	Width	Thickness
2 sides	475mm (1ft 7in)	170mm (6¾in)	16mm (⅝in)
2 ends	250mm (10in)	156mm (6¼in)	16mm (⅝in)
1 hinging rail	250mm (10in)	91mm (3⅝in)	16mm (⅝in)
1 lid	325mm (1ft 1in)	228mm (8⅞in)	16mm (⅝in)
2 clamps	250mm (10in)	38mm (1½in)	16mm (⅝in)
1 ply bottom	406mm (1ft 4¼in)	250mm (10in)	6mm (¼in)
12 dowels	38mm (1½in)	8mm (5/16in) diameter	
6 dowels for lid	25mm (1in)	8mm (5/16in) diameter	
STOOL			
4 legs	250mm (10in)	32mm (1¼in)	23mm (⅞in)
2 rails	400mm (1ft 4in)	32mm (1¼in)	20mm (¾in)
2 end rails	250mm (10in)	25mm (1in)	16mm (⅝in)
2 top rails	225mm (9in)	20mm (¾in)	20mm (¾in)
TRAY			
2 sides	225mm (9in)	38mm (1½in)	8mm (5/16in)
2 ends	200mm (8in)	38mm (1½in)	8mm (5/16in)
2 divisions	225mm (9in)	25mm (1in)	6mm (¼in)
1 ply bottom	225mm (9in)	188mm (7½in)	4mm (3/16in)
2 fillets	400mm (1ft 4in)	13mm (½in)	6mm (¼in)

1 strip of piano hinge 220mm (8¾in) long

Tools not in Basic Kit

Shoulder plane – for finishing shoulders on carcase ends, and clamped ends.
Bullnose plane – to finish stopped rebate on sides.
Router – for finishing grooves on carcase.

Shaped Woodware

The making of small pieces of shaped woodware can be both fascinating and stimulating. The economy of timber and the individual character of each piece are cardinal features. Small and irregularly shaped pieces of hardwood can be purchased from timber merchants at a reasonable price. A variety of woods, including English walnut, sycamore, cherry, pear, elm, lime, African walnut, teak and mahogany, can be used. Defects such as knots and shakes often direct the ultimate shape. Sometimes knots are surrounded by interesting grain formation, and the removal of a defect can often produce an interesting form. Apparently straight-grained wood can, during the process of shaping, produce a delightful enrichment of figure. It is this kind of discovery that makes one aware of the beauty of wood.

This chopping board and dish are both symmetrical about a centre line. They give good practice in the use of the carving gouge.

Tools needed

Few tools are required to begin with. Four carving gouges – a 10mm (⅜in) and 16mm (⅝in) wide with fairly flat curvature, and 6mm (¼in) and 13mm (½in) half round – will cover most requirements. Others can be added as the need arises. A 200mm (8in) half-round fine rasp and a 200mm (8in) medium wood file. Flat and round bottom spokeshaves. A range of glasspaper in grades from middle 2 to 0. A cabinet scraper, ground to suit the particular shape required.

General Procedure

1. Select a suitable piece of wood. Study the grain formation – it may suggest a shape – and, using a piece of chalk, make a freehand sketch of the proposed form, which need not be symmetrical. The illustration conveys the idea.
2. Commence shaping by hollowing out the dish to required depth – a 16mm (⅝in) fairly flat gouge is ideal. A mallet may be used on the gouge for the major part of this work, finishing with fine gouge cuts, using hand pressure. Difficult grain, when encountered, can be overcome by gouging at right angles to the grain.
3. Clean up with scraper and glasspaper, commencing with middle 2 and finishing with flour grade.
4. Outside shaping: bow saw to shape, finishing bevels with spokeshaves and glasspaper, rounded edges with spokeshaves, files and glass-paper.
5. *Finish:* one coat of white polish lightly rubbed down with flour glasspaper, and waxed.

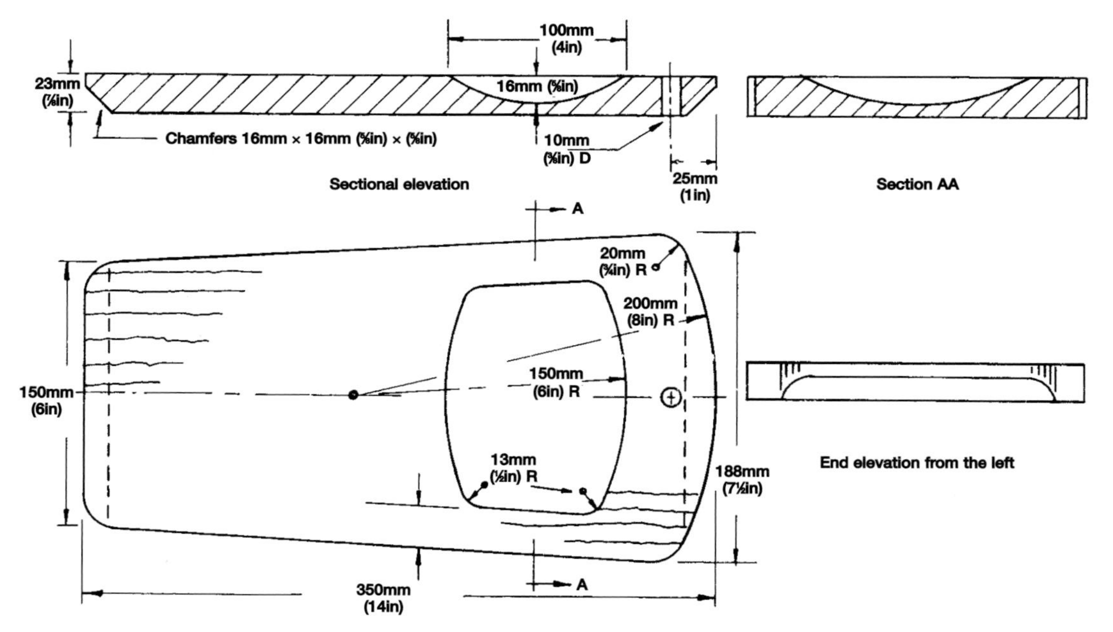

Plan of chopping board

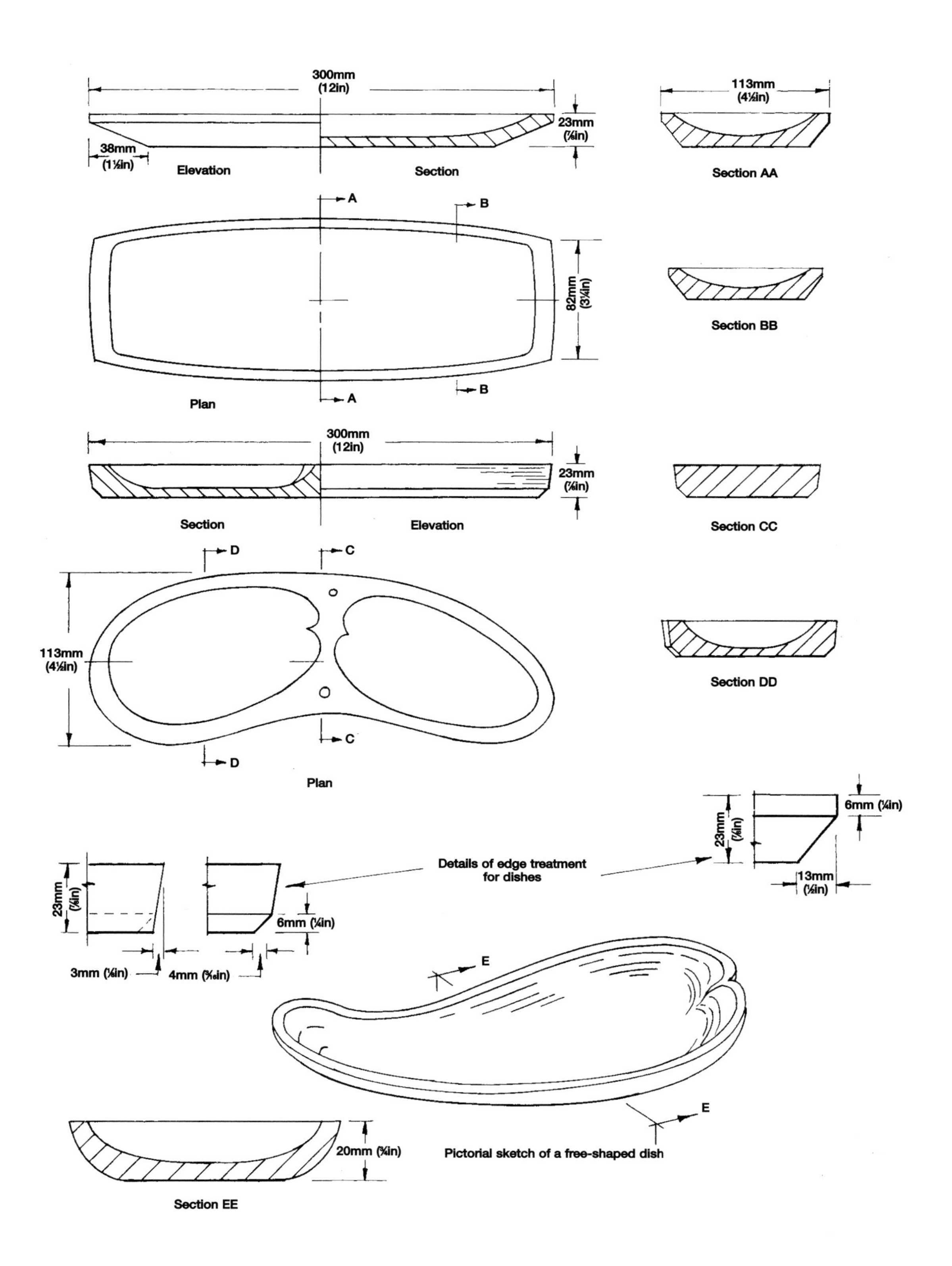
300mm
(12in)
23mm
(⅞in)
38mm
(1½in)
Elevation
Section
113mm
(4½in)
Section AA
A
B
82mm
(3¼in)
Section BB
Plan
300mm
(12in)
23mm
(⅞in)
Section
Elevation
Section CC
D
C
113mm
(4½in)
Section DD
Plan
6mm (¼in)
23mm
(⅞in)
Details of edge treatment
for dishes
13mm
(½in)
23mm
(⅞in)
6mm (¼in)
3mm (⅛in)
4mm (³⁄₁₆in)
E
20mm (¾in)
Pictorial sketch of a free-shaped dish
Section EE

Small Tiled Tray

This small tray looks attractive when made in teak or walnut, and fitted with suitable plain or decorative tiles. The tiles, which may vary from 3mm to 9mm (⅛in to ⅜in) in thickness, are inlaid and glued or cemented into the base. The tray ends are shaped and carved to form the handles, and the feet are simply housed and glued into the base. It is exciting to try out different designs for the base, feet and handles, such as to arrange for the base to have one tile only, leaving the remainder of the tray carved as on page 87.

Method

1. Prepare the material.
2. Mark out shape of tray and position of tiles – it is advisable to take dimensions from the tiles. Gauge down the length, and make firm cut lines at ends of tray.
3. Cramp firmly to bench and remove waste as suggested (figure 1 shows a simple method of making recess for the tiles). Divide the base into a number of equal parts. Chop out carefully alternate spaces (the drawing gives the idea) and finish to depth with a router. Eliminate the waste strips one at a time. This method gives support for the router.
4. Fit tiles and mark positions.
5. Cut grooves for feet.
6. Shape ends and form handles, clean up for polishing.
7. Glue in feet and flush ends.
8. Glue in tiles, using a proprietary cement or use a mixture of Unibond and Sirapite. Clean off surplus cement.
9. *Finish:* oil or white polish as desired.

Suggested Material

Elm, teak or walnut.

Cutting list

Description	Length	Width	Thickness
1 base	400mm (1ft 4in)	132mm (5¼in)	20mm (¾in)
2 feet	150mm (6in)	16mm (⅝in)	6mm (¼in)
3 tiles	100mm (4in)	100mm (4in)	

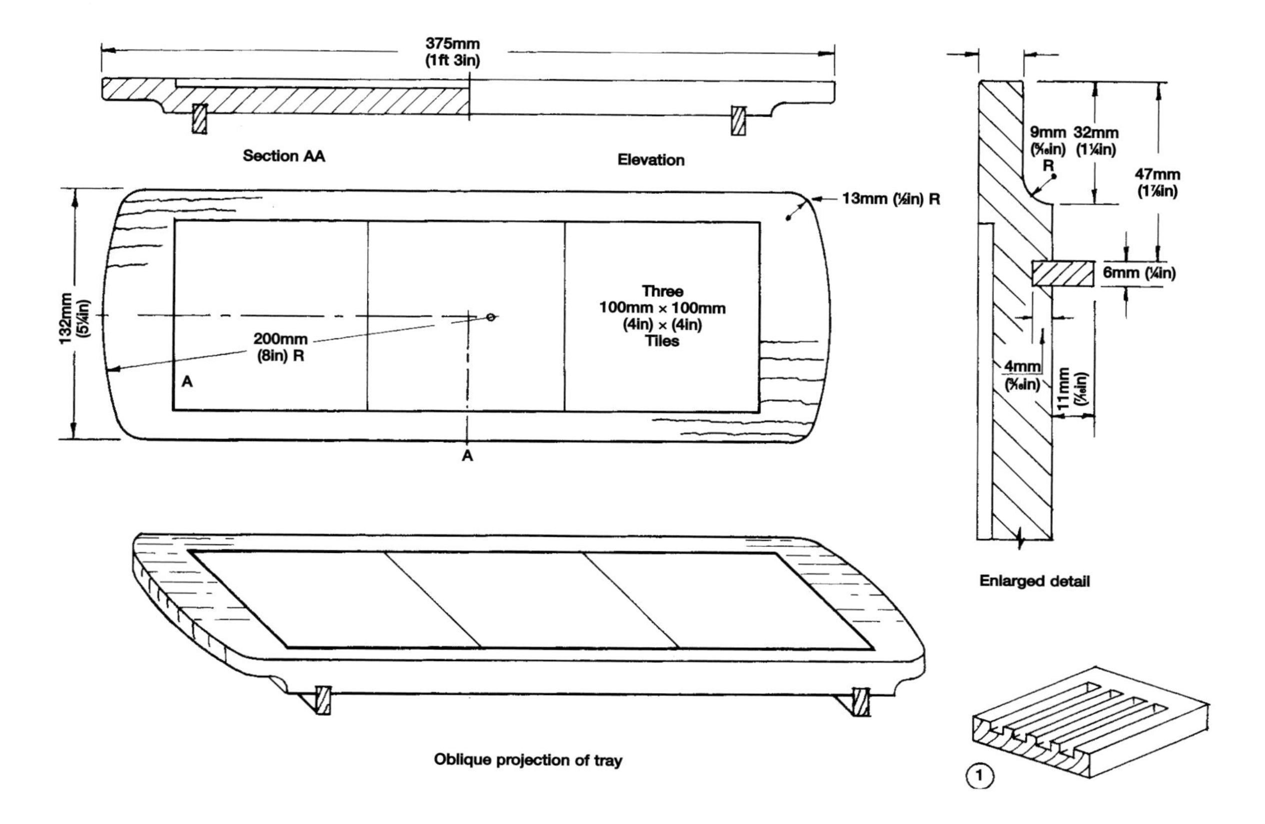
375mm
(1ft 3in)
Section AA
Elevation
13mm (½in) R
132mm
(5¼in)
200mm
(8in) R
A
A
Three
100mm × 100mm
(4in) × (4in)
Tiles
9mm
(⅜in)
R
32mm
(1¼in)
47mm
(1⅞in)
6mm (¼in)
4mm
(³⁄₁₆in)
11mm
(⁷⁄₁₆in)
Enlarged detail
Oblique projection of tray
1

Serving Tongs

A useful pair of serving tongs.

Method

1. Prepare material.
2. Taper handle as shown in detail A.
3. Mark out length of sides, glue and cramp to handle.
4. Drill for 3mm ($\frac{1}{8}$in) pins and glue in.
5. Taper sides and shape ends as shown in elevation.
6. Round end of handle.
7. Clean up, and wipe over with olive oil.

Suggested Material

Sycamore, maple or walnut.

Cutting list

Description	Length	Width	Thickness
2 sides	200mm (8in)	20mm ($\frac{3}{4}$in)	2mm ($\frac{3}{32}$in)
1 handle	38mm (1$\frac{1}{2}$in)	23mm ($\frac{7}{8}$in)	16mm ($\frac{5}{8}$in)
pins	50mm (2in)	3mm ($\frac{1}{8}$in) diameter	

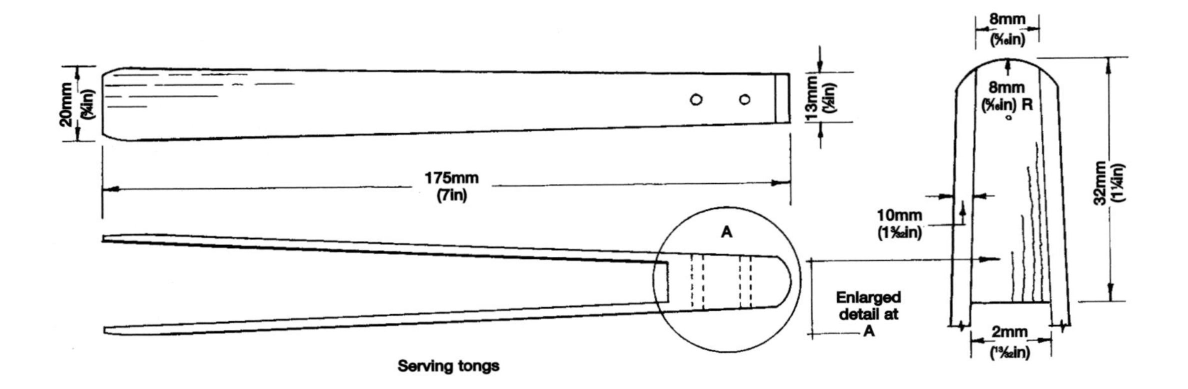

Serving tongs

Salad Servers

Salad servers can be fashioned into many exciting shapes. The spoon and fork shown in the drawing are simple to make, and provide an excellent introduction to shaped woodware.

Method

1 Prepare material.
2 Mark out length, thickness of each end, and taper as shown in the elevation.
3 Run a centre line, in pencil, down the length, and mark off dimensions as shown in plan and section.
4 Using a 16mm (⅝in) flat gouge, hollow out to a depth as shown in elevation and section.
5 Cut to outline of plan, and clean up with spokeshave, file and glasspaper.
6 Shape outside of spoon, using spokeshave, rasp, file and glasspaper.
7 To make fork, proceed as for spoon, mark out for prongs, cut with a coping saw and clean up with a file and glasspaper.
8 *Finish:* wipe over with olive oil.

Suggested Material

Walnut.

Cutting list

Description	Length	Width	Thickness
spoon	225mm (9in)	41mm (1⅝in)	13mm (½in)
fork	225mm (9in)	41mm (1⅝in)	13mm (½in)

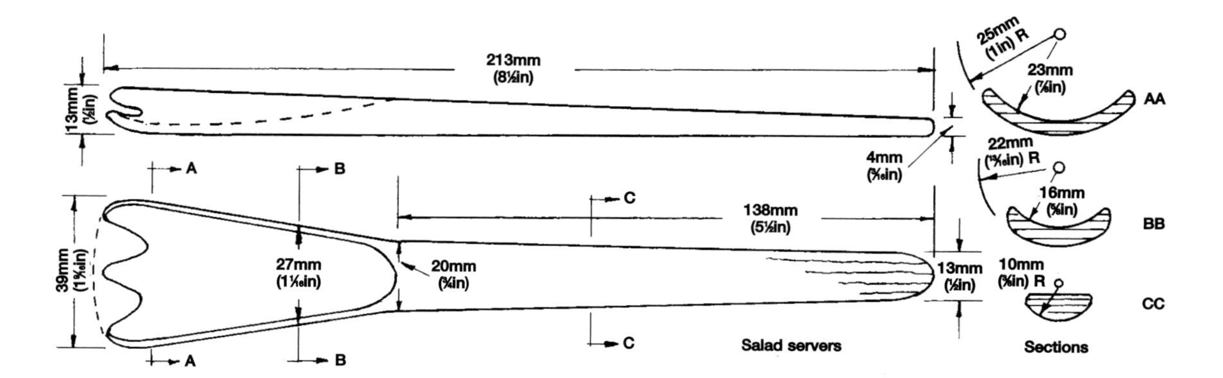

Small Garden Chair

A set of these small chairs, used with the table shown on page 179, would be ideal for meals in the garden. Painted white they would look delightful; alternatively, for a bold effect, each chair and the table could be painted a different colour. Designed as an introduction to chair-making, the chair is simple to make. It has a rectangular seat frame and square shoulders, the slats giving a diminished look to the seat. It provides good practice in setting out, the making and fitting of braces, and introduces simple jig-making. The back rails consist of three 4mm (3/16in) laminations glued up in a shaped former or jig, as shown in the drawing. A laminated rail is superior in strength to a rail cut out of the solid, as it eliminates short grain. The chair gives the student an opportunity to practise the technique of boring holes, using brass cups and screws, and the proper use and care of the screwdriver, and the use of waterproof glues.

Note: for painted work, omit the brass cups, countersink the screws slightly below the surface, and 'stop up' with a suitable filler in order to provide a flush surface.

Method

1. Prepare the material, arrange and match the grain.
2. Set out back and front legs in pairs (handed), showing position of mortises, sight lines, floor line and total height of chair. (See pages 57, 59 and 151 for further information on setting out.)
3. Set out side rails in pairs and diminish as shown in drawing.
4. Set out back and front rails.
5. Set mortise gauge to a 6mm (1/4in) mortise chisel and gauge all mortises and tenons. Note that the front and back rails are set in, and adjust the mortise gauge accordingly.
6. Cut mortises and tenons, and fit side frames. Test for wind. Chamfer rails and diminish inside of legs including slope for back.
7. Clean up inner surfaces and glue up side frames. Flush off and clean up both sides when glue is dry.
8. Make jig for back rails to a radius of 975mm (3ft 3in) and allow for the thickness of three laminations (see drawing). Candle grease rubbed over the inner surfaces of the jig, will prevent the rails adhering to the jig should surplus glue flow between them. Paper placed between the jig and rail surfaces will also give good protection. (For further information on jigs and their construction, see page 167.)
9. Glue up laminations in jig, commence cramping from the centre and work outwards, three or four 150mm (6in) 'G' cramps will be sufficient for this operation.
10. Fit front and back rails and chamfer. Complete the chamfering on side frames and glue up. Test for square and alignment. Make, fit and glue in angle braces.
11. Cut off horns and flush all joints.
12. Chamfer and clean up slats. Note housing at back legs and fitting of slat. Bore for cups and screws, and screw in back and front slats. Equally spacing remaining four slats, leaving waste on, fix with steel screws. For good appearance keep all screw slots in the same direction.

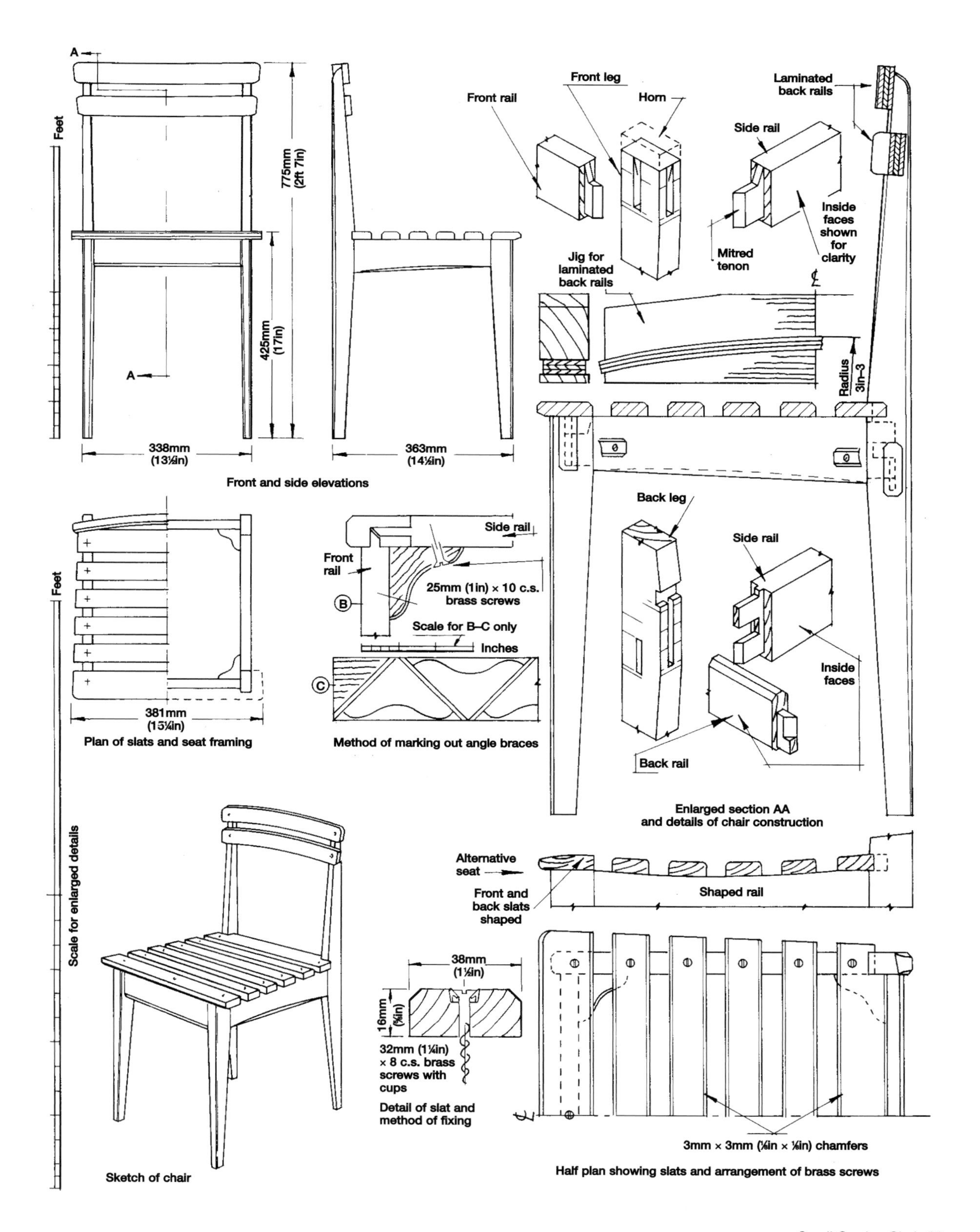

Feet
775mm
(2ft 7in)
425mm
(17in)
338mm
(13⅜in)
363mm
(14½in)
Front and side elevations
Front rail
Front leg
Horn
Laminated
back rails
Side rail
Inside
faces
shown
for
clarity
Mitred
tenon
Jig for
laminated
back rails
Radius
3in–3
Back leg
Side rail
Inside
faces
Back rail
Enlarged section AA
and details of chair construction
Side rail
Front
rail
25mm (1in) × 10 c.s.
brass screws
Scale for B–C only
Inches
Method of marking out angle braces
381mm
(15¼in)
Plan of slats and seat framing
Scale for enlarged details
Alternative
seat
Front and
back slats
shaped
Shaped rail
38mm
(1½in)
16mm
(⅝in)
32mm (1¼in)
× 8 c.s. brass
screws with
cups
Detail of slat and
method of fixing
3mm × 3mm (⅛in × ⅛in) chamfers
Half plan showing slats and arrangement of brass screws
Sketch of chair

13 Lay a straight edge on the seat and mark slats to length. Remove slats, cut to length and clean up end grain with a block plane. Re-fix slats using brass cups and screws.

14 Clean up back laminated rails, cut to length and shape. Bevel back legs to suit rails and fix with cups and screws (see enlarged details).
Fitting brass cups and screws: It is advisable to bore into a scrap piece of wood and test the diameter and depth of hole required for the cups. The cups are driven into the holes and should finish flush with the top of the slats. A depth gauge fitted to the bit controls the depth of boring. A cup below the surface of the wood constitutes poor workmanship. To prevent brass screws from shearing, and to keep the slots free from burr, drive in steel screws first. Then remove and replace them with brass screws. Dipping the thread of steel or brass screws in Russian tallow or Vaseline assists in the driving and removing of screws, and prevents steel screws rusting.
Note: a separate detail shows a seat with shaped side rails.

15 *Finish:* Oak, varnished. Teak, oiled. Selected pine, painted.

Suggested Material

Oak, teak or selected pine.

Cutting list

Description	Length	Width	Thickness
2 back legs	800mm (2ft 8in)	45mm (1¾in)	23mm (⅞in)
2 front legs	425mm (1ft 5in)	45mm (1¾in)	23mm (⅞in)
2 side rails	350mm (1ft 2in)	70mm (2¾in)	23mm (⅞in)
1 back rail	325mm (1ft 1in)	56mm (2¼in)	20mm (¾in)
1 front rail	325mm (1ft 1in)	56mm (2¼in)	20mm (¾in)
6 laminations for back rails	425mm (1ft 5in)	45mm (1¾in)	4mm (3/16in)
4 seat slats	388mm (1ft 3½in)	38mm (1½in)	16mm (⅝in)
1 front slat	400mm (1ft 4in)	56mm (2¼in)	16mm (⅝in)
1 back slat	375mm (1ft 3in)	50mm (2in)	16mm (⅝in)
1 piece for brackets	250mm (10in)	45mm (1¾in)	20mm (¾in)
jig in breech	425mm (1ft 5in)	88mm (3½in)	50mm (2in)

screws, eight, 50mm (1in) × 10 countersunk brass screws
screws, thirteen, 32mm (1¼in) × 8 countersunk brass screws with cups

Tools not in Basic Kit

Shoulder plane – for finishing rail shoulders.
Block plane – to clean up ends of slats.

Tiled Table

Select the tiles, plain or decorated, to harmonize with the wood used for the table frame. It is advisable to purchase the tiles before making the table, so that any variations in size of tiles can be allowed for in the setting out.

Proportion and simplicity is the keynote of the design. It incorporates basic stool-construction techniques and introduces a rebated top rail, necessitating a special arrangement of the secret haunch (see pages 137 and 153, and note tenon proportions). A separate detail (figure 3) shows a simple alternative to the tiled top. The depth of the rebate is increased to take 13mm (½in) Formica faced multi-plywood.

Note: generally tenons are first sawn down their length and all ploughing, rebating and moulding, if any, is completed before removing the tenon cheeks.

Method

1. Prepare material and arrange to the best advantage. Note rail and tenon proportions, and the position of the secret haunch (see page 134 for further information on stool construction).
2. Set out legs in pairs (see page 58 for information on setting out).
3. Set out long and short rails in pairs.
4. Set mortise gauge to a 6mm (¼in) mortise chisel and gauge all mortises and tenons.
5. Cut mortises and haunchings.
6. Saw down the tenons. Work plough grooves to take the fillets or tongues for the base (see figures 1 and 2). Work rebates for the tiles. Do not remove the tenon cheeks at this stage.
7. With a thumb gauge and pencil mark out the cavetto mouldings on the bottom and top edges of the rails. Chamfer down to pencil lines, and work cavetto with a moulding plane to suit the radius. Make rubber to fit mouldings, and clean up carefully with glasspaper.
8. Saw down the shoulders to remove the tenon cheeks, cut tenons to size and make the haunchings.
9. Mark length of tenons and mitre the ends (see section AA).
10. Fit all joints, set out and work grooves and rebates on end of legs (see isometric view of joint).
11. Cut legs at floor line, mark out and taper legs on the inside.
12. Clean up all inside surfaces, mask joints and polish.
13. Glue up the two side frames, test legs for alignment.
14. Flush all joints and clean up.
15. Cut multi-ply base to size and make the tongues. Fit and try table together complete with end rails.

    Note: if fillets are used to support the base as shown in diagram 2, the table can be glued up without the base. Fillets and base are added later.
16. Glue up end rails and base, test for alignment.
17. Flush all joints, and complete moulding at top of legs – a 6mm (¼in) scribing gouge is useful here.
18. Complete polishing.
19. Arrange and glue tiles to base (see page 88, step 8).

Suggested Material

Sapele, oak or beech.

Cutting list

Description	Length	Width	Thickness
4 legs	438mm (1ft 5½in)	32mm (1¼in)	32mm (1¼in)
2 side rails	625mm (2ft 1in)	75mm (3in)	20mm (¾in)
2 end rails	325mm (1ft 1in)	75mm (3in)	20mm (¾in)
1 piece of plywood for base	600mm (2ft)	300mm (12in)	13mm (½in) multi-ply
8 tiles	150mm (6in)	150mm (6in)	varies

Tools not in Basic Kit

Shoulder plane – for finishing rail shoulders.
Plough – for ploughing grooves in rails to take base.
Moulding plane (Round) – for cavetto mouldings on rails.

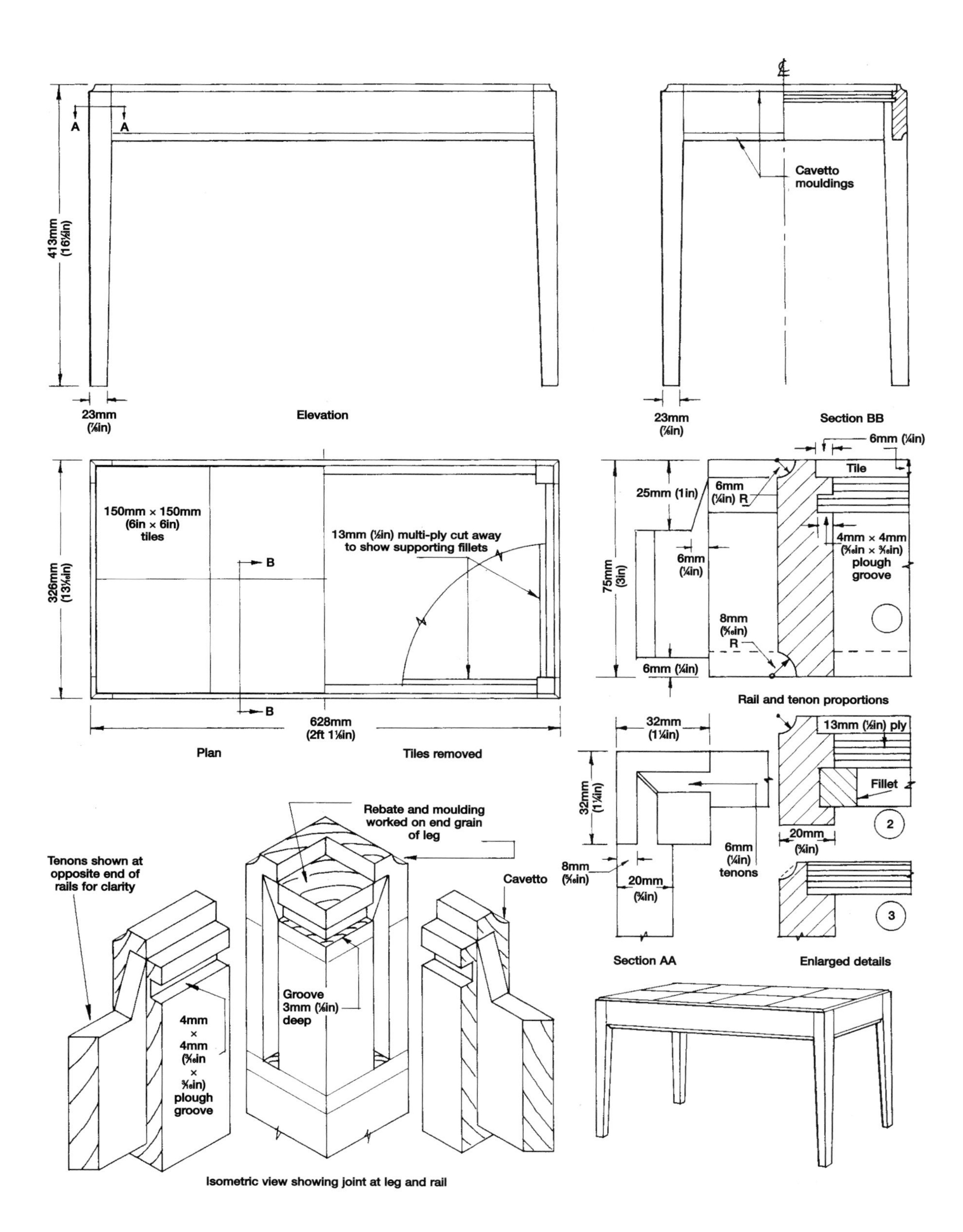

413mm (16½in)
A
A
23mm (⅞in)
Elevation
Cavetto mouldings
23mm (⅞in)
Section BB
150mm × 150mm (6in × 6in) tiles
13mm (½in) multi-ply cut away to show supporting fillets
B
B
326mm (13⅞in)
628mm (2ft 1⅛in)
Plan
Tiles removed
6mm (¼in)
Tile
25mm (1in)
6mm (¼in) R
6mm (¼in)
75mm (3in)
4mm × 4mm (³⁄₁₆in × ³⁄₁₆in) plough groove
8mm (⁵⁄₁₆in) R
6mm (¼in)
Rail and tenon proportions
32mm (1¼in)
32mm (1¼in)
6mm (¼in) tenons
8mm (⁵⁄₁₆in)
20mm (¾in)
Section AA
13mm (½in) ply
Fillet
2
20mm (¾in)
3
Enlarged details
Rebate and moulding worked on end grain of leg
Tenons shown at opposite end of rails for clarity
Cavetto
Groove 3mm (⅛in) deep
4mm × 4mm (³⁄₁₆in × ³⁄₁₆in) plough groove
Isometric view showing joint at leg and rail

Small Coffee Table

This is a delightful small table of pleasing proportions. It emphasises restraint in the use of material and simplicity in design. The choice of colour for the Formica top should be carefully considered in relation to the wood used so as to produce a satisfactory colour harmony.

The table necessitates neat and accurate craftsmanship, and provides good experience in setting out, shaping, gluing up and finishing. Note tenon proportions and shaping of legs. For splayed work it is good practice to make a full-sized detail drawing, from which all bevels can be accurately obtained. The separate detail drawing of leg and end rail conveys the idea.

Method

1 Prepare the material, arrange and match the grain.
2 Set out the legs in pairs. A separate drawing (enlarged details) shows tenon proportions, shaping of legs and top rails.
3 Set out in pairs the long and short rails – the shoulders are not square on the long rails. Set mortise gauge to a 6mm (¼in) mortise chisel and gauge mortises and tenons for side frames.
4 Adjust mortise gauge and mark out mortises on legs for end rails. Make a further adjustment and gauge tenons on end rails.
5 Cut all mortises and tenons, and plough the long rails to take the top before removing tenon cheeks.
6 Fit side frames together and test for wind.
7 Taper inside of legs, stopping at quadrant as indicated by dotted lines (see enlarged details).
8 Taper inside of legs below end rails.
9 Work waggon bevels on the bottom edge of side rails, and bevels on the inside top edge. Clean up all inner edges, mask joints and polish.
10 Glue up side frames, and test legs for wind. Flush off when glue is set, polish inside.
11 Shape end rails and make saw kerfs for wedges. Clean up and polish.
12 Cut plywood top to size, and plough grooves to receive the lipping. The grooves are continued round the top and stop at the leg position. Glue on the Formica.

Note: the following information for fixing Formica, or other types of plastic sheet can be applied to all the designs in this book incorporating laminated plastic-faced veneer, as these use relatively small pieces and require no special equipment for gluing up.

Adhesives for bonding (for normal domestic uses).

The solvent adhesives – one solution cement impact type – are simple to use. Adhesion is instantaneous and prolonged pressure is unnecessary.

The synthetic resin cements are heatproof and reliable in damp situations. Evenly spread cramping pressure is essential. The method of cramping as used in caul veneering could be adopted. (For information on caul veneering see page 161.)

Application: Before gluing, lightly glasspaper plastic veneer and plywood base, and clean surface free from dust.

13 Lay the side frames on a cutting board and using a 6mm (¼in) scribing

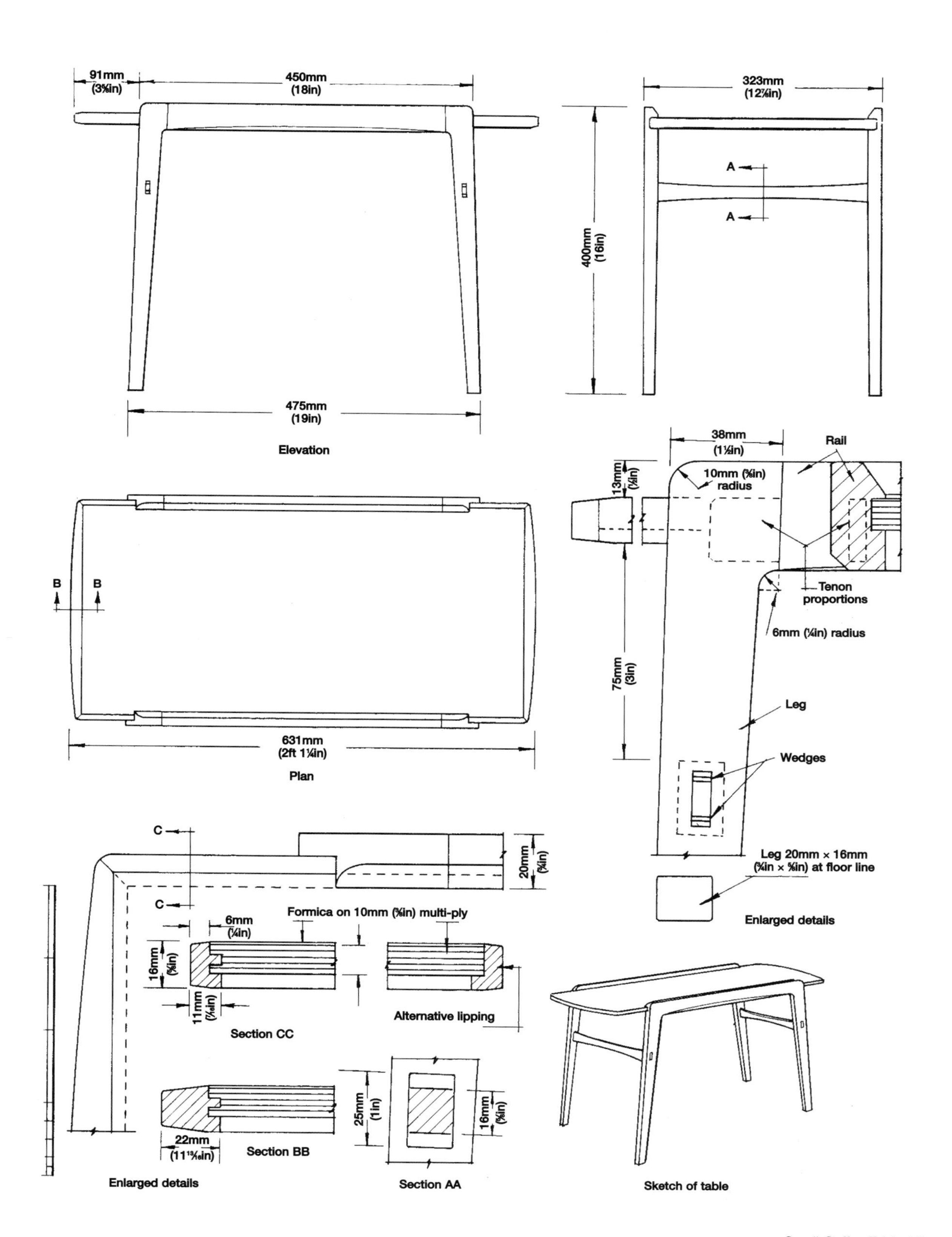
91mm
(3⅝in)
450mm
(18in)
475mm
(19in)
Elevation
323mm
(12⅞in)
A
A
400mm
(16in)
631mm
(2ft 1¼in)
Plan
B
B
38mm
(1½in)
Rail
13mm
(½in)
10mm (⅜in)
radius
Tenon
proportions
6mm (¼in) radius
75mm
(3in)
Leg
Wedges
Leg 20mm × 16mm
(¾in × ⅝in) at floor line
Enlarged details
C
C
20mm
(¾in)
Formica on 10mm (⅜in) multi-ply
6mm
(¼in)
16mm
(⅝in)
11mm
(7⁄16in)
Section CC
Alternative lipping
22mm
(11 13⁄16in)
Section BB
25mm
(1in)
16mm
(⅝in)
Section AA
Enlarged details
Sketch of table

gouge, pare out the 6mm (¼in) radius between leg and rail. Clean up with glasspaper and polish.

14 Try table together and make any necessary adjustments. Remove horns, round top corners and continue bevel along the top edge. Clean up and polish.

15 Glue up table, carefully driving in wedges. Leave top cramped up until dry.

16 Fit lipping, mitre and glue up. Clean up and complete polishing.

Suggested Material

Guarea, mahogany, afrormosia.

Cutting list

Description	Length	Width	Thickness
4 legs	425mm (1ft 5in)	38mm (1½in)	20mm (¾in)
2 side rails	450mm (1ft 6in)	38mm (1½in)	20mm (¾in)
2 end rails	338mm (1ft 1½in)	25mm (1in)	16mm (⅝in)
1 top	600mm (2ft)	300mm (12in)	10mm (⅜in)
1 piece Formica	600mm (2ft)	300mm (12in)	1.6mm (1/16in)
2 end lippings	325mm (1ft 1in)	22mm (13/16in)	16mm (⅝in)
1 to cut 4 side lippings	400mm (1ft 4in)	16mm (⅝in)	11mm (7/16in)

Tools not in Basic Kit

Plough – for making grooves in long rails, lipping and ends of top.
Shoulder plane – for cleaning up rail shoulders.
Mitre cut – for making mitres on lipping.
Mitre shooting board – for planing mitres.

Tea Trolley

A small, well-proportioned trolley incorporating decorative plastic-surfaced shelves with open ends designed for easy cleaning, is here shown. Other design features include shaped bottom rails, waggon bevels on side and end rails, tapered legs with decorative horns, which make comfortable handles for pushing the trolley. The horns could be removed, in which case the top edges of the framing could have a treatment similar to the coffee table on page 99.

The main constructional features, which can be seen in the drawings, are the two mortised-and-tenoned side frames. These are made and glued up separately, and the shelves which consist of 13mm (½in) multi-ply, Formica faced, are tongued into the frames and subsequently lipped on the exposed edges.

Note: in order to obtain accurate shoulder lengths and bevels of the side rails it is advantageous to make a full-sized working drawing of the elevation as shown in section AA. A sheet of 6mm (¼in) birch plywood is excellent for this purpose as it can be used on both sides. When a new drawing is required the pencil lines are easily removed with a scraper or by glasspapering. The advantages in setting out are obvious: the legs and rails can be placed in the correct position on the board, and all sight lines, mortises and shoulder lines accurately taken off. The small coffee table on page 99, and the tea trolley make an excellent introduction to full-sized workshop drawing. (For the use of rods see page 119.)

Method

1 Prepare material, arrange and match the grain.
2 Set out legs in pairs, and make taper.
3 Set out in pairs top side rails and bottom side rails. Use a bevel for marking out shoulder lines.
4 Set out end rails – four together – and gauge all mortises and tenons, adjust gauge as necessary for end rails.
5 Cut all mortises and tenons. Before removing tenon cheeks from the side rails, plough the 10mm (⅜in) grooves to take the shelves.
6 Finish shoulders to cut line with a shoulder plane.
7 Fit side frames together, and check alignment.
8 Shape top of legs. Shape bottom side rails and work waggon bevels as indicated in drawing.
9 Bevel inside edges of top rails and work waggon bevels on the lower edges.
10 Make waggon bevels on the end rails.
11 Clean up all inner surfaces, including end rails, mask joints and polish.
12 Prepare for gluing up the side frames, adjust to correct positions four 600mm (2ft) sash cramps and have cramping blocks ready, glue up. Use a squaring rod and make a diagonal test for square (see page 145). Leave to dry.
13 Flush all joints on side frames, mark out and continue grooves across legs, and make notches to receive lipping. Make stop chamfers on inside of legs.
14 Cut shelves to size and work rebate to make tongues. Plough ends for lipping.
15 Glue on Formica veneer. (For method of gluing, see page 98.)
16 Fit in shelves and end rails. Cramp up dry and test, make any necessary adjustments.

17 Polish end rails. Glue up, carefully removing surplus glue.
18 Fit lipping, mitre and glue up.
19 Complete polishing, and bore holes to take wheel fittings.

Suggested Material

Guarea, oak or teak.

Cutting list

Description	Length	Width	Thickness
4 legs	600mm (2ft)	38mm (1½in)	23mm (⅞in)
4 side rails	475mm (1ft 7in)	35mm (1⅜in)	23mm (⅞in)
4 end rails	400mm (1ft 4in)	32mm (1¼in)	16mm (⅝in)
1 top shelf	600mm (2ft)	375mm (15in)	13mm (½in) multi-ply
1 bottom shelf	575mm (1ft 11in)	375mm (15in)	13mm (½in) multi-ply
2 pieces Formica	600mm (2ft)	375mm (15in)	1.6mm (1/16in)
4 lippings	575mm (1ft 11in)	16mm (⅝in)	18mm (11/16in)

4 rubber tyred castors 63mm (2½in) diameter
Eight 38mm (1½in) × 8 countersunk brass screws, screw through end rails into shelves, two at each rail.

Tools not in Basic Kit

Shoulder plane – for cleaning up rail shoulders.
Plough – for making grooves in long rails and at ends of shelves.
Mitre cut – for cutting mitres on lipping.
Mitre shooting board – for planing mitres on lipping.

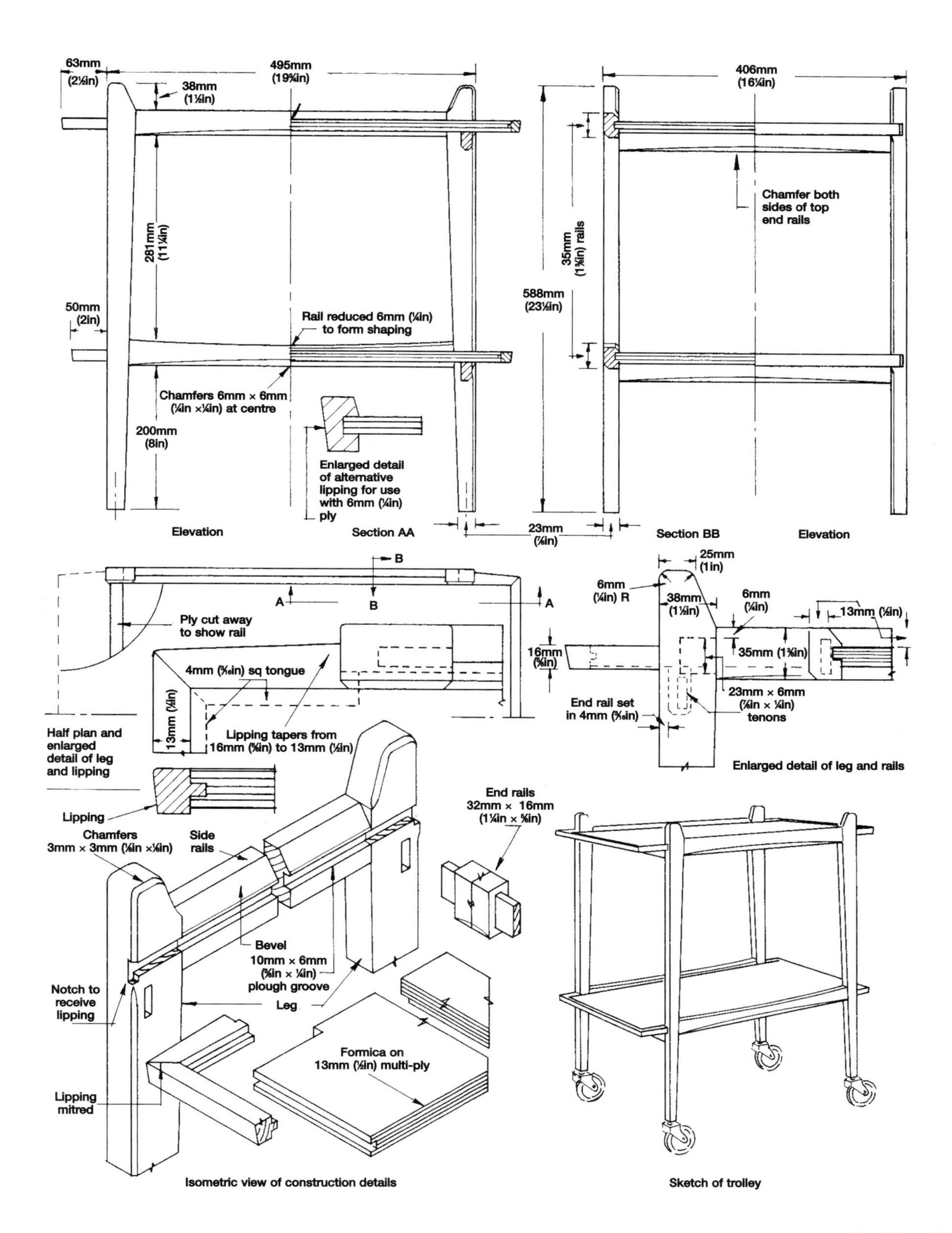

63mm
(2½in)
495mm
(19¾in)
38mm
(1½in)
281mm
(11¼in)
50mm
(2in)
Rail reduced 6mm (¼in)
to form shaping
Chamfers 6mm × 6mm
(¼in ×¼in) at centre
200mm
(8in)
Enlarged detail
of alternative
lipping for use
with 6mm (¼in)
ply
Elevation
Section AA
406mm
(16¼in)
Chamfer both
sides of top
end rails
35mm
(1⅜in) rails
588mm
(23⅛in)
23mm
(⅞in)
Section BB
Elevation
Ply cut away
to show rail
4mm (3/16in) sq tongue
13mm (½in)
Lipping tapers from
16mm (⅝in) to 13mm (½in)
Half plan and
enlarged
detail of leg
and lipping
Lipping
25mm
(1in)
6mm
(¼in) R
38mm
(1½in)
6mm
(¼in)
13mm (½in)
16mm
(⅝in)
35mm (1⅜in)
23mm × 6mm
(⅞in × ¼in)
tenons
End rail set
in 4mm (3/16in)
Enlarged detail of leg and rails
End rails
32mm × 16mm
(1¼in × ⅝in)
Chamfers
3mm × 3mm (⅛in ×⅛in)
Side
rails
Bevel
10mm × 6mm
(⅜in × ¼in)
plough groove
Notch to
receive
lipping
Leg
Formica on
13mm (½in) multi-ply
Lipping
mitred
Isometric view of construction details
Sketch of trolley

Wall Writing Cabinet

A compact writing cabinet in oak with sycamore interior is shown. The carcase is through-dovetailed – a decorative treatment – and the top front edges are mitred at the corners so that the chamfers can be neatly carried round. The flap consists of a panelled frame with a decorative inlaid escutcheon of rosewood. Leather or PVC can be glued on the inside for the writing surface. The pigeon-hole unit is in sycamore and the drawers are fitted with rosewood handles. Within the dimensional limits the cabinet gives the student an opportunity to incorporate his own innovations. Separate details show alternative designs for the flap and mouldings.

Method

1 Prepare material for the carcase; select and match the grain. Number the joints for easy identification. For application of face side marks in relation to shaped work, see page 107.
2 Mark out ends in pairs, set out and cut the dovetails.
3 Mark out pins at top and bottom.
4 Complete dovetailing, try joints – fitting where necessary – rebate for back (see diagram) and assemble carcase.
5 Flush joints on top edge, round the bottom corners and make the inner chamfers on carcase edges.
6 Mark out and make pen groove in bottom: use a firmer gouge and clean up with shaped rubber and glasspaper. Work plough groove in bottom for division and make grooves in carcase to receive ends. Cut division to length, shape and round top edge and fit.
7 Clean up all inner surfaces, mask joints where necessary and polish. Glue up.
8 Make external chamfers. Clean up carcase and polish. Fit back and screw up temporarily.
9 Prepare material for pigeon-hole unit. The unit is slip dovetailed into the top and slides in from the back.
   Note: the unit could be made and fitted to the carcase top before assembling carcase. The drawings show all constructional details. The joints are designed and arranged to give the maximum strength to the unit. The bottom is through dovetailed to the ends, the shelves and division are secured with a number of small through tenons, known as 'pinning'. The joint is not housed between the mortises. The vertical division is a continuous member and is pinned into bottom and top shelves (see separate detail showing division and mitre). The middle shelf is pinned to the ends, the tenons being halved at the vertical division.
10 Set out ends in pairs, marking dovetails, and position of mortises.
11 Mark out shelves, and gauge all mortises and tenons for pinning. Mark out pins and complete dovetailing.
12 Cut all joints for pinning, cut mitres on edge (use a mitre template) and try together, fitting where necessary.
13 Round the front edges and clean up all inner surfaces. Mask the joints where necessary and polish all inside surfaces. Glue up and, when dry, clean up exterior surfaces and complete polishing. Mark out position of housing on carcase to receive slip dovetails, and fit unit.
14 Prepare material for flap, arrange and match the grain, taking particular

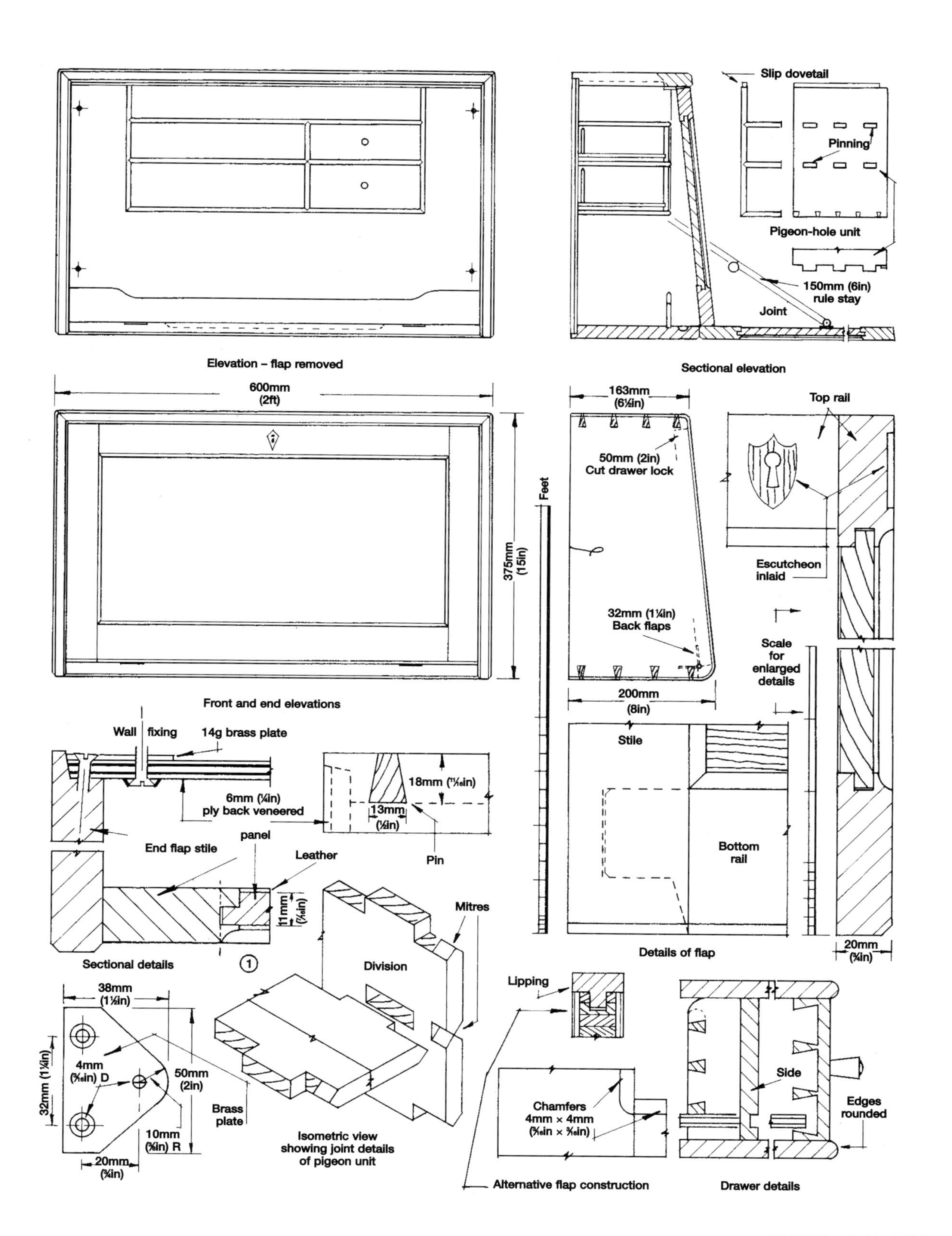
Elevation – flap removed
Slip dovetail
Pinning
Pigeon-hole unit
150mm (6in) rule stay
Joint
Sectional elevation
600mm (2ft)
375mm (15in)
Front and end elevations
Feet
163mm (6½in)
50mm (2in) Cut drawer lock
32mm (1¼in) Back flaps
200mm (8in)
Top rail
Escutcheon inlaid
Scale for enlarged details
Stile
Bottom rail
20mm (¾in)
Details of flap
Wall fixing
14g brass plate
6mm (¼in) ply back veneered
End flap stile
panel
Leather
11mm (7⁄16in)
18mm (11⁄16in)
13mm (½in)
Pin
Sectional details
1
Mitres
Division
38mm (1½in)
32mm (1¼in)
4mm (5⁄32in) D
50mm (2in)
10mm (⅜in) R
20mm (¾in)
Brass plate
Isometric view showing joint details of pigeon unit
Lipping
Chamfers 4mm × 4mm (5⁄32in × 5⁄32in)
Alternative flap construction
Side
Edges rounded
Drawer details

care with stiles and panel. (See page 199 for setting out technique.)

15 Set out stiles in pairs and check with carcase.

16 Set out top and bottom rails. Mark sight lines – in pencil – to give the inside dimensions of frame, add the depth of moulding to obtain the shoulder lines.

Note: the shoulders are square, with the mitre running right through (see dotted line in figure 1).

17 Gauge and cut mortises and tenons, complete ploughing, and work moulding before removing tenon cheeks.

18 Make mitres on rails and stiles, and fit together.

19 Cut panels to size and work rebate to form tongue. Careful fitting of the panel is essential (see pages 118–122).

20 Clean up panel and mouldings, polish.

21 Glue up flap. To allow for possible movement the solid panel is not glued in.

22 Flush all joints. Remove horns and carefully fit flap, a close joint is desirable.

23 Fix flap stop under top. Screw on back and fix metal hanging plates.

24 *Hinging:* brass back flaps – mark out position on flap, cut recesses and fit hinge. Offer up flap to carcase and mark positions of back flaps. Cut out recesses and fit hinge, adjusting as necessary (see page 173 on locks and hinges).

25 Fit lock and inlaid escutcheon.

26 Screw on brass rule stay.

27 Make and fit drawers (see page 145).

28 Complete all polishing.

Suggested Material

Quartered oak, for carcase and flap.

Cutting list

Description	Length	Width	Thickness
Carcase			
2 sides	400mm (1ft 4in)	200mm (8in)	18mm (11/16in)
1 bottom	625mm (2ft 1in)	178mm (7 1/8in)	18mm (11/16in)
1 top	625mm (2ft 1in)	166mm (6 5/8in)	18mm (11/16in)
1 back	600mm (2ft)	375mm (15in)	6mm (1/4in) oak-faced ply
Flap			
2 stiles	375mm (1ft 3in)	47mm (1 7/8in)	20mm (3/4in)
1 top rail	550mm (1ft 10in)	47mm (1 7/8in)	20mm (3/4in)
1 bottom rail	550mm (1ft 10in)	56mm (2 1/4in)	20mm (3/4in)
1 panel	500mm (1ft 8in)	263mm (10 1/2in)	11mm (7/16in)
1 flat strip sycamore	600mm (2ft)	20mm (3/4in	4mm (3/16in)
1 partition sycamore	600mm (2ft)	50mm (2in)	6mm (1/4in)
escutcheon oddment of rosewood			

To give the student an opportunity to prepare his own, the cutting list for the pigeon-hole unit has been omitted.

Bureau Bookcase

This is an unusual design combining bureau and bookcase. Two small handles replace the traditional lock. It gives good practice in shaped work and veneering.

Method

1. Prepare material for carcase, select and match the grain, taking into consideration the shaping of the ends.

   Note: in shaped work it is often necessary to select or make a datum line from which all squaring or setting out can be taken. The obvious choice for a datum line in this example is the back edge of the bureau, which is easily identified by face side and face edge marks, from which all squaring can be done.
2. Pair up the sides, mark out the shape on one and set out the shelf positions.
3. *Sides:* carefully bore two 16mm (⅝in) diameter holes at each tenon position and remove the waste to form the shaped mortise.
4. Cut stopped housings and finish to correct depth with a router. See step 9.
5. Work rebates for plywood back.
6. *Sides:* bow saw one to shape, clean up with steel jack plane and spokeshaves. Use finished side as a template and mark out the opposite side.
7. Cut shelves to length, and fit those to be tenoned into the housing and with an awl mark round the inside of mortise to give position of shaped tenons.
8. Cut tenons and shape, make saw kerfs for wedges.
9. The two shelves below the flap can be dovetail housed (see page 135).
10. Fit shelves. Make housings to receive top fillet, and assemble carcase dry. Rebate top fillet and cut to length.
11. Mark out depth of round with a pencil gauge and shape front edges of sides, and shelves, as shown in separate drawing. Clean up all inner surfaces, mask joints where necessary and polish.
12. Cut wedges and prepare for gluing up. Glue up and test for square and alignment.
13. Fit back and screw in temporarily.
14. Prepare material for pigeon-hole unit. The unit is through dovetailed with mitred front edges. Mark out, cut dovetails and pins. Make stopped housings to receive shelf and divisions.
15. Cut and fit shelf and divisions. Assemble unit dry and flush joints. Make waggon bevels on inner edges. Clean up all inner surfaces, mask joints where necessary and polish. Glue up.
16. Prepare material for flap.
17. Cut laminboard to size, making allowance for lipping, and plough grooves to take lipping.
18. Veneer both sides of flap. When laid vertically stripy oak veneer makes an attractive finish. (See page 161 for veneering.) Clean up edges, fit and mitre lipping.
19. Carefully flush lippings on outside of flap, clean up and polish.
20. Fix stop under top shelf. Fit flap taking care to maintain an equal margin on lipping.
21. Fit back flaps and rule joint stays.

22 Turn handles and fit to flap. Polish and glue in.
23 Screw pigeon-hole unit to top shelf. Polish carcase back and top fillet and screw in.
24 Glue on leather or PVC inside flap, for writing surface. Clean up where necessary, and complete polishing.

Suggested Material

Oak, with walnut for lippings, handles and wedges. Sapele, with rosewood contrasts.

Cutting list

Description	Length	Width	Thickness
Carcase			
2 sides	120mm (4ft)	288mm (11½in)	20mm (¾in)
1 bottom shelf	713mm (2ft 4½in)	250mm (10in)	20mm (¾in)
1 shelf	700mm (2ft 4in)	225mm (9in)	20mm (¾in)
1 shelf	700mm (2ft 4in)	200mm (8in)	20mm (¾in)
1 shelf	713mm (2ft 4½in)	238mm (9½in)	20mm (¾in)
1 top shelf	713mm (2ft 4½in)	195mm (7¾in)	20mm (¾in)
1 top fillet	713mm (2ft 4½in)	23mm (⅞in)	20mm (¾in)
Pigeon hole unit			
3 shelves	463mm (1ft 6½in)	145mm (5¾in)	13mm (½in)
2 ends	163mm (6½in)	145mm (5¾in)	13mm (½in)
1 division	150mm (6in)	145mm (5¾in)	13mm (½in)
1 flap laminboard	675mm (2ft 3in)	288mm (11½in)	16mm (⅝in)
1 stop	675mm (2ft 3in)	20mm (¾in)	6mm (¼in)
2 lippings walnut	700mm (2ft 4in)	20mm (¾in)	15mm (9/16in)
2 lippings walnut	325mm (1ft 1in)	20mm (¾in)	15mm (9/16in)
1 back plywood	1125mm (3ft 9in)	700mm (28in)	6mm (¼in)
1 piece for handles walnut	100mm (4in)	25mm (1in)	25mm (1in)

veneer as required, either oak or sapele
oddments of walnut for wedges
1 pair of 38mm (1½in) brass back flaps
1 pair of 150mm (6in) rule joint stays

Tools not in Basic Kit

Plough – for making grooves to take lippings.
Router – for finishing housings to depth.
Mitre cut – for cutting mitres on lipping.
Mitre shooting board – for finishing mitres.

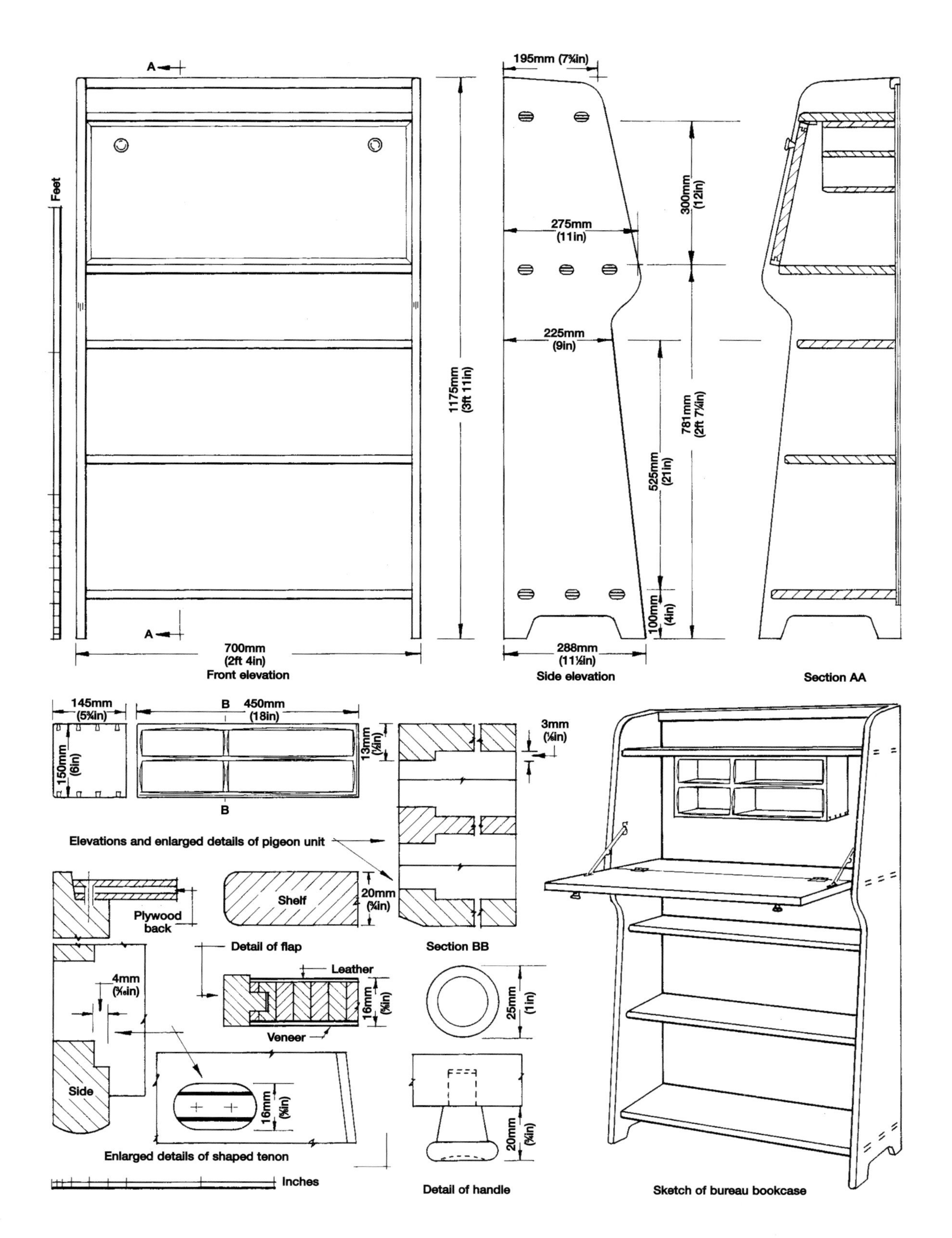

A
Feet
195mm (7¾in)
300mm (12in)
275mm (11in)
225mm (9in)
1175mm (3ft 11in)
781mm (2ft 7¼in)
525mm (21in)
100mm (4in)
700mm (2ft 4in)
Front elevation
288mm (11½in)
Side elevation
Section AA
145mm (5¾in)
B
450mm (18in)
150mm (6in)
13mm (½in)
3mm (⅛in)
Elevations and enlarged details of pigeon unit
Shelf
20mm (¾in)
Plywood back
Detail of flap
Section BB
Leather
4mm (3⁄16in)
16mm (⅝in)
Veneer
25mm (1in)
Side
16mm (⅝in)
20mm (¾in)
Enlarged details of shaped tenon
Inches
Detail of handle
Sketch of bureau bookcase

Cabinet Construction

A designer cannot have too much information on timber – its strength, workability, colour, weight, availability – or its various man-made forms such as veneer, plywood, blockboard, chipboard or plastic-faced sheets. In fact, as wide an acquaintance as possible with processes and materials of all kinds is an essential part of the designer's equipment. In addition, a good designer must also possess originality, inspiration and good judgement, for without these qualities they cannot make the best use of their knowledge.

Box Construction

The main feature of the sideboard illustrated is the carcase. The carcase is dovetailed together in a boxlike form, the natural movement of the wood taking place in its width. Suitable joints are indicated and these are incorporated in various designs shown in this book.

Stand

The carcase is fixed to a stand which consists of four legs and rails mortised and tenoned together. For all practical purposes the shrinkage of timber in its length is negligible. The drawing shows the grain direction. The grain of the carcase and end rails of the stand are at right angles to each other. It is obvious that the stand if screwed to the carcase through the end rails, prevents the natural movement of the wood. According to conditions the shrinkage on a wide carcase could well be 4mm (3⁄16in) or more. To prevent possible splitting of the carcase, screw the stand to the carcase through the front rail. Elsewhere fix with wood buttons or slotted metal plates.

Frame construction

A frame is designed to break up large surface areas of wood into smaller units and thus minimise the effect of shrinkage and warping, and yet provide strength in both length and width. The sideboard is fitted with a panelled back – a mortised and tenoned frame with panels. This makes a first-class finish and gives rigidity to the carcase. A variety of doors and panelling are included in this category.

Framed carcase construction

This consists basically of mortised and tenoned frames with panels. The frames can be assembled in a variety of ways to form the carcase. The small cupboard with drawer illustrated opposite and the linen chest on page 119 are good examples.

Table or Framed Work

Based on mortise and tenon joints this covers a variety of jobs. Included in this heading are stools, chairs, tables and stands. The cabinet on stand (illustrated opposite) has been designed to incorporate the basic features of cabinet construction, as follows: box construction – dovetailed carcase; frame construction – panelled back; a table or framed work based on the mortise and tenon joint – stand for carcase.

The student should develop a sense of design and make drawings and models (to a suitable scale) of various arrangements of the basic cabinet features. Good proportion is essential. Full-size detail drawings of panel treatments, solid or plywood, mouldings, leg and edge treatments are all useful exercises.

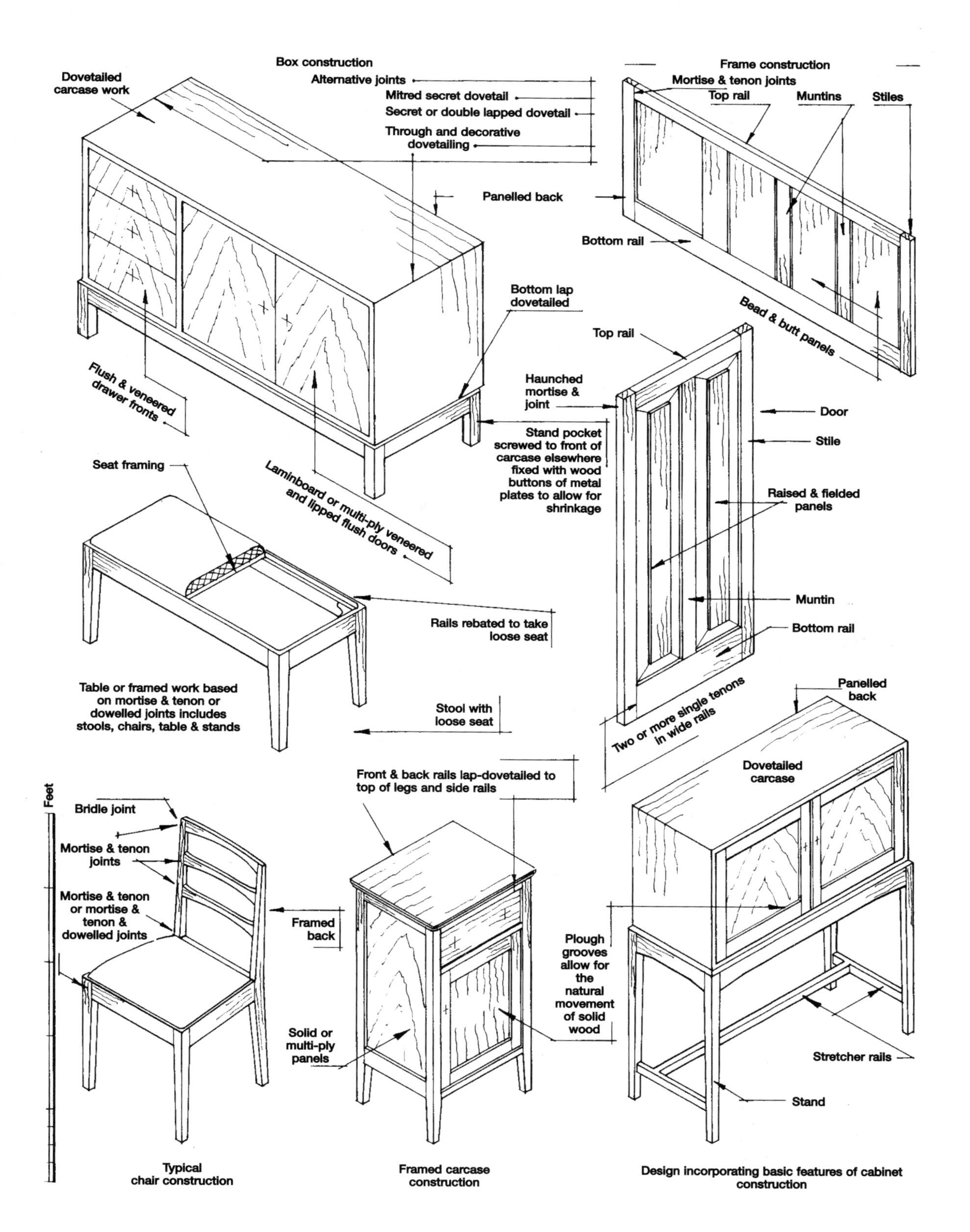

Box construction
Dovetailed carcase work
Alternative joints
Mitred secret dovetail
Secret or double lapped dovetail
Through and decorative dovetailing
Panelled back
Frame construction
Mortise & tenon joints
Top rail
Muntins
Stiles
Bottom rail
Bead & butt panels
Bottom lap dovetailed
Flush & veneered drawer fronts
Laminboard or multi-ply veneered and lipped flush doors
Top rail
Haunched mortise & joint
Door
Stile
Stand pocket screwed to front of carcase elsewhere fixed with wood buttons of metal plates to allow for shrinkage
Seat framing
Raised & fielded panels
Rails rebated to take loose seat
Muntin
Bottom rail
Table or framed work based on mortise & tenon or dowelled joints includes stools, chairs, table & stands
Stool with loose seat
Two or more single tenons in wide rails
Panelled back
Dovetailed carcase
Front & back rails lap-dovetailed to top of legs and side rails
Feet
Bridle joint
Mortise & tenon joints
Mortise & tenon or mortise & tenon & dowelled joints
Framed back
Plough grooves allow for the natural movement of solid wood
Solid or multi-ply panels
Stretcher rails
Stand
Typical chair construction
Framed carcase construction
Design incorporating basic features of cabinet construction

Dressing & Writing Table Compactum

A neat compactum of pleasing proportions and simplicity of line is shown. It provides good accommodation for books and dressing table requirements, and has a useful tray. The main design features are the unusual shaping of the end rails, and the long bevel with decorative dowelling at the top of the legs, the tray-like appearance of the top, and the plastic faced lids. It gives good practice in the use of a variety of materials and in the technique of dowelling and hinging. It demands neat and accurate craftsmanship.

Method

1. Prepare material. Select and match the grain.
2. Set out the legs in pairs, and taper inside of legs to 28mm (1⅛in).
3. Set out the end rails in pairs and gauge for mortises and tenons.
4. Cut mortises and tenons. Make grooves for tray runners in one end rail and in one side of division. Rebate end rails for bottom.
5. Shape stretchers and assemble end frames, fitting as necessary. Taper legs below long rails to make 23mm (⅞in) at floor line.
6. Clean up all inner surfaces, rounding edges as shown in separate detail.
7. Mask joints where necessary and polish all inner surfaces.
8. Glue up end frames, and test for alignment.
9. Set out front and back rail. Bore holes for division and make housings.
10. Rebate rails for bottom, and cut shoulders to form tongues.
11. Make round tenons on division and fit to back and front rails. Make saw kerfs for wedges.
12. Flush joints on the inside of end frames and make grooves to receive the back and front rails. Cut stretcher to length and make tenons. Make saw kerfs for wedging. Assemble framing dry, fitting as necessary.
13. Cut bottom to size, house in 3mm (⅛in) at legs and prepare for screwing.
14. Saw off horns on the end frames. Clean up and round corners. Bevel inside of top rails. Clean up all inner surfaces. Mask joints where necessary and polish.
15. Prepare for gluing up. Have sash cramps ready adjusted, wedges cut, and screws for fixing bottom to hand.
16. When dry remove cramps and bore for the dowels at front and back rails.
17. Plane long bevel at top of legs.
18. Fit and dowel top fillet to back rail. Bevel front of fillet to make stop for flap, and glue in.
19. Cut laminboard to size, make plough groove and fit lipping to lids. Note the front lippings are not mitred; they are applied after fixing plastic sheets.
20. Glue plastic faced sheets to lids. Fit and glue in front lipping.
21. Carefully fit lids. Mark out for butts and hinge.
22. *Tray:* plough grooves and make mouldings. Fit bottom, cut mitres, and glue up. When dry reinforce mitres with veneer keys (see page 68).
23. Fix mirror with corner plates.
24. Clean up as necessary and complete polishing.

Suggested Material

Sapele with rosewood contrasts (pellets over dowels, wedges at stretcher rails, and front lipping) with black plastic faced lids. Other suitable but more expensive woods are afrormosia, teak and black bean.

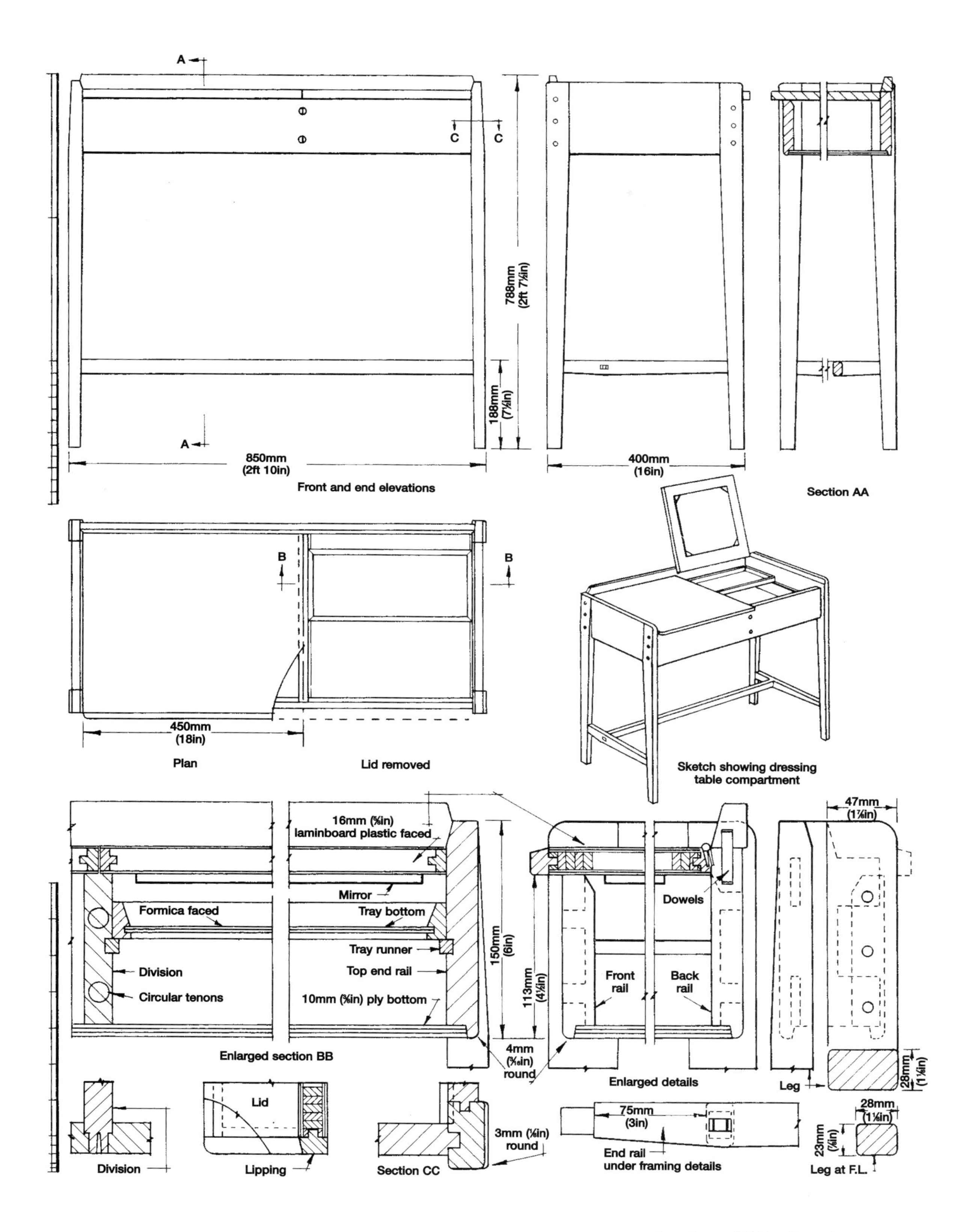
A
C
C
788mm
(2ft 7⅛in)
188mm
(7⅛in)
A
850mm
(2ft 10in)
Front and end elevations
400mm
(16in)
Section AA
B
B
450mm
(18in)
Plan
Lid removed
Sketch showing dressing
table compartment
16mm (⅝in)
laminboard plastic faced
Mirror
Formica faced
Tray bottom
Tray runner
Division
Top end rail
Circular tenons
10mm (⅜in) ply bottom
150mm
(6in)
113mm
(4½in)
4mm
(3⁄16in)
round
Enlarged section BB
Dowels
Front
rail
Back
rail
Enlarged details
47mm
(1⅞in)
28mm
(1⅛in)
Leg
Lid
Division
Lipping
Section CC
3mm (⅛in)
round
75mm
(3in)
End rail
under framing details
28mm
(1⅛in)
23mm
(⅞in)
Leg at F.L.

Cutting list

Description	Length	Width	Thickness
4 legs	800mm (2ft 8in)	47mm (1⅞in)	28mm (1⅛in)
2 end rails	400mm (1ft 4in)	150mm (6in)	23mm (⅞in)
1 back rail	850mm (2ft 10in)	132mm (5¼in)	23mm (⅞in)
1 front rail	850mm (2ft 10in)	113mm (4½in)	23mm (⅞in)
1 division	413mm (1ft 4½in)	103mm (4⅛in)	20mm (¾in)
1 top fillet	850mm (2ft 10in)	32mm (1¼in)	25mm (1in)
1 stretcher	850mm (2ft 10in)	32mm (1¼in)	20mm (¾in)
2 stretchers	400mm (1ft 4in)	32mm (1¼in)	20mm (¾in)
1 bottom plywood	850mm (2ft 10in)	400mm (16in)	10mm (⅜in)
1 lid laminboard plastic faced	825mm (2ft 9in)	388mm (15½in)	16mm (⅝in)
2 lippings	825mm (2ft 9in)	20mm (¾in)	20mm (¾in)
4 lippings	400mm (1ft 4in)	20mm (¾in)	20mm (¾in)
2 tray runners	400mm (1ft 4in)	10mm (⅜in)	10mm (⅜in)
2 tray sides	650mm (2ft 2in)	25mm (1in)	13mm (½in)
1 tray bottom plastic faced plywood	338mm (1ft 1½in)	150mm (6in)	4mm (3/16in)
1 to cut tray ends	325mm (1ft 1in)	25mm (1in)	13mm (½in)
12 dowels	75mm (3in)	6mm (¼in) diameter	
1 pair of 50mm (2in) solid brass butts			
4 mirror corner plates			

Tools not in Basic Kit

Shoulder plane – for cleaning up rail shoulders.
Plough – for making grooves for tray bottom and runners.

Student's Desk and Drawing Table

This design meets the requirements of students of art and technical subjects. The main feature is the unusual dual purpose function of the lid. To convert the desk into a drawing table, simply pull the lid forward between the side frames; adjust the saw-tooth supports to desired position, lift lid and allow it to recline on supports. It has a commodious well. The lid is of gaboon-faced laminboard with leather or PVC covering for the desk surface.

Method

1 Prepare material; select and match the grain.
2 Set out the legs in pairs, and make taper on the inside.
3 Set out the end rails in pairs. Gauge legs and rails for mortises and tenons.
4 Cut mortises and tenons. Make a buttressed groove in the top rails to receive the slide (see separate drawing for enlarged constructional details).
Note: plough a 5mm (3/16in) groove and bevel sides with a side rebate plane, opening up the groove to 10mm (3/8in) wide on the outside. Make a template out of 3mm (1/8in) plywood for testing accuracy of groove. The template can be used when marking out for sliding rail.
5 Make rebates for bottom. Assemble frames, fitting as necessary.
6 Mark out for chamfers, using a pencil gauge, chamfer rails and legs, stopping chamfers on the legs and inside of bottom rails at the sight lines.
7 Clean up inner surfaces, mask where necessary and polish.
8 Glue up end frames, check alignment, and leave to dry.
9 Flush all joints, and complete chamfering on inside of frames, making the quadrant with a rat-tail file and glasspaper.
10 Set out long rails, cut shoulders and make tongues. Work rebates for bottom, rebate top edge of front rail.
11 Make housings on end frames to receive front and back rails and fit. Extend buttressed groove through the back leg. Stop grooves at the inside front rail. A separate drawing (enlarged constructional details) conveys the idea.
12 Mark out plywood bottom and fit. House in at leg not more than 3mm (1/8in) deep. Mark out positions, drill and countersink for 23mm (7/8in) × 8 brass screws.
13 Mark out stretcher rail, make chamfers and fit. Assemble table, fitting as necessary.
14 Bevel outside edges of end frames. Clean up all inner surfaces, mask where necessary and polish.
15 Glue up, screw bottom in position and leave to dry.
16 Mark out position of dowels. Bore the holes to receive the dowels and carefully drive in. Flush dowels and wedges. Complete stopped chamfering on stretcher rails.
17 Mark out and cut sliding rail to length, carefully fitting (see figure 1) into buttressed groove. Rail should fit well and slide smoothly. Lubricate with candle wax.
18 Mark out, cut and fit back fillet. Brass screw cups are ideal for use in this situation and provide a neat finish.
19 Cut laminboard to make lid and plough for lippings. Make and fit lippings, mitring the corners. Allow for the thickness of leather or PVC covering on the top or desk side of lid.

20 Fit lid. Mark out position of back flaps, cut recesses in lid and fit hinges. Locate lid on the desk marking out position of hinges on sliding rail. Cut recesses and fit hinges. Test lid for accuracy.
21 Glue on leather or PVC.
22 Set out adjustable supports, and make sawtooth slots. Cut to length and fit hinges. Bore holes in supports, locate position and screw to sides with 38mm (1½in) × 10 brass round head screws. Fit washers under screw head and between end and supports.
23 Complete cleaning up and polishing where necessary.

Suggested Material

Columbian pine with walnut lippings, dowels and wedges.

Cutting list

Description	Length	Width	Thickness
4 legs	800mm (2ft 8in)	56mm (2¼in)	24mm (15/16in)
2 end rails	400mm (1ft 4in)	145mm (5¾in)	24mm (15/16in)
1 front rail	750mm (2ft 6in)	132mm (5¼in)	24mm (15/16in)
1 back rail	750mm (2ft 6in)	103mm (4⅛in)	24mm (15/16in)
2 bottom rails	400mm (1ft 4in)	34mm (1 5/16in)	22mm (13/16in)
2 stretchers	775mm (2ft 7in)	34mm (1 5/16in)	22mm (13/16in)
1 bottom plywood	750mm (2ft 6in)	400mm (16in)	10mm (⅜in)
1 sliding rail beech	750mm (2ft 6in)	63mm (2½in)	28mm (1⅛in)
1 fixing fillet	750mm (2ft 6in)	28mm (1⅛in)	25mm (1in)
1 lid gaboon-faced laminboard	750mm (2ft 6in)	413mm (16½in)	20mm (¾in)
2 lippings walnut	750mm (2ft 6in)	23mm (⅞in)	11mm (7/16in)
2 lippings walnut	425mm (1ft 5in)	23mm (⅞in)	11mm (7/16in)
4 supports beech	300mm (1ft)	23mm (⅞in)	20mm (¾in)
2 supports beech	125mm (5in)	23mm (⅞in)	20mm (¾in)
12 dowels	70mm (2¾in)	10mm (⅜in) diameter walnut	

Oddments of walnut to make the wedges
Three 38mm (1½in) solid brass back flaps, and screws
Twenty-four 23mm (⅞in) × 8 countersunk brass screws for bottom
Four 50mm (2in) × 8 countersunk brass screws and cups
Leather or PVC to cover top – fit neatly inside lippings

Tools not in Basic Kit

Shoulder plane – for cleaning up rail shoulders.
Side rebate plane – for bevelling groove.

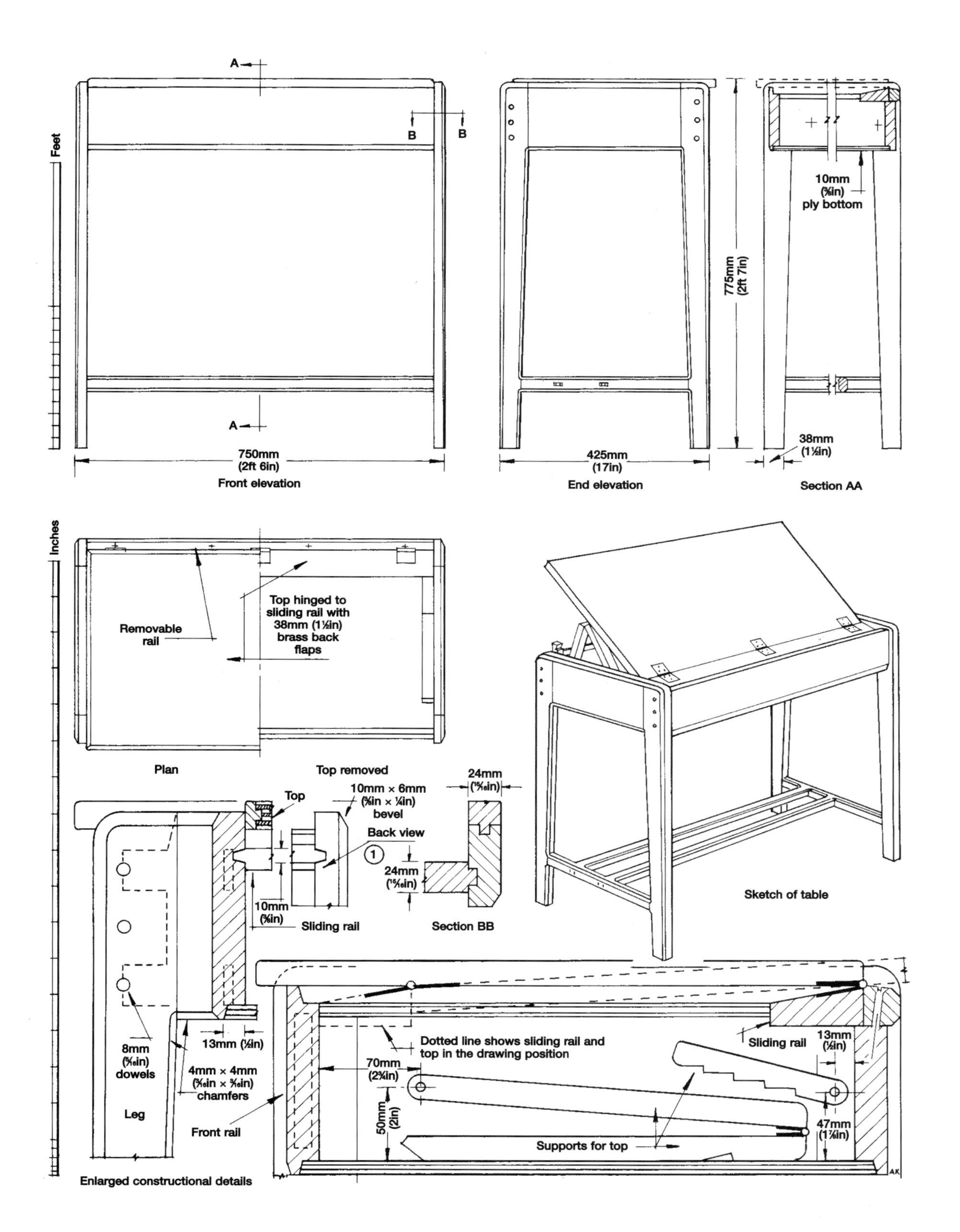

A
B
B
Feet
A
750mm
(2ft 6in)
Front elevation
775mm
(2ft 7in)
425mm
(17in)
End elevation
10mm
(⅜in)
ply bottom
38mm
(1½in)
Section AA
Inches
Removable
rail
Top hinged to
sliding rail with
38mm (1½in)
brass back
flaps
Plan
Top removed
Sketch of table
Top
10mm × 6mm
(⅜in × ¼in)
bevel
Back view
24mm
(15/16in)
24mm
(15/16in)
10mm
(⅜in)
Sliding rail
Section BB
8mm
(5/16in)
dowels
13mm (½in)
4mm × 4mm
(3/16in × 3/16in)
chamfers
Leg
Front rail
Dotted line shows sliding rail and
top in the drawing position
70mm
(2¾in)
50mm
(2in)
Supports for top
Sliding rail
13mm
(½in)
47mm
(1⅞in)
Enlarged constructional details

Linen Chest

Designed to give generous storage space, this oak linen chest, left in its natural colour, makes an attractive piece of furniture.

The main constructional features are the mortised-and-tenoned framed carcase with legs, and the flush panelled bottom. Decorative treatment includes stop chamfering, raised and fielded panels, decorative stops and tapered chamfering at bottom of the legs. It incorporates many sound principles of craftsmanship. The making of a rod – full-sized horizontal and vertical sections, drawn on a rod or thin piece of wood, showing shoulder lines, mortises and tenons, etc. – and the subsequent setting out of the job, give valuable experience. The drawings show many alternative treatments, including the use of manufactured boards. These treatments should be carefully studied and used as a nucleus for new designs.

Method

1 Make full-size working rods 1–5.

2 Prepare material for the framed carcase, arrange and match the grain to the best advantage.

3 Set out the legs in pairs, use rod 1.

4 Set out the long rails in pairs, use rod 2. Use a marking knife for marking out the shoulder lines. A pencil for setting out positions of the mortises and sight lines. (See isometric drawing on page 121.)

5 Set out short rails in pairs, use rod 4.

6 Set out mortises, use rod 1.

7 Set mortise gauge to an 8mm (5/16in) mortise chisel and gauge mortises and tenons.

8 Cut mortises and tenons. Work all plough grooves before removing tenon cheeks.

Note: the grooves are stopped on the legs. If taken through at the top rail allow for square haunching on tenon.

9 Carefully fit all joints, testing for squareness and alignment as shown on page 59, and assemble dry.

10 Prepare panels for carcase. Sound seasoned material should be used in which case the minimum of shrinkage will occur. However, in a damp atmosphere the panels are liable to expand. This expansion must be allowed for, and for this reason the panels should be set out 1mm (1/32in) short in the direction of the grain and 3mm (1/8in) narrow in the width. Matching up the grain and colour is an essential feature in panelled work of this description. A panel if carelessly positioned can have that upside-down appearance; this should be avoided. Select three panels for the front and stand them in their relative positions against the framing. View from a distance, arranging as necessary.

11 *Fitting panels:* prepare a piece of hardwood about 75mm (3in) long × 50mm (2in) × 25mm (1in) and plough a groove (the same size and depth as in the panelling) in one edge. This is called a mullet and is used for testing, to ensure a well fitting panel. Gauge panel for depth and width of fielding. Adjust rebate plane and work recessing or sinking to form the fielded panel (details can be seen opposite). Test frequently with mullet to ascertain panel edge thickness. Plane the sharp edges off the outside of

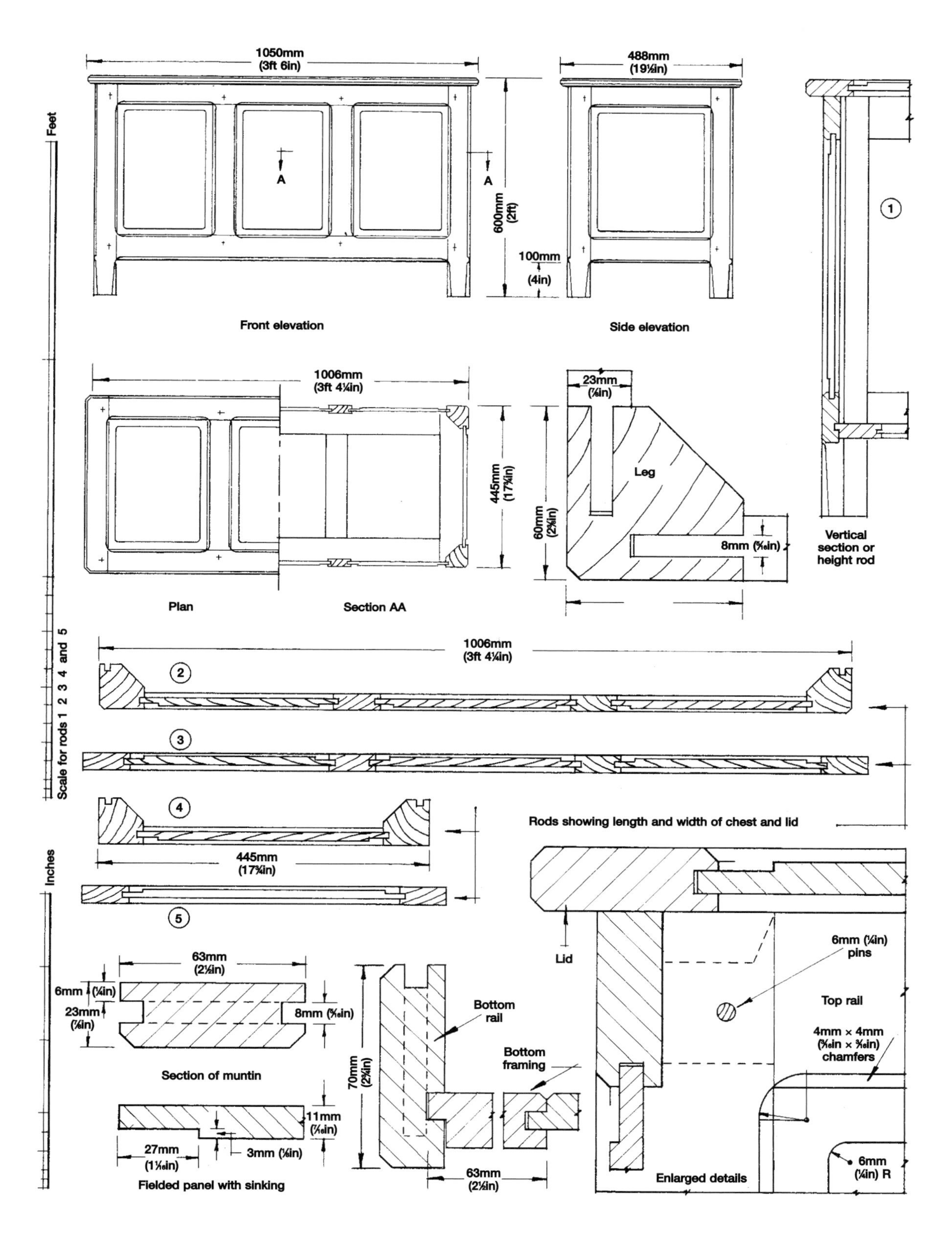
1050mm
(3ft 6in)
488mm
(19¼in)
A
A
600mm
(2ft)
100mm
(4in)
Front elevation
Side elevation
1
Vertical
section or
height rod
1006mm
(3ft 4¼in)
445mm
(17⅝in)
Plan
Section AA
23mm
(⅞in)
60mm
(2⅜in)
Leg
8mm (5⁄16in)
Feet
Scale for rods 1 2 3 4 and 5
Inches
1006mm
(3ft 4¼in)
2
3
4
445mm
(17⅝in)
5
Rods showing length and width of chest and lid
Lid
6mm (¼in)
pins
Top rail
4mm × 4mm
(5⁄32in × 5⁄32in)
chamfers
6mm
(¼in) R
Enlarged details
63mm
(2½in)
6mm (¼in)
23mm
(⅞in)
8mm (5⁄16in)
Section of muntin
70mm
(2¾in)
Bottom
rail
Bottom
framing
63mm
(2½in)
11mm
(7⁄16in)
27mm
(11⁄16in)
3mm (⅛in)
Fielded panel with sinking

panels, this assists the entry of the panels. The panels should be hand tight, forcing will bruise and fracture the groove walls.

12 On completion of the mulletting of the panels, chamfer legs on the inside and assemble carcase dry, fitting as necessary.
Note: mark the panel edges for easy identification when gluing up.

13 Mark position of plough grooves on legs, and house in 6mm (¼in) deep to receive panelled bottom.

14 Pencil gauge and work all stopped chamfers.

15 Carefully round the corners of the fielded panel and clean up sinking: a piece of soft wood about 75mm (3in) × 25mm (1in) × 10mm (⅜in) with a piece of No 0 glasspaper glued round it makes a good rubber and helps to maintain clean sharp arrises.

16 Clean up panels and all inner edges. Mask joints as necessary and give panels and all inner edges a rub over with white french polish.

17 Glue up front and back frames with appropriate legs.
Note: panels are not glued in.
Gluing-up technique: Lay the framing on three 50mm × 75mm (2in × 3in) bearers on the bench, this supports each end and the centre of the framing and will accommodate two sash cramps, one for each muntin on the underside of the framing. Two 1200mm (4ft) sash cramps can then be placed over bottom and top rails for cramping up the legs. Test all joints for flatness with a straight edge – a carelessly placed cramping block can pull a leg, rail or stile out of alignment when pressure is applied. It is wise not to allow glue, Scotch or Resin, to come in contact with the sash cramps. Make a habit of sliding a piece of paper between cramps and work. Leave to dry.

18 Prepare material for lid and bottom, select and match the grain.

19 Set out lid, use rods 3 and 5. Gauge and cut the mortises and tenons. Proceed as for main framing and glue up.

20 Set out and make bottom framing. The panels are flush on the inside and must be carefully fitted. Work a chamfer round the panels and on both edges of muntins. Stop chamfers at the sight lines on the framing preparatory to making a mason's mitre.

21 Prepare for, and polish. Glue up and leave to dry. Make mason's mitres on bottom.

22 Flush off joints on front and back framing.

23 Mark out and fit bottom.

24 Assemble carcase dry, adjusting as necessary and prepare for gluing up.

25 Glue up. Test for square and alignment and leave to dry.

26 Make pins. Split a piece of 8mm (5/16in) straight grain oak into a number of approximately 8mm (5/16in) square pieces. Chisel off the corners and drive through a 6mm (¼in) dowel plate to make 6mm (¼in) pins.

27 Using a brace and a 6mm (¼in) twist bit bore for pins. Chisel a point on the pins, glue and carefully drive in.

28 Flush all joints and pins, and work chamfers on the lid. Make decorative stops on legs (see alternative stops in figures 1 and 2). Mark out for butts and hinge lid.

29 Clean up and give a light rub over with polish. Cut down with flour glasspaper and finish with wax polish.

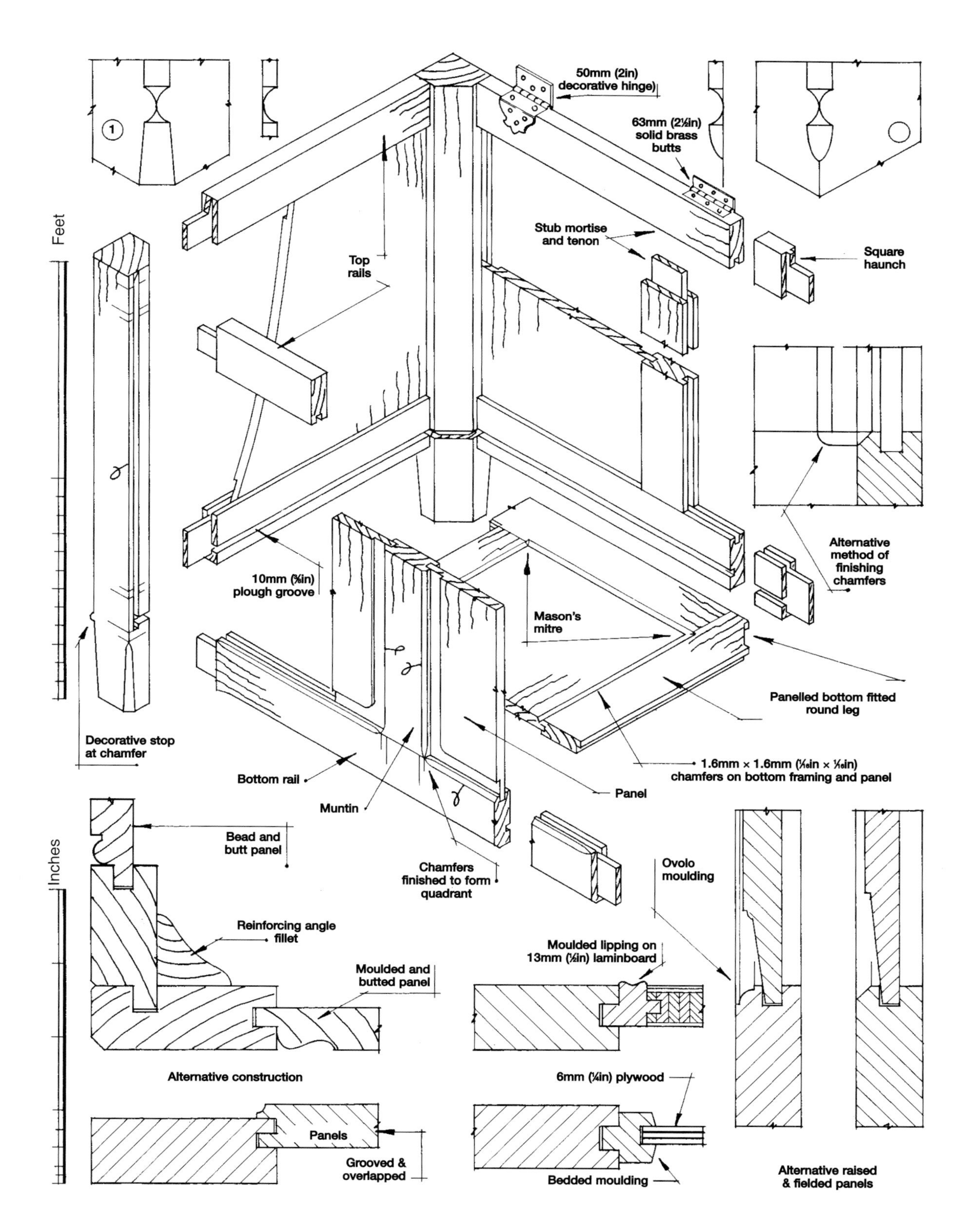
50mm (2in) decorative hinge
63mm (2½in) solid brass butts
Stub mortise and tenon
Square haunch
Top rails
Feet
Alternative method of finishing chamfers
10mm (⅜in) plough groove
Mason's mitre
Panelled bottom fitted round leg
Decorative stop at chamfer
1.6mm × 1.6mm (1/16in × 1/16in) chamfers on bottom framing and panel
Bottom rail
Panel
Muntin
Bead and butt panel
Chamfers finished to form quadrant
Ovolo moulding
Inches
Reinforcing angle fillet
Moulded lipping on 13mm (½in) laminboard
Moulded and butted panel
Alternative construction
6mm (¼in) plywood
Panels
Grooved & overlapped
Bedded moulding
Alternative raised & fielded panels

Suggested Material

Oak.

Cutting list

Description	Length	Width	Thickness
Carcase			
4 legs	600mm (2ft)	60mm (2⅜in)	60mm (2⅜in)
2 top rails	1000mm (3ft 4in)	60mm (2⅜in)	23mm (⅞in)
2 top rails	475mm (1ft 7in)	60mm (2⅜in)	23mm (⅞in)
2 bottom rails	1000mm (3ft 4in)	70mm (2¾in)	23mm (⅞in)
2 bottom rails	475mm (1ft 7in)	70mm (2¾in)	23mm (⅞in)
4 muntins	450mm (1ft 6in)	63mm (2½in)	23mm (⅞in)
6 panels	375mm (1ft 3in)	275mm (11in)	11mm (7⁄16in)
2 panels	375mm (1ft 3in)	365mm (13¾in)	11mm (7⁄16in)
Top			
2 rails	1025mm (3ft 5in)	63mm (2½in)	23mm (⅞in)
2 stiles	513mm (1ft 8½in)	63mm (2½in)	23mm (⅞in)
2 muntins	450mm (1ft 6in)	63mm (2½in)	23mm (⅞in)
3 panels	388mm (1ft 3½in)	288mm (11½in)	11mm (7⁄16in)
Bottom			
2 rails	975mm (3ft 3in)	63mm (2½in)	20mm (¾in)
2 stiles	450mm (1ft 6in)	63mm (2½in)	20mm (¾in)
2 muntins	375mm (1ft 3in)	56mm (2¼in)	20mm (¾in)
3 panels	325mm (1ft 1in)	235mm (11in)	13mm (½in)
32 pins	38mm (1½in)	6mm (¼in) diameter	

Three 63mm (2½in) long solid brass butts and screws

Tools not in Basic Kit

Shoulder plane – for cleaning up rail shoulders and sinkings to panels.
Plough – for making grooves to take panels.
Scratch stock – for finishing stopped plough grooves on legs.

Casket

Made in oak with contrasting walnut lippings and inlay, this design is suitable for a presentation casket. Two designs are shown in the drawing, but within the dimensional limits there is ample scope for creating individual designs. It gives the woodworker an opportunity to make the mitred secret dovetail joint as used in first-class cabinet work. Practice is also provided in inlaying strings, making of a shaped plinth and lid, sawing off and hinging the lid.

Method

1. Prepare material, select and match the grain. *Note:* sides and ends could be cut out of one length, and arranged to obtain continuity of grain. Figures 1 and 2 on page 125 show alternative dovetail arrangement, the latter making the better job.
2. Pair up and mark to length the sides and ends. Cut to length and plane accurately to the cut line.
3. Mark out for mitred secret dovetail joint and remove waste to make laps.
4. Mark out and cut pins.
5. Locate ends on sides, mark out and make tails.
6. Carefully pare and plane mitres on lap and edges of casket, and assemble, fitting as necessary.
7. Flush top and bottom edges of carcase. Work grooves in sides, ends and top. Make a test piece before ploughing.
8. Work rebates for bottom.
9. Fit top and assemble dry, fitting as necessary.
10. Clean up. Mask joints and polish inner surfaces. Glue up carcase taking care to prevent glue entering tongue and lipped joint of top.
11. Veneer both sides of bottom. Fit, clean up and polish.
12. Glue in bottom and cramp up.
13. Using a cutting gauge and scratch stock, mark out and prepare for stringing. Finish corners with a sharp chisel. Mitre and glue in stringing.
14. Chamfer the top edge of carcase and work cavetto moulding.
15. Mark out for tapering on carcase and plane off.
16. Clean up and lightly rub over with white polish.
17. Saw off, clean up and fit lid.
18. Mitre and glue on lipping. When dry bore for decorative dowels.
19. Mitre and glue in locating bead.
20. Mark out position of butts, cut recesses and hinge lid. Note chamfering at back of casket and the setting in of hinge knuckle. This forms a stop for the lid.
21. Shape, mitre and glue plinth in position. Leave to dry.
22. Bore for 3mm (⅛in) wood pins and glue in. Flush off and clean up plinth.
23. Finish as for wax polish.

Suggested Material

Oak with walnut contrasts and rosewood strings.

Cutting list

Description	Length	Width	Thickness
2 sides	300mm (1ft)	91mm (3⅝in)	18mm (1 1⁄16in)
1 for 2 ends	300mm (1ft)	91mm (3⅝in)	18mm (1 1⁄16in)
1 top	275mm (11in)	125mm (5in)	13mm (½in)
2 plinths walnut	300mm (1ft)	20mm (¾in)	18mm (1 1⁄16in)
1 for 2 plinths walnut	325mm (1ft 1in)	20mm (¾in)	18mm (11⁄16in)
1 bottom plywood	275mm (11in)	125mm (5in)	6mm (¼in)
2 pieces veneer cut	275mm (11in)	125mm (5in) oak double knife	
2 lippings walnut	450mm (1ft 6in)	15mm (9⁄16in)	3mm (⅛in)
2 locating beads walnut	400mm (1ft 4in)	16mm (⅝in)	3mm (⅛in)
2 strings	375mm (1ft 3in)	1.6mm (1⁄16in)	
10 pins	32mm (1¼in)	3mm × 3mm (⅛in × ⅛in) oak	
10 decorative dots knitting needle)	13mm (½in) (these can be cut from a white plastic		

1 pair of 38mm (1½in) brass butts and screws

Tools not in Basic Kit

Shoulder plane – for finishing mitres.
Plough – for grooving top.
Scratch stock – for inlaying stringing.
Moulding plane, round – for making cavetto.

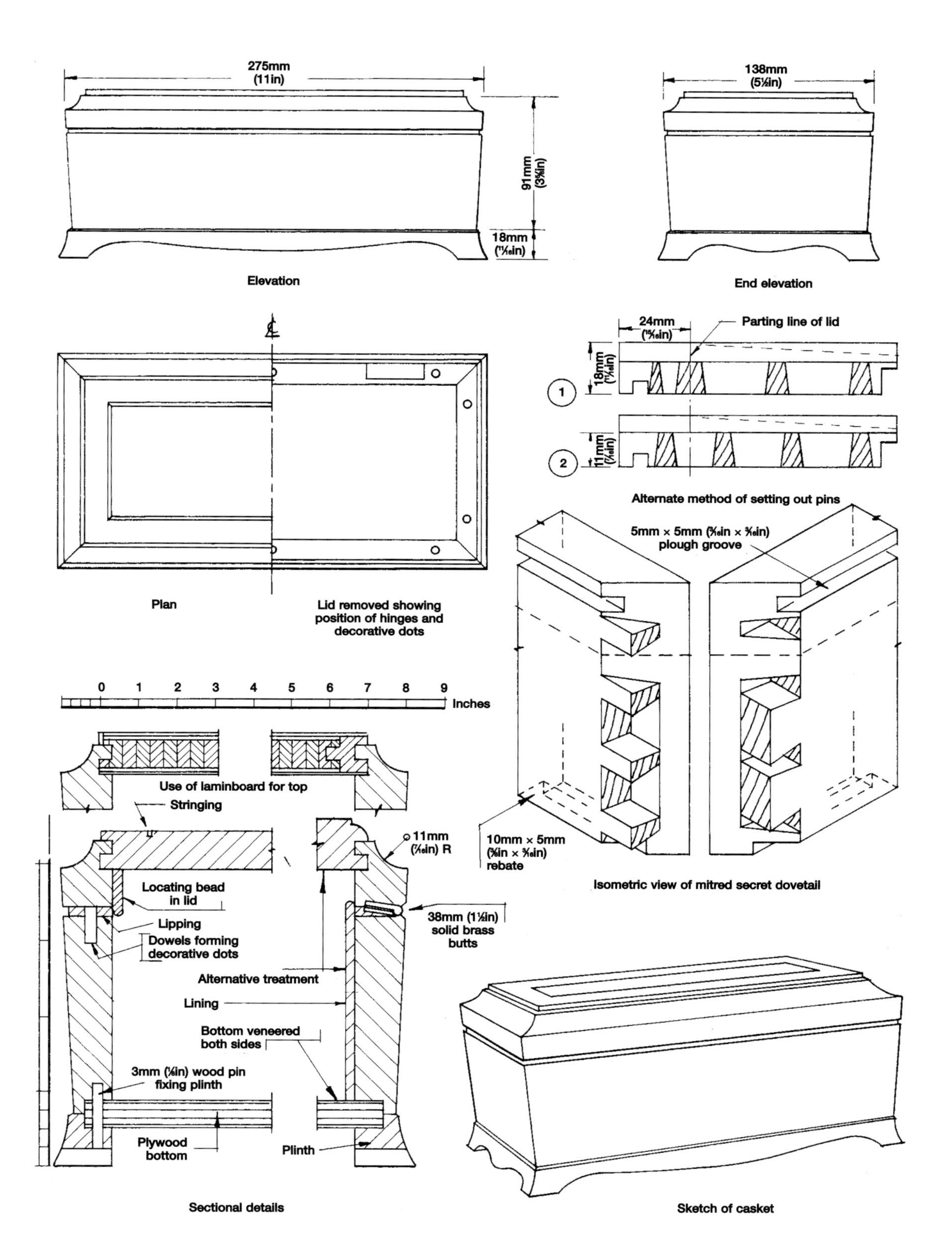
275mm
(11in)
138mm
(5½in)
91mm
(3⅝in)
18mm
(11/16in)
Elevation
End elevation
24mm
(15/16in)
Parting line of lid
18mm
(11/16in)
1
11mm
(7/16in)
2
Alternate method of setting out pins
Plan
Lid removed showing
position of hinges and
decorative dots
0 1 2 3 4 5 6 7 8 9
Inches
5mm × 5mm (3/16in × 3/16in)
plough groove
Use of laminboard for top
Stringing
11mm
(7/16in) R
10mm × 5mm
(⅜in × 3/16in)
rebate
Locating bead
in lid
Isometric view of mitred secret dovetail
Lipping
38mm (1½in)
solid brass
butts
Dowels forming
decorative dots
Alternative treatment
Lining
Bottom veneered
both sides
3mm (⅛in) wood pin
fixing plinth
Plywood
bottom
Plinth
Sectional details
Sketch of casket

Wall Fitment

A small cabinet of useful proportions fitted with an adjustable shelf is shown. It is designed to take plywood or glass sliding doors. The plywood doors incorporate neat sunk finger pulls backed with a decorative veneer.

The main constructional feature is the box carcase with secret lapped dovetail joints. The dovetailing is specially arranged (see page 129) to accommodate the grooves; this plate also gives full constructional details of joints and particulars of sliding doors. The top half shows details of a secret or double lapped dovetail joint. The pins are set out in the usual manner except for a slight modification to accommodate the varying depths of grooves. This gives a first class finish. The drawings in the lower half give details of a simple lapped dovetail joint. It shows the grooves covered by a large pin. This treatment simplifies the construction and makes it suitable for the young woodworker with less experience. In this case the glass or wood panels butt against the carcase side. A separate detail shows an alternative treatment for a loose piece to accommodate the top plough grooves. This is particularly suitable in situations where the glass must not be lifted out, or where the top is too thin to receive a deep groove.

Method

1. Prepare material, arrange and match the grain. Number corners for easy identification.
2. Pair up and mark out length of top and bottom. Square up ends.
3. Pair up and mark out length of sides, deducting 10mm ($\frac{3}{8}$in) from the overall length to allow for laps, and square up ends. Adjust cutting gauge as necessary and gauge for dovetailing.
4. Check with plough iron, for size of groove, 6mm ($\frac{1}{4}$in) plate glass needs a small clearance for smooth running. Gauge and plough for grooves.
5. Set out pins on sides. Make allowance for depth of grooves in top and bottom of the carcase. See isometric views of joints.
6. Cut pins. Using an awl mark out dovetails from the pins (see page 39).
7. Rebate for back.
8. Cut dovetails and assemble carcase, adjusting as necessary.
9. Flush all joints. Work mouldings on the inside edges.
10. Mark out and bore for 8mm ($\frac{5}{16}$in) supporting dowels for adjustable shelves.
11. Clean up all inner surfaces. Mask as necessary and polish.
12. Prepare for gluing, and glue up. Check carefully for straightness of top, bottom and sides. A misplaced sash cramp can cause bowing. Too much strain on a cramp can have similar results. Remove surplus glue and leave to dry.
13. Work moulding on outer edges. Fit and screw in back.
14. Clean up and complete polishing of carcase.
15. Prepare doors, lightly rounding edges. Mark out and make aperture for finger grip.
    Note: to make shape bore a small hole and cut out waste with a coping saw, carefully bevelling with a file. Finish with glasspaper.
16. Cut recesses to receive veneer backing and glue in.
17. Try doors in grooves, adjusting as necessary. Clean up and polish.

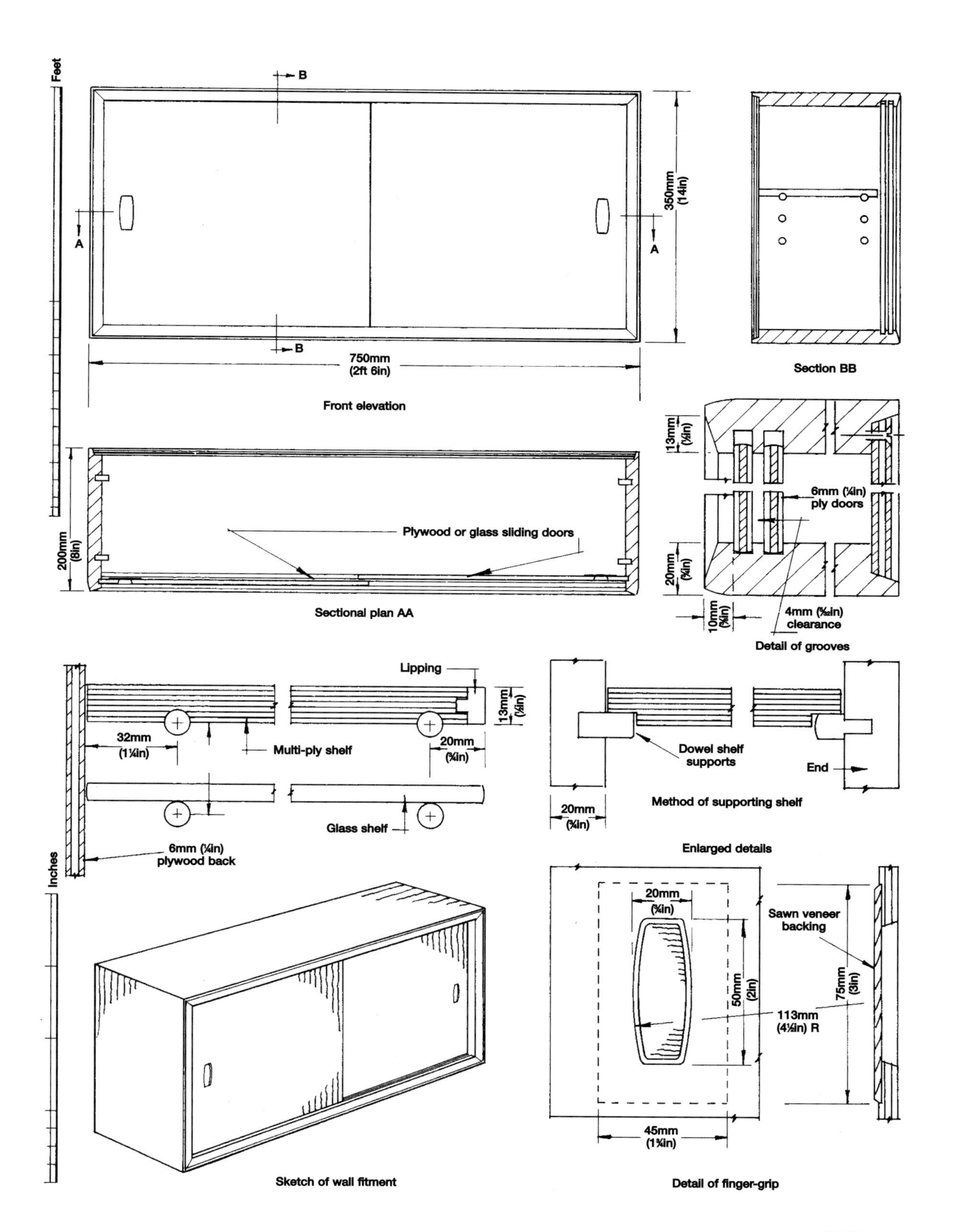

Sketch of wall fitment

Detail of finger-grip

18 Prepare shelf and plough front edge. Make lipping, fit and glue in.
19 Mark out dowel positions on end of shelf. Cramp a spare piece of wood to the end of the shelf and bore holes in end for dowel location. Make dowels and complete polishing.
20 Screw on mirror plates, packing out to make flush with ends, and bore through the back to receive fixing screws; 50mm (2in) × 10 round head screws with washers make a neat finish to the interior.

Suggested Material

With glass doors, sapele carcase with back veneered sycamore. Finish natural colour, wax polished. With plywood doors, selected faced plywood or veneer as desired, with contrasting backing to finger pulls. Alternatively use parana or Columbian pine, left natural colour and lightly polished. Use parana pine or ramin for a painted finish.

Cutting list

Description	Length	Width	Thickness
1 top	775mm (2ft 7in)	200mm (8in)	20mm (¾in)
1 bottom	775mm (2ft 7in)	200mm (8in)	20mm (¾in)
2 ends	363mm (1ft 2½in)	200mm (8in)	20mm (¾in)
1 back plywood	750mm (2ft 6in)	350mm (14in)	6mm (¼in)
2 doors plywood	325mm (1ft 1in)	370mm (14¾in)	6mm (¼in)
veneer backing for finger grips	45mm (1¾in)	75mm (3in)	2mm (3/32in)
1 shelf laminboard	725mm (2ft 5in)	153mm (6⅛in)	13mm (½in)
1 lipping	725mm (2ft 5in)	16mm (⅝in)	11mm (7/16in)
2 doors plate glass with ground handles and polished edges	320mm (1ft ¾in)	366mm (14⅝in)	6mm (¼in)
1 shelf plate glass	710mm (2ft 4⅜in)	160mm (6⅜in)	6mm (¼in)
2 pairs 50mm (2in) brass mirror plates			

Tools not in Basic Kit

Shoulder plane – for cleaning up dovetail laps.
Plough – for making grooves to take sliding doors.

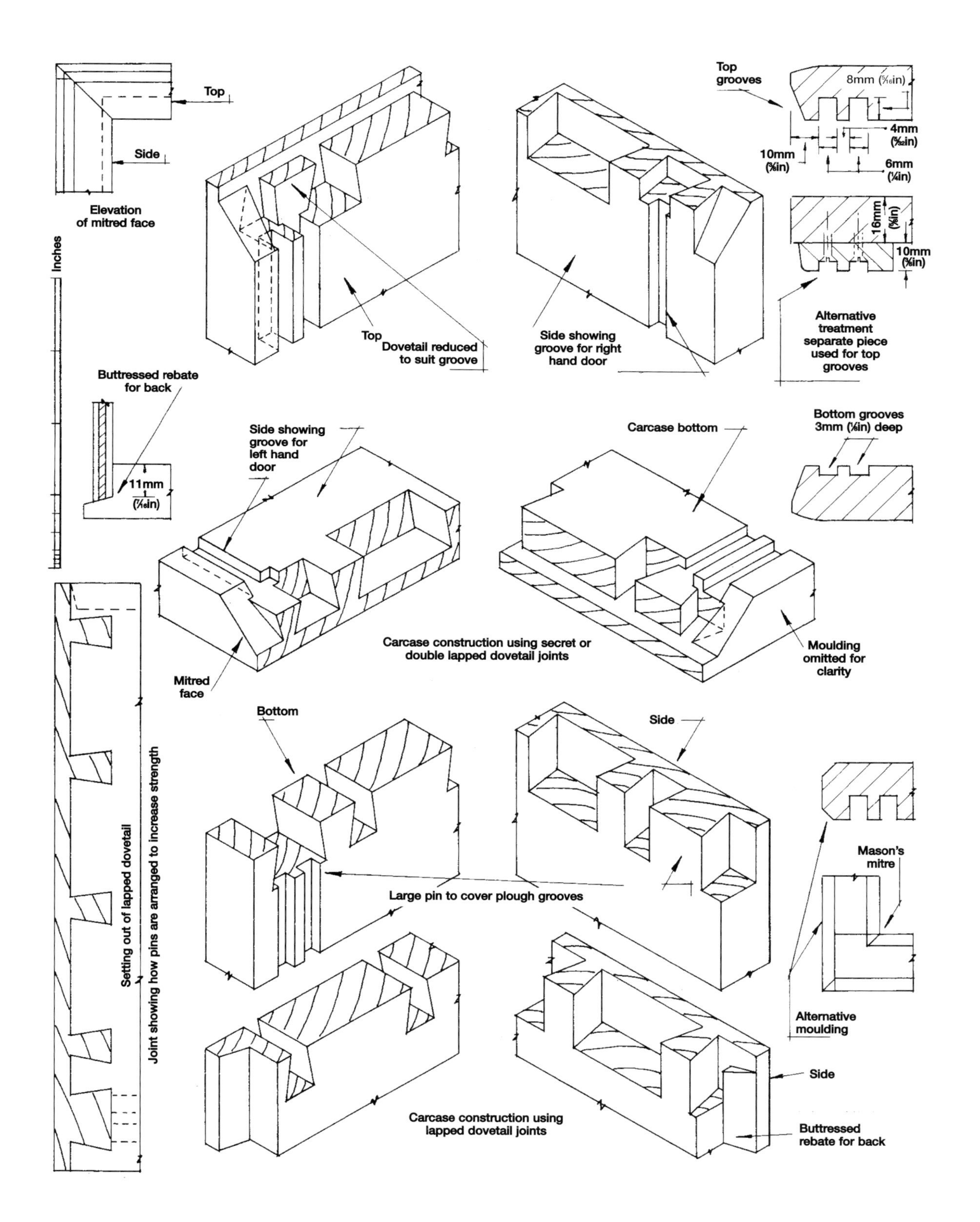

Top
Side
Elevation of mitred face
Inches
Top
Dovetail reduced to suit groove
Side showing groove for right hand door
Top grooves
8mm (5/16in)
4mm (5/32in)
10mm (3/8in)
6mm (1/4in)
16mm (5/8in)
10mm (3/8in)
Alternative treatment separate piece used for top grooves
Buttressed rebate for back
11mm (7/16in)
Side showing groove for left hand door
Carcase bottom
Bottom grooves 3mm (1/8in) deep
Carcase construction using secret or double lapped dovetail joints
Mitred face
Moulding omitted for clarity
Bottom
Side
Setting out of lapped dovetail
Joint showing how pins are arranged to increase strength
Mason's mitre
Large pin to cover plough grooves
Alternative moulding
Side
Carcase construction using lapped dovetail joints
Buttressed rebate for back

Small Bookcase with Drawers

This small cabinet is particularly useful where space is limited. It has two drawers and, for its size, good accommodation for books.

The carcase is in mahogany – many different arrangements are possible – with a separate recessed plinth veneered in Australian walnut, with the grain running vertically. The handles are shaped and veneered in walnut, the grain being arranged to run horizontally. The drawer fronts are veneered in fiddle-back sycamore. The design incorporates, with an economical use of timber, a wide variety of joints used in box carcase and drawer construction. To understand the principles of construction, the student should make a careful study of the joints and appreciate their application to furniture making.

Note: in large carcases, such as a sideboard, a small dovetail near the front and back edges helps to overcome any tendency for the corners to curl away (see separate drawing on page 135).

Method

1. Prepare material, select and match the grain to the best advantage. Number joints for easy identification.
2. Pair up and mark out sides.
3. Cut sides to length, square up ends, and rebate for back. Mark out for pins.
4. Mark out top, shelves and bottom. Cut to length and plane ends square. Gauge for dovetailing.
5. Remove waste to make top lap and clean up rebate with a shoulder plane. Work rebate for back.
6. Cut pins on sides and mark out dovetails from them.
7. Cut dovetails. Fit carcase joints, adjusting as necessary.
8. Cut shouldered dovetail housing for shelves, finishing 4mm (3/16in) deep with a router.
9. Dovetail ends of shelves to fit housings. Slide into respective positions adjusting as necessary.

   Note: mark end of shelves and housings for easy identification when assembling.
10. Mark out vertical drawer division and gauge for twin tenons. Gauge top and drawer shelf for mortises.
11. House drawer shelf 3mm (1/8in) deep to receive drawer guide. Fit vertical drawer division into top and shelf.
12. Mortise drawer shelf to receive stops.
13. Clean up all inner surfaces. Mask joints as necessary and polish. Prepare for gluing up.
14. Glue in shelves. Glue and assemble the bottom. Apply glue to top and drawer division. Assemble, and cramp up, carefully check for square and alignment.
15. Set out plinth. Make mitred secret dovetail on front and lap dovetail at back.
16. Assemble plinth, fitting as necessary.
17. Glue up plinth and leave to dry.
18. Make fixing blocks. Bore three holes in each block. The blocks are glued and screwed to the plinth. Make an allowance for shrinkage by elongating the holes in the side and back blocks before fixing to carcase.

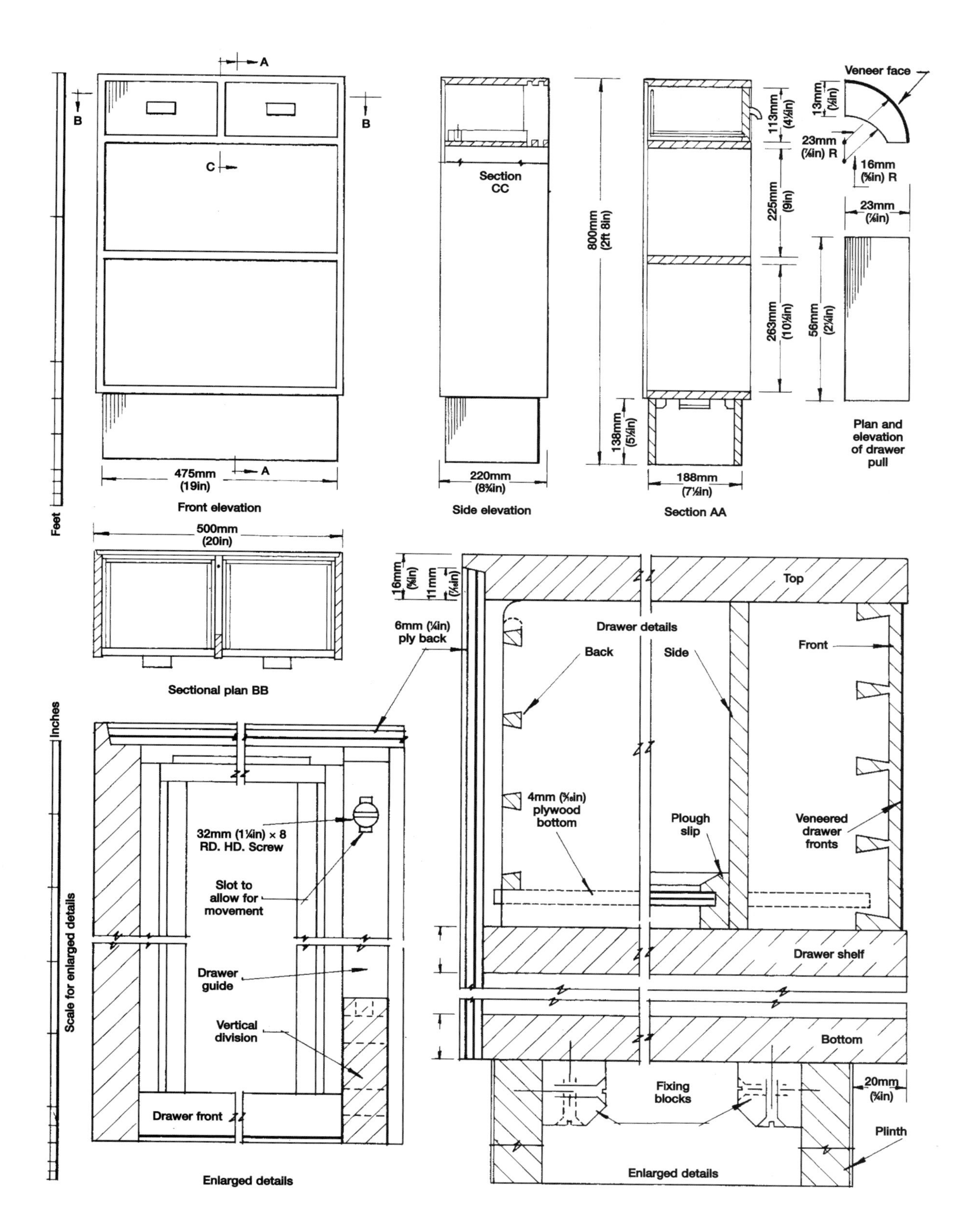
A
B
B
C
475mm
(19in)
A
Front elevation
Section
CC
220mm
(8¾in)
Side elevation
800mm
(2ft 8in)
113mm
(4½in)
225mm
(9in)
263mm
(10½in)
138mm
(5½in)
188mm
(7½in)
Section AA
Veneer face
13mm
(½in)
23mm
(⅞in) R
16mm
(⅝in) R
23mm
(⅞in)
56mm
(2¼in)
Plan and elevation of drawer pull
Feet
500mm
(20in)
Sectional plan BB
Inches
Scale for enlarged details
16mm
(⅝in)
11mm
(7/16in)
6mm (¼in)
ply back
32mm (1¼in) × 8
RD. HD. Screw
Slot to
allow for
movement
Drawer
guide
Vertical
division
Drawer front
Enlarged details
Top
Drawer details
Back
Side
Front
4mm (3/16in)
plywood
bottom
Plough
slip
Veneered
drawer
fronts
Drawer shelf
Bottom
Fixing
blocks
20mm
(¾in)
Plinth
Enlarged details

19 Flush joints of plinth, finishing with a toothing plane to provide a key for the veneer. Apply veneer, grain running vertically (see page 161 for veneering technique).
20 Flush joints on carcase. Fit back, bore holes for screws, clean up and polish. Screw back in place.
21 Make and fit drawer stops. Screw on plinth. Fit drawer guide. Glue tenon only, and allow for shrinkage by slot screwing at the back.
22 Clean up carcase and polish.
23 Make and carefully fit the drawers. Note the drawer fronts are veneered, grain running vertically. The fronts are set back 1.6mm (1/16in) (see page 144 for drawer construction).
24 Shape and veneer the handles and screw or dowel to drawer fronts.
25 Clean up and complete polishing.

Gluing-up Technique

For general carcase work or framing.

On completion of fitting the joints assemble carcase or framing. Test for square and make any necessary adjustments at this stage. A badly cut dovetail, a stub tenon touching the bottom of a mortise, shoulders not square, are the results of poor craftsmanship. Cramps will not correct errors of this description.

Prepare blocks and adjust cramps. Make a trial run through of the gluing-up procedure for the particular job in hand before applying glue. Inadequate preparation usually results in panic – a dash for extra cramps, a hammer, blocks of wood, etc.

Notes on glues

A good quality animal glue – Scotch or French – can be used successfully for most domestic furniture.

Advantages: one of the cheapest glues to use. It has non-staining properties and is very strong. Excellent for making rubbed joints, and veneering particularly by the hammer method. Make sure the glue kettle is kept clean. The glue should be clean and fresh. On no account must the glue burn, as burning destroys its adhesive qualities. Always use a clean brush. The brush should be washed out with hot water after use and not left in the pot. Glue up in a warm workshop free from draughts. It is helpful to warm the joints immediately before applying the glue, this prevents the glue from chilling rapidly.

Disadvantages: not resistant to dampness. Comparatively short assembly time.

Synthetic resin glues

Advantages: strength, high resistance to water and heat. Mainly free from staining. Longer period for gluing up. Setting time can be extended according to type of hardener. Can be obtained in powder form, ready for use by adding water, or in two distinct parts, glue and hardener.

Disadvantages: expensive to use, particularly in the smaller quantities. Surplus glue dries very hard and is difficult to remove. Tends to dull tools.

Suggested Material

Carcase, mahogany. Drawer fronts, fiddle-back sycamore, veneer. Handles (finished), walnut veneer. Plinth (finished), Australian walnut veneer.

Cutting list

Description	Length	Width	Thickness
Carcase			
2 sides	675mm (2ft 3in)	220mm (8¾in)	16mm (⅝in)
1 top	525mm (1ft 9in)	220mm (8¾in)	16mm (⅝in)
2 shelves	500mm (1ft 8in)	220mm (8¾in)	16mm (⅝in)
1 bottom	500mm (1ft 8in)	211mm (8 7⁄16in)	16mm (⅝in)
1 back plywood	675mm ((2ft 3in)	500mm (20in)	6mm (¼in)
1 vertical division	150mm (6in)	50mm (2in)	16mm (⅝in)
1 drawer guide	175mm (7in)	25mm (1in)	16mm (⅝in)
Plinth			
1 front	500mm (1ft 8in)	138mm (5½in)	16mm (⅝in)
1 back	500mm (1ft 8in)	138mm (5½in)	16mm (⅝in)
2 ends	200mm (8in)	138mm (5½in)	16mm (⅝in)
2 pieces veneer Australian walnut	150mm (6in)	500mm (20in)	
2 pieces veneer Australian walnut	150mm (6in)	225mm (9in)	
Drawers			
2 fronts	225mm (9in)	116mm (4⅝in)	16mm (⅝in)
4 sides	213mm (8½in)	116mm (4⅝in)	6mm (¼in)
2 backs	225mm (9in)	95mm (3¾in)	6mm (¼in)
4 plough slips	213mm (8½in)	20mm (¾in)	10mm (⅜in)
2 drawer bottoms	225mm (9in)	213mm (8½in)	4mm (3⁄16in)
1 for drawer stops	100mm (4in)	20mm (¾in)	6mm (¼in)
2 pieces fiddle-back sycamore veneer	125mm (5in)	250mm (10in)	
1 piece for handles	125mm (5in)	23mm (⅞in)	23mm (⅞in)
8 fixing blocks	63mm (2½in)	23mm (⅞in)	23mm (⅞in)

Tools not in Basic Kit

Shoulder plane – for cleaning up dovetail laps and mitres.
Router – for finishing housings to depth.
Plough – for grooves in plough slip and drawer fronts.
Toothing plane – for keying drawer fronts and plinth.
Veneering hammer – for laying veneers.
Veneer knife – for jointing veneer.

Hall Seat

This well-proportioned hall seat is suitable where space is limited. It would also serve as a telephone table, being fitted with a drawer and open shelf. It has interesting leg and rail treatments.

Method

1 Prepare material for stool. Arrange and match the grain.
2 Set out legs in pairs (see separate drawing of enlarged details showing tenon proportions).
3 Set out long and short rails in pairs. Spring (or bend) a batten and mark out shape on rails.
4 Set mortise gauge to an 8mm (5/16in) mortise chisel and gauge all mortises and tenons.
5 Cut mortises and haunchings (see isometric drawing on page 231). The leg haunchings at carcase end are taken up to top of rail.
6 Saw down the tenons. Work rebates for the loose seat.
Note: the rebates are stopped on the long rails. Fig. 1 shows the dovetailed top rail with fillet, which is glued to the rail and forms the rebate adjacent to the drawer carcase. Chopping out with a 25mm (1in) chisel, remove as much as possible of the rebate up to the stop. Clean up to the gauge lines with shoulder and bull-nose planes.
7 Saw down the shoulders to remove the tenon cheeks, cut tenons to size and make the haunchings. See step 5.
8 Mark length of tenon and mitre the ends.
9 Fit all joints, set out and work rebates on the end of two legs. Dovetail top rail into side rails.
10 Cut legs at floor line, mark out and taper legs on the inside. Round corners of leg as shown in separate detail.
11 Cut and shape rails. Bevel top and bottom edges.
12 Clean up all inner surfaces, mask joints and polish.
13 Glue up the two side frames, test legs for alignment and leave to dry.
14 Flush joints on side frames. Glue up end rails and dovetailed top rail. Test for square and alignment.
15 Shape and fit brackets.
16 Flush all joints and complete bevelling round top of legs.
17 To complete the loose seat rebate, glue fillet on dovetailed top rail.
18 Complete the polishing.
19 Prepare material for the drawer carcase.
20 Set out length of top and bottom. Cut and plane ends square.
21 Set out sides, cut to length and plane ends square.
22 Gauge and mark out for through dovetailing. Rebate for panelled back. Note mitres at top of rebate. Cut dovetails and mark out pins.
23 Cut pins, removing greater part of waste with a coping saw, and finish to cut line with a paring chisel.
24 Mark out drawer rail, cut tenons and make mortises in carcase sides. The tenons are arranged to give the maximum strength and gluing surfaces. The tenons also counteract possible warping of the rail.
25 House carcase ends for drawer runner.
26 Mark out for the drawer framing and plough for dust boards.

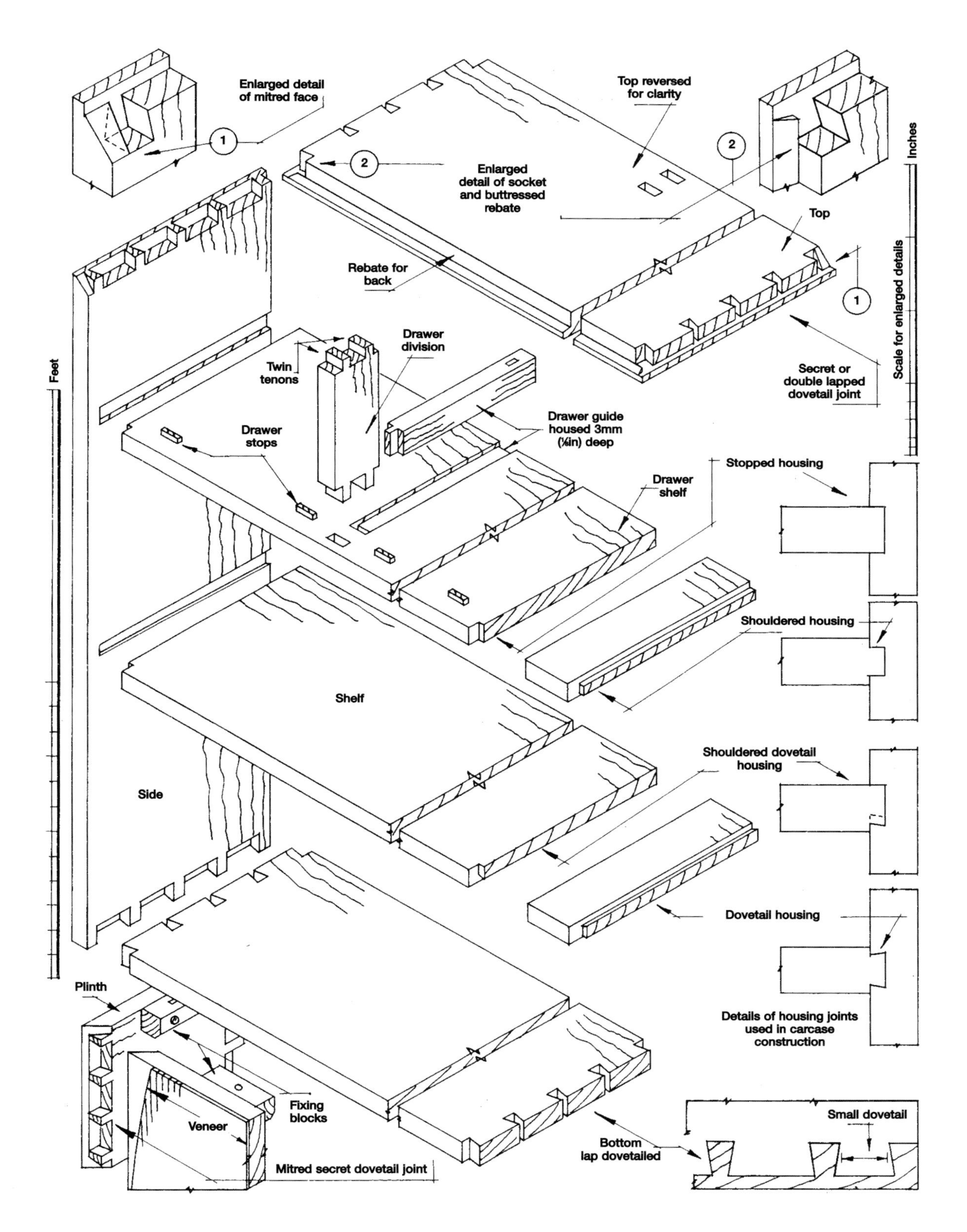
Enlarged detail of mitred face
1
2
Top reversed for clarity
2
Enlarged detail of socket and buttressed rebate
Top
Inches
Scale for enlarged details
1
Rebate for back
Secret or double lapped dovetail joint
Drawer division
Twin tenons
Feet
Drawer guide housed 3mm (⅛in) deep
Drawer stops
Stopped housing
Drawer shelf
Shouldered housing
Shelf
Shouldered dovetail housing
Side
Dovetail housing
Details of housing joints used in carcase construction
Plinth
Fixing blocks
Veneer
Small dovetail
Bottom lap dovetailed
Mitred secret dovetail joint

Note: as the weight of the drawer is supported by the drawer framing, the 'housing' in of the drawer runners prevents any possible distortion of the framing. Allowance must be made for the opposite grain directions. The drawer runners will not shrink in their length. The carcase will of course contract or expand in its depth or distance from back to front. To counteract the effect of this movement only the front portion including the tenons of the drawer runners are glued, and a clearance of approximately 4mm (3/16in) should be allowed between the framing and the panelled back. This arrangement allows the carcase to contract or expand freely without splitting and prevents the back from being forced off. Carefully note grain direction, as given in the separate detail isometric view showing carcase construction. (Compare this with carcase shown on page 135.)

27 Assemble carcase including drawer framing, adjusting as necessary.
28 Clean up all inner surfaces, mask joints as necessary and polish.
29 Glue up. When dry flush all joints and work chamfers, rounding corners as shown on isometric detail.
30 Prepare material for the panelled back.
31 Set out stiles and rails in pairs.
32 Gauge for and cut mortises and tenons, and plough for panel.
33 Fit panel, and work beads on the long edges. Work the bead 1mm (1/32in) below panel surface to prevent the bead from losing its shape when the framing is cleaned up. See figure 2 for alternative back treatment.
34 Make loose seat framing and glue and screw on plywood. (For upholstery details see page 151.)
35 Make and fit drawer. Note the extension of the drawer front over the drawer rail to serve as a drawer pull.
36 Glue and screw fixing blocks to stool. Elongate the screw holes to allow for shrinkage, and screw on the carcase.
37 Complete polishing.

Suggested Material

Guarea, afrormosia or oak.

Cutting list

Description	Length	Width	Thickness
Stool			
4 legs	438mm (1ft 5½in)	35mm (1⅜in)	35mm (1⅜in)
2 rails	800mm (2ft 8in)	82mm (3¼in)	23mm (⅞in)
2 end rails	325mm (1ft 1in)	82mm (3¼in)	23mm (⅞in)
1 top rail	325mm (1ft 1in)	45mm (1¾in)	16mm (⅝in)
1 top fillet	325mm (1ft 1in)	32mm (1¼in)	16mm (⅝in)
brackets	325mm (1ft 1in)	56mm (2¼in)	20mm (¾in)
Carcase			
1 top	350mm (1ft 2in)	300mm (12in)	16mm (⅝in)
1 bottom	350mm (1ft 2in)	300mm (12in)	16mm (⅝in)
2 ends	275mm (11in)	300mm (12in)	16mm (⅝in)
1 drawer rail	325mm (1ft 1in)	38mm (1½in)	16mm (⅝in)

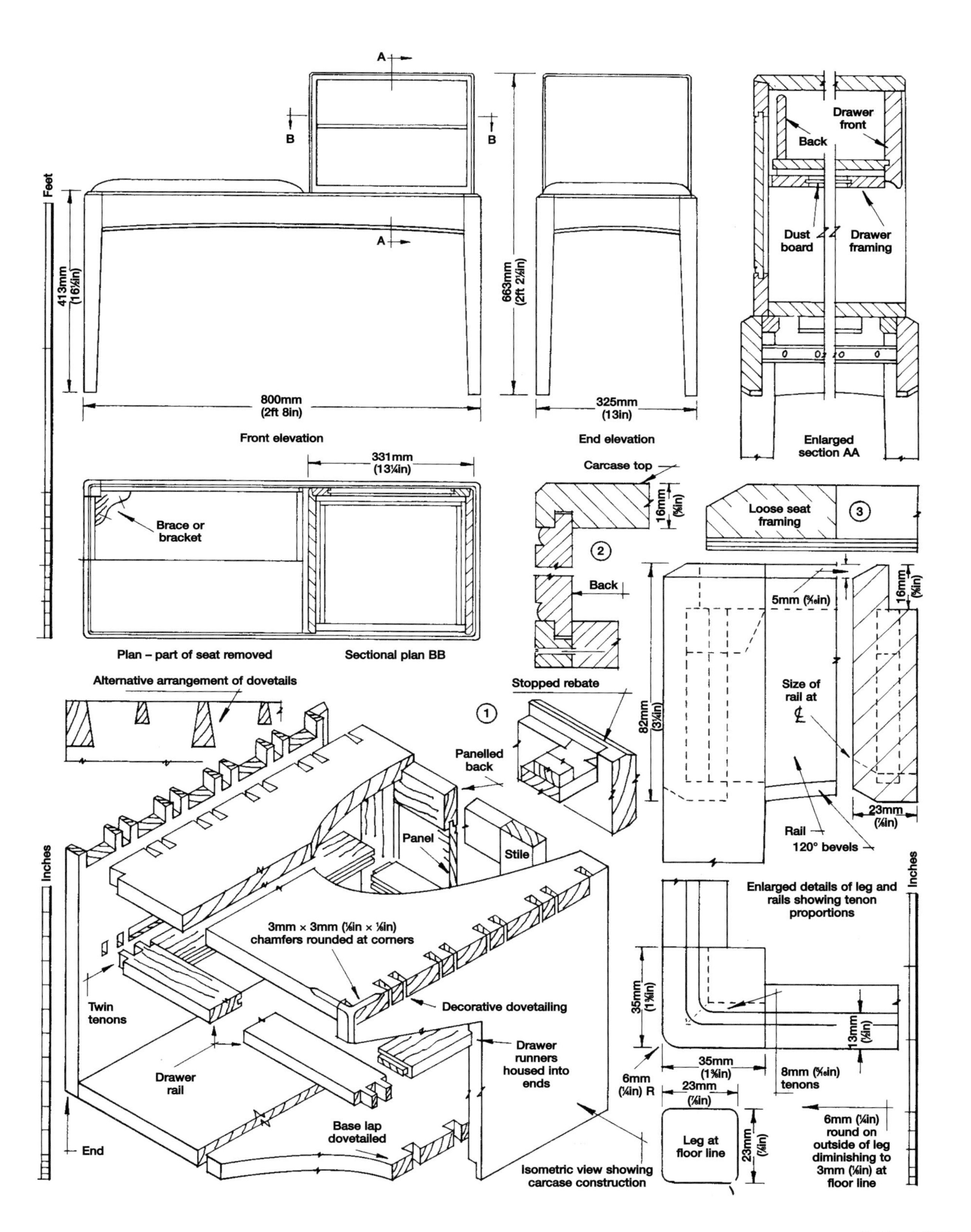
Feet
413mm
(16½in)
A
B
B
A
663mm
(2ft 2½in)
800mm
(2ft 8in)
325mm
(13in)
Front elevation
End elevation
Drawer front
Back
Dust board
Drawer framing
Enlarged section AA
331mm
(13¼in)
Brace or bracket
Plan – part of seat removed
Sectional plan BB
Carcase top
16mm (⅝in)
Loose seat framing
Back
5mm (3/16in)
16mm (⅝in)
Alternative arrangement of dovetails
Stopped rebate
Panelled back
82mm (3¼in)
Size of rail at ℄
23mm (⅞in)
Panel
Stile
Rail
120° bevels
Inches
Enlarged details of leg and rails showing tenon proportions
3mm × 3mm (⅛in × ⅛in) chamfers rounded at corners
Twin tenons
Decorative dovetailing
35mm (1⅜in)
13mm (½in)
Drawer runners housed into ends
Drawer rail
35mm (1⅜in)
8mm (5/16in) tenons
6mm (¼in) R
23mm (⅞in)
Base lap dovetailed
Leg at floor line
23mm (⅞in)
6mm (¼in) round on outside of leg diminishing to 3mm (⅛in) at floor line
End
Isometric view showing carcase construction
Inches

2 drawer runners	250mm (10in)	38mm (1½in)	16mm (⅝in)
1 back rail	250mm (10in)	38mm (1½in)	16mm (⅝in)
1 dust board	250mm (10in)	200mm (8in)	4mm (3/16in)
drawer material	order as required		
panelled back	order as required		
Loose seat frame			
2 rails	450mm (1ft 6in)	45mm (1¾in)	20mm (¾in)
2 end rails	300mm (1ft)	45mm (1¾in)	20mm (¾in)
1 bottom plywood	450mm (1ft 6in)	300mm (12in)	4mm (3/16in)

Tools not in Basic Kit

Shoulder plane – for cleaning up shoulders and rebates.
Plough – for grooving dust board and back.
Bullnose plane – for finishing stop rebates.
Round moulding plane – for pull on drawer front.

Side Table

This could be used as a small writing table. It is a good example of table-frame and drawer construction. It gives the student an opportunity to acquire workshop experience and techniques and to become familiar with cabinet-making terms. The design includes two drawers with handles inlaid with rosewood or leather and features a subtle use of chamfers. An alternative treatment making use of lipped and veneered multi-ply is shown in a detail drawing. Leather or PVC covering, which makes an excellent writing surface, could be used instead of veneer.

Design and Modelmaking

To gain experience in design, it is suggested that the student or craftsman should make a thorough study of the drawings, and design several alternative side tables of various sizes. The drawer fronts, for example, could be arranged to run through and conceal the drawer division. The legs could be moulded, and the stretcher rails shaped, repositioned or even omitted.

Building up a design

When originating, or modifying a design the importance of making good freehand sketches cannot be over emphasised. A light colour wash often helps to distinguish various materials, particularly when arranging for colour harmony.

Scale models and drawings

From the freehand sketches scale drawings can be developed – 40mm (1½in) to 300mm (1ft) is quite suitable for this exercise. From these drawings an appreciation of the general form and proportion of the job can be obtained. A model in balsa wood is easily made and gives an excellent three-dimensional view of the design. Any modification should be incorporated at this stage and the final scale drawing made.

Method

1. Prepare material for table framing. Arrange and match the grain. For setting out technique see exploded isometric view of end framing.
2. Pair up the legs and set out.
3. Set out end and back rails, and gauge mortises and tenons.
4. Set out front drawer rails. Mark out dovetails.
5. Set out vertical drawer division and gauge mortises and tenons.
6. Gauge mortises and tenons for drawer rail.
7. Cut mortises and tenons. Work rebate in back and end rails, and fit joints.
8. Cut dovetails on top front rail. Position rail over top of leg and mark round dovetail. Cut and remove sockets. Try together, fitting as necessary.
   Note: it is preferable to fit the small dovetails in the end rails after gluing up the end frames.
9. Taper inside of legs. Fit stretcher rails, work chamfers, and assemble end frames.
10. Clean up all inner surfaces, mask as required and polish.
11. Glue up end frames, and leave to dry.
12. Complete marking out of the drawer framing. Check dimensions with end frame.

13 Plough for dust boards and fit panels.

14 Dovetail one end of drawer division into back rail. Tongue the opposite end into the vertical drawer division.

15 Tongue and fit end kickers. Dovetail and tongue centre kicker. Arrange for the fixing of the top.

16 Cut mortises in rail for drawer stops. Assemble table framing, checking all joints, adjusting as necessary. Note housings in legs to take drawer framing.

17 Cut and fit long stretcher rail, and work chamfers.

18 Drawer framing is screwed to back and end rails. Bore and countersink for screws.

19 Clean up all inner surfaces, mask joints as necessary, and polish.

20 Glue up drawer framing. When dry, flush surfaces.
Gluing up technique: Glue up in the following stages; glue mortises and tenons at back rail, front drawer rail, and stretcher rail. Assemble and lightly cramp up. Glue up vertical drawer division, and slide dovetail and twin tenons into position. Glue kickers to top front rail. Glue dovetails and tenons and drive home front rail and centre kicker. Complete cramping up. Screw up drawer framing and kickers. Carefully check for square and alignment. Remove all surplus glue and leave to dry.

21 Remove horns and flush top of table, testing with a straight edge.
It is interesting to compare the two previous carcases of dovetailed-box carcase construction with the table framing. Shrinkage is practically eliminated owing to the frame construction technique. Since the grain of the end rails runs parallel to the drawer runners and kickers, no provision for shrinkage is needed. The drawer framing is grooved to take the ply panel or dust board. The panels could be in solid wood, as the grooves allow for any movement. However, for the fixing of a solid top provision must be made for movement. The isometric view on page 143 shows method of fixing the top. The top is fastened with screws through the front rail, buttons on the back rail and screws through slots in the kickers. With shallow drawers some difficulty might be encountered with this method of fixing the top. Holes large enough to take a small screwdriver through the drawer framing directly under the buttons (as shown in drawing) is one solution. They would also serve as a useful source of ventilation.
Another satisfactory method is to radius the end of the buttons. The buttons are screwed on the underside of the top. The top is located and screwed through the front rail, the button being tapped round on the screw into the mortise. Slotted metal plates are sometimes used.

22 Fix top and glue in drawer stops and guide.

23 Prepare drawer material. Carefully match and arrange the fronts.

24 Set out drawers. Cut all dovetails and plough front. Round top edge of drawer back, and clean up all inner surfaces. Mask joints and polish. (For further information on drawer construction, see page 145.)

25 Glue up and test for square. When dry glue in plough slips.

26 Fit bottom. Clean up, polish and screw bottom to back of drawer.

27 Carefully flush dovetails and fit drawers. A well fitted drawer should slide easily without slackness in either direction – sideways or up and down.

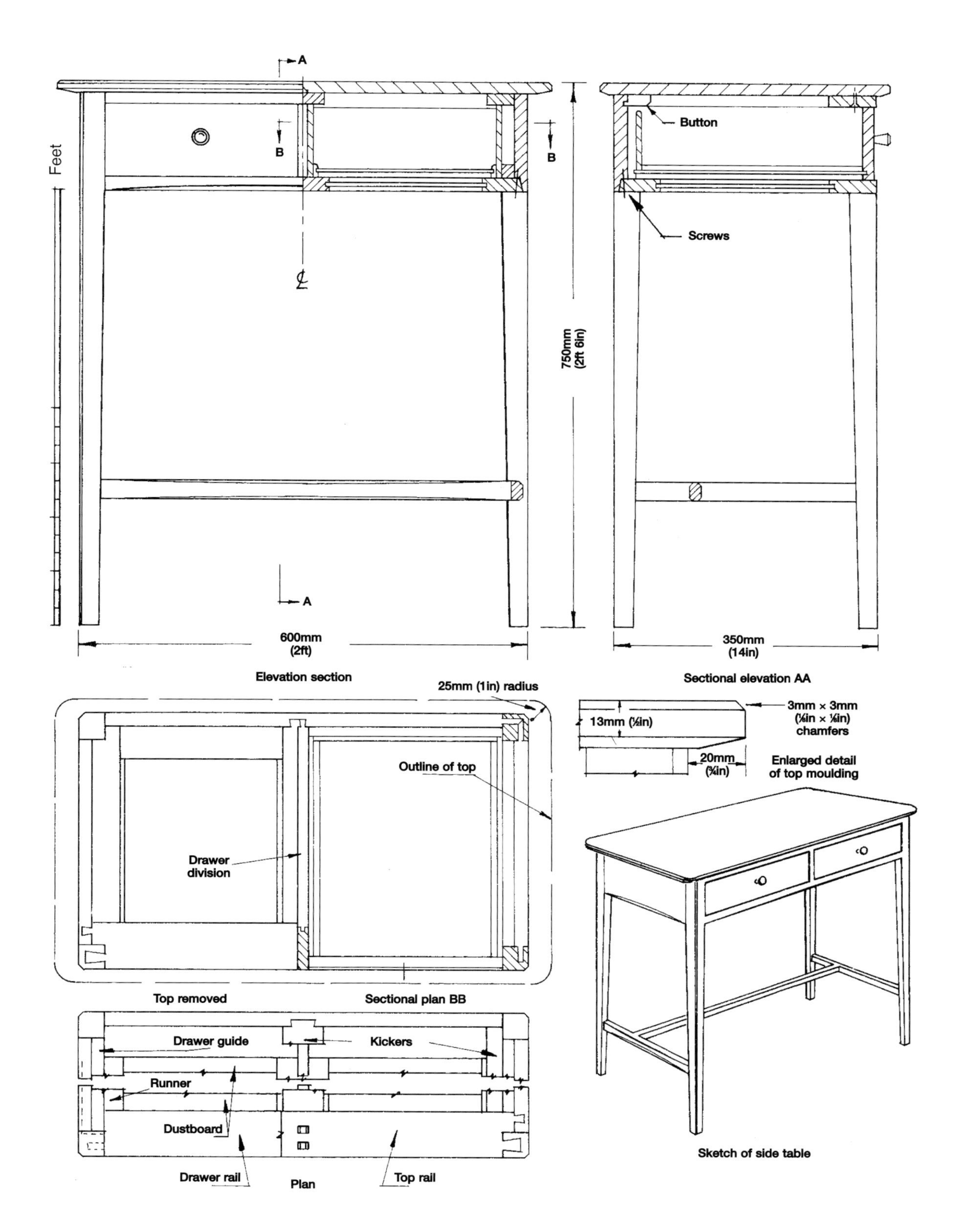
A
B
B
Button
Screws
Feet
750mm
(2ft 6in)
A
600mm
(2ft)
350mm
(14in)
Elevation section
Sectional elevation AA
25mm (1in) radius
13mm (½in)
3mm × 3mm
(⅛in × ⅛in)
chamfers
20mm
(¾in)
Enlarged detail
of top moulding
Outline of top
Drawer
division
Top removed
Sectional plan BB
Drawer guide
Kickers
Runner
Dustboard
Drawer rail
Plan
Top rail
Sketch of side table

28 Complete the polishing. The drawer sides need only a light rub over with white polish. Cut this down with flour glasspaper. The drawer runners and guides can be lubricated with a small quantity of candle grease.

29 Make, polish and fix handles to drawer fronts.

Note: a screw driven into the handle position makes an excellent temporary pull during drawer fitting.

Suggested Material

Sapele, oak or black bean.

Cutting list

Description	Length	Width	Thickness
4 legs	775mm (2ft 7in)	35mm (1⅜in)	35mm (1⅜in)
2 end rails	350mm (1ft 2in)	135mm (5⅜in)	20mm (¾in)
1 back rail	600mm (2ft)	135mm (5⅜in)	20mm (¾in)
1 bottom drawer rail	600mm (2ft)	63mm (2½in)	20mmm (¾in)
1 top drawer rail	600mm (2ft)	63mm (2½in)	16mm (⅝in)
Drawer framing			
1 drawer runner	325mm (1ft 1in)	73mm (2⅞in)	20mm (¾in)
2 drawer runners	325mm (1ft 1in)	56mm (2¼in)	20mm (¾in)
1 back rail	600mm (2ft)	56mm (2¼in)	20mm (¾in)
2 dust boards plywood	225mm (9in)	250mm (10in)	4mm (3/16in)
2 kickers	325mm (1ft 1in)	38mm (1½in)	16mm (⅝in)
1 kicker	325mm (1ft 1in)	56mm (2¼in)	16mm (⅝in)
1 vertical division	150mm (6in)	56mm (2¼in)	16mm (⅝in)
1 drawer division	300mm (1ft)	103mm (4⅛in)	16mm (⅝in)
2 drawer guides	300mm (1ft)	23mm (⅞in)	16mm (⅝in)
2 stretcher rails	350mm (1ft 2in)	25mm (1in)	16mm (⅝in)
1 stretcher rail	600mm (2ft)	25mm (1in)	16mm (⅝in)
1 top	675mm (2ft 3in)	388mm (15½in)	16mm (⅝in)
Drawers			
2 drawer fronts	275mm (11in)	106mm (4¼in)	16mm (⅝in)
4 sides	325mm (1ft 1in)	106mm (4¼in)	8mm (5/16in)
2 backs	275mm (11in)	88mm (3½in)	8mm (5/16in)
4 plough slips	325mm (1ft 1in)	20mm (¾in)	10mm (⅜in)
2 bottoms plywood	250mm (10in)	313mm (12½in)	4mm (3/16in)
handles	100mm (4in)	23mm (⅞in)	23mm (⅞in)
1 drawer stop	125mm (5in)	20mm (¾in)	6mm (¼in)

Tools not in Basic Kit

Shoulder plane – for cleaning up rail shoulders.

Plough – for grooves in dustboards, drawer fronts and plough slips.

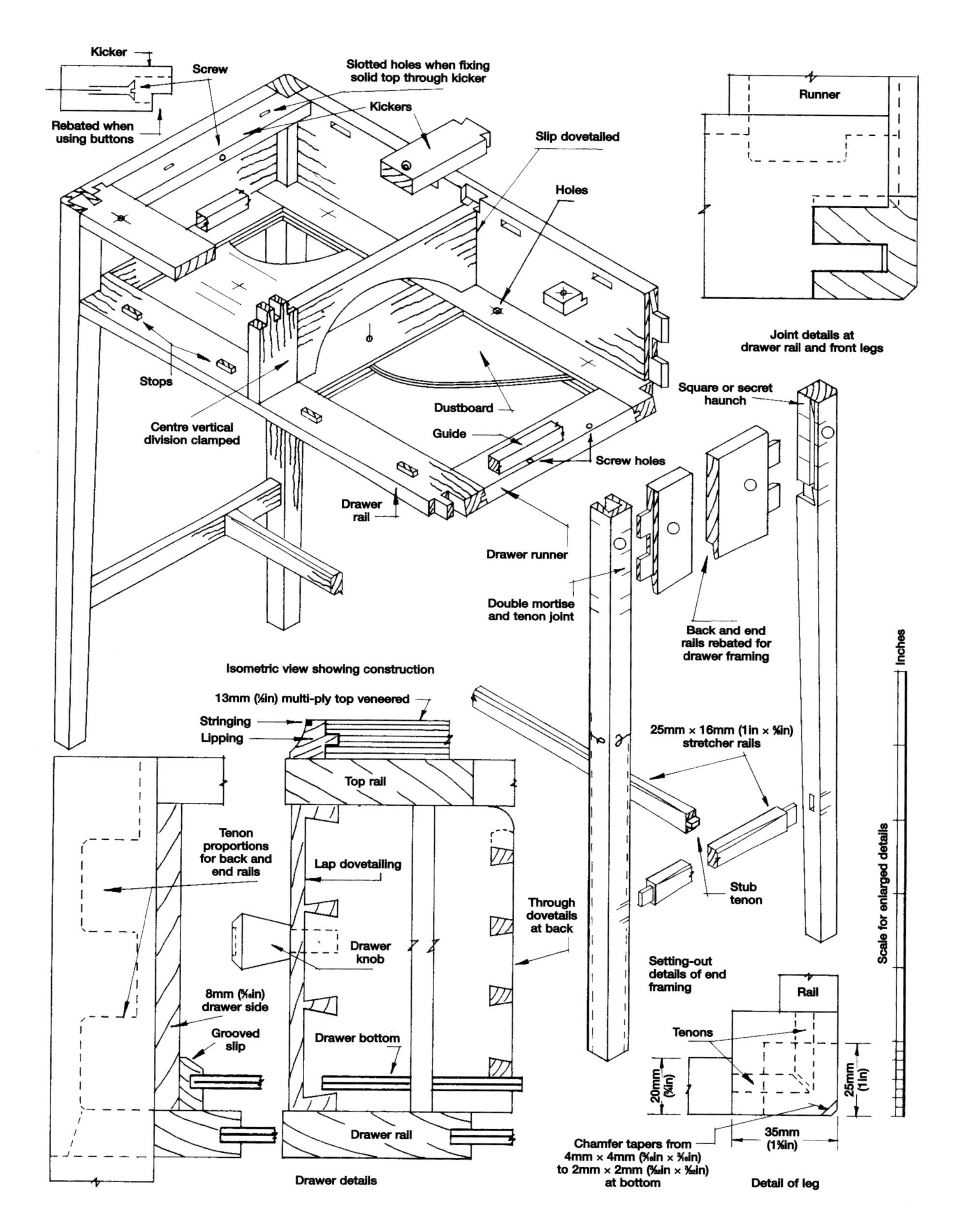
Kicker
Screw
Rebated when using buttons
Slotted holes when fixing solid top through kicker
Kickers
Slip dovetailed
Holes
Runner
Joint details at drawer rail and front legs
Square or secret haunch
Stops
Centre vertical division clamped
Dustboard
Guide
Screw holes
Drawer rail
Drawer runner
Double mortise and tenon joint
Back and end rails rebated for drawer framing
Isometric view showing construction
13mm (½in) multi-ply top veneered
Stringing
Lipping
Top rail
Tenon proportions for back and end rails
Lap dovetailing
Through dovetails at back
Drawer knob
8mm (⅜in) drawer side
Grooved slip
Drawer bottom
Drawer rail
Drawer details
25mm × 16mm (1in × ⅝in) stretcher rails
Stub tenon
Setting-out details of end framing
Inches
Scale for enlarged details
Rail
Tenons
20mm (¾in)
25mm (1in)
35mm (1⅜in)
Chamfer tapers from 4mm × 4mm (3/16in × 3/16in) to 2mm × 2mm (3/32in × 3/32in) at bottom
Detail of leg

Drawer Construction

The drawings give details of drawer setting-out and alternative treatments to plough slips, drawer bottoms and dovetail proportions. The chief features of a dovetailed drawer are the lapped dovetail joint at the front and the through dovetailing at the drawer back. In the front note how the bottom dovetail conceals the plough groove. In fine work the pins almost taper to a point. This makes a neat and decorative finish, and is particularly satisfying to all who appreciate hand-made furniture. The function of a drawer slip is to increase the strength of the drawer side. It practically doubles the running area, thus reducing wear on the drawer edge. The various types of drawer slips may be compared:

1. *The quadrant finish:* this can be used with ply or solid wood bottoms.
2. *The cavetto finish:* the drawer side is rebated to take the slip. This allows the moulding to run out without a feather edge. Easy to keep clean.
3. *The beaded finish:* this is arranged to give a flush surface on the inside, and makes a first class finish when using solid wood. The bead is decorative and breaks the joint between slip and bottom.

The isometric view (figure 1) and the adjacent section give details of a carcase suitable for fixing to a table frame. It could be made longer to incorporate two drawers.

Method

1. Prepare drawer material, leave the front and sides a 1.6mm (1/16in) full. Arrange and match the grain, and number pieces for easy identification.
2. Square one end of drawer front and fit to carcase, making a slight taper as shown in figure 1 – a shaving is quite sufficient.
3. Cut drawer front to length and plane end as before.
   Note: the drawer front should be a good fit, and the inside surface should only just enter the carcase.
4. Mark out and cut drawer sides to length and plane ends square.
5. Mark out and cut drawer back to length and plane ends square. For setting out drawer, see separate detail – gauging and setting-out dovetail joints.
6. The diagram shows clearly the gauging technique. Set the cutting gauge to A, and gauge lightly round the front ends of the drawer sides. With the same setting, gauge the inside of the drawer fronts.
7. Re-set the gauge to B, which is the thickness of the material, and gauge drawer front, sides and back. Re-set gauge to C, and gauge position of back on sides. It also gives the top edge of the plough groove.
8. Mark out and cut the dovetails. A pair or more of sides can be sawn together.
9. Mark out and cut the pins.
10. Plough the front groove and round the top edge of back (see figure 2). Clean up all inner surfaces, assemble drawer, adjusting as necessary. Mask all joints and polish.
11. Glue up, test for square (see figure 3) and leave to dry.
12. Make plough slips. Cut, fit and glue to drawer sides. Small thumb screws are useful for cramping plough slips to drawer sides.

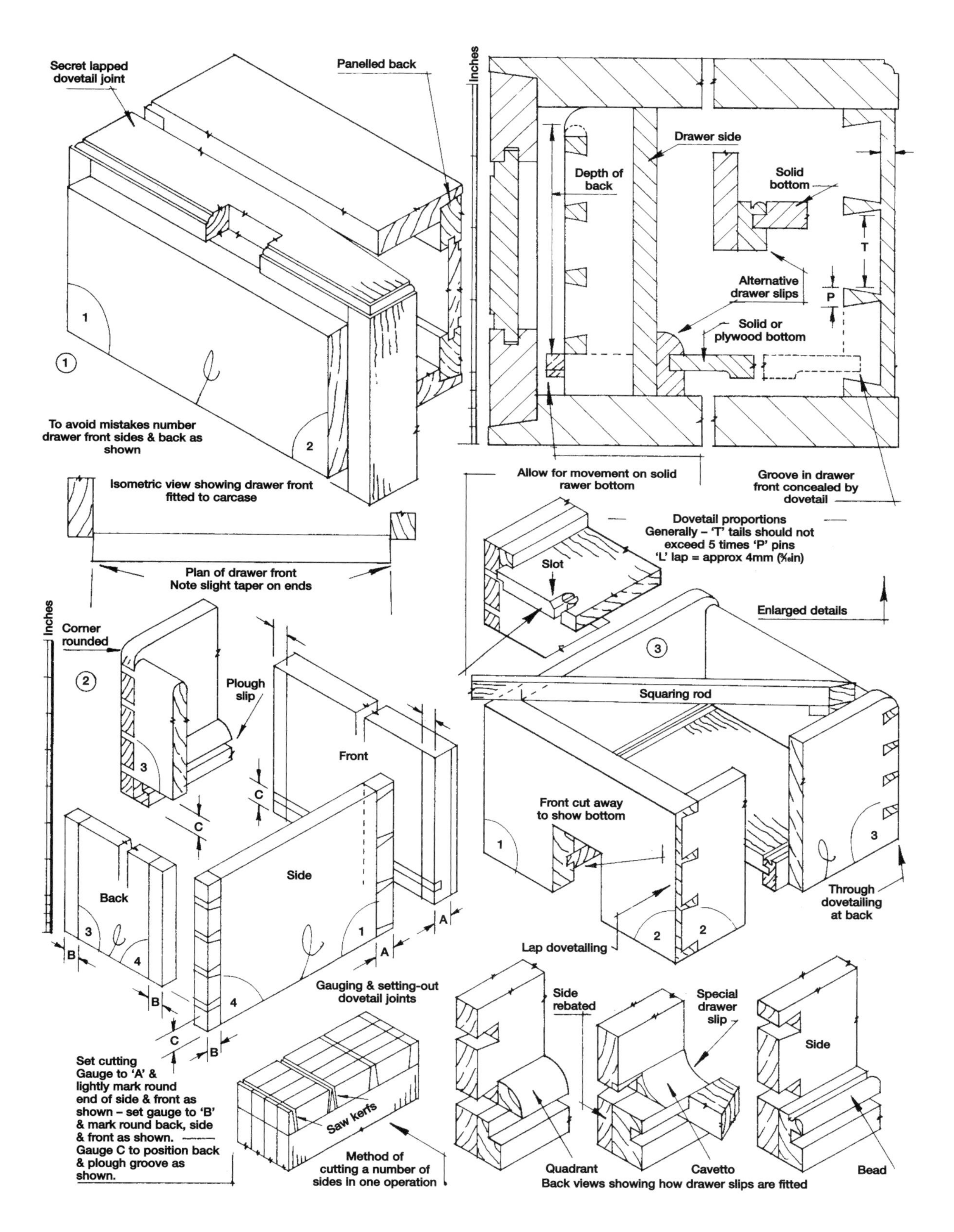

Secret lapped dovetail joint
Panelled back
1
To avoid mistakes number drawer front sides & back as shown
2
Isometric view showing drawer front fitted to carcase
Plan of drawer front
Note slight taper on ends
Inches
Drawer side
Depth of back
Solid bottom
T
Alternative drawer slips
P
Solid or plywood bottom
Allow for movement on solid rawer bottom
Groove in drawer front concealed by dovetail
Dovetail proportions
Generally – 'T' tails should not exceed 5 times 'P' pins
'L' lap = approx 4mm (³⁄₁₆in)
Slot
Enlarged details
3
Squaring rod
Front cut away to show bottom
Through dovetailing at back
Lap dovetailing
Inches
Corner rounded
Plough slip
Front
C
Back
Side
A
B
4
Gauging & setting-out dovetail joints
Set cutting Gauge to 'A' & lightly mark round end of side & front as shown – set gauge to 'B' & mark round back, side & front as shown. Gauge C to position back & plough groove as shown.
Saw kerfs
Method of cutting a number of sides in one operation
Side rebated
Special drawer slip
Side
Quadrant
Cavetto
Bead
Back views showing how drawer slips are fitted

13 Fit drawer bottom. Polish and screw to drawer back. For solid wood slot the bottom to receive the screws. With the bottom fixed the drawer is well braced and can be fitted without straining the joints.

14 *Fitting drawers:* small drawers can often be supported in the vice, the other side being supported by a bearer screwed or cramped to the bench. For larger drawers, two pieces of 50mm × 25mm (2in × 1in) planed material cramped or screwed to the bench gives good support during planing. (For further information see step 27 on page 140.)

Notes on dovetail proportions

A satisfactory slope for dovetails is 1:7 for dovetails in hardwoods, and 1:5½ for dovetails in softwoods. Other proportions can be seen in the drawing. The lap is shown as approximately 4mm (3/16in) which is suitable for dovetailing in 16mm–20mm (⅝in–¾in) material. This of course can vary according to circumstances. For a small drawer with a 13mm (½in) front a 3mm (⅛in) lap would be satisfactory. The lap should not exceed one-third of the thickness of the drawer front.

Dining Chair

This design is one of a series introducing basic features of chair-construction and design. The chair is well proportioned, light and well braced. It is economical to make as the laminated rails and the side frames use the minimum amount of timber. The side frames are connected together with front and back rails of different lengths to form the seat taper. The seat is supported by fillets and the front and back rails, which the seat runs over.

Note: To obtain accurate angles and shoulder lengths, prepare full-size working drawings showing plan, front and side elevations. Prepare template for back legs. Take as a datum line the vertical line passing through the shoulder. The 75mm (3in) and 70mm (2¾in) dimensions give outside points of the back legs. From the given details complete the marking out of the template. Cut and finish accurately to size. Plywood 4mm (3⁄16in) thick is suitable for template making.

Method

1. Prepare material, select and match the grain. Arrange material carefully to minimise short grain. Apply template and mark out the back legs. Cut to shape, leaving the shoulders full as shown by dotted lines and finishing the 8mm (5⁄16in) radius after gluing up.
2. Set out back and front legs in pairs.
3. Set out side rails, taking the shoulder lines from the plan – cut to shape and work the grooves for side fillets.
4. Gauge mortises and tenons.
5. Cut mortises and tenons, and assemble side frames, fitting as necessary.
6. Set out front and back rails, adjusting sliding bevel to correct angle, gauge for tenons and prepare for dowelling.
7. Make a template for the seat angle approximately the size of a brace, and use to obtain chisel alignment when mortising.
8. Make a template for the dowel centres, locate carefully, mark centres and bore holes. A simple jig to ensure the correct angle could be used when boring the holes.
9. Clean up inner edges, and work rounds on rails and legs. Polish as necessary.
10. Glue up side frames, check for alignment and leave to dry.
11. Flush joints on frames. Cut dowels to length and assemble chair, fitting as necessary and checking angles with template.
12. Shape front and back rails.
13. Remove horns on side frames and clean up end grain and round corners. With a scribing gouge carefully pare out the 8mm (5⁄16in) radius and clean up with file and glasspaper.
14. Clean up all inner surfaces. Mask joints as required and polish.
15. Glue up, test for square and alignment and leave to dry.
16. Mark out, cut to shape and fit the braces. Glue and screw into position.
17. Glue in seat fillets.
18. Prepare jig for laminating back rail (see page 92).
19. Glue up laminations to form back rails and leave to dry.
20. Shape back rails, and round the edges.

21 Fit rails to back legs – note how legs are bevelled to fit curve of back – and screw into position.
22 Clean up and polish. Re-fix, and insert dowels to conceal screw heads as shown.
23 Make loose seat frame. This can be dowelled or mortised and tenoned together.
24 Nail on rubber webbing and complete upholstery. (For further information see page 151.) To prevent the seat sliding it can be fastened with small buttons, or secured through the braces.

Suggested Material

Afrormosia, teak or guarea

Cutting list

Description	Length	Width	Thickness
2 back legs	838mm (2ft 9½in)	75mm (3in)	23mm (⅞in)
2 front legs	463mm (1ft 6½in)	50mm (2in)	23mm (⅞in)
2 side rails	400mm (1ft 4in)	66mm (2⅝in)	23mm (⅞in)
1 top front rail	425mm (1ft 5in)	28mm (1⅛in)	23mm (⅞in)
1 top back rail	350mm (1ft 2in)	28mm (1⅛in)	23mm (⅞in)
1 bottom front rail	425mm (1ft 5in)	35mm (1⅜in)	23mm (⅞in)
1 bottom back rail	350mm (1ft 2in)	35mm (1⅜in)	23mm (⅞in)
6 laminations for chair back rails	450mm (1ft 6in)	45mm (1¾in)	4mm (3/16in)
1 to cut 4 braces	300mm (1ft)	56mm (2¼in)	16mm (⅝in)
2 seat fillets	250mm (10in)	16mm (⅝in)	16mm (⅝in)
Beech dowelling	425mm (1ft 5in)	6mm (¼in) diameter	

Loose seat frame

1 front rail	425mm (1ft 5in)	50mm (2in)	20mm (¾in)
1 back rail	350mm (1ft 2in)	50mm (2in)	20mm (¾in)
2 side rails	400mm (1ft 4in)	50mm (2in)	20mm (¾in)

rubber webbing approximately 2100mm × 38mm (7ft × 1½in)

Tools not in Basic Kit

Shoulder plane – for cleaning up rail shoulders.
Block plane – for cleaning up end grain of seat rails.
Plough – for making groove for seat fillet.

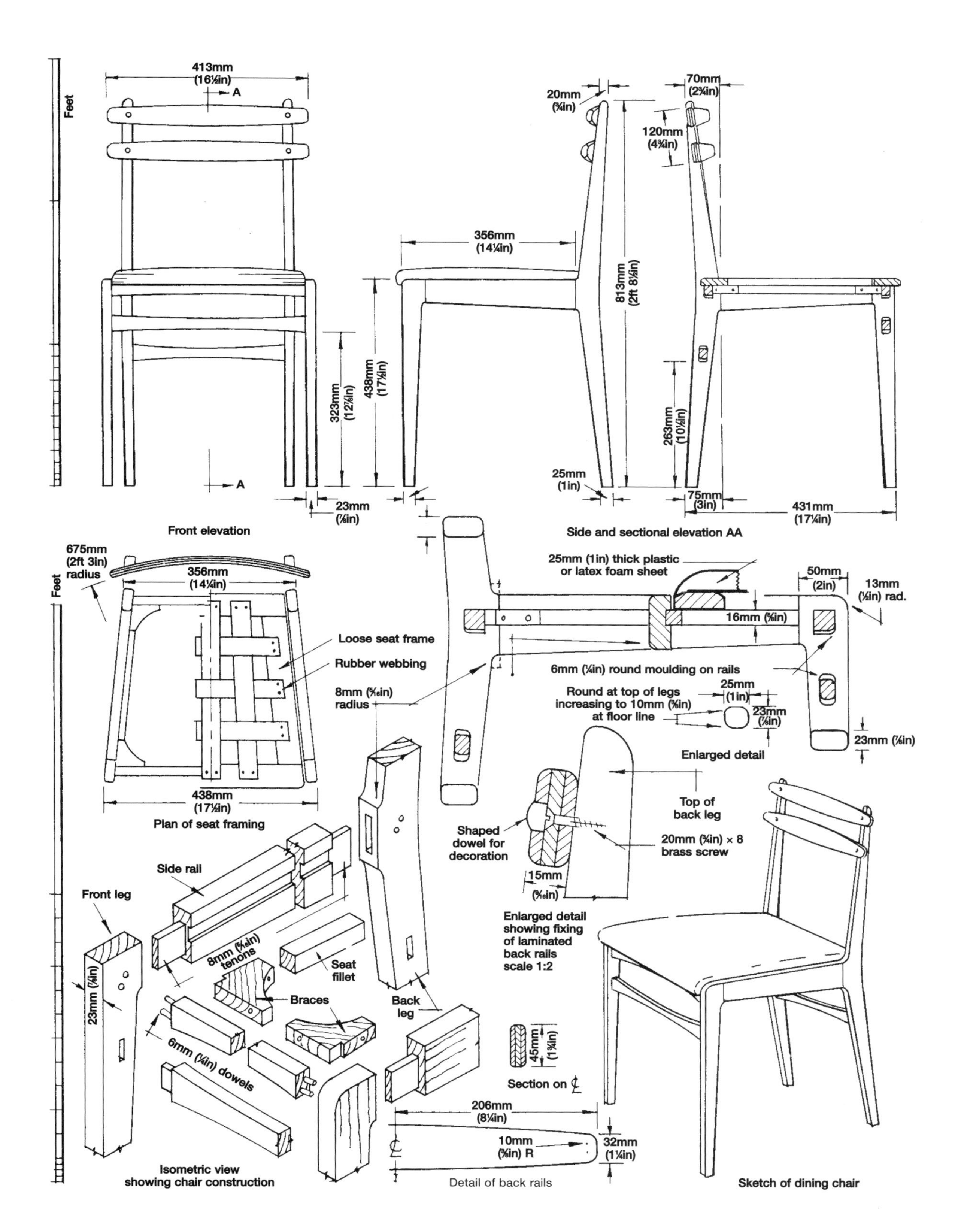

413mm
(16¼in)
A
Feet
20mm
(¾in)
70mm
(2¾in)
120mm
(4¾in)
356mm
(14¼in)
813mm
(2ft 8½in)
438mm
(17½in)
323mm
(12¾in)
263mm
(10½in)
25mm
(1in)
A
23mm
(⅞in)
75mm
(3in)
431mm
(17¼in)
Front elevation
Side and sectional elevation AA
675mm
(2ft 3in)
radius
356mm
(14¼in)
25mm (1in) thick plastic
or latex foam sheet
50mm
(2in)
13mm
(½in) rad.
16mm (⅝in)
Loose seat frame
Rubber webbing
6mm (¼in) round moulding on rails
8mm (5⁄16in)
radius
Round at top of legs
increasing to 10mm (⅜in)
at floor line
25mm
(1in)
23mm
(⅞in)
23mm (⅞in)
Enlarged detail
438mm
(17½in)
Plan of seat framing
Top of
back leg
Shaped
dowel for
decoration
20mm (¾in) × 8
brass screw
Side rail
15mm
(9⁄16in)
Front leg
Enlarged detail
showing fixing
of laminated
back rails
scale 1:2
8mm (5⁄16in)
tenons
Seat
fillet
23mm (⅞in)
Braces
Back
leg
45mm
(1¾in)
6mm (¼in) dowels
Section on ℄
206mm
(8¼in)
10mm
(⅜in) R
32mm
(1¼in)
Isometric view
showing chair construction
Detail of back rails
Sketch of dining chair

Dining Chair

Chair design and making

Every opportunity should be taken to study the historical background and development of chairs, and the way in which changing fashions, social conditions and the introduction of new materials affected design. The enormous variety of new materials, processes and techniques available today offer tremendous scope to versatile designer-craftspeople.

Using the main dimensions given in the drawing opposite, make sketches of alternative designs. Scale models in balsa wood (75mm to 300mm/3in to 1ft), scale drawings, full-size drawings, templates, and mock ups (usually in soft wood) to give a full-size three-dimensional aspect of an arm or leg, all contribute to the production of a successful design.

Compare this chair, which has the back shaped in solid wood, with the previous chair using side frame technique. It should be noted that the back and front seat rails have square shoulders, and that the back and front of the chair are assembled as separate frames. The front and side seat rails are rebated to take the loose seat.

Construction

The front legs are mortised to receive the rails – note the angle and arrangement of tenons. The double mortise and tenon joints at the back legs add considerable strength to the chair back. A good alternative is the chairmaker's technique of tenoning in the long rails and dowelling in the short rails. (This method is shown on page 153.) The chair back is mainly mortised and tenoned together, with the exception of the top rail which is dowelled. Worth considering is the method where the mortises for side rails are cut square with the legs – see separate detail drawing. To gauge the tenons square with the shoulder, carefully pare off side rail (see dotted line) and make square to shoulder line. Gauge off this surface.

Prepare full-size working drawings – a plan and two elevations with a separate detail showing the setting out of the back legs; page 151 should be carefully studied. The dotted line shows the extent of fairing in to the back rails. This is done after the back framing is assembled. The main datum line passes along the shoulder line. A thin batten or a 600mm (2ft) steel rule could be used for fairing in the shape of the back legs. On completion of the working drawings, prepare the necessary templates out of to 4mm (3/16in) plywood as follows:

1. A template for marking out of back legs. The rail position, and the shoulder line for the top rail can be shown on the template.
2. An edge template for the top rail. Made to a sweep of 675mm (2ft 3in) radius and 23mm (7/8in) wide to mark out the rail thickness. It is used for marking out the lower rail and the horizontal rails forming the splats.
3. A face template for the top rail. Can be made in cardboard or stiff paper, and is used for marking out the elevation of the top rail.

Method

1. Prepare material, select and match the grain. Mark out and cut the back legs. Finish to template. The waste from the back leg can be used to support the leg when mortising.

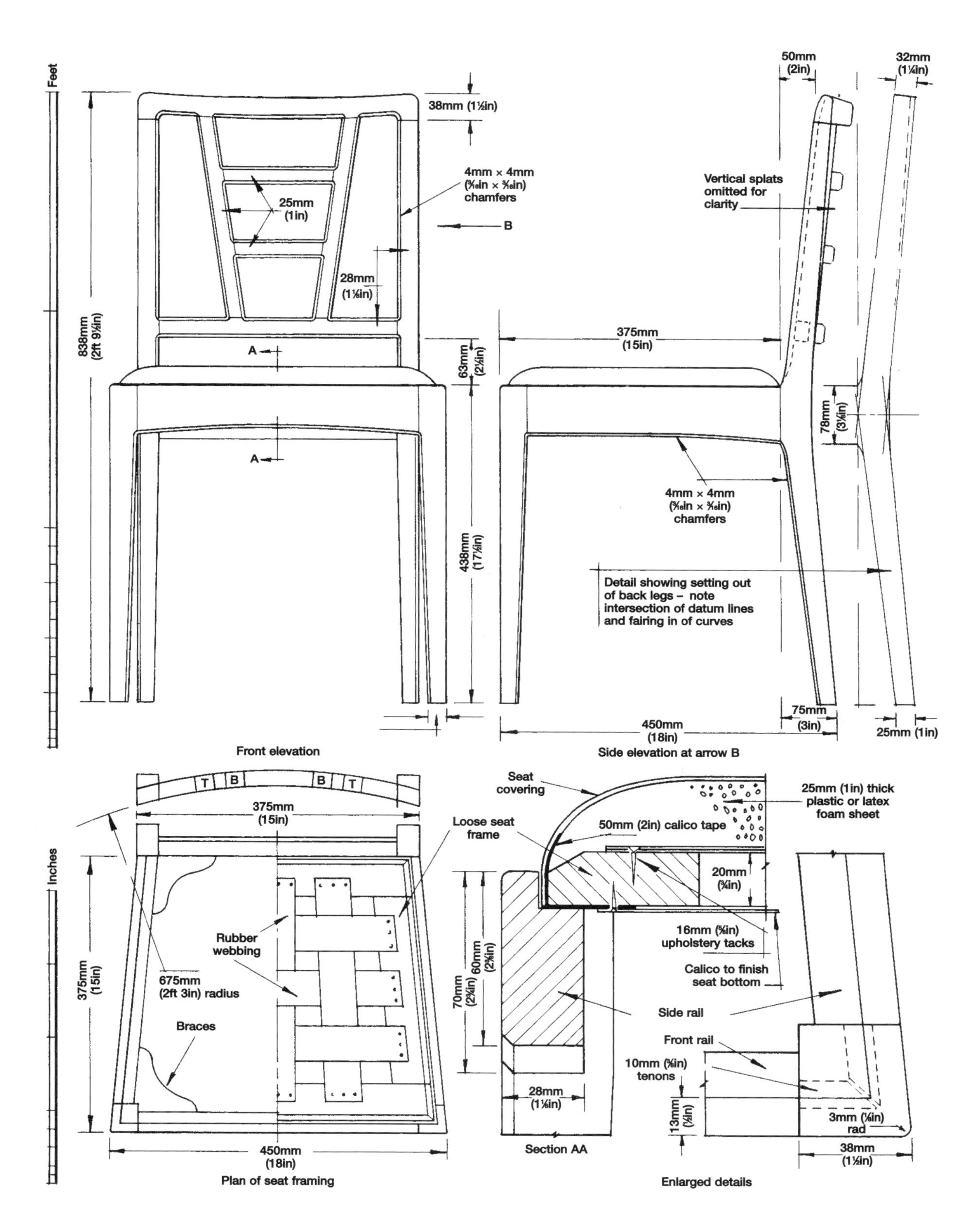

Feet
Inches
38mm (1½in)
4mm × 4mm
(3⁄16in × 3⁄16in)
chamfers
25mm
(1in)
B
28mm
(1⅛in)
838mm
(2ft 9½in)
A
63mm
(2½in)
438mm
(17½in)
Front elevation
50mm
(2in)
32mm
(1¼in)
Vertical splats
omitted for
clarity
375mm
(15in)
78mm
(3⅛in)
4mm × 4mm
(3⁄16in × 3⁄16in)
chamfers
Detail showing setting out
of back legs – note
intersection of datum lines
and fairing in of curves
450mm
(18in)
75mm
(3in)
25mm (1in)
Side elevation at arrow B
T
B
375mm
(15in)
Rubber
webbing
675mm
(2ft 3in) radius
Braces
450mm
(18in)
Plan of seat framing
Seat
covering
Loose seat
frame
50mm (2in) calico tape
25mm (1in) thick
plastic or latex
foam sheet
20mm
(¾in)
16mm (⅝in)
upholstery tacks
Calico to finish
seat bottom
70mm
(2¾in)
60mm
(2⅜in)
Side rail
Front rail
10mm (⅜in)
tenons
28mm
(1⅛in)
13mm
(½in)
3mm (⅛in)
rad
38mm
(1½in)
Section AA
Enlarged details

2 Set out back and front legs in pairs making allowance for the rebate.
3 Set out front and back seat rails – shoulders are square – and shape the front rail.
4 Set out the side rails, taking correct length and bevel for shoulders from the plan, and cut to shape.
5 Gauge mortises and tenons.
Note: the front legs can be bevelled or they can be left square for mortising, in which case the mortise gauge must be re-adjusted to allow for the bevel.
6 Cut mortises and tenons. (See figure 1 on page 153 for application of template when making mortises and fitting rails.) Make rebates on front and side seat rails.
7 Assemble seat framing, fitting as necessary.
8 Taper the front legs and work the chamfers and rebates on them. Clean up inner surfaces and polish.
9 Glue up front frame, and leave to dry.

Setting out and fitting of the back frame

The exploded views on page 153 give full particulars of joints and setting out. The back frame with the exception of the seat rail is shaped, and it should be noticed that the tenons on the bottom rail are square off the shoulder line and not parallel to the curve. The mortises and tenons for the horizontal splats can run parallel to the curve. To allow the assembled splats to drop into the mortises in the bottom rail and for the top rail to locate and complete the chair back the tenons must be shaped as shown in the separate drawing giving the setting out of back framing.

10 Using the template mark out and clean up the top, bottom, and two small rails.
Note: clean up the top rail to the edge template before marking out with the face template.
11 Complete the shaping of the top rail – except for the length and the inside radius which should be left full at this stage. Plan of the shaped back can be seen on page 151, and the mortise positions for the splats are located as T for top, and B for bottom mortises respectively.
12 Set out top and bottom rails, and gauge mortises and tenons.
13 Clean up shoulders at top of back legs, and bore for dowel holes. Bore holes for dowels in the top rails and fit dowels.
14 Cut mortises and tenons, and fit bottom and top rails to back legs and assemble, complete with bottom seat rail.
Note: bottom rail is set back to accommodate the curve.
15 Lightly cramp up. Square frame and locate vertical splats in the correct position and mark shoulder lines.
16 Cut tenons on splats. Clean up the shoulders carefully and assemble to back frame.
17 Complete the marking out, cut the mortises and tenons for horizontal splats.
18 Clean up all inner surfaces. Work as much as possible of the chamfering, mask all joints and polish.

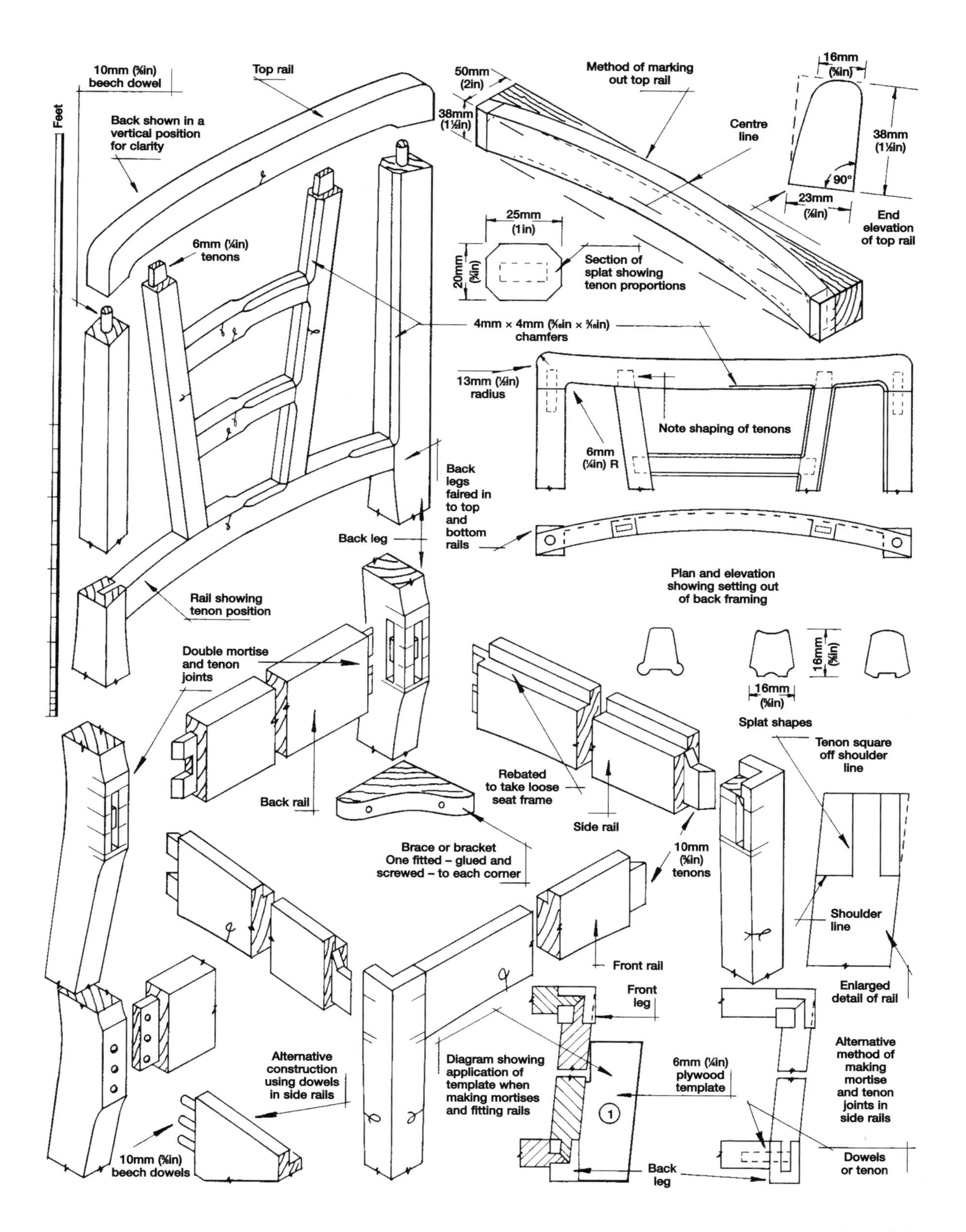
10mm (⅜in) beech dowel
Top rail
Feet
Back shown in a vertical position for clarity
6mm (¼in) tenons
50mm (2in)
38mm (1½in)
Method of marking out top rail
Centre line
16mm (⅝in)
38mm (1½in)
90°
23mm (⅞in)
End elevation of top rail
25mm (1in)
20mm (¾in)
Section of splat showing tenon proportions
4mm × 4mm (³⁄₁₆in × ³⁄₁₆in) chamfers
13mm (½in) radius
Note shaping of tenons
6mm (¼in) R
Back legs faired in to top and bottom rails
Back leg
Plan and elevation showing setting out of back framing
Rail showing tenon position
16mm (⅝in)
16mm (⅝in)
Splat shapes
Double mortise and tenon joints
Back rail
Rebated to take loose seat frame
Side rail
Tenon square off shoulder line
Brace or bracket One fitted – glued and screwed – to each corner
10mm (⅜in) tenons
Shoulder line
Front rail
Front leg
Enlarged detail of rail
Alternative construction using dowels in side rails
Diagram showing application of template when making mortises and fitting rails
6mm (¼in) plywood template
1
Alternative method of making mortise and tenon joints in side rails
10mm (⅜in) beech dowels
Back leg
Dowels or tenon

19 Glue up the back frame, test for square and alignment, and leave to dry.
20 Flush all joints on back frame. Complete chamfering on frame, using a file to form a mason's mitre. Finish carefully with glasspaper, including fairing in of the legs, and complete the polishing.
21 Prepare side rails for gluing up. Make and shape braces.
22 Glue up chair, test for square and alignment and leave to dry.
23 Fit and screw in braces. Flush joints and complete all chamfering.
24 Complete shaping of the top rail, fairing in as necessary. Complete polishing.
25 Make loose seat frame. The frame can be dowelled or mortised and tenoned. Details of upholstery are given on page 151. If a firm seat is preferred, glue a 4mm (3/16in) plywood bottom to the seat frame, filling in the seat frame with 25mm (1in) foam rubber sheet.

Suggested Material

Oak or walnut.

Cutting list

Description	Length	Width	Thickness
2 back legs	825mm (2ft 9in)	82mm (3¼in)	32mm (1¼in)
2 front legs	475mm (1ft 7in)	38mm (1½in)	38mm (1½in)
2 side rails	400mm (1ft 4in)	78mm (3⅛in)	28mm (1⅛in)
1 front rail	450mm (1ft 6in)	70mm (2¾in)	28mm (1⅛in)
1 back rail	450mm (1ft 6in)	78mm (3⅛in)	28mm (1⅛in)
dowel, beech	100mm (4in)	10mm (⅜in) diameter	
1 top rail	400mm (1ft 4in)	50mm (2in)	38mm (1½in)
1 bottom rail	375mm (1ft 3in)	45mm (1¾in)	28mm (1⅛in)
2 splats	325mm (1ft 1in)	25mm (1in)	20mm (¾in)
1 splat	200mm (8in)	32mm (1¼in)	25mm (1in)
1 splat	175mm (7in)	32mm (1¼in)	25mm (1in)
1 for 4 braces	350mm (1ft 2in)	75mm (3in)	23mm (⅞in)
Loose seat frame			
1 front rail beech	450mm (1ft 6in)	50mm (2in)	20mm (¾in)
1 back rail beech	375mm (1ft 3in)	50mm (2in)	20mm (¾in)
2 side rails beech	350mm (1ft 2in)	50mm (2in)	20mm (¾in)

Tools not in Basic Kit

Mortise chisel – for mortises in legs.
Compass plane – for shaping rails.
Shoulder plane – for cleaning up rail shoulders.
Block plane – for cleaning up end grain of back legs to make shoulder for dowels.
Bow saw – for shaped work on back legs and rails.

Easy Chair

This chair introduces the basic features of lounge chair construction. The main constructional features are the two side frames, with applied shaped arm rests. The two side frames are connected together with rails, and the seat and back framing. The legs and rails are shaped and rounded on the edges. The ease with which rubber webbing is fixed and the use of foam rubber has a revolutionary effect on the methods of upholstery.

Method

Prepare full-size working drawings. Make plywood templates for the back and front legs, arm rests, and back top rail.

1. Prepare material, arrange and match the grain.
2. Using the templates, mark out the legs.
3. Set out the side frames in pairs.
4. Cut mortises and tenons.
5. Shape the legs, leaving the shoulders long where they are radiused to meet the rails.
6. Fit joints and assemble frames. Locate on full-size drawing, adjusting as necessary.
7. Set out front seat rail, cut tenons and shape. Cut mortises in front legs to receive rail and fit.
8. Set out seat framing. Cut mortises and tenons and assemble frame.
9. Shape stiles and top rail, and set out back framing. Cut mortises and tenons and assemble frame, adjusting as necessary (see enlarged details in figure 1).
10. Make plough groove and cut tenons on bottom rail of back frame.
    Note: as a decorative feature the tenons could be taken through the bottom rail and wedged.
11. Mark out the arm rest, using the template, and bow saw to shape. Clean up with flat and round bottom spokeshaves.
12. Carefully gauge for thickness of arm rests on top rail of side frames – note bird's-mouth at end – remove waste and test with straight edge.
13. Clean up all inner surfaces and round edges. Mask joints as necessary and polish.
14. Glue up side frames, check shape with full-size working drawings. Test for alignment and leave to dry.
15. Clean up all inner surfaces on the back and seat frames, mask joints and polish. Glue up seat frame, test for square and alignment, leave to dry.
16. Glue up back frame, test for square and alignment, leave to dry.
17. Complete side frames. Clean up 6mm (¼in) radius with a scribing gouge, finishing carefully with a file and glasspaper.
18. Cut back frame support to length and fit dowels, use a template to ensure accurate fitting of dowels. Make round on top edge of rail and clean up.
19. Dish the front rail of the seat framing. Remove horns and clean up all round. Make tongue on top edge of back rail.
20. Shoot back framing to size, checking with seat frame, and assemble chair. Drill screw holes in seat frame, and fit tongue to groove in back frame.
21. Screw seat frame temporarily in position. Test chair for square and alignment.
22. Fitting rubber webbing. Mark out and cut the 4mm (3⁄16in) mortises in the seat frame to take the webbing (figure 2 in the enlarged detail drawing).

23 Fit arm rests, dropping neatly into the birds-mouthed ends. Mark out for 6mm (¼in) dowels, carefully locating positions and bore for dowels.
24 Cut dowels to length, and try arm rests in position dry. Clean up and glue in arm rests, cramping up as necessary.
25 Prepare for gluing up of the complete chair. Glue seat and back framing into position and cramp up. Screw seat frame to bottom rail. Although the frames ensure squareness carefully check for alignment and leave to dry. To secure the back frame, screw through the back rail into the stiles of the back frame. The screws should be sunk in and pelleted.
26 Clean up as necessary, and complete polishing.
27 Cut dowels to length and fit webbing, tensioning the webbing as recommended by the manufacturers (see figure 2). Figure 3 shows the webbing anchored with a steel clip which is mortised into the seat framing.
28 Make loose covers to fit the foam rubber cushions. The loose covers should be made 6mm (¼in) smaller in the length and width.

Suggested Material

Mahogany, afrormosia or teak with rosewood arms.

Cutting list

Description	Length	Width	Thickness
4 legs	550mm (1ft 10in)	45mm (1¾in)	23mm (⅞in)
2 top rails	650mm (2ft 2in)	45mm (1¾in)	23mm (⅞in)
2 bottom rails	700mm (2ft 4in)	56mm (2¼in)	23mm (⅞in)
1 front seat rail	550mm (1ft 10in)	56mm (2¼in)	23mm (⅞in)
1 back rail	525mm (1ft 9in)	45mm (1¾in)	23mm (⅞in)
2 arms	525mm (1ft 9in)	63mm (2½in)	16mm (⅝in)
Seat frame			
1 front rail	550mm (1ft 10in)	45mm (1¾in)	23mm (⅞in)
1 back rail	500mm (1ft 8in)	56mm (2¼in)	23mm (⅞in)
2 side rails	600mm (2ft)	45mm (1¾in)	23mm (⅞in)
Back frame			
2 stiles	650mm (2ft 2in)	45mm (1¾in)	23mm (⅞in)
1 top rail	500mm (1ft 8in)	56mm (2¼in)	23mm (⅞in)
1 bottom rail	550mm (1ft 10in)	50mm (2in)	23mm (⅞in)
4 splats	625mm (2ft 1in)	32mm (1¼in)	16mm (⅝in)
1 foam rubber cushion	600mm (2ft)	500mm (20in)	100mm (4in)
1 foam rubber cushion	550mm (1ft 10in)	500mm (20in)	100mm (4in)
rubber webbing	3150mm (10ft 6in)	50mm (2in)	
1 dowel rod	600mm (2ft)	6mm (¼in)	

Tools not in Basic Kit

Shoulder plane – for cleaning up rail shoulders.
Plough – for making groove in back frame.
Block plane – for cleaning up end grain of supporting rail for back frame

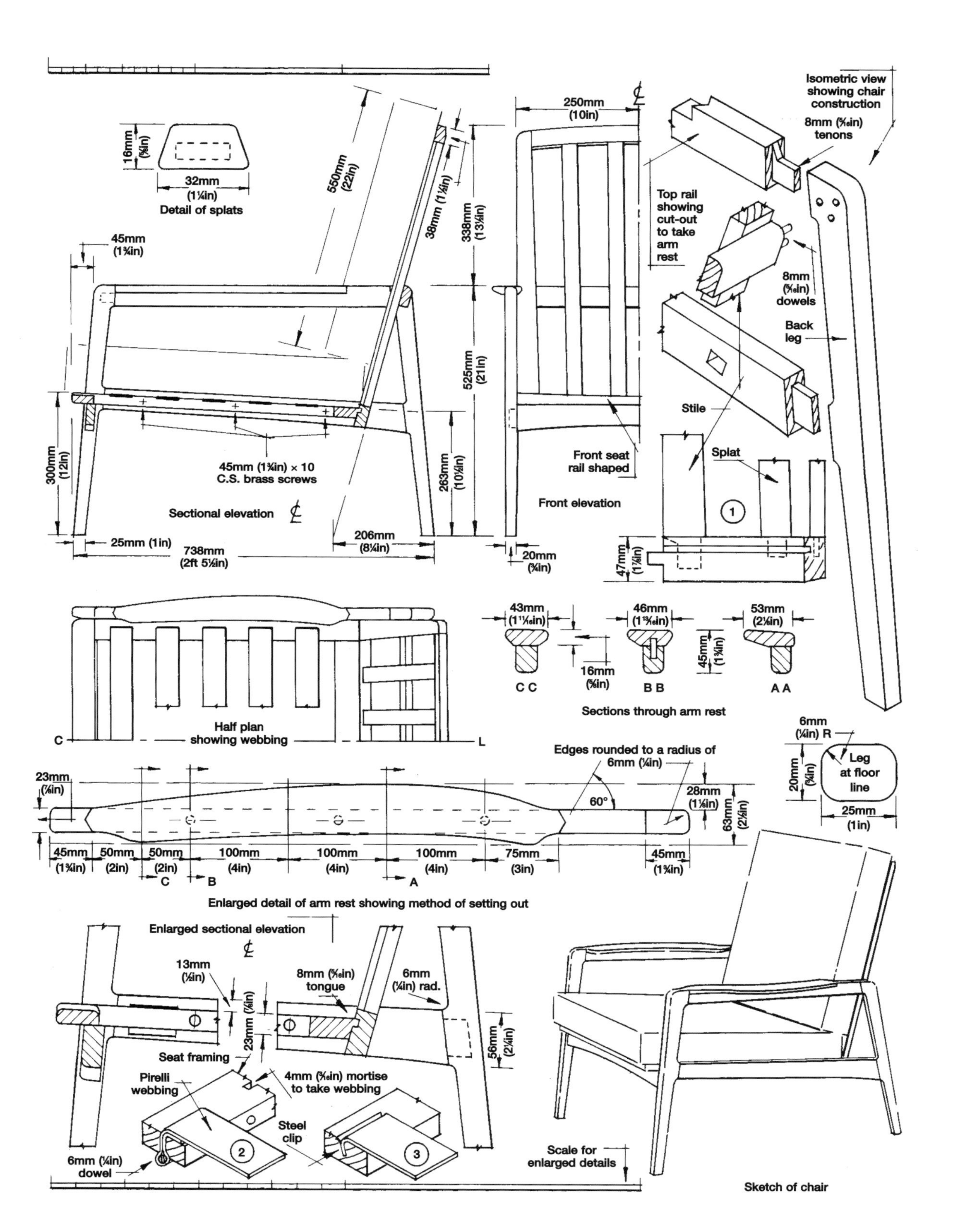

Isometric view showing chair construction
8mm (5/16in) tenons
250mm (10in)
16mm (⅝in)
32mm (1¼in)
Detail of splats
550mm (22in)
38mm (1½in)
338mm (13½in)
Top rail showing cut-out to take arm rest
8mm (5/16in) dowels
Back leg
45mm (1¾in)
525mm (21in)
Stile
Splat
Front seat rail shaped
300mm (12in)
45mm (1¾in) × 10 C.S. brass screws
263mm (10½in)
Sectional elevation
Front elevation
25mm (1in)
738mm (2ft 5½in)
206mm (8¼in)
20mm (¾in)
47mm (1⅞in)
1
43mm (1 11/16in)
16mm (⅝in)
C C
46mm (1 13/16in)
45mm (1¾in)
B B
53mm (2⅛in)
A A
Sections through arm rest
Half plan showing webbing
C
L
6mm (¼in) R
Leg at floor line
20mm (¾in)
25mm (1in)
Edges rounded to a radius of 6mm (¼in)
23mm (⅞in)
28mm (1⅛in)
60°
63mm (2½in)
45mm (1¾in)
50mm (2in)
50mm (2in)
100mm (4in)
100mm (4in)
100mm (4in)
75mm (3in)
45mm (1¾in)
C
B
A
Enlarged detail of arm rest showing method of setting out
Enlarged sectional elevation
13mm (½in)
8mm (5/16in) tongue
6mm (¼in) rad.
23mm (⅞in)
56mm (2¼in)
Seat framing
Pirelli webbing
4mm (3/16in) mortise to take webbing
Steel clip
2
3
6mm (¼in) dowel
Scale for enlarged details
Sketch of chair

Wood Turning

These designs give practice in a variety of lathe techniques, e.g. turning between centres, face plate work, long boring for table lamps, the making of napkin rings and egg cups. They encourage work of a decorative and experimental nature. No attempt has been made to describe actual turning techniques, tools, etc. There are books available dealing with the art of wood turning.

Small table with turned legs

A feature of this table is the thick top with a Formica surface. It looks well with mahogany legs and lipping. Beech, sycamore or birch dowels make a suitable contrast.

The frame is bridle-jointed – to simplify the job it could be halved at the corners – and four 20mm (¾in) diameter holes are bored in the frame to receive the legs. The legs are turned between centres, and a 20mm (¾in) pin is made at the top, for fixing into the frame.

Note: figure 1 shows the base of a leg chamfered. Care must be taken in boring the holes for the dowel rods, which must be at right angles to each other. A simple jig could be developed to ensure accuracy of boring. Alternative lippings are shown, as is also an alternative to mitring the corners. Before gluing on the multi-ply top, rebate the frame to form the groove.

Note: plastic-faced hardboard would make an excellent surface for the top. (See page 98 for details of fixing Formica.) Prepare the lipping and glue to frame and multi-ply. If loose tongues are used, they must be glued all round. Glue in dowel rails, and assemble frame. Glue pins and fix top, checking legs for alignment. Weight down with books and leave to dry.

Note: a saw kerf for wedging could be made down the pin, the frame being attached to the legs and wedged before gluing on the multi-ply.

Table Lamps

The making of table lamps, with or without bases, provides a great variety in design. Simple shapes often produce delightful grain effects. The design showing the 20mm (¾in) pieces planted on makes an attractive finish, particularly when oak is used for the main column and walnut for the planted pieces. The second small table lamp looks very attractive when made in laburnum. The taller of the table lamps shown opposite has four rosewood inlaid lines. This interesting feature presents no difficulty if a jig is prepared. The jig consists of a box to hold the column, with a small bolt passing through. Alternatively it could be wedged and cramped in the box. A scratch stock with a cutter suitable for the inlay is made to drop over the box. The stock is worked up and down the length of the box to work the groove to take the string. Some pleasing arrangements can be achieved by this method. Baize glued to the base is advantageous – it prevents the base from scratching polished surfaces. It should be set in slightly from the outside.

Bowl Turning

This technique introduces face plate work and offers scope for variety and individual work. Figure 2 shows a bowl with a contrasting wood on the base. Napkin rings and egg cups can be turned successfully when held in an egg cup chuck. Jigs play an important part in turning. Very often a jig has to be designed to hold a particular job.

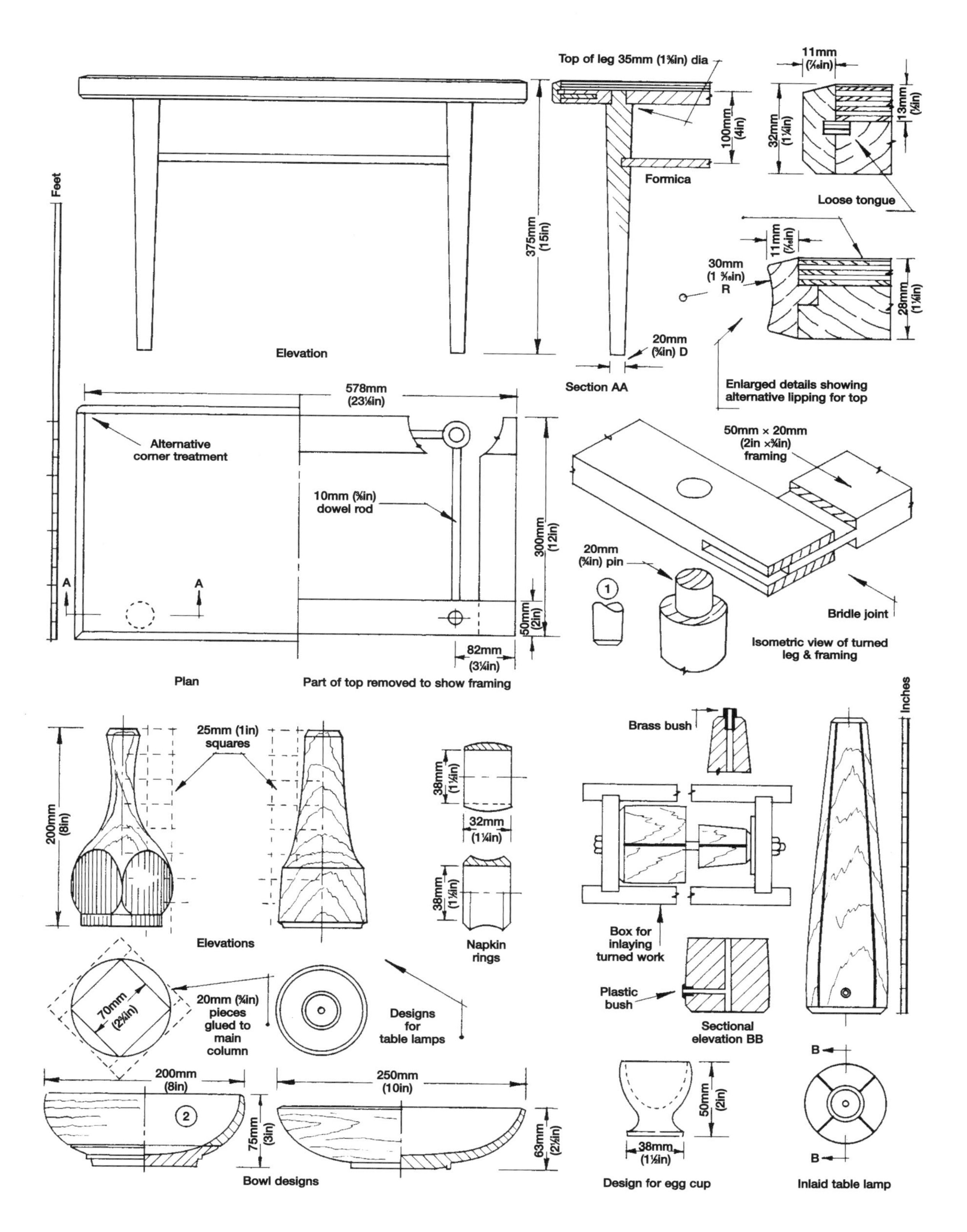
Top of leg 35mm (1⅜in) dia
11mm (7/16in)
32mm (1¼in)
13mm (½in)
100mm (4in)
Formica
Loose tongue
Feet
375mm (15in)
Elevation
11mm (7/16in)
30mm (1 3/16in) R
28mm (1⅛in)
20mm (¾in) D
Section AA
Enlarged details showing alternative lipping for top
578mm (23⅛in)
Alternative corner treatment
10mm (⅜in) dowel rod
300mm (12in)
50mm (2in)
82mm (3¼in)
A
A
50mm × 20mm (2in ×¾in) framing
20mm (¾in) pin
1
Bridle joint
Isometric view of turned leg & framing
Plan
Part of top removed to show framing
25mm (1in) squares
200mm (8in)
38mm (1½in)
32mm (1¼in)
38mm (1½in)
Elevations
Napkin rings
Brass bush
Box for inlaying turned work
Plastic bush
Sectional elevation BB
Inches
70mm (2¾in)
20mm (¾in) pieces glued to main column
Designs for table lamps
200mm (8in)
250mm (10in)
2
75mm (3in)
63mm (2½in)
Bowl designs
50mm (2in)
38mm (1½in)
Design for egg cup
B
B
Inlaid table lamp

Polishing: it is advisable not to attempt french polishing whilst the work is revolving. A satisfactory method is to lightly apply white polish with a rag to the finished job. Allow polish to dry, start the lathe and hold a piece of clean linen firmly on the work for approximately half a minute. Stop the lathe and lightly cut down with flour glasspaper or wire wool. Wire wool should not be used on oak as the fine particles remaining on the job may cause staining if the wood is not absolutely dry. Re-start the lathe and use the linen again: this produces a good finish and in effect fills the grain. Wax polish could be applied and burnished on the lathe.

Cutting list

Description	Length	Width	Thickness
Table			
4 legs	375mm (1ft 3in)	35mm (1⅜in)	35mm (1⅜in)
2 rails	600mm (2ft)	50mm (2in)	20m (¾in)
2 rails	313mm (1ft ½in)	50mm (2in)	20m (¾in)
2 lippings	625mm (2ft 1in)	32mm (1¼in)	11mm (7/16in)
2 lippings	350mm (1ft 2in)	32mm (1¼in)	11mm (7/16in)
2 dowel rods	425mm (1ft 5in)	10mm (⅜in) diameter	
2 dowel rods	275mm (11in)	10mm (⅜in) diameter	
1 top multi-ply	600mm (2ft)	300mm (12in)	13mm (½in)
1 piece of Formica	600mm (2ft)	300mm (12in)	1.6mm (1/16in)
oddments of plywood for loose tongues			
Table lamps			
1 column oak	275mm (11in)	70mm (2¾in)	70mm (2¾in)
4 laminations walnut	113mm (4½in)	100mm (4in)	20mm (¾in)
1 column laburnum	275mm (11in)	95mm (3¾in)	95mm (3¾in)
1 column beech or sycamore	375mm (1ft 3in)	82mm (3¼in)	82mm (3¼in)
4 lines rosewood	325mm (1ft 1in)	3mm (⅛in)	3mm (⅛in)
Bowls			
1 disc mahogany	200mm (8in) diameter		53mm (2⅛in)
1 disc sycamore	200mm (8in) diameter		23mm (⅞in)
1 disc walnut	250mm (10in) diameter		63mm (2½in)
Egg cups			
1 for 4 egg cups walnut	250mm (10in)	50mm (2in)	50mm (2in)
Napkin rings			
1 for 6 rings walnut	250mm (10in)	50mm (2in)	50mm (2in)

Veneering

There are two main methods of laying veneer by hand: with the veneering hammer, using single or double knife-cut veneer; and caul veneering, which is suitable for sawn veneers, built up patterns, and veneers which are difficult to lay, or which have a tendency to cockle. A small hand-veneer press, such as the kind used in bookbinding, is useful.

Method

For hammer veneering and the method of making a veneer joint:

1. Prepare the groundwork. Make sure it is perfectly flat. With a toothing plane, key the groundwork, planing diagonally and in opposite directions to make a good keyed surface. Usually softwoods absorb more glue than hardwoods, and when laying veneers on yellow or selected pine, it is advisable to size (a weak solution of glue) the groundwork to prevent the greater part of the glue being absorbed by the softwood. Gaboon faced laminboard, which makes an excellent groundwork for veneer, comes into this category and should be toothed and sized. Good quality multi-ply also makes an excellent groundwork for veneering. To counteract the 'pull' of veneer, which tends to warp the ground as it dries, it is advisable to veneer both sides of the ground whenever possible.
2. Make sure everything required is ready and within reach. Fresh, hot and fairly thin glue is a necessity; tools and apparatus needed are, veneer hammer, swab, flat-iron ready heated, knife, straight edge, gummed paper strip, 'G' cramps, glasspaper and clean hot water.
3. Arrange and match the grain of the veneer to be jointed. Mark out centre line on ground and identify the veneer to prevent mistakes.
4. Glue the ground (figure 1). Lightly damp the face of the veneer with hot water to prevent the veneer from curling when the glue is applied. The veneer must be kept as dry as possible. Excess of water causes expansion and the subsequent shrinkage upon drying may induce splitting. Apply glue to the veneer, locate on the groundwork, and press out the glue with the hammer (figure 1). Commence at the centre and work backwards and forwards in a zigzag fashion until the air and surplus glue are forced out at the edges.
5. Test by tapping with the fingers for air pockets. If any, lightly damp the veneer and pass the hot flat-iron over quickly and lightly. Keep the flat-iron clean and shiny on the sole, always have a sheet of No 2 glasspaper to clean it on.
6. Apply the other half of the veneer and match carefully, making allowances for the lap (figure 2). Jointing the veneer (figures 3 and 3A). Locate the straight edge on the joint line, hold or cramp firmly in place. Keeping the knife close to the straight edge and with a firm and even pressure cut through the two thicknesses of veneer. It may be necessary to go over the joint again before removing the waste. Peel off top waste (figure 4) lift veneer and peel off inner waste. If difficulty is experienced in lifting the veneer, damp the joint and quickly warm with the flat-iron. Press the joint down with the veneering hammer, run the flat-iron down the joint and squeeze out the surplus glue (figure 5). To prevent the joint opening during drying, tape over with gummed paper, see figure 5.

7 Remove all surplus veneer and glue immediately after jointing the veneer, see figure 6. Use a 25mm (1in) or 32mm (1¼in) bevelled edge chisel, let the bevel rub the edge and cut through the waste. The work must rest on a firm flat surface.

Caul Veneering

The casket, illustrated in the diagram, combines hammer and caul veneering.

Prepare ground as for hammer veneering. Carefully cut out the veneer and build up the pattern as shown by lightly gluing the upper face of the veneer to a sheet of cartridge paper. Weight down and leave to dry. Glue the top of the lid and the veneer and locate, covering with paper. Cramp the caul, which should be heated in advance, over the veneer. The heat and pressure from the caul warms the glue and forces it to the outside.

Cleaning up

Clean up edges with a plane. Use a scraper to clean off the gummed paper and glue; never use a plane. Carefully glasspaper the surface with No 1½ grade, wrapped round a cork rubber. Then finish glasspapering in the direction of the grain, working through the various grades down to flour grade.

Polish with white french polish, rub down with flour glasspaper or wire wool. Finish as for wax.

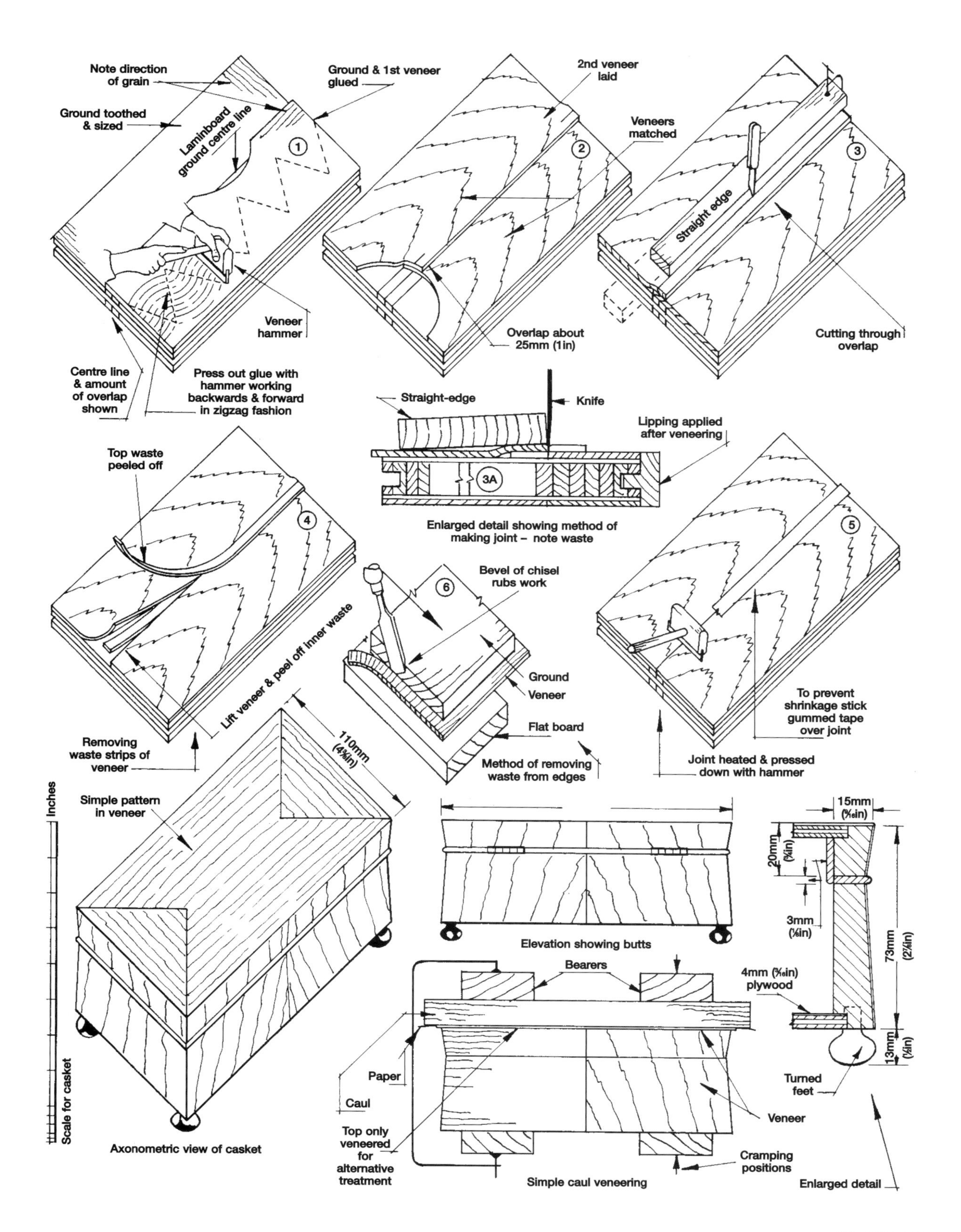
Note direction of grain
Ground & 1st veneer glued
Ground toothed & sized
Laminboard ground centre line
1
Veneer hammer
Centre line & amount of overlap shown
Press out glue with hammer working backwards & forward in zigzag fashion
2nd veneer laid
Veneers matched
2
Overlap about 25mm (1in)
Straight edge
3
Cutting through overlap
Straight-edge
Knife
Lipping applied after veneering
3A
Enlarged detail showing method of making joint – note waste
Top waste peeled off
4
Lift veneer & peel off inner waste
Removing waste strips of veneer
6
Bevel of chisel rubs work
Ground
Veneer
Flat board
Method of removing waste from edges
5
To prevent shrinkage stick gummed tape over joint
Joint heated & pressed down with hammer
110mm (4⅜in)
Simple pattern in veneer
Inches
Scale for casket
Axonometric view of casket
Elevation showing butts
Bearers
4mm (³⁄₁₆in) plywood
Paper
Caul
Top only veneered for alternative treatment
Veneer
Cramping positions
Simple caul veneering
15mm (⁹⁄₁₆in)
20mm (¾in)
3mm (⅛in)
73mm (2⅞in)
13mm (½in)
Turned feet
Enlarged detail

Laminating and Bent Woodwork

Laminated Candleholder

Wood laminating is an interesting technique of bending and shaping thin strips or laminations of wood on formers or jigs. On removal from the jig very little attention is necessary, apart from cleaning up the edges, and preparing for polishing. The article retains its shape and saves hours of cutting out and shaping. The technique has the added advantage of eliminating short grain. Laminating and bending of wood offers a tremendous variety in the field of design. The laminations must be cut out of straight-grained timber. Some suitable woods are beech, sycamore, ash, American elm, oak, maple, gaboon, mahogany, walnut and yew. The candleholder is made up of four laminations, consisting of two laminations of mahogany and two of beech.

Method

1. Make a full-size drawing of the jig, and mark out the position of the four laminations. The small cramping block must be shaped to fit the bottom lamination.
2. Prepare jig to the given dimensions; beech or any mild working hardwood is suitable. The jig serves a dual purpose: it is used for bending, and for boring the 11mm (7/16in) diameter holes. Cut to shape with a bow saw, and clean up with flat and round bottom spokeshaves.
3. The laminations if cut clean with a planer type of circular saw can be used straight from the machine. If the saw marks are pronounced remove with a finely set smoothing plane. Cut the laminations to length, place in jig and try up dry. Note the piece of rubber webbing used as a pressure pad. This takes up any small discrepancies.
4. Rub candle grease over the cramping surfaces of the jig. Apply resin glue to the laminations and cramp up. Check pack for flushness. Wipe off surplus glue and leave to dry.
5. Remove job from the jig and saw to length. Replace and cramp up in vice. Clean edges and finish to width. Bore the holes using the jig to locate them.
6. Using the flat bottom spokeshave shape the holder and clean up with glasspaper ready for polishing.

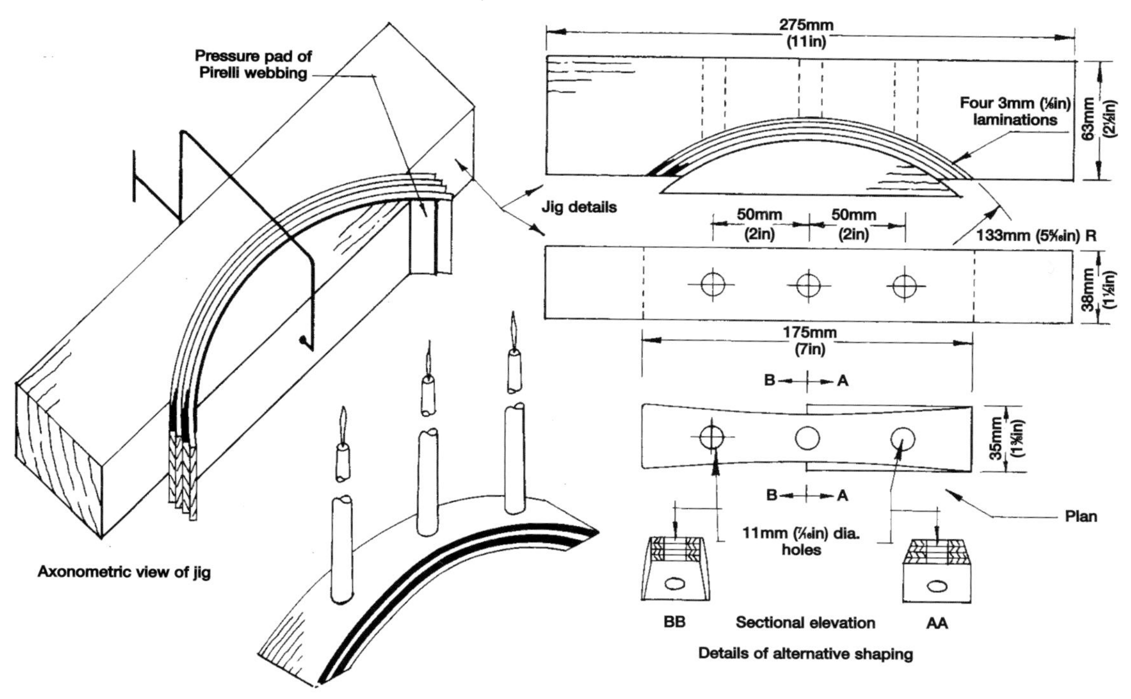
Pressure pad of
Pirelli webbing
Axonometric view of jig
Jig details
275mm
(11in)
Four 3mm (⅛in)
laminations
63mm
(2½in)
50mm
(2in)
50mm
(2in)
133mm (5¼in) R
38mm
(1½in)
175mm
(7in)
B A
35mm
(1⅜in)
B A
Plan
11mm (7/16in) dia.
holes
BB
Sectional elevation
AA
Details of alternative shaping
Isometric sketch of laminated candle holder

Bracket for Wall Light

Wall lights make a charming addition to the decor of a room. The wall bracket illustrated consists of a shaped base to which is tenoned a laminated bracket to hold the lamp fittings. Oak is suggested for the base with oak and walnut contrasting laminations.

Method

1. Prepare a full-size working drawing of the bracket. The laminations are tapered towards the lamp fitting and allowances must be made for this on the jig.
2. Prepare the jig to the given dimensions. Bow saw to shape and clean up with spokeshaves. Well glue and screw fixed piece to jig. Note how the loose piece slides between the jig ends.
3. Taper laminations and cut off to jig lengths. Insert laminations and cramp up dry.
4. To prevent the job adhering to the jig, rub candle grease over the cramping surfaces and base of the jig. Apply resin glue to the laminations and locate in jig. Place pressure pad and sheet of paper against sliding part of jig. Cramp up and wipe off surplus glue. Leave to dry.
5. Remove cramps, clean up and bevel edges. This can be done successfully by holding together the jig and the job in the vice. Simply pack up the job to the height required. Mark out length of job off jig and cut tenon. Cut bracket to length and round the edges. Bore holes for the flex and clean up for polishing.
6. Set out base, cut mortise and fit bracket. Bore holes in the back and make slots for fixing.
7. Shape base and work chamfers. Clean up and polish.
8. Glue in bracket and leave to dry. Bore hole for flex in base. Screw on brass nipple, wire up and fix lampholder. Note: light fittings should only be added to existing circuits

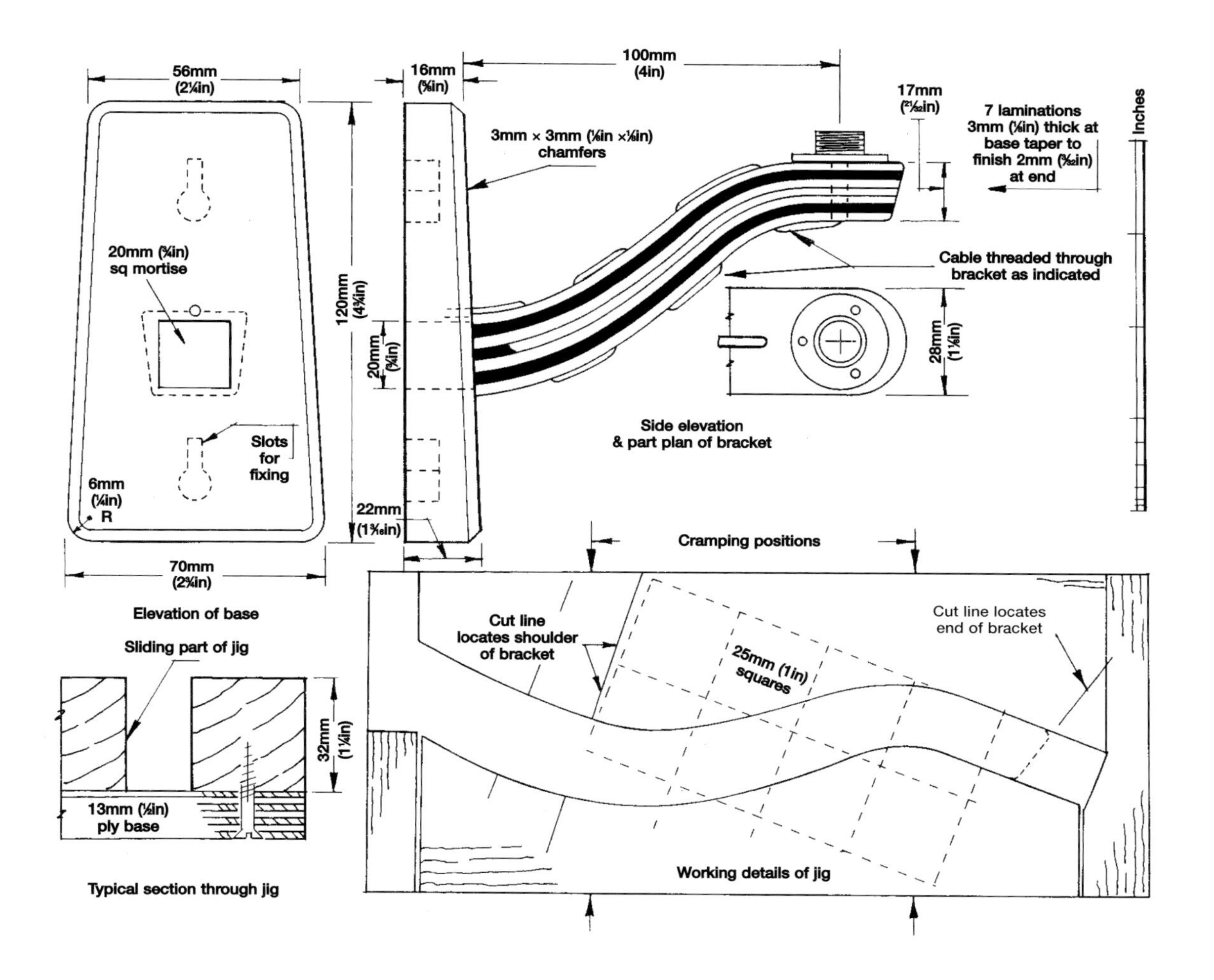
56mm
(2¼in)
16mm
(⅝in)
100mm
(4in)
17mm
(²¹⁄₃₂in)
7 laminations
3mm (⅛in) thick at
base taper to
finish 2mm (³⁄₃₂in)
at end
Inches
3mm × 3mm (⅛in × ⅛in)
chamfers
20mm (¾in)
sq mortise
120mm
(4¾in)
20mm
(¾in)
Cable threaded through
bracket as indicated
28mm
(1⅛in)
Side elevation
& part plan of bracket
Slots
for
fixing
6mm
(¼in)
R
22mm
(1⁵⁄₁₆in)
70mm
(2¾in)
Elevation of base
Cramping positions
Sliding part of jig
32mm
(1¼in)
13mm (½in)
ply base
Typical section through jig
Cut line
locates shoulder
of bracket
25mm (1in)
squares
Cut line locates
end of bracket
Working details of jig

Elliptical Tray

This useful elliptical tray made up of three laminations, which can be in contrasting woods, has a plastic-faced bottom. The same technique can be used for the making of a circular tray or a child's hoop. A separate detail shows a section suitable for a mirror frame. Using this principle a variety of useful articles can be made. The former or jig is robust and consists of two pieces of 13mm (½in) multi-ply glued together. To save the gluing up operation 25mm (1in) multi-ply could be used. The centre is removed to give good cramping facilities. The author used 2.8mm (7/64in) beech and mahogany laminations; these bent round successfully without steaming or soaking.

Method

1. Mark out the ellipse on the plywood and bow saw to shape, clean up outside edge with a flat bottom spokeshave. Use this as a template and mark out the second piece of ply, glue and cramp up jig. Clean up and apply candle grease to the outer edge. The jig has been designed for the use of 75–100mm (3–4in) thumb screws of which 12–14 would be necessary.
2. *Splicing:* traditionally both ends of the laminations should be tapered to form the splice and this involves great accuracy in measurement. *Procedure for bending and splicing:* the first lamination is simply butted – this could be spliced if desired – see figure 1. The author developed a simple technique for splicing the laminations which brings this type of work within the scope of young students. This is a modified splice, which can be used in curved work of a continuous nature. Splice one end of the second lamination, see separate drawing showing method of holding. The block is held in the vice and the lamination can be cramped or nailed to the block. Use a sharp steel smoothing plane to make the splice.
3. Glue the outside of the first and the inside of the second lamination, and wrap completely round the jig. Glue the splice (see figure 2, noting how the end runs over the splice and also see the waste strip for cramping). Cramp up firmly, working from the splice towards the overhanging end, and leave to dry.
4. Clean off overhanging portion of splice (see dotted line in figure 2) and fair in to the curve.
5. Prepare the third lamination, splice one end and glue up as for previous lamination and leave to dry. Note how the splices are staggered (see figure 3).
6. Remove cramps, clean off waste at splice and fair in.
7. Clean up the edges and outside of the rim while still on the jig.
8. Remove from the jig. With a cutting gauge remove the waste to form a rebate for the bottom.
9. Clean up inside, round the edges as required and polish.
10. Using the rim as a template mark out the shape and fit the bottom. Glue and screw into position. Cut out six 25mm (1in) diameter discs of baize and glue them to the bottom at equal spacing round the edge.

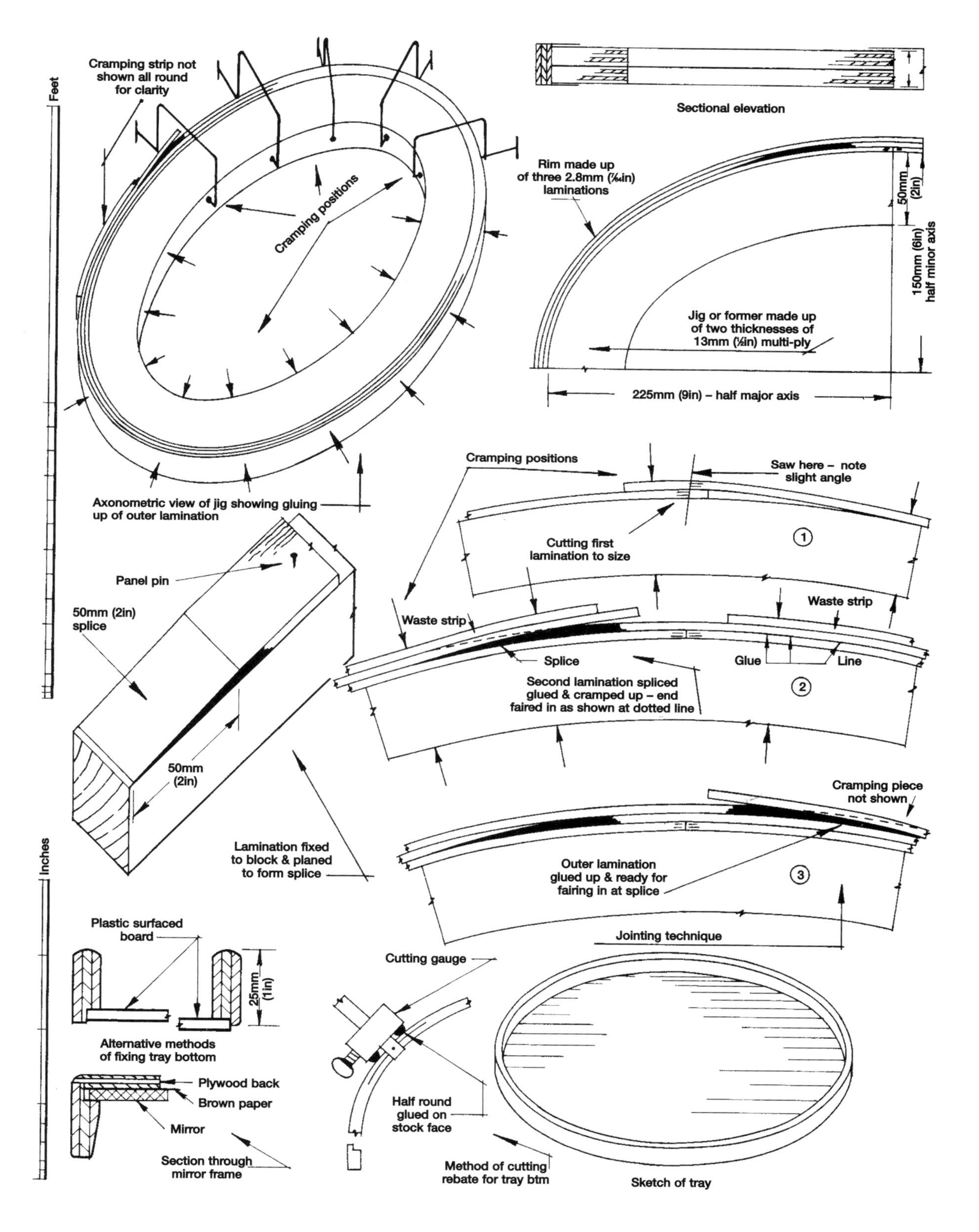

Feet
Cramping strip not shown all round for clarity
Cramping positions
Axonometric view of jig showing gluing up of outer lamination
Sectional elevation
Rim made up of three 2.8mm (⅛in) laminations
50mm (2in)
150mm (6in) half minor axis
Jig or former made up of two thicknesses of 13mm (½in) multi-ply
225mm (9in) – half major axis
Cramping positions
Saw here – note slight angle
Cutting first lamination to size
1
Panel pin
50mm (2in) splice
Waste strip
Waste strip
Splice
Glue
Line
Second lamination spliced glued & cramped up – end faired in as shown at dotted line
2
50mm (2in)
Cramping piece not shown
Lamination fixed to block & planed to form splice
Outer lamination glued up & ready for fairing in at splice
3
Jointing technique
Inches
Plastic surfaced board
25mm (1in)
Alternative methods of fixing tray bottom
Plywood back
Brown paper
Mirror
Section through mirror frame
Cutting gauge
Half round glued on stock face
Method of cutting rebate for tray btm
Sketch of tray

Table with Laminated Legs

The drawings give full details of the making of a jig and the method of gluing-up laminations to make table legs. These laminated legs are suitable for table tops up to 325mm (13in) in width. Cut in two they could be used as separate legs for wider tables, by screwing them to the top at any desired angle. Made in beech and carefully used the jig could be used repeatedly with very little deterioration; for economy the jig could be made of pine with only the cramping blocks in beech.

Method

1 Prepare the base of 13mm (½in) multi-ply and make a full-size plan of the former on the top surface. Using this as a rod, set out and cut all joints. Glue up frame with resin glue and pin the top joints. Cut out housings for slides. Glue and screw frame to base.

2 Set out the thickness of the five laminations plus one for the supporting piece, and make the corner cramping blocks in beech. Prepare the straight cramping blocks in beech. The blocks are numbered 1, 2, 3 and two each of Nos 2 and 3 are required. Make slides in beech. Candle grease the base and cramping surfaces of the jig.

3 Prepare straight-grained laminations for bending.

Note on bending technique: in general terms the thinner the laminations, the easier they are to bend. For example, a piece of single knife cut veneer can be bent into a small radius. Furthermore if damped the veneer could be bent into a much smaller radius without fracturing. The timbers of a boat, say, of 25mm × 20mm (1in × ¾in) can only be bent into a small radius when steamed; this is known as hot bending. It will be apparent from these observations that according to the thickness, the bending of laminations to small radius may require heating. Another factor to consider is that some woods are more suitable for bending. It is generally advisable to make a trial bend, and very often a slight thinning of the laminations eliminates difficulty.

The author used 3mm (⅛in) beech laminations with 3mm (⅛in) sapele for the inner and outer laminations as a contrast, and steamed the laminations for 15 minutes before bending. A box made of 10mm (⅜in) marine quality plywood about 150mm (6in) square and 1200mm (4ft) in length makes an excellent steam chest or chamber. An empty 4.5 litre (one gallon) oil can (the type with a flat top) makes a useful steam boiler. This can be heated over a gas ring, and the steam fed into the box with a tube. Arrange for a sliding door at one end. 13mm (½in) dowel rods at 225mm (9in) intervals through the box sides make good shelf accommodation. For steaming wood allow approximately 1 hour for 25mm (1in) of thickness. Another method is to drop the laminations into a bath or copper of hot water, or cover them over with rags soaked in boiling water and leave for 20 minutes.

4 Have all cramps and jigs ready. After steaming or bending assemble the pack of six laminations, this includes the supporting one. Centre the pack over the jig and working quickly position and cramp number 1 block to the jig. Pull both ends round smartly and lightly cramp blocks 3 at the bottom end. Locate corner blocks 2, so that they almost touch number 1 block, and cramp up tight. Position all cramps and tighten up from the

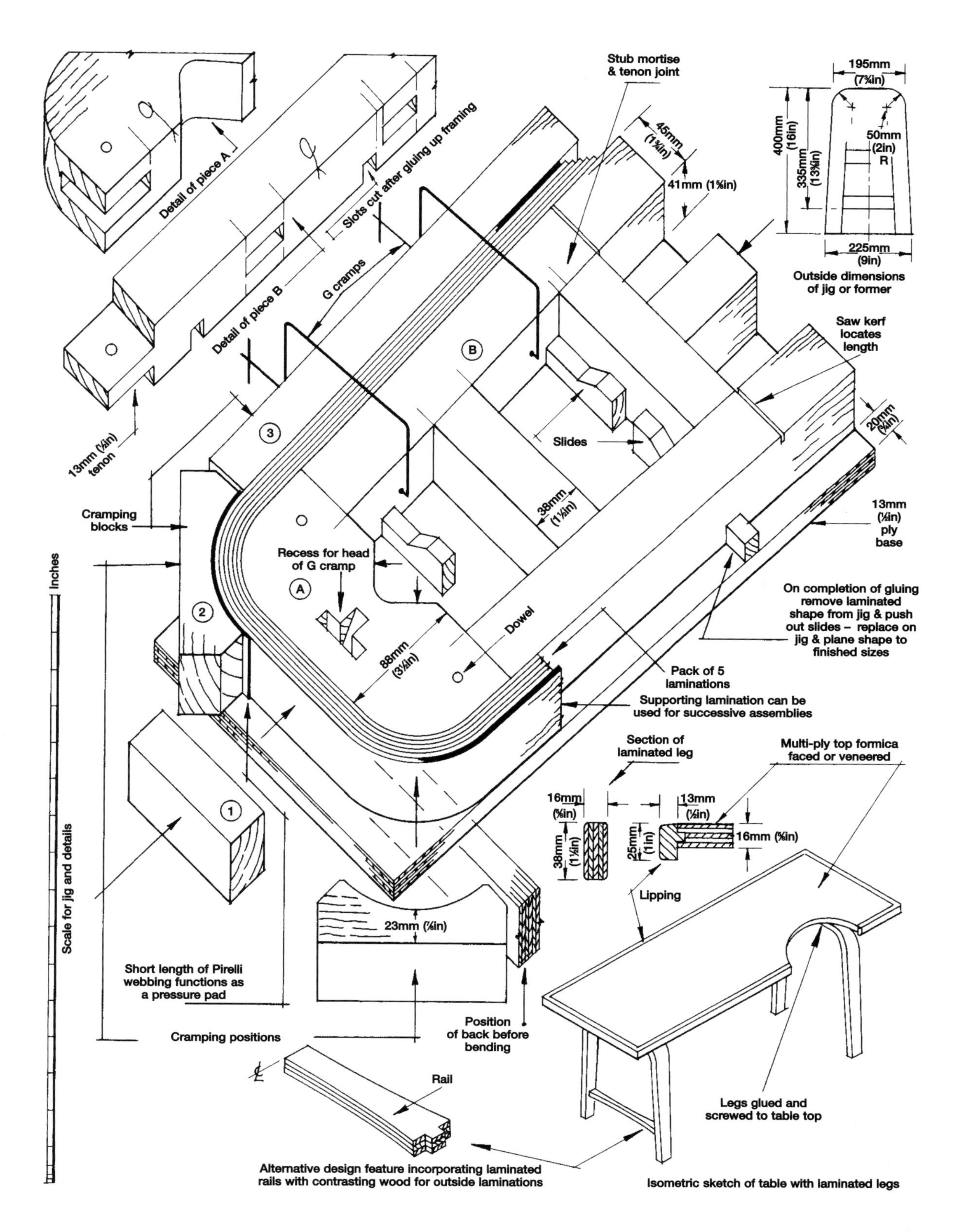
Detail of piece A
Slots cut after gluing up framing
Detail of piece B
G cramps
Stub mortise & tenon joint
45mm (1¾in)
41mm (1⅝in)
195mm (7¾in)
400mm (16in)
335mm (13⅜in)
50mm (2in) R
225mm (9in)
Outside dimensions of jig or former
Saw kerf locates length
20mm (¾in)
13mm (½in) tenon
B
3
Slides
Cramping blocks
38mm (1½in)
13mm (½in) ply base
Inches
Recess for head of G cramp
A
2
Dowel
88mm (3½in)
On completion of gluing remove laminated shape from jig & push out slides – replace on jig & plane shape to finished sizes
Pack of 5 laminations
Supporting lamination can be used for successive assemblies
Section of laminated leg
Multi-ply top formica faced or veneered
1
16mm (⅝in)
13mm (½in)
38mm (1½in)
25mm (1in)
16mm (⅝in)
Lipping
Scale for jig and details
23mm (⅞in)
Short length of Pirelli webbing functions as a pressure pad
Cramping positions
Position of back before bending
Rail
Legs glued and screwed to table top
Alternative design feature incorporating laminated rails with contrasting wood for outside laminations
Isometric sketch of table with laminated legs

radius working down to the bottom. Leave to dry out, check after 24 hours and remove from the jig. The inside surfaces may still be damp and must not be glued up in such condition. Tie a piece of string round the bottom of the laminations and fan open at the top. This allows the inside surfaces to dry out without the laminations springing open.

5 When thoroughly dry, glue laminations and cramp up as before, remove all surplus glue and leave to dry. On removal from the jig the legs should retain their shape.
6 Push out the slides to convert into a cleaning up jig. Flush and taper laminations, and cut to length, clean up for polishing.
7 Repeat for second leg.
8 Prepare top and screw on legs.

Fitting Hinges and Locks

For first-class cabinet work only the best hinges and locks should be considered. Brass butt (solid drawn) hinges are widely used in cabinet-making and joinery.

Procedure for fitting door to carcase

(See diagram showing sequence.)

1. Remove horns of door, and plane hanging stile to fit carcase.
2. Plane door to width, working carefully to ensure equal width of stiles and making a slight angle on the inside to prevent binding.
3. Plane bottom edge to fit carcase.
4. Plane top edge and fit to carcase. The door should be fitted so as to allow a thin piece of veneer to be slipped under the bottom rail. A piece of cartridge paper makes a good gauge for the width clearance.

Procedure for fitting the butts

The position of the hinge in relation to the top and bottom rails is clearly shown opposite.

1. Protect door with a piece of baize and place in vice. Mark out position of butts in pencil and cut lines.
2. Set marking gauge to pin centre and knuckle thickness respectively and carefully gauge on hanging stile.
3. Make saw kerfs with dovetail saw and chisel out waste.
4. Fit in butts and screw to stile.
5. Place door in aperture, with flanges out. Slip a thin piece of veneer under the bottom rail to give the necessary clearance.
6. Mark the position of the butts on the carcase side. Adjust gauge to allow for set in of door and gauge for flanges. Use a pencil to mark face line of door at butt recesses.
7. Remove waste and fit butts. Fix with one screw in each and try door. Adjust as necessary and complete screwing. Note the alternative hinging positions and the separate detail showing an efficient form of ball catch.

Procedure for fitting a drawer lock.

1. Position lock and mark out as shown in drawing.
2. Set gauge and mark pin centre. Bore hole for escutcheon and remove waste with keyhole saw and chisel.
3. Mark out and cut recesses for body and plate of lock.
4. Screw on lock, and smear end of bolt with oilstone grease. Position drawer and turn key so that the bolt marks drawer rail. Cut mortise to receive bolt with drawer lock chisel. A separate detail shows setting out technique for a rule joint stay.

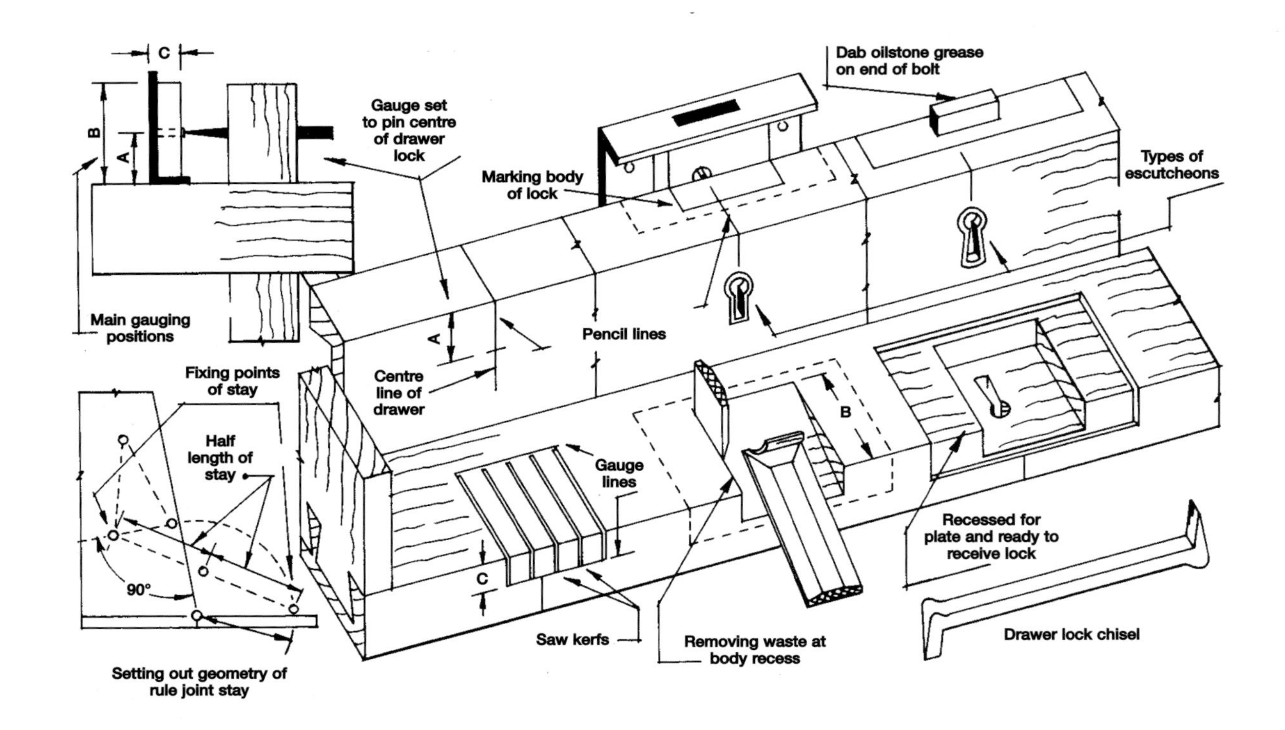
C
B
A
Gauge set to pin centre of drawer lock
Main gauging positions
Marking body of lock
Dab oilstone grease on end of bolt
Types of escutcheons
Pencil lines
A
Centre line of drawer
Fixing points of stay
Half length of stay
90°
Setting out geometry of rule joint stay
B
Gauge lines
C
Saw kerfs
Removing waste at body recess
Recessed for plate and ready to receive lock
Drawer lock chisel

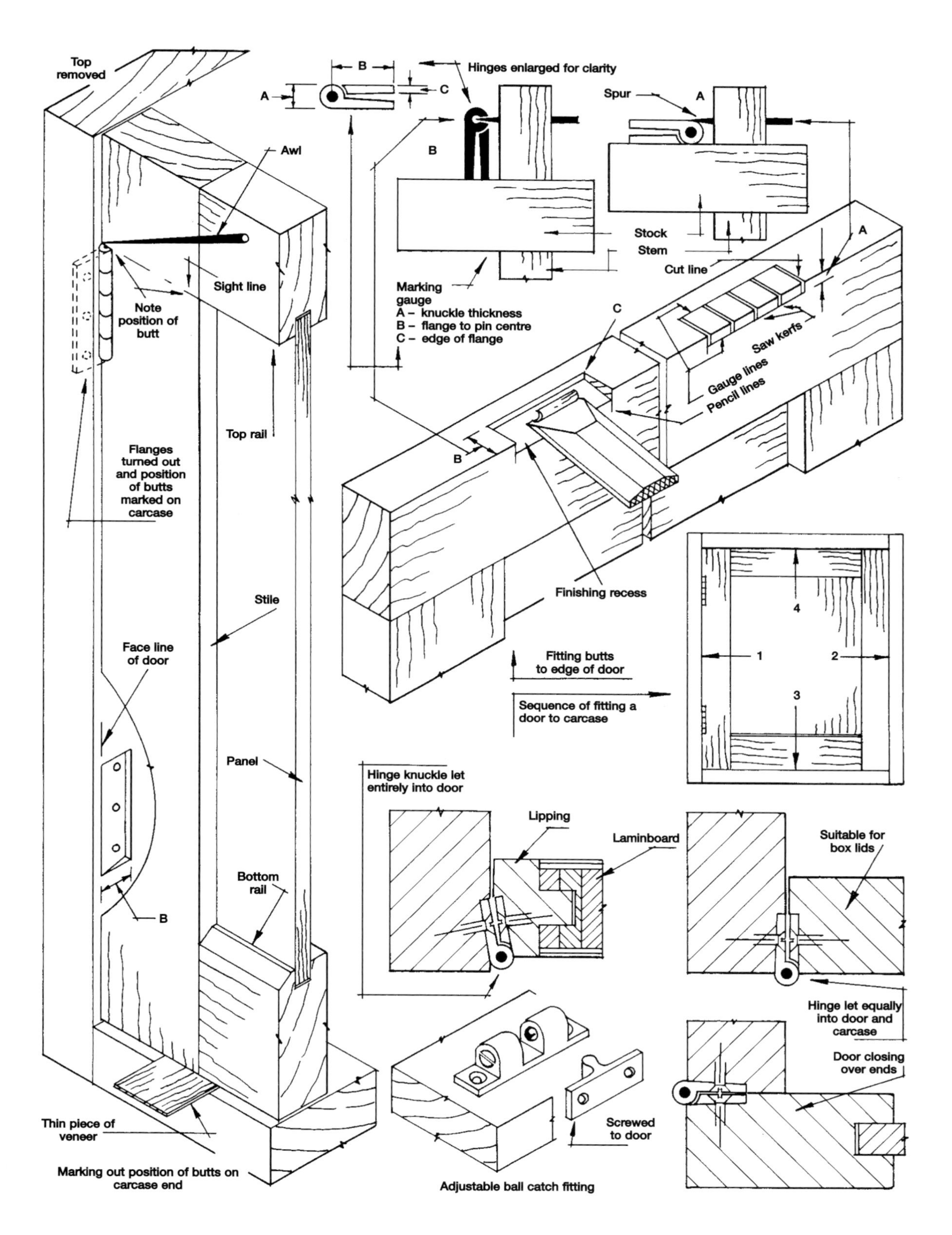
Top removed
Awl
Sight line
Note position of butt
Flanges turned out and position of butts marked on carcase
Top rail
Stile
Face line of door
Panel
Bottom rail
B
Thin piece of veneer
Marking out position of butts on carcase end
B
A
C
Hinges enlarged for clarity
B
Spur
A
Stock
Stem
Marking gauge
A – knuckle thickness
B – flange to pin centre
C – edge of flange
Cut line
A
C
Saw kerfs
Gauge lines
Pencil lines
B
Finishing recess
Fitting butts to edge of door
Sequence of fitting a door to carcase
4
1
2
3
Hinge knuckle let entirely into door
Lipping
Laminboard
Suitable for box lids
Hinge let equally into door and carcase
Door closing over ends
Screwed to door
Adjustable ball catch fitting

Workshop-made Tools & Appliances

The following simple tools can be made, rather than purchased:

Scratch Stock: Most useful for scratching in grooves to receive inlays, strings and bandings. It is also used for making small runs of special mouldings which would not be economical to produce by machine. It consists of two pieces of wood shaped and screwed together to form a stock which is held firmly against the edge or side of the job. Old scrapers make excellent material for the cutters. The cutter is sharpened by filing across at right angles, thus enabling the scratch to be used on both the forward and backward movements. To make a groove to receive strings or bandings, cut and file the cutter to the exact width of string. Try out on a small piece of wood and test for size. It should be finger tight.

Veneer Hammer: A necessity when veneering by hand. It is used for pressing down the veneer and squeezing out the glue. It consists of a head shaped to form a comfortable grip for the hand, and a handle which is fixed to the head by wedging. The head is grooved to take the brass strip which should not be less than 1.6mm (1⁄16in) thick.

Try Square: This type of try square is useful when setting out and testing work. It also serves a useful purpose as a 60° set square. The stock should be in hardwood. It is ploughed to receive the plywood blade which is glued in.

Bench Hook: This is used to hold wood when sawing on the bench. It can be used on either side and the front and back members should be glued and dowelled on. It wears well when made in beech.

Dowelling Technique: Figure 1 shows a section through a dowelled joint. The saw kerf or groove allows the surplus glue to escape. Without this groove the surplus glue can build up in the cavity and the dowel acting as a piston could produce sufficient pressure to fracture and split the wood. The groove is not necessary when through dowelling as in the bench hook.

Mitre Template: When mouldings are stuck, i.e. worked in the solid, for doors, windows and frames, the mouldings are usually mitred or scribed. The template is made out of one piece of wood (any suitable hardwood) and the ends are cut and planed at 45°. The diagrams opposite show mitring and scribing technique.

Box Square: The square is made out of one piece of hardwood. It is particularly useful for setting out work where there would be no bearing surface for the stock of a normal try square, as is the case with material already moulded for window sashes, etc.

Winding Strips: Used for testing work for wind or twist. These strips are placed one at each end of the work and are sighted across the top edges, which will be parallel when the work is flat. The small insets when made of bone or white plastic material, aid sighting.

Centre Square: Particularly useful for finding centres when working with cylindrical material. Accurate setting out and boring of holes are essential.

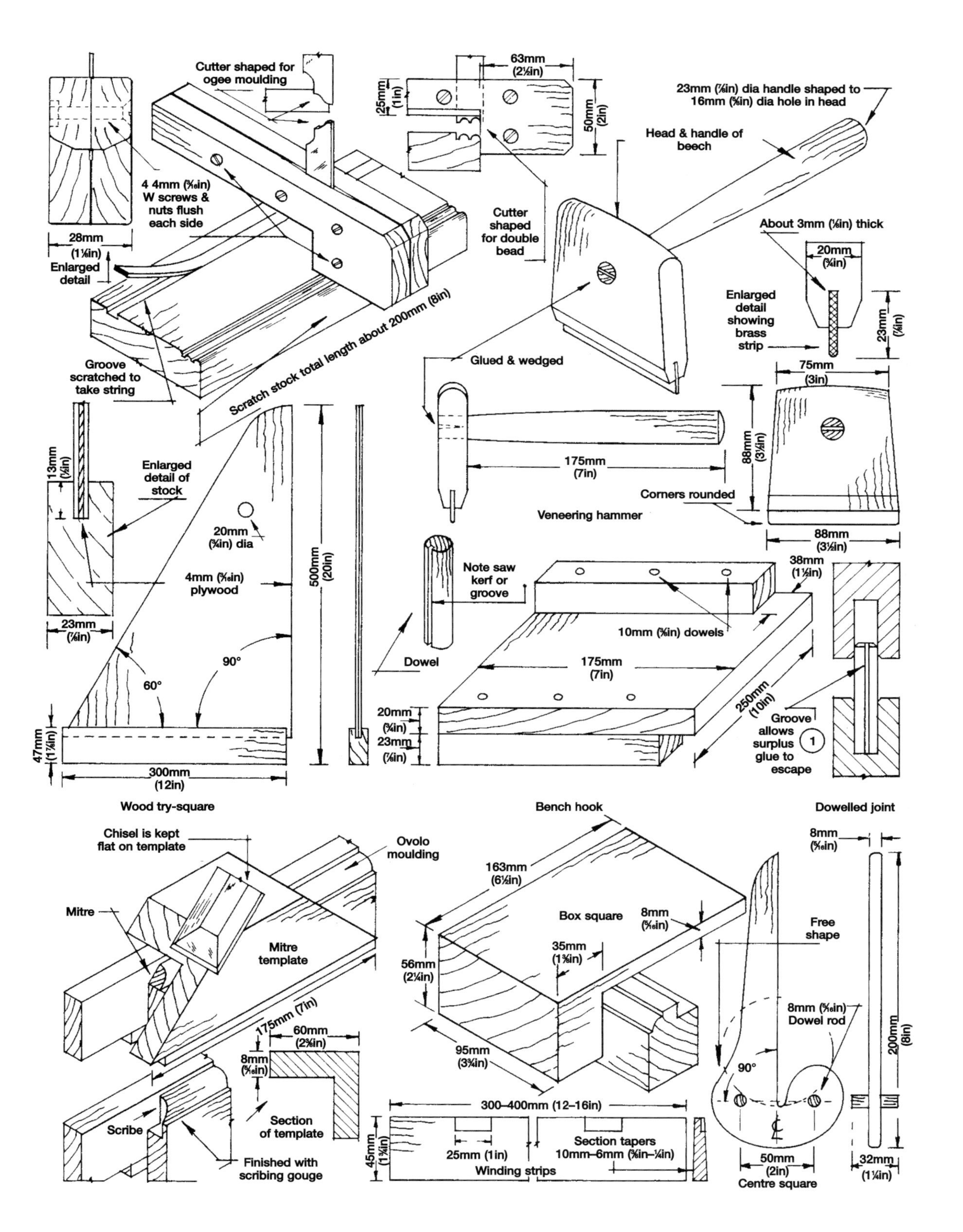

Cutter shaped for ogee moulding
28mm (1⅛in)
Enlarged detail
4 4mm (3⁄16in) W screws & nuts flush each side
Groove scratched to take string
Scratch stock total length about 200mm (8in)
63mm (2½in)
25mm (1in)
50mm (2in)
Cutter shaped for double bead
23mm (⅞in) dia handle shaped to 16mm (⅝in) dia hole in head
Head & handle of beech
About 3mm (⅛in) thick
20mm (¾in)
Enlarged detail showing brass strip
23mm (⅞in)
Glued & wedged
75mm (3in)
88mm (3½in)
175mm (7in)
Corners rounded
Veneering hammer
88mm (3½in)
13mm (½in)
Enlarged detail of stock
20mm (¾in) dia
4mm (3⁄16in) plywood
500mm (20in)
23mm (⅞in)
90°
60°
47mm (1⅞in)
300mm (12in)
Wood try-square
Note saw kerf or groove
Dowel
38mm (1½in)
10mm (⅜in) dowels
175mm (7in)
250mm (10in)
20mm (¾in)
23mm (⅞in)
Groove allows surplus glue to escape
1
Bench hook
Dowelled joint
Chisel is kept flat on template
Ovolo moulding
Mitre
Mitre template
175mm (7in)
60mm (2⅜in)
8mm (5⁄16in)
Section of template
Scribe
Finished with scribing gouge
163mm (6½in)
Box square
8mm (5⁄16in)
35mm (1⅜in)
56mm (2¼in)
95mm (3¾in)
300–400mm (12–16in)
45mm (1¾in)
25mm (1in)
Section tapers 10mm–6mm (⅜in–¼in)
Winding strips
8mm (5⁄16in)
Free shape
8mm (5⁄16in) Dowel rod
200mm (8in)
90°
50mm (2in)
Centre square
32mm (1¼in)

Slatted Garden Table

This is a table to match the garden chair shown on page 93. Its design gives the student practice in setting out, joint proportioning, chamfering, and the fitting of brass cups and screws.

Method

1 Prepare the material, select and match the grain.
2 Set out the legs in pairs (see page 57 for information on setting out).
3 Set out the long and short rails in pairs and number joints for ease of identification during fitting.
4 Set out the bottom rails and stretcher.
5 Set mortise gauge to an 8mm (5/16in) mortise chisel and, noting that the rails are set in from the legs and adjusted to suit, gauge all mortises and tenons with exception of stretcher rail, which has 10mm (3/8in) shouldered tenons. Adjust mortise gauge accordingly.
6 Cut all mortises, haunchings and tenons and assemble table, fitting as necessary. Cut dovetails on centre rail, mark out and fit to side rails.
7 Using a thumb gauge, mark out and work the bevels on the top rails.
8 Mark out and work the chamfers on the stretcher and bottom rails. Care is needed with the making of the stopped chamfers.
9 Clean up inner surfaces, including rail surfaces, and make tapered chamfers on inside of legs. Cut leg to floor line and make a 3mm (1/8in) chamfer all round. This prevents the legs splintering when the table is dragged or pushed.
10 Glue and cramp up the two end frames. Test for square and alignment. Clean off surplus glue and leave to dry.
11 Glue and cramp up the stretcher and the long rails. Drive in the wedges at the bottom rails. Test for square and alignment and leave to dry.
12 Cut off horns and flush top edges with trying plane. Test with a straight edge. Chamfer legs at the corners.
13 Prepare slats, leaving them long at this stage, and mark centres for screws. Bore for brass cups and screws (see step 14 on page 94 for fitting of cups).
14 Position slats. Using steel screws, screw on outside slats, make a small gauge to fit the gap and screw on remainder of slats.
15 Mark out length of slats and square across. Remove slats, cramp together and saw off ends. Clean up and chamfer ends.
16 Round the corners of the outside slats and complete the chamfering, clean up.
17 Re-fix the slats with brass cups and screws.
18 Finish as for small garden chair.

Suggested Material

Oak, teak or selected pine.

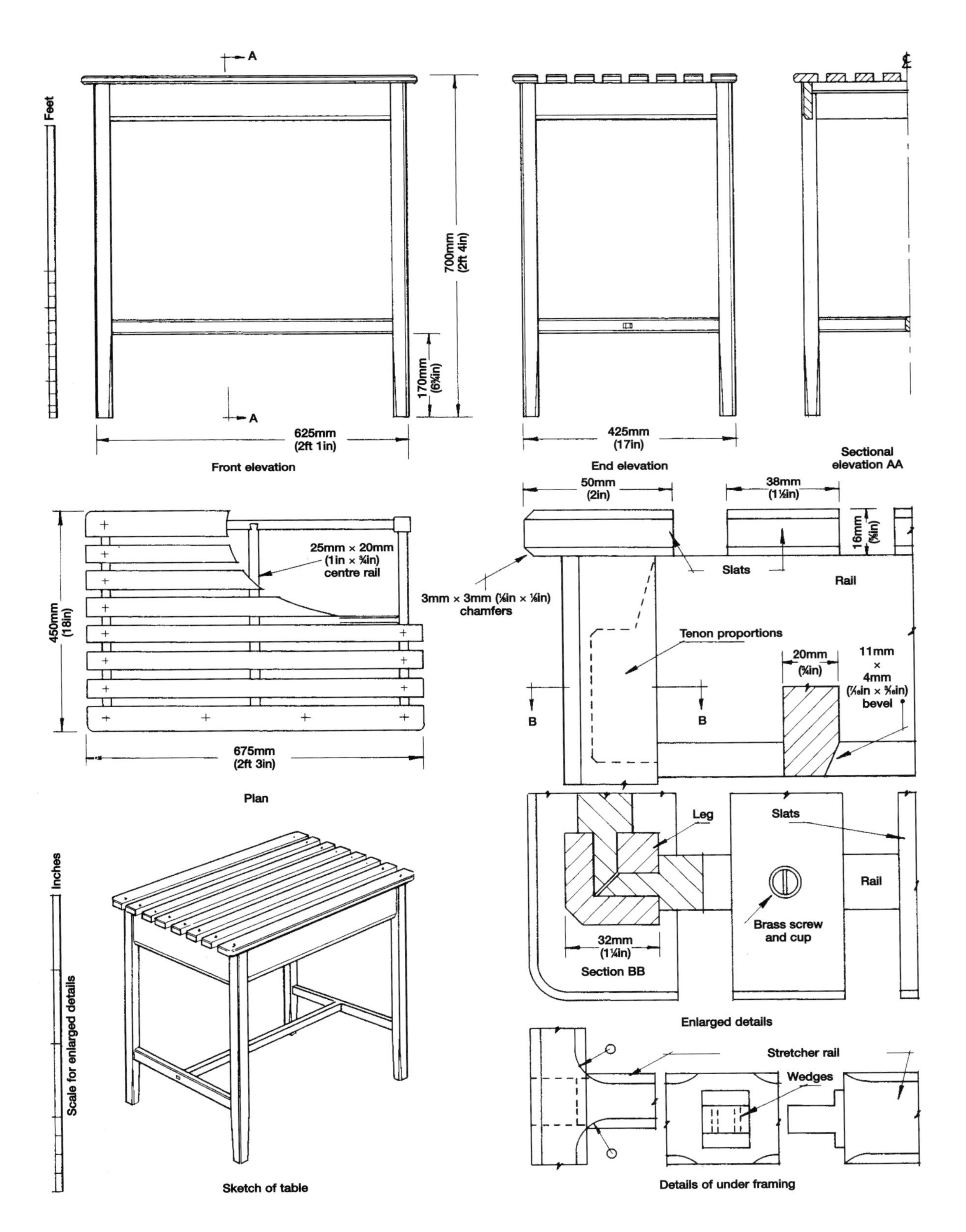
A
700mm
(2ft 4in)
170mm
(6¾in)
A
625mm
(2ft 1in)
Front elevation
425mm
(17in)
End elevation
Sectional
elevation AA
Feet
450mm
(18in)
25mm × 20mm
(1in × ¾in)
centre rail
675mm
(2ft 3in)
Plan
50mm
(2in)
38mm
(1½in)
16mm
(⅝in)
Slats
Rail
3mm × 3mm (⅛in × ⅛in)
chamfers
Tenon proportions
20mm
(¾in)
11mm
×
4mm
(7⁄16in × 5⁄32in)
bevel
B
B
Leg
Slats
Rail
Brass screw
and cup
32mm
(1¼in)
Section BB
Enlarged details
Inches
Scale for enlarged details
Stretcher rail
Wedges
Details of under framing
Sketch of table

Cutting list

Description	Length	Width	Thickness
4 legs	725mm (2ft 5in)	32mm (1¼in)	32mm (1¼in)
2 side rails	625mm (2ft 1in)	75mm (3in)	20mm (¾in)
2 end rails	425mm (1ft 5in)	75mm (3in)	20mm (¾in)
1 centre rail	425mm (1ft 5in)	25mm (1in)	20mm (¾in)
2 end rails	425mm (1ft 5in)	32mm (1¼in)	20mm (¾in)
1 stretcher rail	625mm (2ft 1in)	32mm (1¼in)	20mm (¾in)
2 slats	700mm (2ft 4in)	50mm (2in)	16mm (⅝in)
6 slats	700mm (2ft 4in)	38mm (1½in)	16mm (⅝in)

20 screws, 32mm (1¼in) × 8 countersunk brass screws with cups

Tools not in Basic Kit

Shoulder plane – for finishing rail shoulders.
Trying plane – for finishing top rails and legs.

Plant Stand

The plant stand is designed to be made in teak or oak for an oil finish, or in pine if a painted finish is desired. A metal tray would be a useful addition.

It has many features incorporating sound joinery practice. The box has sloping ends necessitating special setting out of the dovetails. This is clearly indicated in the separate detail showing dovetails. It can be seen that the dovetails are set out with the centre line of the pins running parallel to the grain. This arrangement eliminates short grain. The through dovetail joint is mitred on the bottom edge to take the plough groove (see page 134 for method). The stand framing has a shaped rail which is dovetailed halved to the top of the legs. This type of joint is often used in the making of mock panelling. The bottom is tongued in with a clearance on the long sides to allow for expansion and has three drainage holes.

Method

1. Prepare the material, arrange and match the grain.
2. Make full-size drawing of the two elevations (see note on page 101).
3. Mark out the sides in pairs – a bevel is needed here – and clean up sloping ends to cut lines. Number all joints for easy identification.
4. Mark out the ends in pairs, cut to length and clean up end grain to cut lines. Bevel top and bottom edges.
5. Set out and cut the dovetails.
6. Mark out and cut pins. Arrange for the mitres on the bottom edge.
7. Assemble box, fitting as necessary. Flush top and bottom edges.
8. Work plough grooves on sides and ends to receive bottom.
9. Cut bottom to size, rebate to form tongue and fit up. Bore drainage holes and open up to larger diameter with a gouge.
10. Clean up all inner surfaces, and glue up box. Do not apply glue to the bottom as it must be free to move.
11. Set out the legs in pairs. Mark out and cut the through mortises for the bottom rails.
12. Set out the bottom rails, cut tenons and shoulders. Shape rails and assemble the end frames. Make saw kerfs for wedges.
13. Mark out, from full-size drawing, the shoulder to form splay on the legs. Remove the waste with panel and tenon saws, finishing to the line with shoulder and smoothing planes.
14. Set out and make the shaped top rails. Cut the dovetails and shoulders (see separate detail showing dovetail halving joint). Position legs, mark out and cut the sockets for the dovetails.
15. Chamfer the top rails. Assemble the dovetail halving joints and shape top of legs to suit.
16. Set out and work chamfers on legs.
17. Flush all joints on the box and clean up. Work the bevels on the top edge.
18. Clean up the legs and prepare for gluing up.
19. Glue up end frames and top rail. Cramp up and drive in wedges at bottom rails. Check for alignment and leave to dry.
20. Bore for dowels and glue in. When dry flush off dowels, and finish stand as for Small Garden Chair.

21 Alternatively, the legs could be screwed and pelleted to the box as shown on page 185.

Note: the stand can be simplified by leaving out the top side rail and extending the legs to within 25mm (1in) of the top.

Suggested Material

Teak, oak or pine.

Cutting list

Description	Length	Width	Thickness
2 sides	700mm (2ft 4in)	145mm (5¾in)	16mm (⅝in)
1 for 2 ends	400mm (1ft 4in)	153mm (6⅛in)	16mm (⅝in)
1 bottom	625mm (2ft 1in)	175mm (7in)	16mm (⅝in)
4 legs	575mm (1ft 11in)	50mm (2in)	23mm (⅞in)
2 top rails	425mm (1ft 5in)	56mm (2¼in)	13mm (½in)
2 bottom rails	250mm (10in)	28mm (1⅛in)	16mm (⅝in)
hand-made dowels	250mm (10in)	10mm (⅜in) diameter	

Tools not in Basic Kit

Shoulder plane – for cleaning up rail shoulders.
Plough – for making grooves for bottom.
10mm (⅜in) scribing gouge – for bevelling drainage holes.
Panel saw – for cutting sides and ends of box.

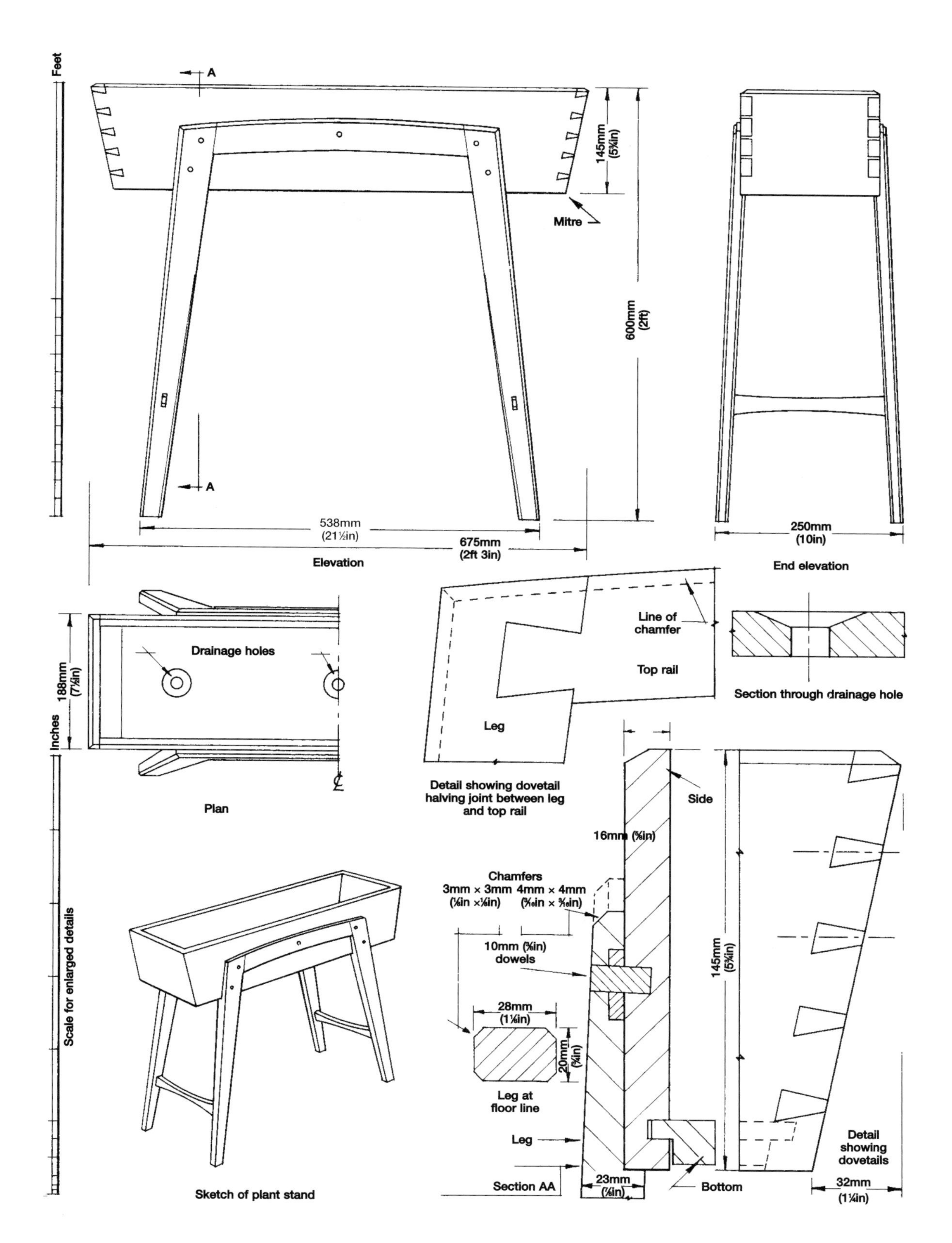
Feet
A
145mm
(5¾in)
Mitre
600mm
(2ft)
A
538mm
(21½in)
675mm
(2ft 3in)
Elevation
250mm
(10in)
End elevation
188mm
(7½in)
Drainage holes
Inches
Plan
Line of
chamfer
Top rail
Leg
Detail showing dovetail
halving joint between leg
and top rail
Section through drainage hole
Side
16mm (⅝in)
Chamfers
3mm × 3mm 4mm × 4mm
(⅛in ×⅛in) (³⁄₁₆in × ³⁄₁₆in)
10mm (⅜in)
dowels
28mm
(1⅛in)
20mm
(¾in)
Leg at
floor line
145mm
(5¾in)
Scale for enlarged details
Leg
Section AA
23mm
(⅞in)
Bottom
Detail
showing
dovetails
32mm
(1¼in)
Sketch of plant stand

Wood Form or Bench

This form provides a good exercise in setting out and shaping and is useful when extra seating accommodation is required. When fitted with a 50mm (2in) foam rubber cushion, the stool makes an excellent seat for the dining recess.

Method

1 Prepare material. Select and match the grain. Make full-size drawings in order to obtain the correct bevels.
2 Set out the ends in pairs (see separate drawing showing enlarged detail of end), taking the correct length and bevels from the full-size elevation.
3 Cut the tenons and complete the shaping of the ends.
4 Set out the top. Square over a line 125mm (5in) from the ends to locate the mortises and with a bevel mark out the splay of the legs on the edge. Square over on the underside of the top. This locates the mortises and gives correct splay.
5 Mark a centre line on the ends and top. Position the ends and mark round the tenons with a marking knife or scriber to give correct mortise dimensions. Set a mortise gauge to the lines already made and transfer these to the top surface. Remember to give the ends an identification mark.
6 Bore a 16mm (⅝in) hole in the centre of the mortise and clean up to the lines with a firmer chisel. Make the housing between the mortises.
7 Assemble ends to top, fitting as necessary. Check for correct splay.
8 Set out the side rails, by turning the form upside down, and cramping them temporarily in position. Mark the housing positions from each side of ends with a marking knife.
9 Gauge depth of housing. Saw shoulders and remove waste. Complete shaping of rails, and work decorative chamfers.
10 Bore for pellets and make screw holes in side rails. Clean up and polish. See figure 2 for details of screwing and pelleting.
11 Make the diagonal saw kerfs in the tenons to receive the wedges. Figure 1 shows an alternative method of wedging. Clean up the ends, mask joints and polish.
12 Round the corners of the top, work chamfers and bore for the screws. Work chamfers on the form ends and taper inside of ends to finish 20mm (¾in) at the floor line. Clean up for polishing, masking the joints as necessary.
13 Cut wedges and make pellets. Prepare for gluing up.
14 Glue up and screw sides to ends. Wedge up the top, gluing in the wedges, and cramp to side rails. Test rail for straightness and drive in screws.
15 Glue in the pellets and leave to dry.
16 Flush off wedges, clean up and complete polishing.

Suggested Material

Columbian pine.

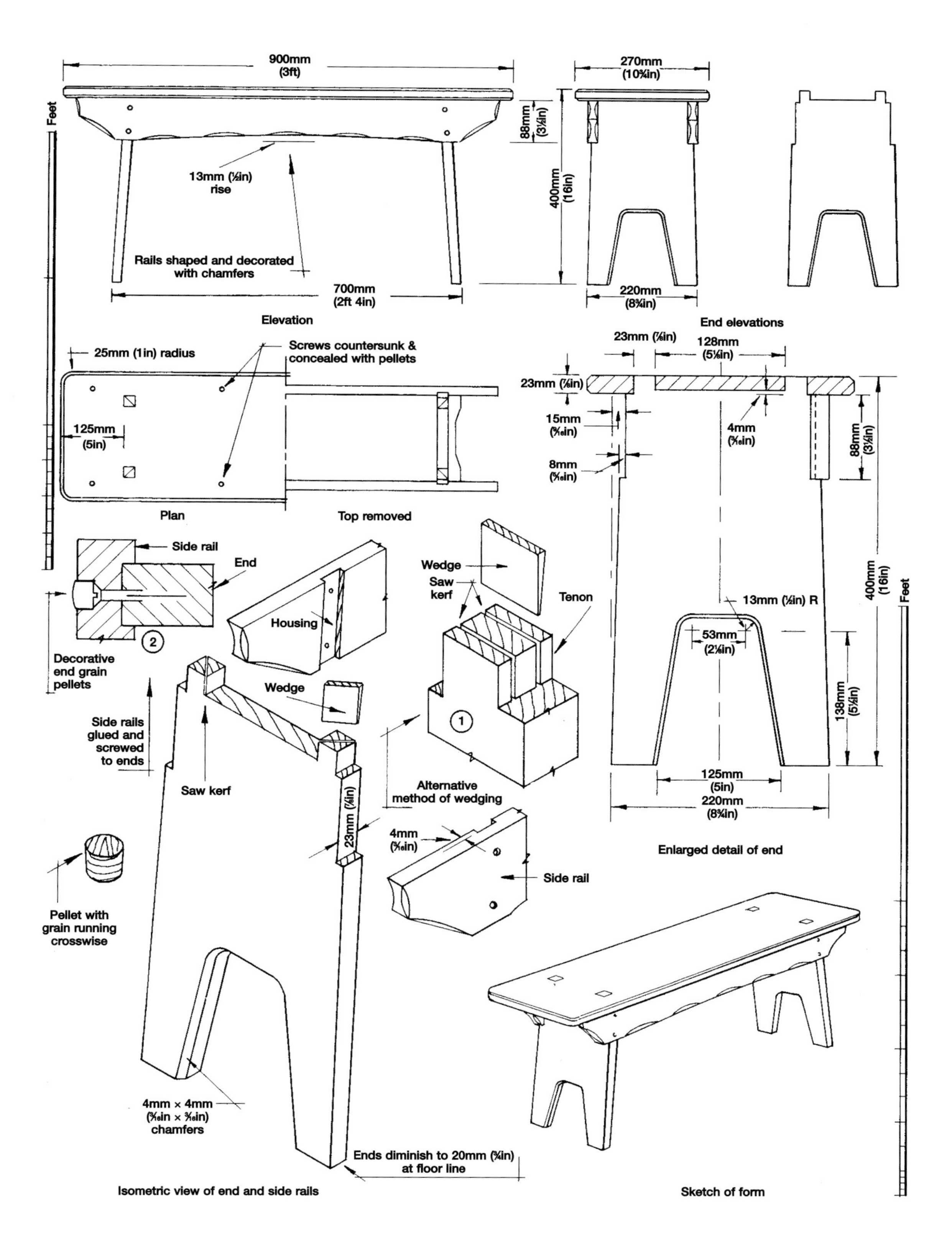

900mm
(3ft)
270mm
(10¾in)
Feet
88mm
(3½in)
400mm
(16in)
13mm (½in)
rise
Rails shaped and decorated
with chamfers
700mm
(2ft 4in)
220mm
(8¾in)
Elevation
End elevations
25mm (1in) radius
Screws countersunk &
concealed with pellets
125mm
(5in)
Plan
Top removed
23mm (⅞in)
128mm
(5⅛in)
23mm (⅞in)
15mm
(⅝in)
4mm
(3/16in)
8mm
(5/16in)
88mm
(3½in)
400mm
(16in)
Feet
13mm (½in) R
53mm
(2⅛in)
138mm
(5½in)
125mm
(5in)
220mm
(8¾in)
Enlarged detail of end
Side rail
End
2
Decorative
end grain
pellets
Housing
Wedge
Saw
kerf
Tenon
Wedge
1
Side rails
glued and
screwed
to ends
Saw kerf
23mm (⅞in)
Alternative
method of wedging
4mm
(3/16in)
Side rail
Pellet with
grain running
crosswise
4mm × 4mm
(3/16in × 3/16in)
chamfers
Ends diminish to 20mm (¾in)
at floor line
Isometric view of end and side rails
Sketch of form

Cutting list

Description	Length	Width	Thickness
2 legs	425mm (1ft 5in)	220mm (8¾in)	23mm (⅞in)
2 side rails	875mm (2ft 11in)	88mm (3½in)	20mm (¾in)
1 top	925mm (3ft 1in)	270mm (10¾in)	23mm (⅞in)

Tools not in Basic Kit

Router, wood or metal – for finishing housings to depth.

Gallows Bracket Table

This space-saving table is particularly suitable for the kitchen or a small dining recess. The table incorporates many interesting features, and is economical in the use of timber. The frame containing the gallows brackets is lap dovetailed at the ends. The back rails are dovetailed into the ends, and provide good fixing facilities. The 23mm (7/8in) diameter bracket pivots are worked on the stile (see enlarged details of joints). The brackets provide a good exercise in setting-out techniques, and give the student an opportunity to make the oblique tenon often used in the art of carpentry and joinery. The top is made up of multi-ply or laminboard and is lipped. It looks well if covered in Formica. A separate detail shows an alternative treatment for the bottom corners.

Method

1. Prepare full-size working drawings (see note on page 101).
2. Prepare the material.
3. Set out the frame and make the lap dovetail joints (see page 144).
4. Mark out the centres for the bracket pins, and bore the 23mm (7/8in) diameter holes.
5. Set out the vertical and horizontal members of the gallows brackets, noting the taper. Set the mortise gauge to a 8mm (5/16in) mortise chisel, gauge the mortises and tenons and make the joints. Make the wedges when cutting out the tenon haunchings. Assemble joints, fitting as necessary.
6. To mark out the brace, place bracket on the full-size drawing and mark off the brace position. Lay the brace in the correct position on the vertical and horizontal members and carefully mark out the length. Mark on a 6mm (1/4in) to give the shoulder length and position of abutment (see enlarged details of joints): note the abutment is square off the edge of the brace.
7. Gauge the oblique mortises and tenons. Make the oblique tenons, finishing accurately to the cut lines with shoulder and block planes.
8. Locate the brace on the horizontal and vertical members, and mark out the shoulder and tenon angles. Cut the mortises and remove the waste to form the brace seating.
9. Assemble brackets complete with brace, fitting as necessary.
10. Clean up all inner surfaces.
11. Glue up brackets and wedge horizontal members, and leave to dry. The brace could be pinned with 4mm (3/16in) dowel pins. Flush all joints and clean up.
12. Cut stiles to the correct length, and remove portion of horn to form pins.
13. Round the back edge of the stiles and complete the pins. Bore a 23mm (7/8in) hole in a spare block of wood and fit the pins.
14. Clean up all inner surfaces of the frame. Assemble the table complete with brackets and test, fitting as necessary.
15. Glue up the frame with the brackets in position. Check for square and alignment and leave to dry.
16. Mark out back rails and cut the dovetails, bevel the top of the bottom rail.
17. Fit the back rails into the frame, screw and glue in position. Stiffen up the frame with 3 screws through the top and the bottom into the back rails. Flush all joints and clean up.

18 Mark out the laminboard and cut to size. Plough for lipping and glue on the Formica.
19 Make, fit, and glue lipping to flap.
20 Fit butts to flap. Locate on frame and complete hanging.
21 Fix to the wall through the back rails.
22 Finish. Painted. Lippings to flap left natural and wax polished.

Suggested Material

Selected pine, for a painted finish.

Cutting list

Description	Length	Width	Thickness
1 top	775mm (2ft 7in)	75mm (3in)	23mm (⅞in)
1 bottom	775mm (2ft 7in)	75mm (3in)	23mm (⅞in)
2 ends	525mm (1ft 9in)	75mm (3in)	23mm (⅞in)
2 back rails	750mm (2ft 6in)	38mm (1½in)	20mm (¾in)
Gallows brackets			
2 stiles	500mm (1ft 8in)	45mm (1¾in)	23mm (⅞in)
2 top rails	400mm (1ft 4in)	45mm (1¾in)	23mm (⅞in)
2 braces	475mm (1ft 7in)	38mm (1½in)	23mm (⅞in)
1 top laminboard	750mm (2ft 6in)	450mm (18in)	20mm (¾in)
2 lippings beech	775mm (2ft 7in)	23mm (⅞in)	16mm (⅝in)
2 lippings beech	475mm (1ft 7in)	23mm (⅞in)	16mm (⅝in)
1 pair 63mm (2½in) solid brass butts			

Tools not in Basic Kit

Shoulder plane – for cleaning up bracket and rail shoulders.
Block plane – for cleaning up end of brace.
Plough – for making grooves for lippings.
23mm (⅞in) Twist or Forstner bit – for boring holes for pins.

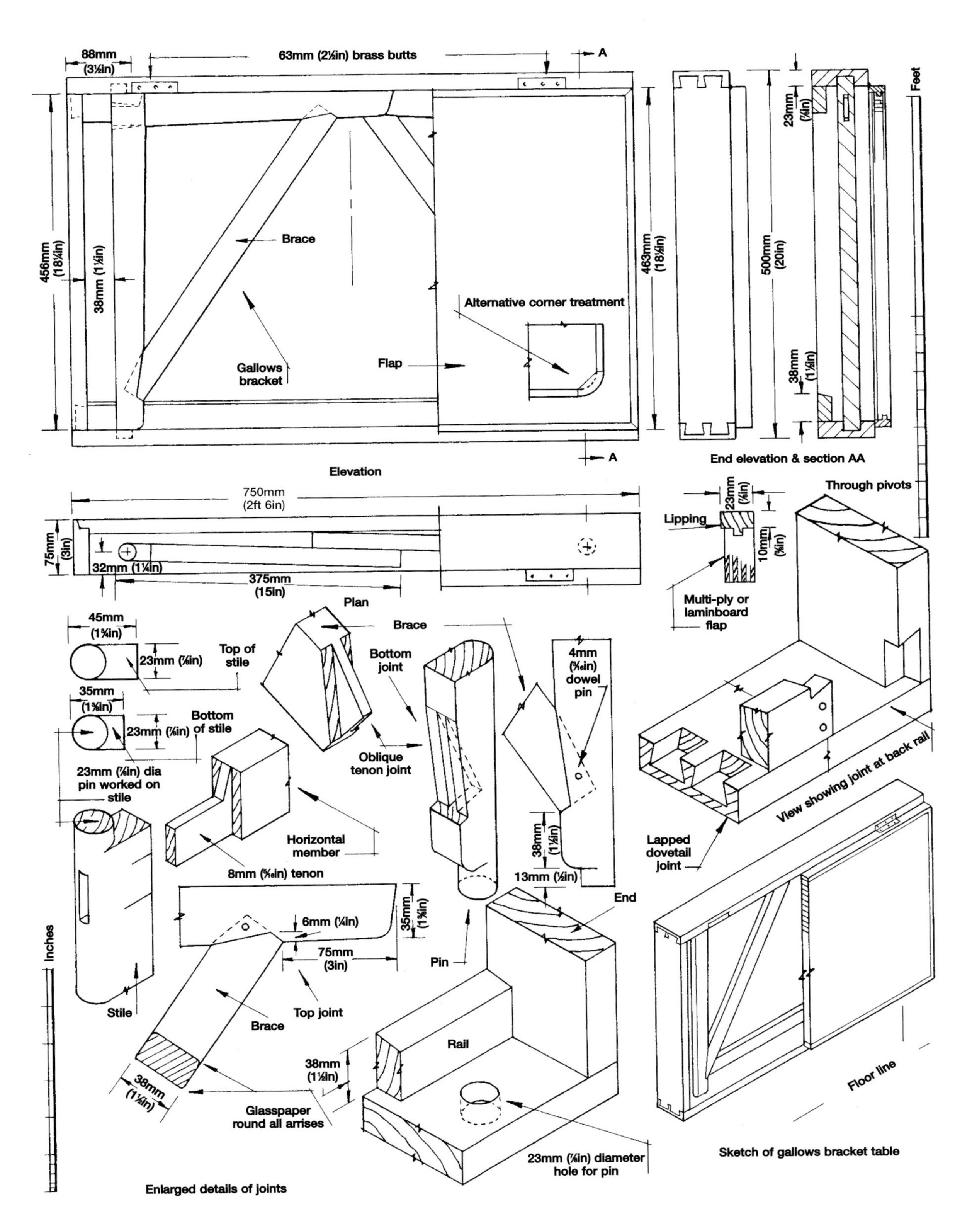

88mm
(3½in)
63mm (2½in) brass butts
A
456mm
(18¼in)
38mm (1½in)
Brace
Alternative corner treatment
Gallows
bracket
Flap
463mm
(18½in)
500mm
(20in)
23mm
(⅞in)
38mm
(1½in)
Feet
A
Elevation
End elevation & section AA
750mm
(2ft 6in)
75mm
(3in)
32mm (1¼in)
375mm
(15in)
Plan
23mm
(⅞in)
Through pivots
Lipping
10mm
(⅜in)
Multi-ply or
laminboard
flap
45mm
(1¾in)
23mm (⅞in)
Top of
stile
35mm
(1⅜in)
23mm (⅞in)
Bottom
of stile
23mm (⅞in) dia
pin worked on
stile
Brace
Bottom
joint
Oblique
tenon joint
4mm
(³⁄₁₆in)
dowel
pin
Horizontal
member
8mm (⁵⁄₁₆in) tenon
38mm
(1½in)
13mm (½in)
End
View showing joint at back rail
Lapped
dovetail
joint
6mm (¼in)
35mm
(1⅜in)
75mm
(3in)
Pin
Inches
Stile
Brace
Top joint
Rail
38mm
(1½in)
38mm
(1½in)
Glasspaper
round all arrises
23mm (⅞in) diameter
hole for pin
Floor line
Sketch of gallows bracket table
Enlarged details of joints

Garden Gate

The designing and construction of gates offers an opportunity for the young woodworker to experiment and develop new designs. Balsa models are invaluable in this development.

The main constructional feature is a braced frame – to support the gate the lower end of the brace should be near the hanging stile – with a thinner bottom rail. The thin rail accommodates the vertical bars which are fixed to the face. The application of a bare-faced tenon is clearly shown in the isometric view of gate construction. The tenons are taken through the stiles and draw-pinned. This is preferable to wedging for gate construction, as the effect of varying weather conditions – alternate expansion and shrinkage – may cause wedges to work loose. Use waterproof glue when gluing up.

Method

1. Prepare the material. For oak select and match the grain.
2. Set out the stiles in pairs.
3. Set out the rails, including the mortise positions in the top rail.
4. Set the mortise gauge to a 13mm (½in) mortise chisel and gauge the mortises and tenons. Re-adjust the gauge and gauge the 8mm (5/16in) mortises in top rail.
5. Cut the mortises and tenons and assemble the gate, fitting as necessary.
6. Fitting the brace: for this particular design the brace finishes against the stile and bottom rail. It can also be moved 25–50mm (1–2in) away from the hanging stile, according to the width of the gate. Taper the brace and place in the correct position on the gate, checking for correct hand, and set out shoulder and mortise positions.
7. Cut brace to length and make the stub tenons.
8. Mortise top rail to take brace. Mortise stile and bottom rail to take stub tenons of brace. To provide a good bearing surface carefully make the mortises fit the tenons. The bottom rail is weathered – a sloping surface to shed the water – and is notched to receive the brace.
9. *Draw-pinning:* bore the 10mm (⅜in) holes in the stiles, keeping the twist bit upright and boring from both sides to prevent splitting. Assemble the gate with brace and fit as necessary. Lightly cramp and square up. Place a twist bit in the holes and give half a turn to locate a centre on the tenons. Remove the stiles and bore through the tenons, adjusting the centre so as to make the hole 1.6mm–3mm (1/16in–⅛in) nearer to the shoulder. When the pin is driven in it draws the stile tight up to the rail shoulders.
10. Make weathering on top rail. Shape decorative horns on stiles, work all chamfers and clean up all inner surfaces.
11. Make pins, which should be split to avoid short grain, and taper the ends.
12. Glue and cramp up. Test for square and alignment and drive in pins. Flush all joints when dry.
13. Gauge and cut tenons on vertical bars. Mark out position on bottom rail, fit and align bars.
14. Bevel bars and work shape on ends. Glue bars in position, and nail up with 56mm (2¼in) oval brads. Punch nails in and turn over on the back.

    Note: if making the gate in oak, secure the bars by screwing through the bottom rail and brace with brass screws.

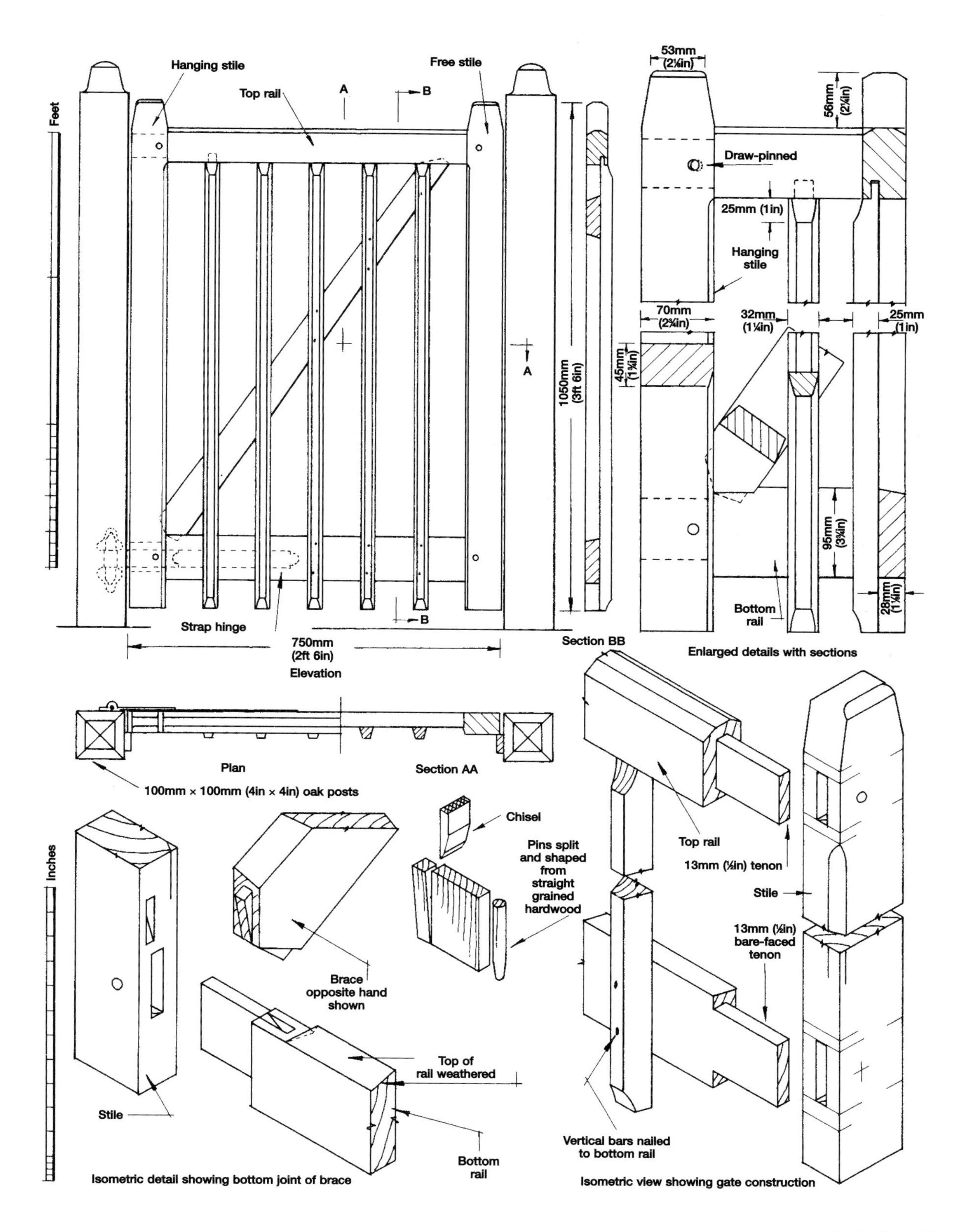

Feet
Hanging stile
Top rail
A
B
Free stile
1050mm
(3ft 6in)
A
Strap hinge
B
750mm
(2ft 6in)
Elevation
Section BB
53mm
(2⅛in)
56mm
(2¼in)
Draw-pinned
25mm (1in)
Hanging
stile
70mm
(2¾in)
32mm
(1¼in)
25mm
(1in)
45mm
(1¾in)
95mm
(3¾in)
28mm
(1⅛in)
Bottom
rail
Enlarged details with sections
Plan
Section AA
100mm × 100mm (4in × 4in) oak posts
Inches
Chisel
Pins split
and shaped
from
straight
grained
hardwood
Brace
opposite hand
shown
Top of
rail weathered
Stile
Bottom
rail
Isometric detail showing bottom joint of brace
Top rail
13mm (½in) tenon
Stile
13mm (½in)
bare-faced
tenon
Vertical bars nailed
to bottom rail
Isometric view showing gate construction

15 Shoot outside edges of gate and prepare for painting. Gate stops on the post are optional.

16 Shape top of posts, cut a batten 10mm (⅜in) wider than the gate and use for testing for correct width when digging holes and plumbing posts.

17 *Finish:* prepare gate for painting. Stop up all holes and prime. Finish colour as desired.

Finish for oak: in outside conditions oak develops a charming silver-grey colour. Owing to the tannic acid present in oak, care must be taken in fastening ironwork. All ironwork should be painted before fixing. Always use brass or galvanised screws.

Suggested Material

Selected pine or oak.

Cutting list

Description	Length	Width	Thickness
2 stiles	1075mm (3ft 7in)	70mm (2¾in)	45mm (1¾in)
1 top rail	763mm (2ft 6½in)	70mm (2¾in)	45mm (1¾in)
1 bottom rail	763mm (2ft 6½in)	95mm (3¾in)	28mm (1⅛in)
1 brace	975mm (3ft 3in)	70mm (2¾in)	28mm (1⅛in)
5 bars	950mm (3ft 2in)	32mm (1¼in)	25mm (1in)
1 for pins	75mm (3in)	50mm (2in)	11mm (7/16in)
2 gate posts oak	1800mm (6ft)	100mm (4in)	100mm (4in)
2 gate stops	1050mm (3ft 6in)	38mm (1½in)	13mm (½in)

1 pair 375mm (15in) strap hinges
1 gate catch as required

Tools not in Basic Kit

Shoulder plane – for cleaning up rail and brace shoulders.

Household Steps

A strong, well-made pair of steps is indispensable for the home decorator. As an exercise in craftwork it incorporates many interesting features, setting out, working to bevels, housing and dowelling. Craft terms which are used in joinery, such as strings, treads, nosings, rise, going, are given. Several methods of securing treads are shown. If simply housed and nailed, reinforce with 4mm (3/16in) diameter tie rods at alternate treads.

Method

1 Prepare material, select and match the grain. The safety factor is important and all material should be carefully examined and rejected if there are any signs of short grain.

2 Set out the strings in pairs. Set bevel and mark out the housings for the treads (see separate drawing illustrating the application of bevels) and work the 6mm (1/4in) bead or chamfer on the edge.

3 Carefully saw the shoulders of the housings. A saw kerf below the gauge line will seriously weaken the steps. Chisel out the housings, finishing with a router.

4 Cut strings to length, checking bevels, and make tongue on top.

5 *Marking out the treads:* lay out the strings – 450mm (18in) at the bottom and 275mm (11in) at the top – and take measurements for the upper edges of the bottom and top treads respectively. Cramp up the four treads and mark out a centre line. Mark out the lengths of the top and bottom treads (see detail of setting out) and apply straight edge to make line AB. This gives the correct length of the upper edge of each tread. Set bevel and mark edges of tread. Cut treads to length and clean up ends.

   Note: if through tenons are preferred make allowances for the extra length.

6 Set out the top piece and make housings to receive strings. Make stopped groove to receive back piece.

7 Assemble strings, treads and top piece, fitting as necessary. Test diagonally for accuracy.

8 Clean up all inner surfaces, including bead or chamfer edge and make nosings on tread.

9 Glue up complete with top piece and wedge or dowel, according to type of joint used.

10 Set out the back framing (see the elevation giving the true shape of the hinged back). Lay the stiles on the steps in their relative positions and locate top and bottom rails. Mark out one stile, and then pair up the opposite hand. Replace the stiles, and mark out the shoulder lengths of rails, making 3mm (1/8in) allowance for cleaning off. Set a bevel and make a cut line for the shoulders.

11 Gauge for 6mm (1/4in) mortises and tenons.

12 Cut mortises and tenons. Assemble frame, adjusting as necessary.

13 Work chamfers and clean up inner surfaces.

14 Glue up – owing to the taper on the back framing use tapered blocks with the sash cramps – and bore holes for the pins. Glue in pins and leave to dry.

15 Make tongue on back piece and shape. Glue and screw to strings and top.

16 Clean up, flushing dowels or wedges, and rounding front and back edges of strings. Note alternative finish to tread nosing.
17 Flush all joints on back framing and remove horns. Shoot edges and fit frame to back piece ready for hinging. Screw on strap hinges. Make 3mm (⅛in) chamfer all round the bottom of the strings and back framing.
18 Bore holes for sash cord, stretch the cord before fixing and knot firmly.
19 *Finish:* painted or varnished.

Suggested Material

Selected pine.

Cutting list

Description	Length	Width	Thickness
2 strings	1200mm (4ft)	88mm (3½in)	22mm (13⁄16in)
1 for 4 treads	1500mm (5ft)	113mm (4¼in)	22mm (13⁄16in)
1 top	375mm (1ft 3in)	145mm (5¾in)	22mm (13⁄16in)
1 back piece	350mm (1ft 2in)	138mm (5½in)	22mm (13⁄16in)
2 stiles	1050mm (3ft 6in)	63mm (2½in)	22mm (13⁄16in)
1 for 2 rails	700mm (2ft 4in)	56mm (2¼in)	22mm (13⁄16in)
1 top rail	275mm (11in)	100mm (4in)	22mm (13⁄16in)
1 pair of 100mm (4in)	strap hinges		
1 piece	300mm (1ft)	8mm (5⁄16in) diameter dowel rod for back framing	
sash cord	1200mm (4ft)		

Tools not in Basic Kit

Shoulder plane – for cleaning up rail shoulders.

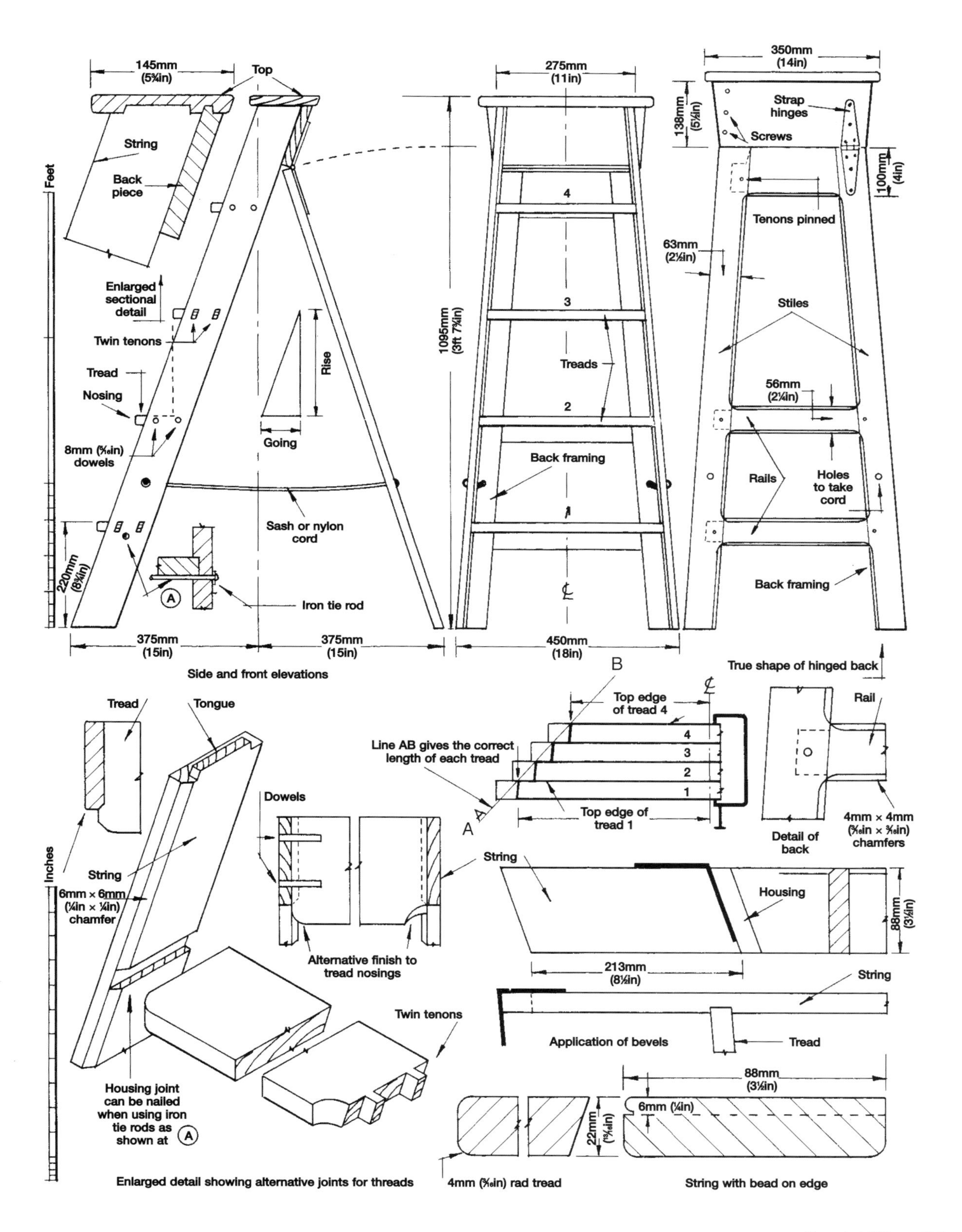
145mm
(5¾in)
Top
String
Back piece
Feet
Enlarged sectional detail
Twin tenons
Tread
Nosing
8mm (⁵⁄₁₆in) dowels
220mm (8¾in)
A
Rise
Going
Sash or nylon cord
Iron tie rod
375mm
(15in)
375mm
(15in)
275mm
(11in)
1095mm
(3ft 7⅛in)
4
3
2
1
Treads
Back framing
450mm
(18in)
350mm
(14in)
138mm
(5½in)
Strap hinges
Screws
100mm
(4in)
Tenons pinned
63mm
(2½in)
Stiles
56mm
(2¼in)
Rails
Holes to take cord
Back framing
True shape of hinged back
Side and front elevations
Tread
Tongue
Inches
String
6mm × 6mm
(¼in × ¼in)
chamfer
Housing joint can be nailed when using iron tie rods as shown at A
Dowels
Alternative finish to tread nosings
Twin tenons
Enlarged detail showing alternative joints for threads
B
A
Top edge of tread 4
Line AB gives the correct length of each tread
Top edge of tread 1
Rail
Detail of back
4mm × 4mm
(⁵⁄₃₂in × ⁵⁄₃₂in)
chamfers
String
Housing
88mm
(3½in)
213mm
(8½in)
String
Application of bevels
Tread
88mm
(3½in)
6mm (¼in)
22mm
(⅞in)
4mm (⁵⁄₃₂in) rad tread
String with bead on edge

Cabinet with Table Flap

This design illustrates a compact cabinet with good shelf accommodation. It is fitted with a hinged table flap which is supported by a leg that folds into the door when not in use. The doors and top are faced with Formica. The cabinet gives the student a chance to gain experience in the use of Formica, laminboard or blockboard, and in the making of a panelled back. It also provides good practice in the setting out and making of doors. A painted finish is suggested, but the top lipping and mouldings to doors, if made in beech, could be left in natural colour for contrast. The inside of the cabinet is to be polished.

Method

1. Make full-size sectional drawings of the plan and elevation. These drawings are used as rods when setting out.
2. Prepare material for the carcase. Arrange for the core of the laminboard to run vertically.
3. Set out ends and bottom; finish to size and plough grooves for lipping.
4. Set out back and front top rails and glue on the bracket pieces: these stiffen up the carcase considerably and are economical in the use of timber.
5. Make lipping for ends and front edge of bottom, fit and glue in, flush off when dry.
6. Set out and cut the dovetails on the top rails.
7. Rebate the ends to take the panelled back. Mark out and cut the dovetail pins to receive the top rails.

   Note: the back rail finishes flush with the rebate, and the front rail is set back to accommodate the doors.
8. Make the housings in the ends and fit the bottom. Make grooves to receive the plinth. Glue and screw on the fillet to carcase ends.
9. Set out and bore the holes for the adjustable shelves. Cut plinth to length, and make tongues to fit grooves.
10. Work chamfers on bottom and top ends. Clean up inner surfaces, mask joints and polish.
11. Glue up the carcase, screw bottom to fillets. Test for square and alignment. Glue up plinth, locate with 'G' cramps and rub in glue blocks at the back. Leave to dry.
12. Prepare material for the panelled back. Set out the stiles in pairs, off the rod, and mark out the muntins. Set out the bottom and top rails in pairs.
13. Cut the mortises and tenons and work grooves for the panels before removing tenon cheeks.
14. Assemble framing, fitting as necessary. Mark out and cut panels to size, remove all sharp edges and fit panels.
15. Clean up panels and inner edges of framing and polish inside surfaces. Glue up framing.
16. Prepare material for the doors. Set out the stiles in pairs, off the rod, and make allowances for the rebate at the meeting stiles (see illustrations).
17. Set out in pairs the top and bottom rails. Cut the mortises and tenons.
18. Make grooves for panels in one door only. Assemble doors, fitting as necessary.
19. Cut multi-ply panel to size, make rebate for planted moulding and glue on Formica. Fit panel in door.

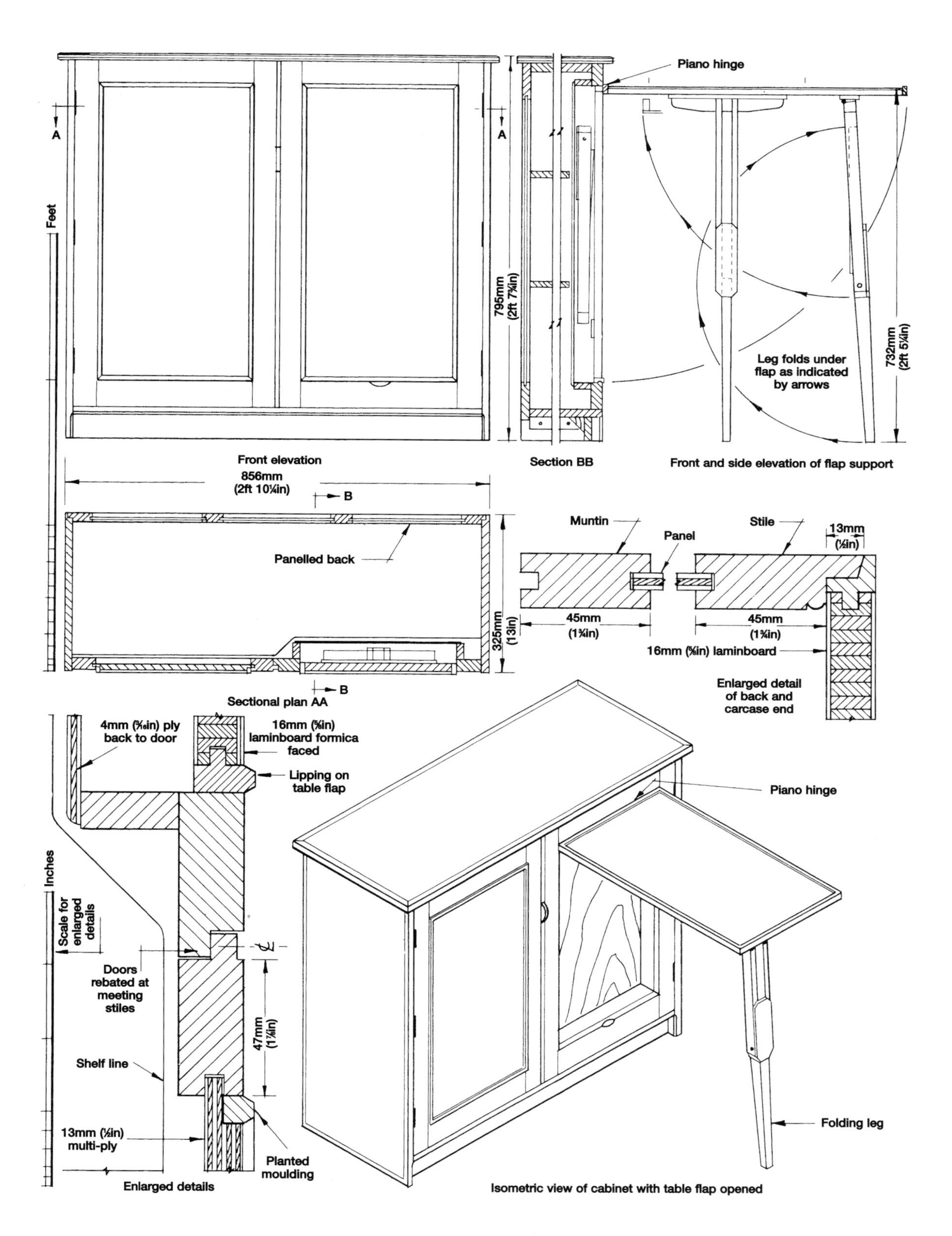

Piano hinge
A
A
Feet
795mm
(2ft 7¼in)
Leg folds under
flap as indicated
by arrows
732mm
(2ft 5¼in)
Front elevation
Section BB
Front and side elevation of flap support
856mm
(2ft 10¼in)
B
Muntin
Stile
Panel
13mm
(½in)
Panelled back
45mm
(1¾in)
45mm
(1¾in)
325mm
(13in)
16mm (⅝in) laminboard
B
Enlarged detail
of back and
carcase end
Sectional plan AA
4mm (⅙in) ply
back to door
16mm (⅝in)
laminboard formica
faced
Lipping on
table flap
Piano hinge
Inches
Scale for
enlarged
details
Doors
rebated at
meeting
stiles
47mm
(1⅞in)
Shelf line
13mm (½in)
multi-ply
Planted
moulding
Folding leg
Enlarged details
Isometric view of cabinet with table flap opened

20 Clean up inner surfaces, polish as necessary, and glue up doors. Test for square and alignment. Mitre, fit and glue in planted moulding. Rebate meeting stiles.
21 Make through dovetail frame behind flap door, dowel and glue on to back of door.
22 Prepare 16mm (5/8in) laminboard for flap. Glue on Formica and fit lippings.
23 Glue on plywood back to flap door.
24 Cut top to length, and plough for lipping. Glue on Formica and fit lipping.
25 Flush all joints on back panelling. Remove horns and fit to carcase with brass cups and screws.
26 Fix top through top rails.
27 Prepare material for leg. Set out bridle joints and leg centre.
28 Make bridle joints. Round top of bottom portion of leg, and make the notch to receive locking piece. Bore hole for 4mm (3/16in) bolt, and assemble leg, fitting as necessary.
29 Glue up complete with locking piece.
30 Make finger grip on bottom rail and portion of flap. Fit flap – a close fit is essential – and hinge it to the door frame.
31 Glue packing piece under flap, and bevel to suit splay of leg. Fit back flaps to piece and complete hinging of the table flap.
32 Fit butts and hang doors. A small finger grip is dovetailed into the edge of the door that opens first.
33 Mark out and cut adjustable shelving. Clean up and polish. Fit supports.
34 *Finish:* painted, with primer and hard gloss. Trim: left in natural colour.

Suggested Material

Selected pine with beech lippings to top and doors.

Cutting list

Description	Length	Width	Thickness
Carcase			
2 sides laminboard	775mm (2ft 7in)	300mm (12in)	16mm (5/8in)
1 bottom laminboard	850mm (2ft 10in)	288mm (11½in)	16mm (5/8in)
1 top laminboard	875mm (2ft 11in)	350mm (14in)	16mm (5/8in)
2 top rails	850mm (2ft 10in)	63mm (2½in)	20mm (¾in)
1 for 4 brackets	600mm (2ft)	75mm (3in)	20mm (¾in)
1 plinth	850mm (2ft 10in)	50mm (2in)	16mm (5/8in)
2 fillets beech	300mm (1ft)	25mm (1in)	25mm (1in)
4 lippings, ends beech	788mm (2ft 7½in)	20mm (¾in)	20mm (¾in)
2 lippings, ends beech	338mm (1ft 1½in)	20mm (¾in)	20mm (¾in)
1 lipping, bottom beech	850mm (2ft 10in)	20mm (¾in)	20mm (¾in)
Panelled back			
2 stiles	775mm (2ft 7in)	56mm (2¼in)	20mm (¾in)
2 for bottom and top rails	825mm (2ft 9in)	75mm (3in)	20mm (¾in)
2 muntins	700mm (2ft 4in)	45mm (1¾in)	20mm (¾in)
3 panels plywood	600mm (2ft)	238mm (9½in)	6mm (¼in)

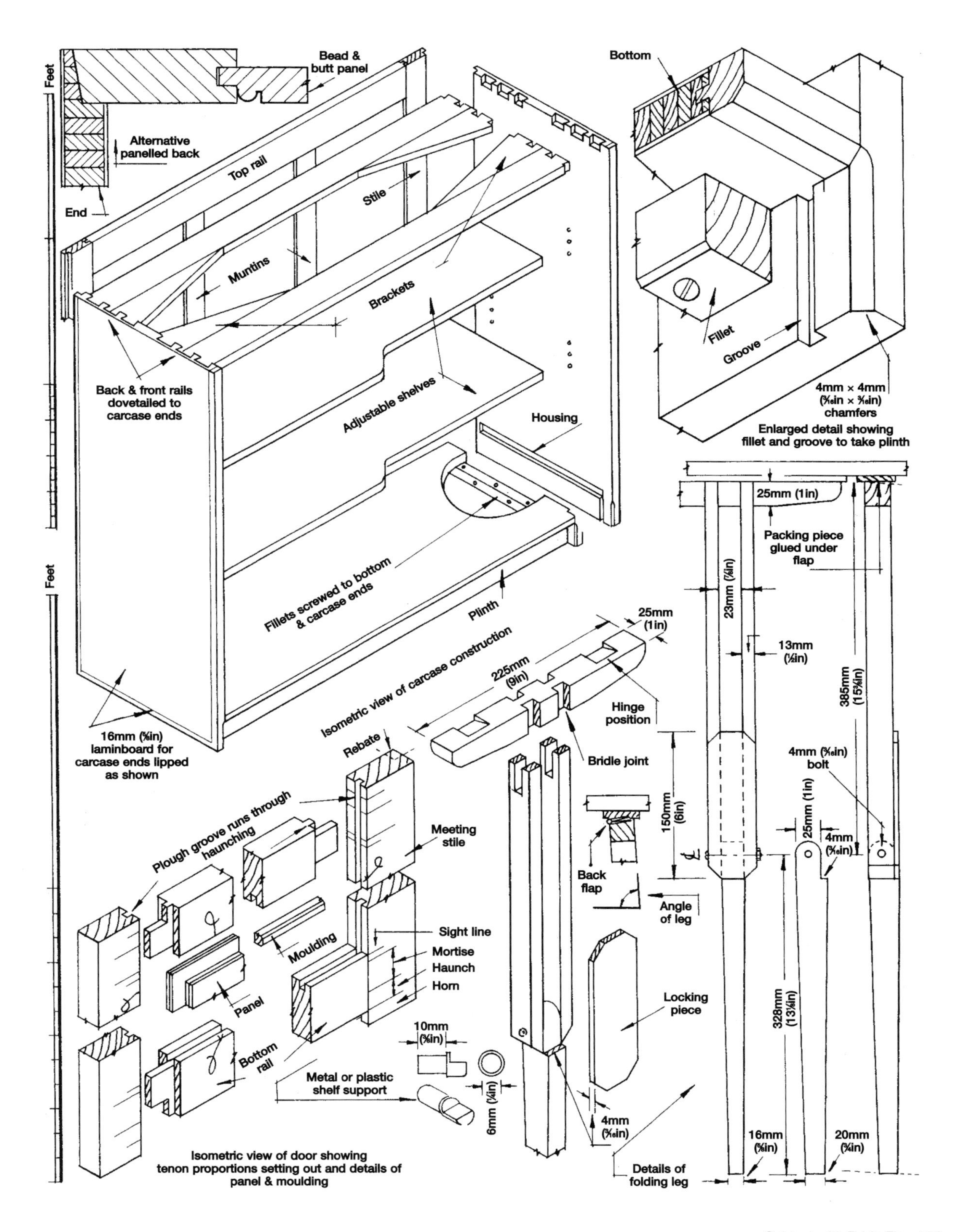

Bead &
butt panel
Alternative
panelled back
End
Feet
Top rail
Stile
Muntins
Brackets
Back & front rails
dovetailed to
carcase ends
Adjustable shelves
Housing
Fillets screwed to bottom
& carcase ends
Plinth
Isometric view of carcase construction
16mm (⅝in)
laminboard for
carcase ends lipped
as shown
Bottom
Fillet
Groove
4mm × 4mm
(³⁄₁₆in × ³⁄₁₆in)
chamfers
Enlarged detail showing
fillet and groove to take plinth
25mm (1in)
Packing piece
glued under
flap
23mm (⅞in)
13mm
(½in)
385mm
(15⅛in)
225mm
(9in)
25mm
(1in)
Hinge
position
Bridle joint
150mm
(6in)
4mm (³⁄₁₆in)
bolt
25mm (1in)
4mm
(³⁄₁₆in)
Back
flap
Angle
of leg
Rebate
Plough groove runs through
haunching
Meeting
stile
Sight line
Mortise
Haunch
Horn
Moulding
Panel
Bottom
rail
Locking
piece
328mm
(13⅛in)
10mm
(⅜in)
Metal or plastic
shelf support
6mm (¼in)
4mm
(³⁄₁₆in)
16mm
(⅝in)
20mm
(¾in)
Isometric view of door showing
tenon proportions setting out and details of
panel & moulding
Details of
folding leg

Description	Length	Width	Thickness
Doors			
2 stiles, meeting	750mm (2ft 6in)	56mm (2¼in)	23mm (⅞in)
2 stiles	750mm (2ft 6in)	50mm (2in)	23mm (⅞in)
2 bottom rails	400mm (1ft 4in)	56mm (2¼in)	23mm (⅞in)
2 top rails	400mm (1ft 4in)	50mm (2in)	23mm (⅞in)
1 panel plywood	638mm (2ft 1½in)	331mm (13¼in)	13mm (½in)
1 panel laminboard	600mm (2ft)	300mm (12in)	16mm (⅝in)
2 pieces Formica	600mm (2ft)	300mm (12in)	
2 lippings, flap, beech	950mm (3ft 2in)	23mm (⅞in)	16mm (⅝in)
2 mouldings beech	950mm (3ft 2in)	11mm (7/16in)	10mm (⅜in)
2 lippings for top	1225mm (4ft 1in)	20mm (¾in)	20mm (¾in)
1 piece for glue blocks	225mm (9in)	45mm (1¾in)	45mm (1¾in)
Framing for well of door			
2 pieces	1000mm (3ft 4in)	34mm (1 5/16in)	13mm (½in)
1 back plywood	650mm (2ft 2in)	350mm (14in)	4mm (3/16in)
Folding leg			
1 bottom piece beech	350mm (1ft 2in)	32mm (1¼in)	23mm (⅞in)
2 top portions beech	425mm (1ft 5in)	25mm (1in)	13mm (½in)
1 top rail beech	250mm (10in)	25mm (1in)	25mm (1in)
1 locking piece beech	175mm (7in)	50mm (2in)	6mm (¼in)
1 top packing piece beech	250mm (10in)	38mm (1½in)	6mm (¼in)
2 shelves plywood	825mm (2ft 9in)	275mm (11in)	13mm (½in)

1 piece of piano hinge 313mm (12½in) long
1 pair of 25mm (1in) back flaps, solid brass
1 56mm (2¼in) round head 4mm (3/16in) metal thread bolt
fittings for adjustable shelves as required

A Small Workshop

A workshop covered in tempered hardboard has much to commend it, particularly when the interior is also clad with hardboard. It gives great rigidity and has good insulating qualities. This principle can be used for larger workshops, in which case the size and number of studs and rafters should be increased. For example use 75mm × 50mm (3in × 2in) studs and rafters for a workshop 3600mm × 2700mm (12ft × 9ft). The workshop consists of four main frames, which are bolted together. The ridge is dovetailed into the gable ends, and the rafters are closed with a collar. The roof is made up of two pieces of framing covered in hardboard. These are simply screwed – from the inside – to the rafters and gable ends. Conventional types of weatherboarding could be used for exterior cladding, with hardboard on the interior.

The workshop stands on 150mm × 100mm (6in × 4in) concrete lintels, and is easily erected or dismantled. Lintels can be purchased ready-made or boxed up and made on the site, in which case reinforce with two 13mm (½in) diameter rods running almost the full length of the box. The student should take note of the various terms used in building, such as lintel, damp proof course, floor joist, sill, plate, stud, post, brace, ridge, rafter, collar, bird's-mouth, finial, barge board and gable.

Before commencing work on the framing, level off site and lay lintels in position.

Method

1. Set out front and back frames. Pair up top plates and sills and mark out position for studs and posts. Make allowances for the window frame. Set out posts, studs, and horizontal rails. Gauge and cut the bridle and mortise and tenon joints. Make the notched joints below the window frame aperture.
2. Assemble frames, adjusting as necessary. Resin glue all joints and nail up the frames (see separate drawing showing nailing technique) and make diagonal test for squareness.
3. Position braces and mark out angles. Cut to size, fit and skew nail to framing.
4. *Setting out frames and gables:* for end frames proceed as for front and back. Note arrangements of the studs at the door aperture and the equal spacing of same at the opposite end.
5. Set out pitch of gable end. Make the halving joints and stub tenons. Mark out the plywood gussets and cut out sockets to take dovetailed ridge. Assemble gables to the end frames, adjusting as necessary. Glue and screw gables to end framing and test for alignment.
6. Assemble the complete framing on the prepared site. 'G' cramp the posts together, mark out and bore the 10mm (⅜in) holes in readiness for bolting up.
7. Preparation of exterior cladding. To prevent the hardboard buckling after fixing, it is necessary to thoroughly wet the inner surface – mesh side – with clean water and leave flat for approximately 20 hours.
8. Give all the framing a coat of clear preservative.
9. Before fixing the hardboard, give some thought as to the most economical method of cutting. Butt joints are unavoidable. When covered with

32mm × 13mm (1¼in × ½in) battens, which can be chamfered or rounded on their edges, they look attractive.

10 Mark out the hardboard and cut to fit. Nail to framing with 25mm (1in) sherardised pins at 63mm (2½in) centres, punching the heads slightly below the surface.

11 Clean up outside edges and apertures, and prepare for erecting. Bore through the hardboard at the bolt holes. Lay strips of roofing felt along the lintels for a damp proof course. Assemble framing and bolt up using washers on the inside.

12 Position and square up framing on the concrete lintels. The weight of the workshop plus the contents is adequate for general stability. In an area subjected to strong winds or gales it is advisable to secure each corner of the workshop to the lintels. This is easily achieved by simply bending 25mm × 3mm (1in × ⅛in) metal strips under the lintels and screwing to the inside of the framing.

13 Cut the ridge to length and dovetail to gable ends. Bevel the top edge of ridge to suit the gables.

14 Mark out the rafters, cut the bird's-mouth, and fit to plate and ridge.

15 Mark out the collar position on the rafters. Cut collar to length, make dovetail halving joint and assemble, fitting as necessary.

16 Bore for the screws and screw rafters to top plate and ridge. Screw collars to rafters.

17 Set out and make the roof panel framing. The rails are stub tenoned into the stiles. The stiffeners are simply notched into the rails and skew nailed. Resin glue and nail the hardboard to the frames.

18 Clean up the edges of the frames and fit to the ridge. Bevel the framing at the eaves. Screw the roof panels to the rafters and the gable ends from the inside.

19 Make ridge moulding or backing piece, painting surfaces before fixing, and screw to the roof.

20 Cut floor joists to size and place in position.

21 Cut flooring to length and nail to joists with 56mm (2¼in) floor brads. Punch the heads slightly below the surface.

Note: to give access to the metal holding strips, arrange for two floor boards – one at each end – to be screwed for easy removal.

22 Set out barge boarding and finial. Make mortise and tenon joints and plough for roof framing. Chamfer the barge boards, paint the mortise and tenon joints and draw pin to finial. Paint edges of roof framing and barge boards. Screw boards to roof framing.

23 Cut covering strips to length, rebate, chamfer and screw to posts.

24 Line interior of workshop with 4mm (3/16in) hardboard (this can be of a cheaper grade – not tempered) making the panels near the bolts removable for easy access to same.

25 Prepare door linings, tongue linings into head, and cut sill round studs. Work throating on sill, paint and fix to bottom plate. Cut linings to fit over sill, paint inner surfaces and nail linings and head to framing.

26 *Finish:* treat all hardboard with a hardboard sealer, and paint or varnish, as desired.

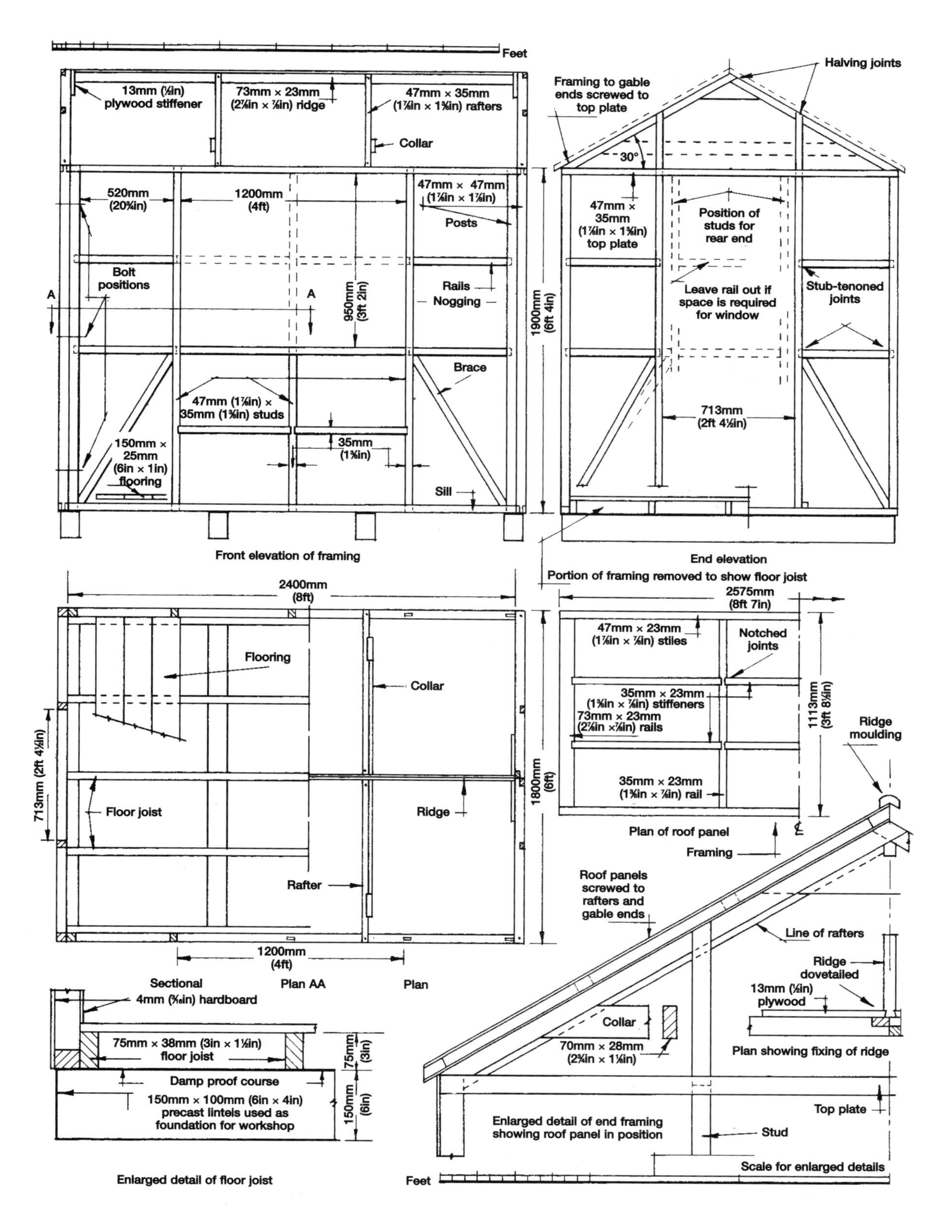
Feet
13mm (½in) plywood stiffener
73mm × 23mm (2⅞in × ⅞in) ridge
47mm × 35mm (1⅞in × 1⅜in) rafters
Collar
520mm (20½in)
1200mm (4ft)
47mm × 47mm (1⅞in × 1⅞in)
Posts
Bolt positions
A
A
950mm (3ft 2in)
Rails
Nogging
Brace
47mm (1⅞in) × 35mm (1⅜in) studs
35mm (1⅜in)
150mm × 25mm (6in × 1in) flooring
Sill
Front elevation of framing
1900mm (6ft 4in)
Framing to gable ends screwed to top plate
Halving joints
30°
47mm × 35mm (1⅞in × 1⅜in) top plate
Position of studs for rear end
Leave rail out if space is required for window
Stub-tenoned joints
713mm (2ft 4½in)
End elevation
Portion of framing removed to show floor joist
2400mm (8ft)
Flooring
Collar
713mm (2ft 4½in)
Floor joist
Ridge
Rafter
1800mm (6ft)
1200mm (4ft)
Sectional
Plan AA
Plan
2575mm (8ft 7in)
47mm × 23mm (1⅞in × ⅞in) stiles
Notched joints
35mm × 23mm (1⅜in × ⅞in) stiffeners
73mm × 23mm (2⅞in × ⅞in) rails
35mm × 23mm (1⅜in × ⅞in) rail
1113mm (3ft 8½in)
Plan of roof panel
Ridge moulding
Framing
Roof panels screwed to rafters and gable ends
Line of rafters
Ridge dovetailed
13mm (½in) plywood
Plan showing fixing of ridge
Collar
70mm × 28mm (2¾in × 1⅛in)
4mm (3/16in) hardboard
75mm × 38mm (3in × 1½in) floor joist
75mm (3in)
Damp proof course
150mm × 100mm (6in × 4in) precast lintels used as foundation for workshop
150mm (6in)
Enlarged detail of floor joist
Enlarged detail of end framing showing roof panel in position
Top plate
Stud
Scale for enlarged details
Feet

Suggested Material

Pine, for framing and flooring. Oak, for barge boards, finial, and covering strips. Exterior cladding, 4mm ($\frac{3}{16}$in) oil-tempered hardboard.
Interior linings, standard hardboard.

When buying prepared timber – machine-planed – the sizes quoted are those of the timber before planing. Thus 50mm × 25mm (2in × 1in) batten planed all round (P.A.R.) will be approximately 47mm × 23mm ($1\frac{7}{8}$in × $\frac{7}{8}$in). The batten will however still be ordered by its original or 'nominal size', that is, 50mm × 25mm (2in × 1in) P.A.R. Sometimes boards are purchased planed on the faces only. These are referred to as planed both sides (P.B.S.) and a nominal 25mm (1in) board will be approximately 23mm ($\frac{7}{8}$in) finished thickness.

Cutting list

Description	Length	Width	Thickness
8 posts	1925mm (6ft 5in)	47mm ($1\frac{7}{8}$in)	47mm ($1\frac{7}{8}$in)
4 sill and top plates	2400mm (8ft)	47mm ($1\frac{7}{8}$in)	35mm ($1\frac{3}{8}$in)
4 sill and top plates	1800mm (6ft)	47mm ($1\frac{7}{8}$in)	35mm ($1\frac{3}{8}$in)
9 studs	1900mm (6ft 4in)	47mm ($1\frac{7}{8}$in)	35mm ($1\frac{3}{8}$in)
8 braces	975mm (3ft 3in)	47mm ($1\frac{7}{8}$in)	35mm ($1\frac{3}{8}$in)
2 studs	900mm (3ft)	47mm ($1\frac{7}{8}$in)	35mm ($1\frac{3}{8}$in)
4 studs gable end	375mm (1ft 3in)	47mm ($1\frac{7}{8}$in)	35mm ($1\frac{3}{8}$in)
5 rails or noggins	2400mm (8ft)	47mm ($1\frac{7}{8}$in)	35mm ($1\frac{3}{8}$in)
4 gable ends	1125mm (3ft 9in)	47mm ($1\frac{7}{8}$in)	35mm ($1\frac{3}{8}$in)
4 rafters	1050mm (3ft 6in)	47mm ($1\frac{7}{8}$in)	35mm ($1\frac{3}{8}$in)
2 collars	1575mm (5ft 3in)	70mm ($2\frac{3}{4}$in)	28mm ($1\frac{1}{8}$in)
1 ridge	2400mm (8ft)	73mm ($2\frac{7}{8}$in)	23mm ($\frac{7}{8}$in)
1 ridge moulding	2500mm (8ft 4in)	38mm ($1\frac{1}{2}$in)	28mm ($1\frac{1}{8}$in)
1 for 2 stiffeners	750mm (2ft 6in)	150mm (6in)	13mm ($\frac{1}{2}$in)
Roof framing			
4 stiles	2600mm (8ft 8in)	47mm ($1\frac{7}{8}$in)	23mm ($\frac{7}{8}$in)
4 rails	1100mm (3ft 8in)	73mm ($2\frac{7}{8}$in)	23mm ($\frac{7}{8}$in)
4 stiffeners	2450mm (8ft 2in)	35mm ($1\frac{3}{8}$in)	23mm ($\frac{7}{8}$in)
4 stiffeners	1100mm (3ft 8in)	35mm ($1\frac{3}{8}$in)	23mm ($\frac{7}{8}$in)
5 floor joists sawn	2400mm (8ft)	75mm (3in)	38mm ($1\frac{1}{2}$in)
17 pieces flooring oak	1725mm (5ft 9in)	145mm ($5\frac{3}{4}$in)	23mm ($\frac{7}{8}$in)
4 barge boards	1125mm (3ft 9in)	63mm ($2\frac{1}{2}$in)	20mm ($\frac{3}{4}$in)
1 finial oak	150mm (6in)	35mm ($1\frac{3}{8}$in)	28mm ($1\frac{1}{8}$in)
4 covering strips oak	1900mm (6ft 4in)	63mm ($2\frac{1}{2}$in)	16mm ($\frac{5}{8}$in)
10 sheets approx.			
oil-tempered hardboard	2400mm (8ft)	1200mm (48in)	

Order hardboard for interior as required
Hardboard sealer, and paint or varnish
Clear preservative for all woodwork

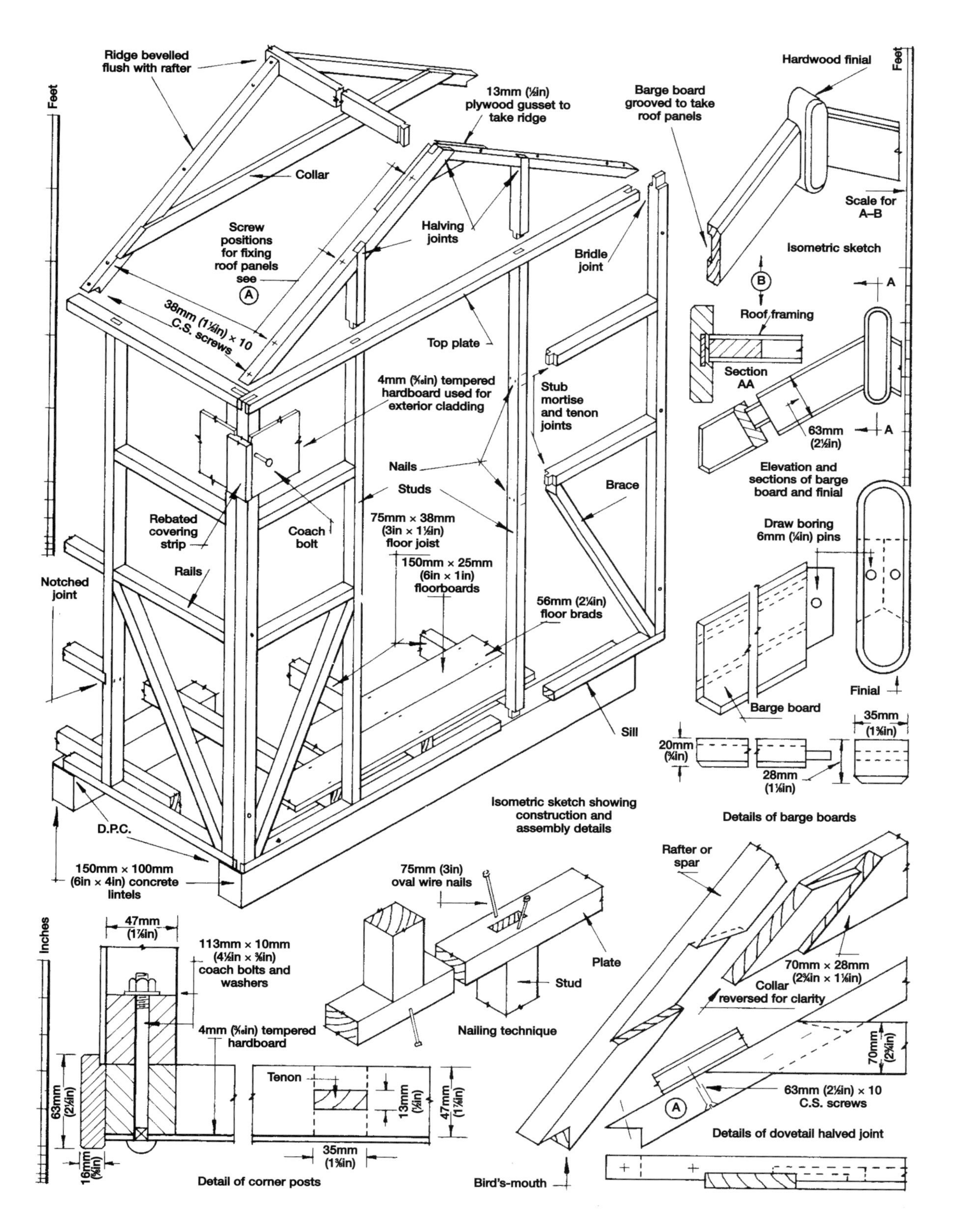

Ridge bevelled flush with rafter
Collar
13mm (½in) plywood gusset to take ridge
Barge board grooved to take roof panels
Hardwood finial
Feet
Scale for A–B
Isometric sketch
Halving joints
Screw positions for fixing roof panels see (A)
38mm (1½in) × 10 C.S. screws
Bridle joint
Top plate
Roof framing
Section AA
63mm (2½in)
Elevation and sections of barge board and finial
4mm (5/32in) tempered hardboard used for exterior cladding
Stub mortise and tenon joints
Nails
Studs
Brace
Draw boring 6mm (¼in) pins
Rebated covering strip
Coach bolt
75mm × 38mm (3in × 1½in) floor joist
150mm × 25mm (6in × 1in) floorboards
56mm (2¼in) floor brads
Notched joint
Rails
Finial
Barge board
Sill
20mm (¾in)
35mm (1⅜in)
28mm (1⅛in)
Details of barge boards
Isometric sketch showing construction and assembly details
D.P.C.
150mm × 100mm (6in × 4in) concrete lintels
Rafter or spar
75mm (3in) oval wire nails
Plate
Stud
Nailing technique
70mm × 28mm (2¾in × 1⅛in)
Collar reversed for clarity
70mm (2¾in)
63mm (2½in) × 10 C.S. screws
Details of dovetail halved joint
Bird's-mouth
Inches
47mm (1⅞in)
113mm × 10mm (4½in × ⅜in) coach bolts and washers
4mm (5/32in) tempered hardboard
63mm (2½in)
16mm (⅝in)
Tenon
13mm (½in)
47mm (1⅞in)
35mm (1⅜in)
Detail of corner posts

Ledged, Braced & Battened Door

This is a light, inexpensive door suitable for the workshop and other outbuildings. The door is made up. of tongued, grooved and vee-jointed battens, fastened together with horizontal members (ledges) and diagonally braced to prevent the door sagging. The braces are often cut straight on to the ledges. In good work the brace is joggled in, thus preventing any possibility of the brace sliding. Alternative batten joints are shown in a separate detail.

Method

1. Prepare the material. Arrange to have battens of equal dimensions on the outside edges. Mark out the tongued and grooved battens and cut to length. Place 75mm × 50mm (3in × 2in) bearers on the bench and lay the battens on top, painting all tongues and grooves, and lightly cramp up. Mark out ledge positions. Cut ledges to length, bevel ends and bore for screws.
2. Screw on ledges, turn over door and nail battens to ledges, clenching nails on the inside.
3. Carefully mark out braces, cut and fit to ledges. Nail battens to braces, and clench nail on the inside.
4. Shoot edges of door and fit to aperture. As the door is exposed to the weather allowances must be made for expansion and paint thickness. Approximately 4mm (3/16in) overall should be satisfactory on the width. Allow for a 1.6mm (1/16in) clearance at the top and 3mm (1/8in) at the bottom.
5. Paint behind the tee hinges and screw to door. Nail on door stops, and position door for fixing. Cut out door linings to receive hinge knuckles and screw hinges to post.
6. Fit dead lock or latch as required.

Suggested Material

Pine

Cutting list

Description	Length	Width	Thickness
6 T.G. & V. battens	1800mm (6ft)	125mm (5in) nominal	20mm (3/4in) nominal
3 ledges	675mm (2ft 3in)	145mm (5 3/4in)	23mm (7/8in)
2 braces	900mm (3ft)	100mm (4in)	23mm (7/8in)

Door linings

Description	Length	Width	Thickness
2 linings	1800mm (6ft)	66mm (2 5/8in)	20mm (3/4in)
1 head	725mm (2ft 5in)	66mm (2 5/8in)	20mm (3/4in)
1 sill oak	800mm (2ft 8in)	78mm (3 1/8in)	28mm (1 1/8in)
1 margin piece oak	700mm (2ft 4in)	35mm (1 3/8in)	13mm (1/2in)

1 pair 450mm (18in) tie or cross garnet hinges

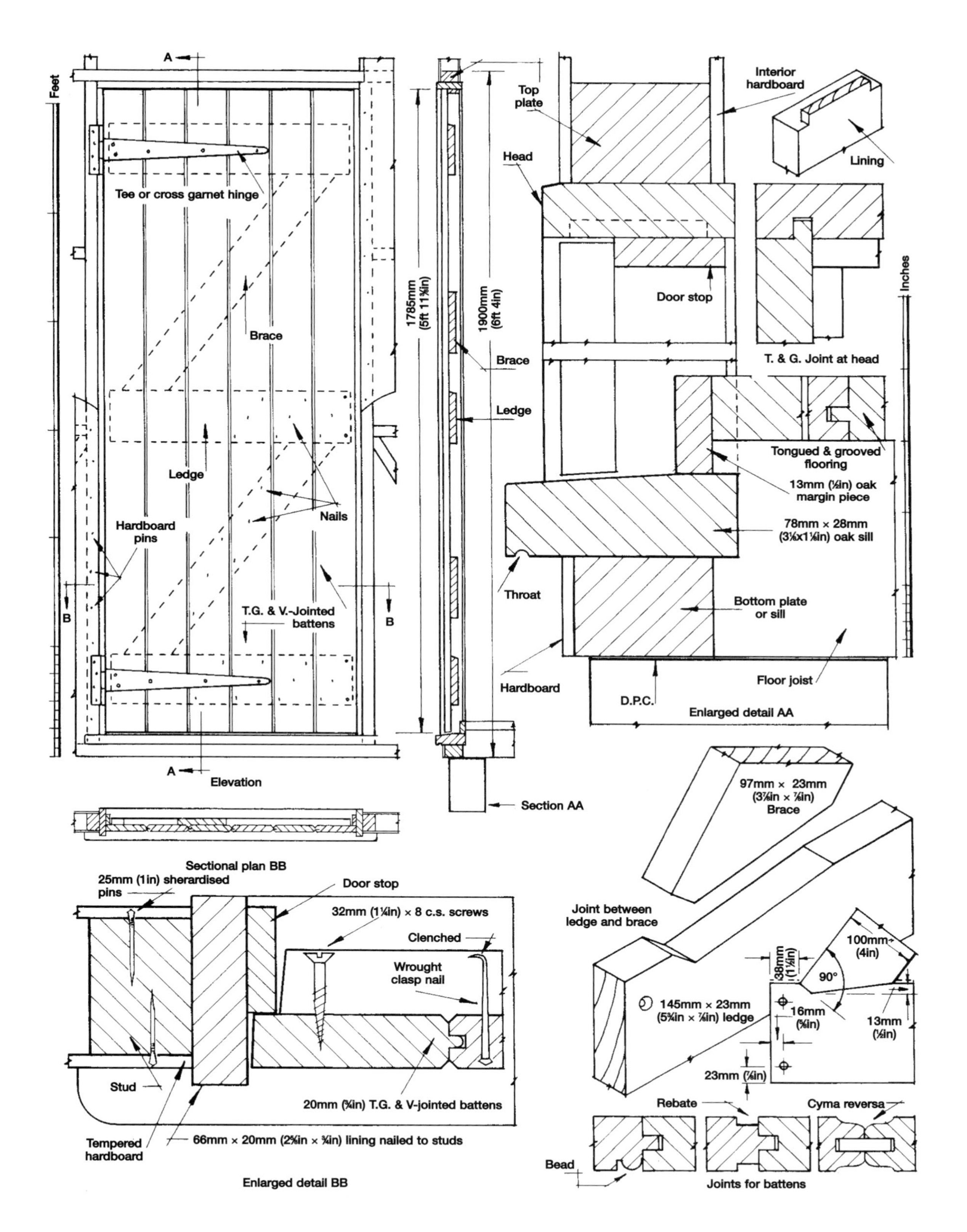
A
Feet
Tee or cross garnet hinge
Brace
Ledge
Nails
Hardboard pins
T.G. & V.-Jointed battens
B
Elevation
1785mm (5ft 11⅜in)
1900mm (6ft 4in)
Brace
Ledge
Section AA
Top plate
Head
Interior hardboard
Lining
Door stop
T. & G. Joint at head
Inches
Tongued & grooved flooring
13mm (½in) oak margin piece
78mm × 28mm (3⅛x1⅛in) oak sill
Throat
Bottom plate or sill
Hardboard
Floor joist
D.P.C.
Enlarged detail AA
Sectional plan BB
25mm (1in) sherardised pins
Door stop
32mm (1¼in) × 8 c.s. screws
Clenched
Wrought clasp nail
Stud
Tempered hardboard
20mm (⅘in) T.G. & V-jointed battens
66mm × 20mm (2⅝in × ⅘in) lining nailed to studs
Enlarged detail BB
97mm × 23mm (3⅞in × ⅞in) Brace
Joint between ledge and brace
38mm (1½in)
100mm (4in)
90°
145mm × 23mm (5¾in × ⅞in) ledge
16mm (⅝in)
13mm (½in)
23mm (⅞in)
Rebate
Cyma reversa
Bead
Joints for battens

Window Frame & Casement Sashes

This frame and sashes have been specially designed for the small workshop. To effect economy, the dimensions of the frame have been kept to a minimum. They give the student an opportunity to gain valuable practical experience in making and working to full-size drawings, the preparation and making of rods, and the setting out of work.

Method

Make a careful study of the drawings overleaf.

1. Prepare full-size height and width rods for the frame and sashes. Strips of plywood are excellent for this purpose.
2. Prepare material to specification. Set out window frame. Lay sill on width rod and mark out mortise positions for jambs and mullions (see mortise positions on rod). Pair up with head and transfer mortise positions.
3. Lay jamb on height rod and mark out shoulder lines. Gauge and cut the mortises and tenons, working rebates and mouldings before removing tenon cheeks.
4. Make weathering at sill, and capillary groove – throating – and plough groove under sill for interior lining (see overleaf for details of joints). Assemble frame fitting as necessary.
5. Clean up all inner surfaces, mouldings and rebates. Glue, cramp and wedge up. Make diagonal test for squareness and check for alignment. Leave to dry.
6. Setting out of casement sashes: lay a stile on the height rod, and mark out the sight lines, and mortise positions for bottom, top rails and horizontal or lay bars. Pair up the remaining stiles and complete marking out.
7. Lay a rail on the width rod and mark out the sight lines, in pencil, and shoulder lines using a marking knife. Complete the marking out of rails and sash bars.
8. Make a careful study of the joints illustrated on page 209. It is interesting to note the scribing for the moulding or sinking, and the method of haunching. The stiles are not cut to form a conventional haunching; instead a spur is left projecting, and the rails are cut to fit over; this is called franking and provides for maximum strength of stile.
9. Gauge and cut mortises and tenons, working rebates and mouldings before cutting shoulders. Assemble sashes, adjusting as necessary.
10. Clean up all inner surfaces, mouldings and rebates. Glue, cramp and wedge up. Test for square and alignment, leave to dry.
11. Fit sashes and work capillary grooves. Fit hinges and hang sashes. Screw on casement fittings.
12. Remove horns at head of frame. Cut sill to fit aperture, and try in frame. Fit as necessary.
13. Paint round edge of frame, and nail to workshop framing. Fix cover fillet on the outside.
14. Finish: give frame and sashes a coat of priming before glazing. On completion of glazing, finish with two coats of flat paint and one coat of hard gloss.

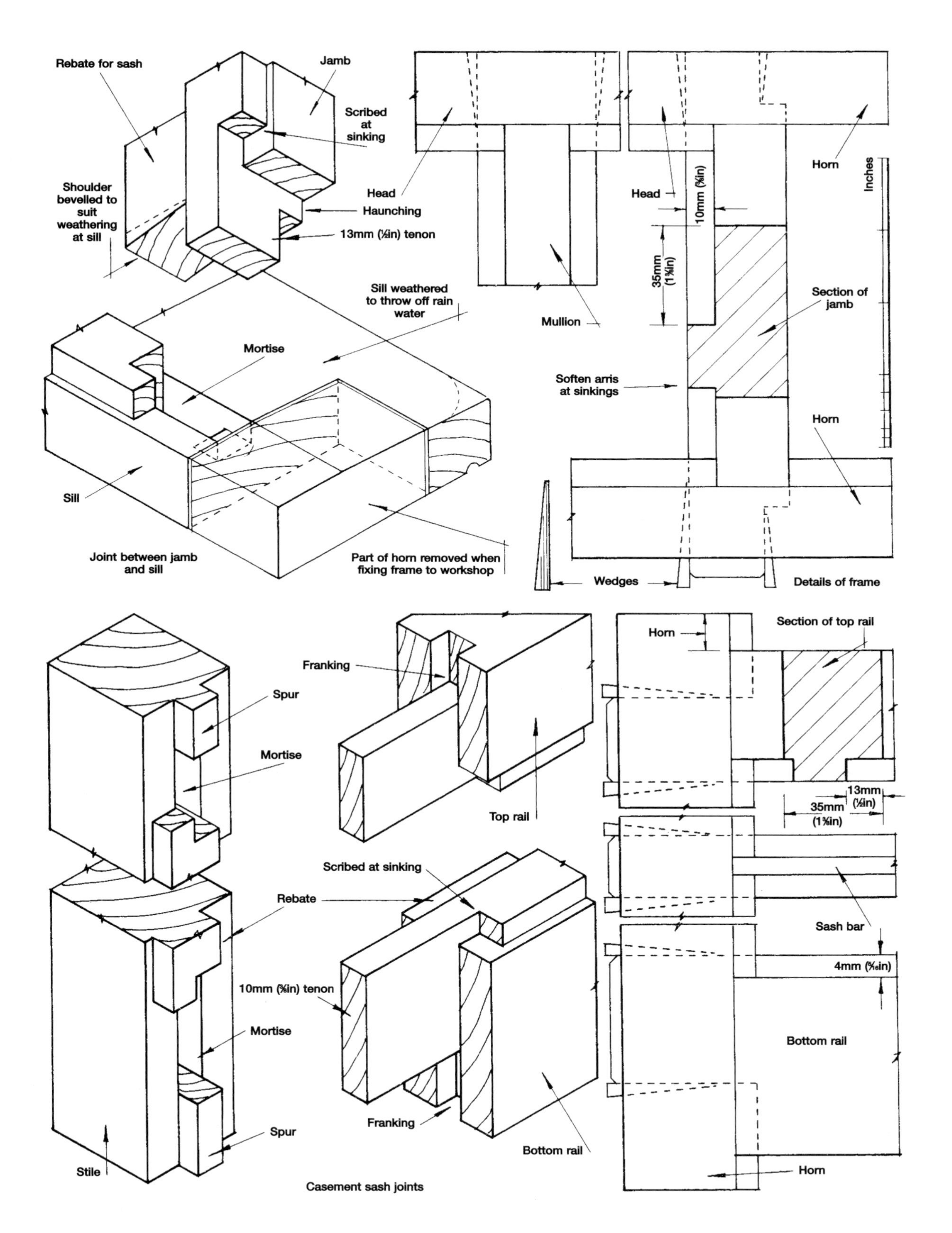
Rebate for sash
Jamb
Scribed
at
sinking
Shoulder
bevelled to
suit
weathering
at sill
Haunching
13mm (½in) tenon
Head
Head
10mm (⅜in)
35mm
(1⅜in)
Horn
Inches
Mullion
Sill weathered
to throw off rain
water
Mortise
Section of
jamb
Soften arris
at sinkings
Horn
Sill
Joint between jamb
and sill
Part of horn removed when
fixing frame to workshop
Wedges
Details of frame
Franking
Spur
Mortise
Top rail
Horn
Section of top rail
13mm
(½in)
35mm
(1⅜in)
Scribed at sinking
Rebate
Sash bar
10mm (⅜in) tenon
4mm (³⁄₁₆in)
Mortise
Bottom rail
Franking
Spur
Bottom rail
Stile
Horn
Casement sash joints

Suggested Material

Selected pine with oak sills.

Cutting list

Description	Length	Width	Thickness
2 jambs	975mm (3ft 3in)	60mm (2⅜in)	35mm (1⅜in)
1 mullion	975mm (3ft 3in)	60mm (2⅜in)	41mm (1⅝in)
1 head	1250mm (4ft 2in)	60mm (2⅜in)	35mm (1⅜in)
1 sill oak	1300mm (4ft 4in)	85mm (3⅜in)	35mm (1⅜in)
Sashes			
4 stiles	950mm (3ft 2in)	47mm (1⅞in)	35mm (1⅜in)
2 bottom rails	575mm (1ft 11in)	70mm (2¾in)	35mm (1⅜in)
2 top rails	575mm (1ft 11in)	47mm (1⅞in)	35mm (1⅜in)
4 sash bars	575mm (1ft 11in)	35mm (1⅜in)	23mm (⅞in)

Tools not in Basic Kit

4mm (3⁄16in) throating plane – for making capillary grooves on frame and sashes.
13mm (½in) and 10mm (⅜in) mortise chisels – for frame and sashes.

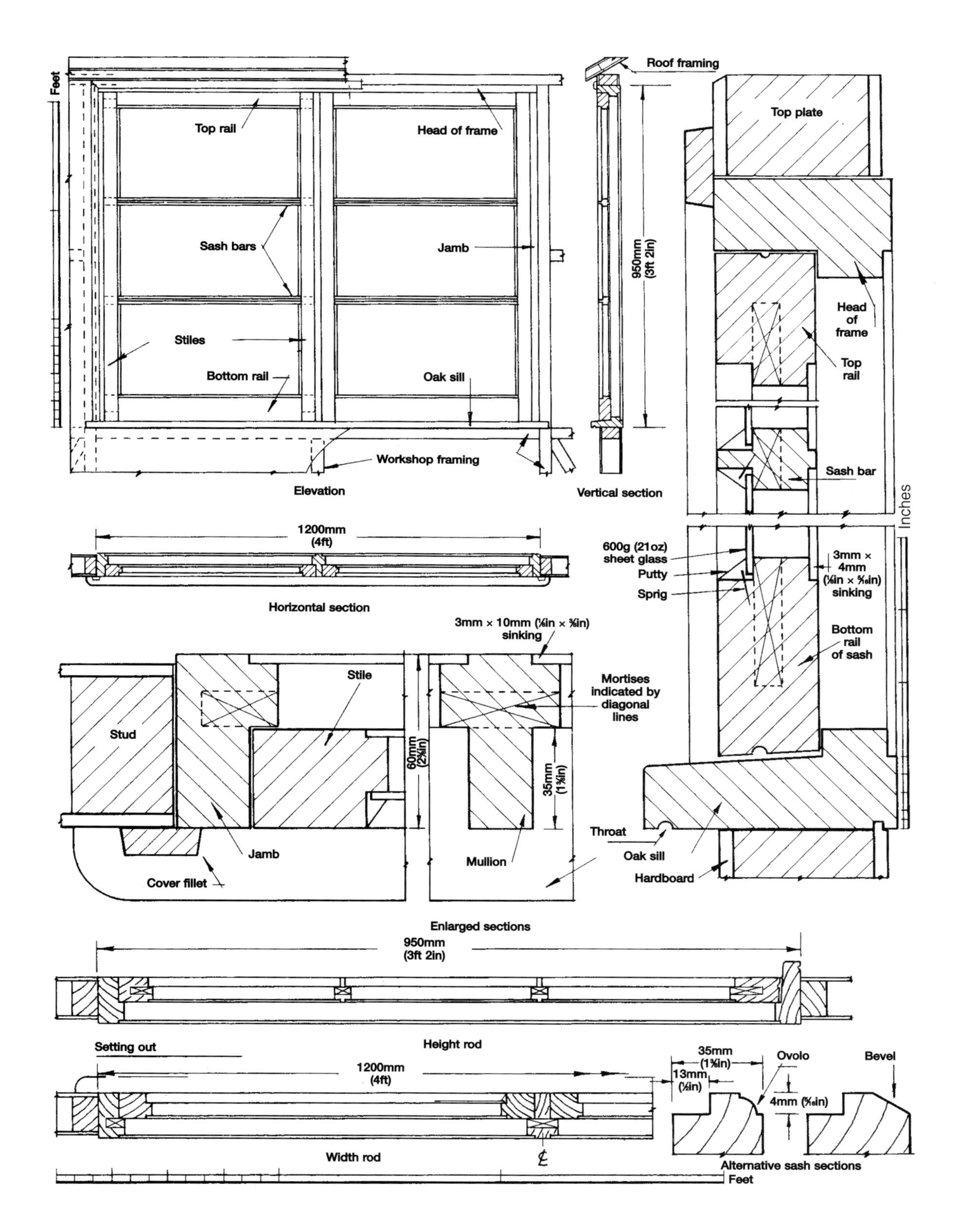
Roof framing
Top plate
Top rail
Head of frame
Sash bars
Jamb
Stiles
Bottom rail
Oak sill
Workshop framing
Elevation
950mm (3ft 2in)
Vertical section
Head of frame
Top rail
Sash bar
Inches
Feet
1200mm (4ft)
Horizontal section
600g (21oz) sheet glass
Putty
Sprig
3mm × 4mm (⅛in × 3⁄16in) sinking
Bottom rail of sash
3mm × 10mm (⅛in × ⅜in) sinking
Stile
Mortises indicated by diagonal lines
Stud
60mm (2⅜in)
35mm (1⅜in)
Throat
Oak sill
Hardboard
Jamb
Cover fillet
Mullion
Enlarged sections
950mm (3ft 2in)
Setting out
Height rod
1200mm (4ft)
Width rod
35mm (1⅜in)
13mm (½in)
Ovolo
Bevel
4mm (3⁄16in)
Alternative sash sections
Feet

Pattern-making and Casting

Pattern-making is a highly skilled branch of woodwork dealing chiefly with the making of patterns so that various metals, rubber and plastics can be cast or moulded into specific shapes. The work demands a high degree of accuracy. The making of patterns, their moulding and finally casting, offers considerable scope for a large variety of interesting work.

The author deals mainly with small-scale pattern-making, suitable for use in schools or the home workshop, and designed several small articles incorporating basic techniques. With the necessary foundry equipment these articles could be cast in a variety of metals. However, where there are limited facilities for casting, a metal with a low melting point has considerable value. A zinc base alloy which has a melting point of about 450°C, and can be melted in a plumber's pot over an ordinary gas ring, makes successful casting possible with very little addition to the equipment of the normal woodwork room. This alloy is reasonably strong and machines quite well. Moulding and casting procedure is only briefly discussed, and for more detailed information, textbooks dealing solely with the subject should be consulted. Full particulars of a pair of moulding boxes, complete with handles and a range of moulding tools are given in the diagrams opposite and overleaf.

Method for Moulding Boxes

1 Prepare material to the given sizes.
2 Mark out the dovetails and cut rebate to groove depth.
3 Cut the dovetails, mark out the pins and make joints.
4 Work plough grooves and assemble boxes, fitting as necessary.
5 Glue up and test for square. When dry, clean up joints and fit boxes. A separate detail shows an alternative method of making the boxes.

Handles for Moulding Boxes

(Solid or one piece pattern in yellow pine or mahogany.)

Method

1 Prepare material to the given sizes.
2 Carefully mark out – note build up of the pattern and the intersections of the centre lines – make allowance for the draft and cut to shape.
3 Glue the separate pieces to the base. Make rubbed joints (use Scotch glue), taking care to locate the centre lines.
4 Carefully clean up and check for correct draft. Make lifting hole in the base of pattern.
5 Glue in leather fillets, or mix up a filler (plaster of Paris) and work in and mould fillets with a 3mm (⅛in) rod. If the plaster of Paris is used it is advisable to give the pattern a light rub over with white polish before working in fillets.
6 Drive a screw through a scrap piece of wood and use this wood as a stand to support the pattern – by the lifting hole – so that it can be painted all over.

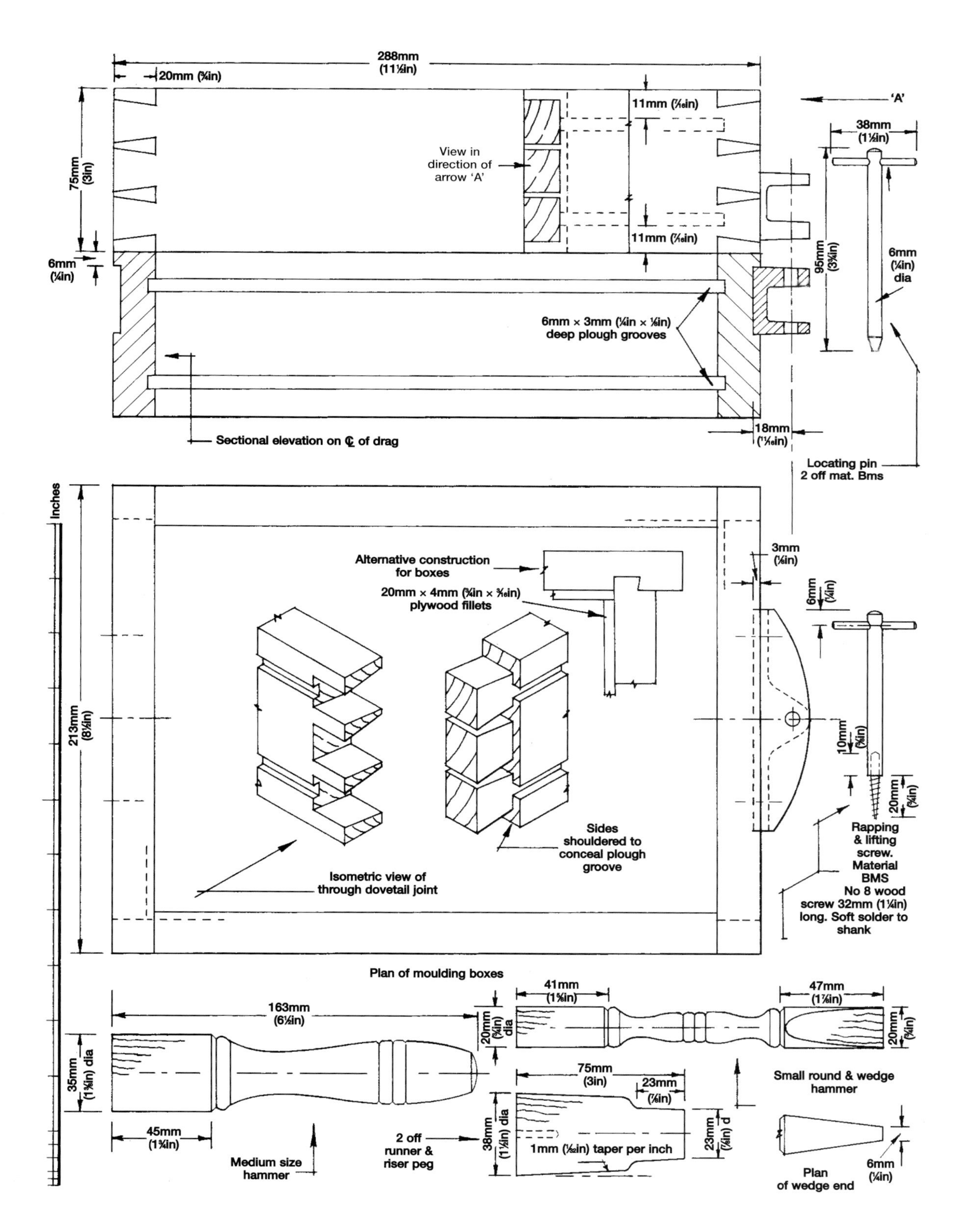

288mm (11½in)
20mm (¾in)
75mm (3in)
6mm (¼in)
11mm (7⁄16in)
'A'
38mm (1½in)
View in direction of arrow 'A'
95mm (3¾in)
6mm (¼in) dia
6mm × 3mm (¼in × ⅛in) deep plough grooves
18mm (11⁄16in)
Sectional elevation on ℄ of drag
Locating pin 2 off mat. Bms
Inches
213mm (8½in)
Alternative construction for boxes
20mm × 4mm (¾in × 3⁄16in) plywood fillets
3mm (⅛in)
6mm (¼in)
10mm (⅜in)
20mm (¾in)
Rapping & lifting screw. Material BMS No 8 wood screw 32mm (1¼in) long. Soft solder to shank
Sides shouldered to conceal plough groove
Isometric view of through dovetail joint
Plan of moulding boxes
163mm (6½in)
35mm (1⅜in) dia
45mm (1¾in)
Medium size hammer
2 off runner & riser peg
41mm (1⅝in)
47mm (1⅞in)
20mm (¾in) dia
20mm (¾in)
75mm (3in)
23mm (⅞in)
38mm (1½in) dia
23mm (⅞in) d
1mm (1⁄32in) taper per inch
Small round & wedge hammer
Plan of wedge end
6mm (¼in)

Method for Moulding

1. Place the drag, joint face down, on a moulding or turnover board, position the pattern – lifting hole on the board – and lightly sprinkle the turnover board with parting sand. Dust pattern with parting powder in muslin bag.
2. Cover the pattern with moulding sand, using a fine sieve (riddle), and carefully ram the sand firmly against pattern. A larger sieve can be used after the initial ramming of the pattern, and the filling up and ramming of the drag should be done in stages.
3. Flush off the sand with a straight edge.
4. Turn over the drag and replace on a clean board lightly sprinkled with parting sand.
5. Assemble cope with locating pins. Sprinkle joint surface with parting sand, and dust patterns with parting powder.
6. Study the diagrams showing general arrangements for mould-making, and suitably position runner and riser pegs.
7. Cover pattern with finely sieved moulding sand, and ram up carefully and firmly round pegs and sides of box.
8. Flush off sand and insert rapping and lifting screws in pegs. Rap carefully in all directions and remove pegs.
9. Lift off cope. Insert rapping and lifting screws in pattern. Rap carefully and lift pattern cleanly from the sand.
10. Cut runner and riser basins. Cut gates, blow out all loose sand and re-assemble moulds.
11. Pour metal with a continuous flow and leave to cool.

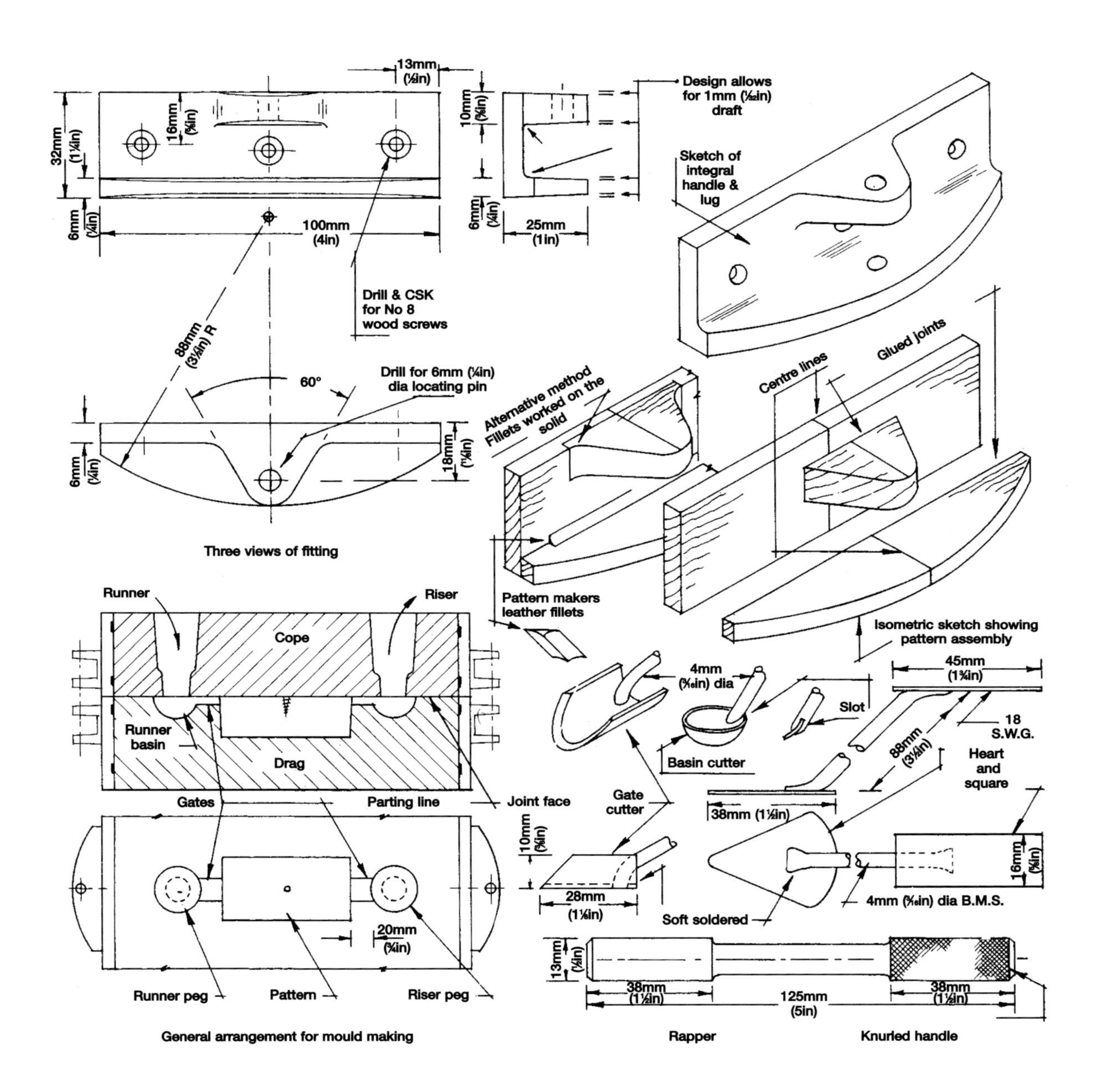
13mm (½in)
Design allows for 1mm (1/32in) draft
32mm (1¼in)
16mm (⅝in)
10mm (⅜in)
6mm (¼in)
100mm (4in)
25mm (1in)
Sketch of integral handle & lug
Drill & CSK for No 8 wood screws
88mm (3½in) R
60°
Drill for 6mm (¼in) dia locating pin
18mm (11/16in)
Three views of fitting
Alternative method Fillets worked on the solid
Centre lines
Glued joints
Pattern makers leather fillets
Isometric sketch showing pattern assembly
Runner
Riser
Cope
Runner basin
Drag
Gates
Parting line
Joint face
Runner peg
Pattern
Riser peg
20mm (¾in)
General arrangement for mould making
4mm (5/32in) dia
Slot
Basin cutter
45mm (1¾in)
18 S.W.G.
88mm (3½in)
Heart and square
Gate cutter
38mm (1½in)
10mm (⅜in)
28mm (1⅛in)
Soft soldered
16mm (⅝in)
4mm (5/32in) dia B.M.S.
13mm (½in)
38mm (1½in)
125mm (5in)
Rapper
Knurled handle

Shelf Bracket

A neat reversible bracket for supporting a teak or other wood shelf is shown. It is attractive when cast in aluminium or P.T.A. alloy and lacquered. The drawings give details of a solid pattern with a loose piece. Use selected pine or mahogany for the flanges and marine quality plywood for the web. Make the pattern to the given specification and fit loose piece as shown. The loose piece converts the pattern into a solid pattern during the process of ramming up the drag. Prepare for painting and make all fillets and radiuses. Paint and leave to dry. A separate details shows the pattern in the drag, and the position of a runner. This small casting can be poured quite successfully with only a runner (note position). A riser position is shown in dotted outline.

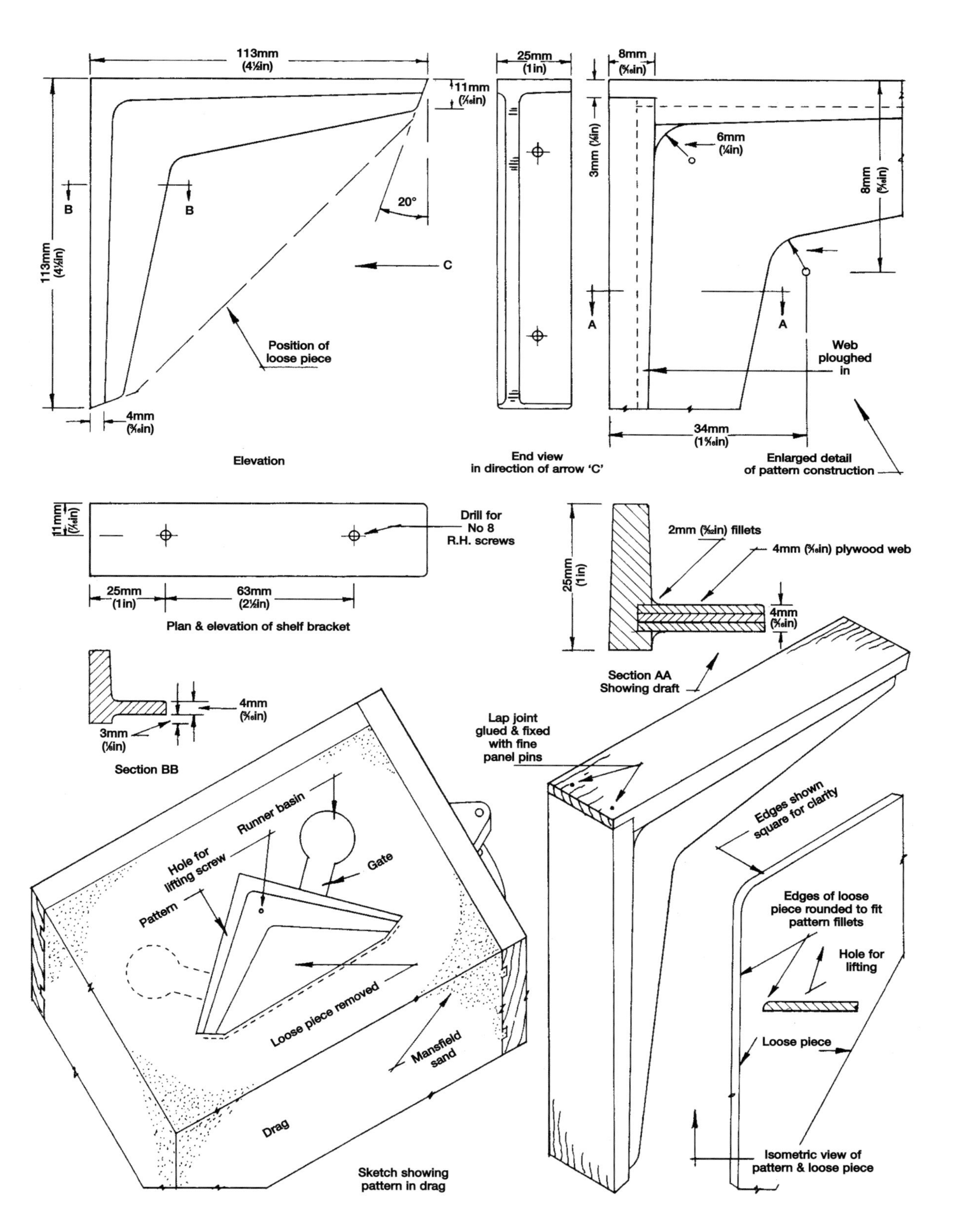
113mm
(4½in)
11mm
(7⁄16in)
113mm
(4½in)
B
B
20°
C
Position of
loose piece
4mm
(3⁄16in)
Elevation
25mm
(1in)
End view
in direction of arrow 'C'
8mm
(5⁄16in)
3mm (⅛in)
6mm
(¼in)
8mm
(5⁄16in)
A
A
Web
ploughed
in
34mm
(1⅜in)
Enlarged detail
of pattern construction
11mm
(7⁄16in)
Drill for
No 8
R.H. screws
25mm
(1in)
63mm
(2½in)
Plan & elevation of shelf bracket
25mm
(1in)
2mm (3⁄32in) fillets
4mm (3⁄16in) plywood web
4mm
(3⁄16in)
Section AA
Showing draft
4mm
(3⁄16in)
3mm
(⅛in)
Section BB
Lap joint
glued & fixed
with fine
panel pins
Runner basin
Hole for
lifting screw
Gate
Pattern
Loose piece removed
Mansfield
sand
Drag
Sketch showing
pattern in drag
Edges shown
square for clarity
Edges of loose
piece rounded to fit
pattern fillets
Hole for
lifting
Loose piece
Isometric view of
pattern & loose piece

Drawer or Door Handle

The designing and making of handles is an important factor in cabinet design. The making of a pattern for a particular design and the subsequent casting and finishing gives one great satisfaction and a sense of achievement. Owing to the shape of the handle illustrated below a split pattern must be used for moulding purposes.

Method

1. Prepare the material, leaving approximately 50mm (2in) longer for holding in the vice.
2. Mark out one piece and carefully, with a marking knife, position the centre lines.
3. Locate both pieces and cramp up. Square over and mark out the other side.
4. Gauge centres and bore for the 4mm (3/16in) dowels. Fit dowels hand tight and leave dry. This enables the pattern to be shaped in one piece (see Door Knocker, step 6 on page 220 for alternative method).
5. On completion of shaping, carefully separate the pattern. Cut and round dowels as shown in given section, and glue in. Split patterns must locate accurately on the pins, and yet separate easily. Make provision for lifting pattern from the sand.
6. Paint pattern red and leave to dry.
7. When preparing for moulding, lay the flat side of the split pattern in the drag – on the moulding board – and proceed with ramming up.
8. On turning over the drag, locate cope and place the other half of the pattern in position.
9. Place riser and runner pegs in position and proceed with ramming up.
10. Rap and remove pegs. Carefully remove cope, so that one half of pattern lifts out with it, and insert rapping and lifting screw in patterns. Rap and carefully remove.
11. Cut basins and gates, blow out all dust, reassemble boxes and prepare for pouring.

Material

Mahogany or cherry wood.

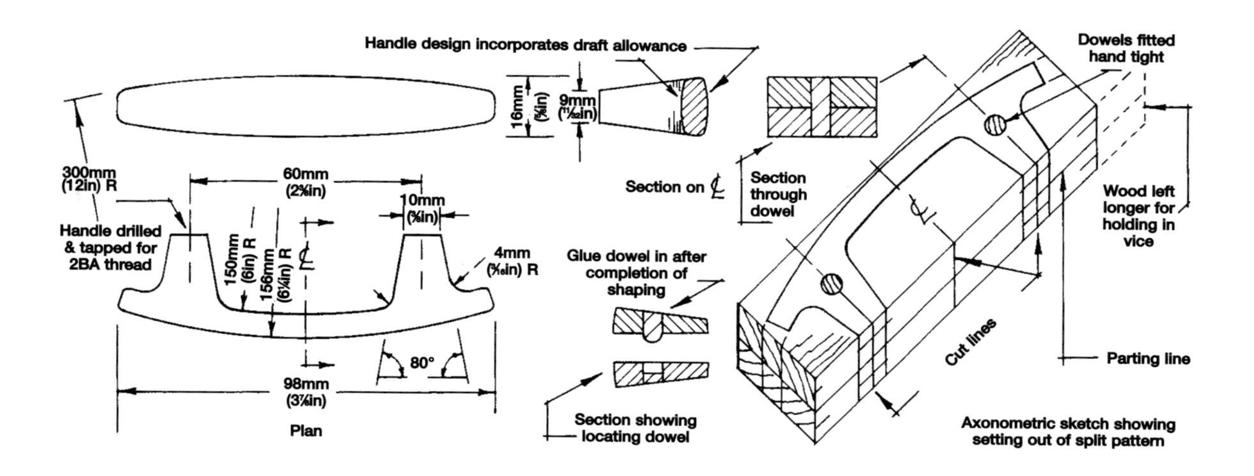

Handle design incorporates draft allowance
300mm (12in) R
60mm (2⅜in)
10mm (⅜in)
Handle drilled & tapped for 2BA thread
150mm (6in) R
156mm (6¼in) R
4mm (3/16in) R
80°
98mm (3⅞in)
Plan
16mm (⅝in)
9mm (11/32in)
Section on ℄
Section through dowel
Glue dowel in after completion of shaping
Section showing locating dowel
Dowels fitted hand tight
Wood left longer for holding in vice
Cut lines
Parting line
Axonometric sketch showing setting out of split pattern

Door Knocker

Suitable for the back or front door, this small knocker provides a good exercise in the making of both solid and split patterns. The designing of a different shape would give the student an opportunity to develop his own design ability. The side elevation of the knocker shows position of the pattern locating pins.

Method

1 Prepare the material.
2 Set out the back plate (solid pattern) and cut in all centre lines.
3 Carefully shape (templates are useful here), working accurately to the drawing.
4 Recess back and complete pattern ready for painting.
5 Set out material for split pattern, leaving wood longer, and proceed as for door handle on page 218.
6 An alternative method for the making of a split pattern, is to glue up the two pieces with a slip of paper between them. Use Scotch glue for this. The pattern is split after shaping and the paper is easily removed. It then requires the locating pins to be inserted. This must be very carefully done (see Boat Hook, step 2, on page 222).

Material

Selected straight-grain mahogany or maple. Leave the wood longer for securing in the vice.

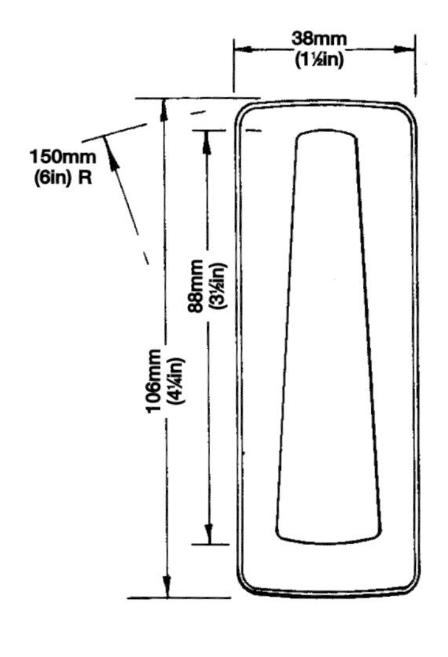

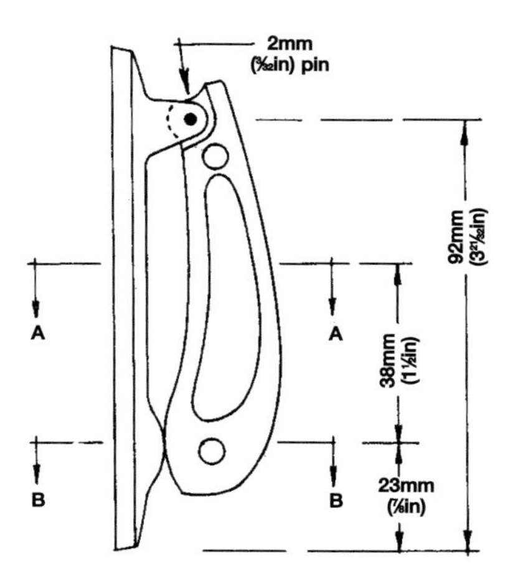

Front and side elevations

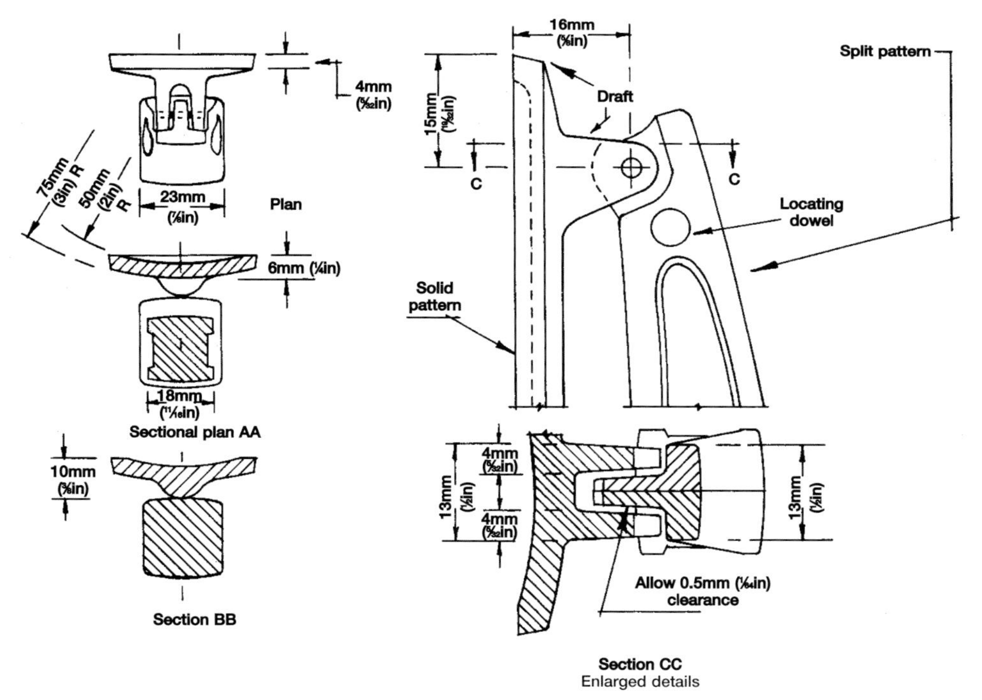

Section CC
Enlarged details

Boat Hook

Usually cast in brass or gunmetal, the boat hook is a good example of a split pattern. It also introduces a core print and core box. The pattern maker allows for the contraction of various metals, and uses contraction rules for this purpose. Owing to the smallness of these castings, the shrinkage, unless for special work, can be ignored.

Method

1. Prepare the material to the given sizes. If the glue and paper technique is used for holding the split pattern, the pattern could be worked on the lathe, leaving only the hook to be shaped by hand.
2. Complete the shaping, split the pattern on the joint line and clean off paper. Mark out pin centres and drive in two small panel pins. Cut off the heads and file to a point. Carefully locate the two halves of the pattern and press firmly together. This will give accurate centres for the holes taking locating pins.
3. Glue in pins, and test pattern for easy withdrawal. Finish – red paint.
4. Prepare material for the core box.
5. Set out and make templates for testing. Remove waste with paring and carving gouges. Bore for locating pins, and test for accuracy. The core box, if securely fixed to a face plate, could be accurately turned on the lathe.
6. Paint core box black.

Material

Selected mahogany. Maple or birch are particularly suitable for turning.

Method for Core Making

1. Mix thoroughly 9 parts dry sharp silica sand, and 1 part moulding sand. Mix a small quantity of plain flour and water (binder) and gradually add to the sand mixture.
2. Close core box and clamp or hold firmly, lightly dust inside with parting powder.
3. Insert sand and ram up firmly in stages.
4. Rap and carefully remove from box.
5. Place in core oven for drying and leave until baked dry; temperature, 200–250°C maximum.
6. Mould up patterns as previously described. Care must be taken in placing header and riser in the most effective positions, and often a trial run is necessary to find same.

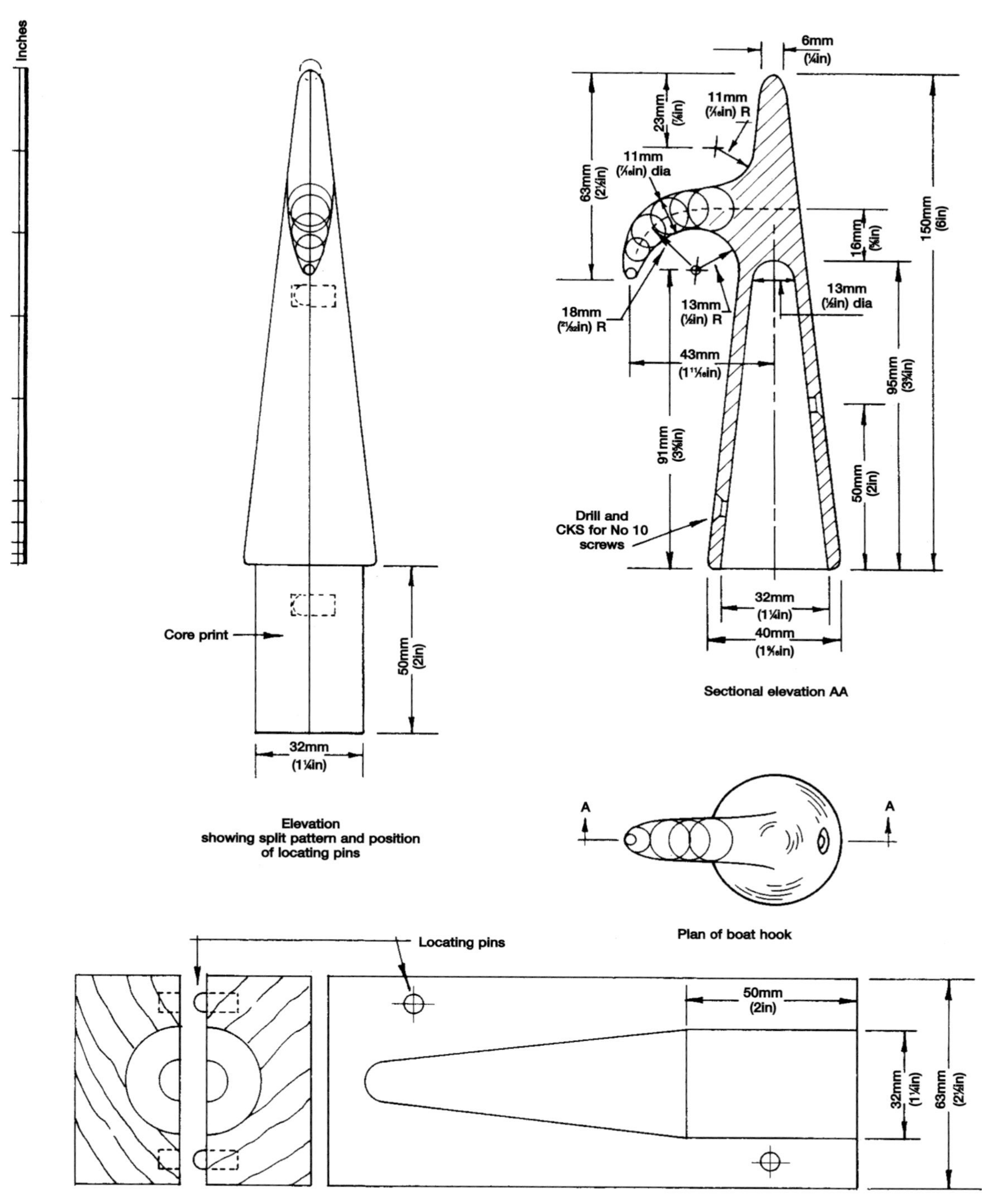

Elevation showing split pattern and position of locating pins

Sectional elevation AA

Plan of boat hook

Detail of core box

Splicing & Scarf (Scarph) Jointing

Splicing

This is a sound and effective method of lengthening timber. When marking out, make the splice 12 times the thickness of the material. Use a sharp trying plane to taper each piece to a feather edge and test with a straight edge. Cramp the material to a straight block of wood to support the splice during planing. A separate detail, opposite, shows the method of cramping up. Prepare two cramping blocks (faces planed true) and cramp splice up dry, adjust as necessary. Glue up splice, using waterproof glue, and place greaseproof paper under the cramping bearers. Carefully locate the splice and cramp up as shown. Should side slip occur, cramp a block on either side to prevent movement. Leave to dry. If properly made the resulting joint should be as strong as the wood.

Splicing of plywood

This is used for boat panels or planks. First mark out the length of the splice – 1 in 9 – and bevel to a feather edge. Then prepare two 75mm × 100mm (3in × 4in) hardwood cramping bearers or pressure bars, and make the top bearer slightly convex on its bottom edge (see figure 1). When cramped up this has the effect of applying pressure all along the splice. Glue and locate the splice on bottom bearer driving in two or three pins to prevent slip. Cramp up – remember to place greaseproof paper under bearers – and leave to dry.

Butt joint

The panels are simply butted, glued and screwed to a plywood jointing strip.

Scarf joint

Chiefly used for lengthening planks in clinker and carvel built boats. The jointing surfaces are usually varnished. Note direction of bevel in relation to the stem. A separate detail shows a pair of planking tongs. These are used when planking up clinker built craft. The tongs slide over the plank and on to the landing and the wedges when lightly driven in cause the ends to grip the landings. Planking tongs are light in weight and are preferable to 'G' cramps.

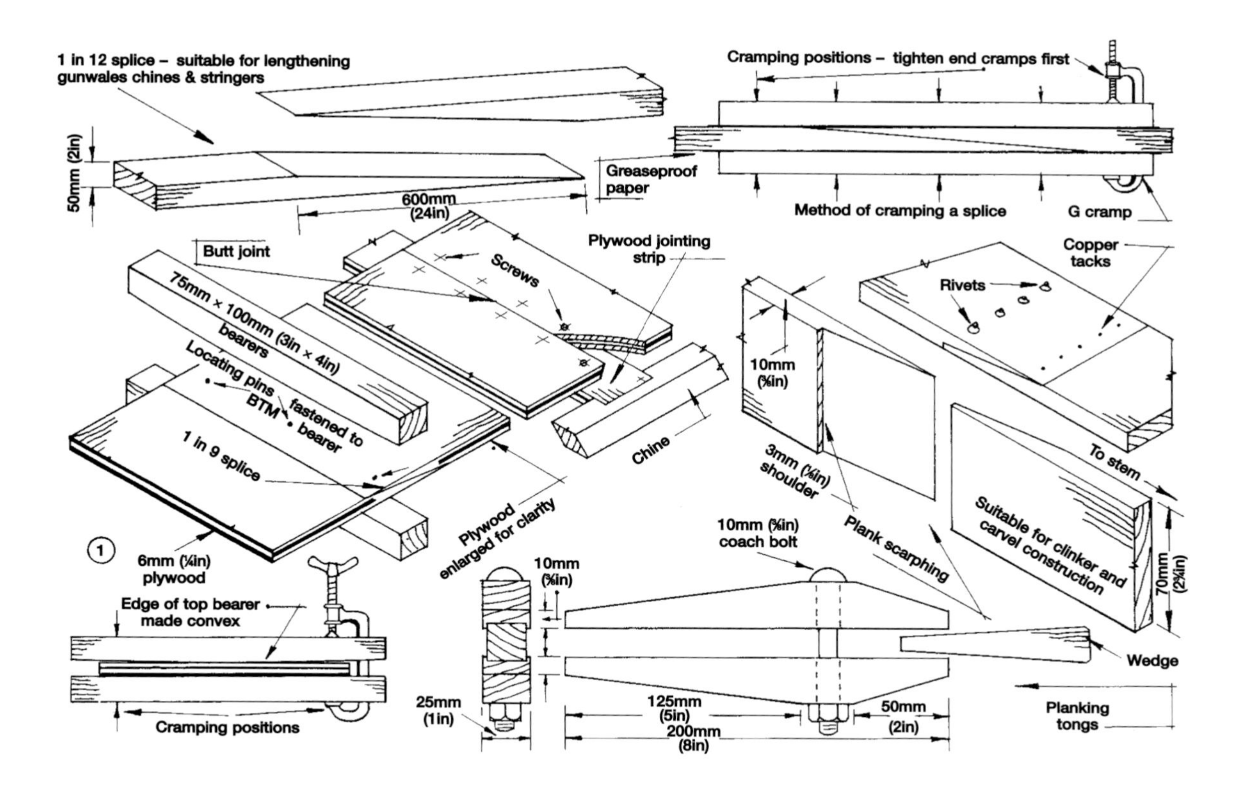

1 in 12 splice – suitable for lengthening gunwales chines & stringers
50mm (2in)
600mm (24in)
Greaseproof paper
Cramping positions – tighten end cramps first
Method of cramping a splice
G cramp
Butt joint
75mm × 100mm (3in × 4in) bearers
Locating pins fastened to BTM • bearer
Screws
Plywood jointing strip
1 in 9 splice
Plywood enlarged for clarity
Chine
1
6mm (¼in) plywood
Copper tacks
Rivets
10mm (⅜in)
3mm (⅛in) shoulder
Plank scarphing
To stem
Suitable for clinker and carvel construction
70mm (2¾in)
Edge of top bearer made convex
Cramping positions
10mm (⅜in) coach bolt
10mm (⅜in)
25mm (1in)
125mm (5in)
200mm (8in)
50mm (2in)
Wedge
Planking tongs

Canoe Paddles

Paddles should be both light and strong. Sitka spruce fulfills these conditions, as for its weight it is one of the strongest of timbers. Once the jig has been made, a paddle with a plywood blade is easy to make.

Method for Plywood Paddle

1. Prepare the jig as shown in separate drawing. Glue and screw the 10mm (⅜in) plywood to the framing. A block of wood approximately 25mm (1in) thick × 175mm (7in), shaped to fit the jig, makes an excellent cramping piece.
2. Cut the 3mm (⅛in) plywood (waterproof grade) to size.
3. Run a toothing plane over the jointing surfaces of the plywood and glue up, using waterproof glue, with a piece of double knife cut veneer in the centre. Note the grain direction.
4. When dry mark a centre line on the plywood and set out the blade. Cut to shape and clean up.
5. Prepare material for the loom, and round as for spar.
6. Fit loom to blade and screw up dry.
7. Round the edges of the blade and fit copper tips.
8. Glue and screw up, taking care to make the screw heads flush.
9. Clean up for varnishing and fit telescopic brass tubing.
10. *Finish:* four coats of yacht varnish.

Spruce Paddle

When made entirely of spruce a paddle is more professional looking than the plywood blade pattern. It gives good practice in shooting joints and gluing up, the setting out of shaped work, the use of special planes for hollowing out, and the making and using of templates. The gluing up frame is an effective method for gluing up several paddles at a time.

Method

1. Prepare the material and glue up as shown opposite. Leave to dry.
2. Mark out the outline of the blade as for the previous paddle and cut to shape.
3. Make an edge template of cardboard and mark out the sweep on each edge.
4. Round the loom and shape the back of the blade.
5. Make templates as required for inside of blade.
6. Clean up hollows with a round bottom plane (these small planes are often made by the woodworker).
7. Round edges and clean up for varnishing. Fit telescopic brass tubing and copper tips.
8. *Finish:* four coats of yacht varnish.

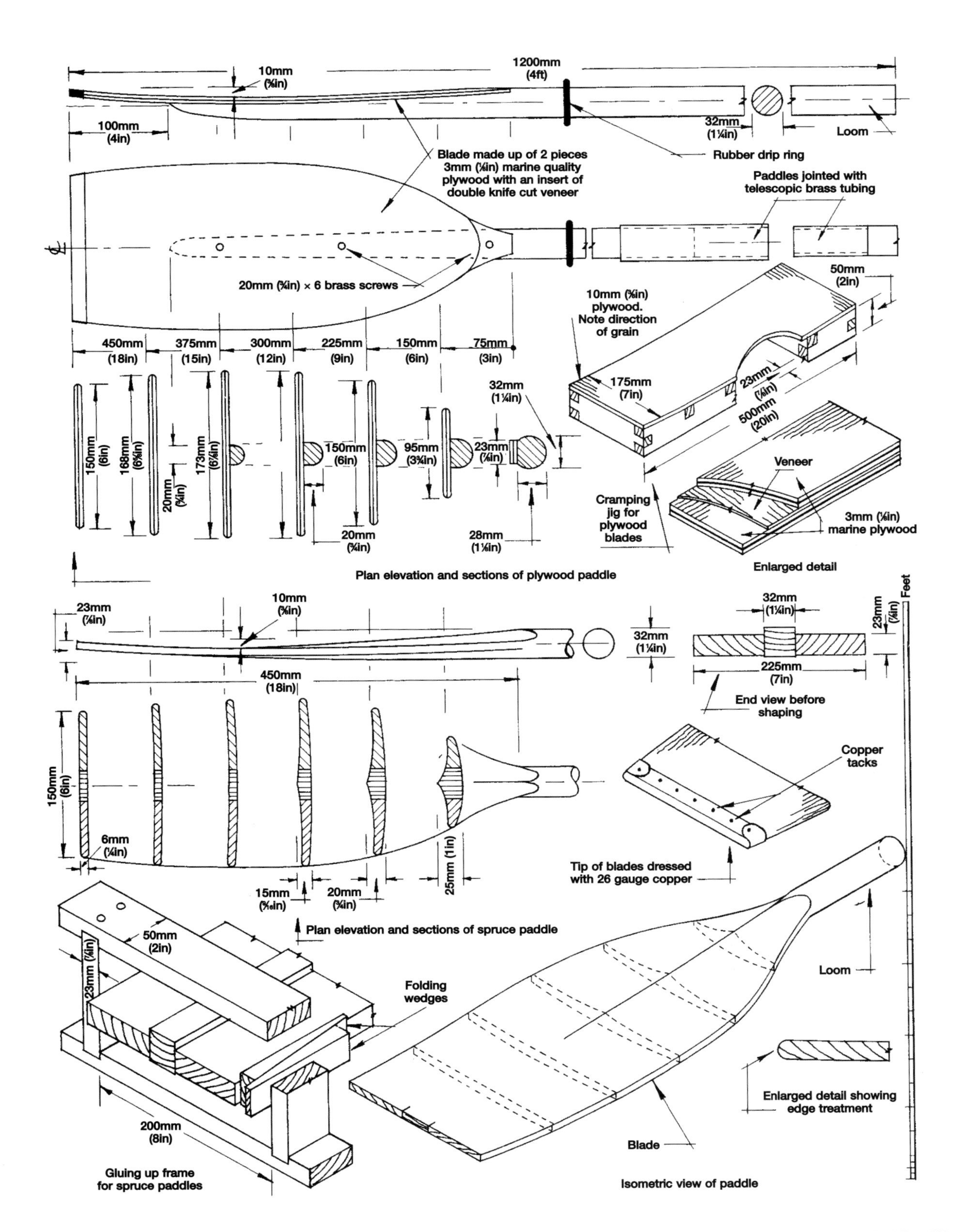
1200mm
(4ft)
10mm
(⅜in)
100mm
(4in)
32mm
(1¼in)
Loom
Blade made up of 2 pieces
3mm (⅛in) marine quality
plywood with an insert of
double knife cut veneer
Rubber drip ring
Paddles jointed with
telescopic brass tubing
20mm (¾in) × 6 brass screws
450mm
(18in)
375mm
(15in)
300mm
(12in)
225mm
(9in)
150mm
(6in)
75mm
(3in)
150mm
(6in)
168mm
(6⅝in)
20mm
(¾in)
173mm
(6⅞in)
150mm
(6in)
95mm
(3¾in)
32mm
(1¼in)
23mm
(⅞in)
20mm
(¾in)
28mm
(1⅛in)
10mm (⅜in)
plywood.
Note direction
of grain
50mm
(2in)
175mm
(7in)
23mm
(⅞in)
500mm
(20in)
Veneer
Cramping
jig for
plywood
blades
3mm (⅛in)
marine plywood
Enlarged detail
Plan elevation and sections of plywood paddle
23mm
(⅞in)
10mm
(⅜in)
32mm
(1¼in)
450mm
(18in)
32mm
(1¼in)
225mm
(7in)
End view before
shaping
23mm
(⅞in)
Feet
150mm
(6in)
6mm
(¼in)
15mm
(⁹⁄₁₆in)
20mm
(¾in)
25mm (1in)
Copper
tacks
Tip of blades dressed
with 26 gauge copper
Plan elevation and sections of spruce paddle
50mm
(2in)
23mm (⅞in)
Folding
wedges
Loom
200mm
(8in)
Enlarged detail showing
edge treatment
Blade
Gluing up frame
for spruce paddles
Isometric view of paddle

Spar or Mast Making

Usually the plans and building instructions for a boat contain the mast specification and this should be strictly adhered to. According to the size and design, masts can be made out of the solid, or built up to make a hollow spar. In the early days of spar making, the spar-maker would shape their mast or spar, starting from the natural round of the tree. After removing the bark they would then proceed to square up and straighten the spar, checking carefully with a chalk line stretched the full length for alignment. Most of the waste would be removed with an adze before finishing with the jack plane. From the square they would then work through the various stages to form the round.

For a small mast, an economical method is to glue up two pieces of sitka spruce – a light and strong wood – taking care to match up the end grain as shown in a separate detail, page 229. After planing the surfaces to make a good joint, glue and cramp up, and leave to dry. Clean up to size and check dimensions. A slight entasis is usually allowed for in the dimensions. To round the spar mark out the octagonal section. A separate detail, opposite, shows the method of marking out with a gauge made by the spar-maker. This is an efficient and accurate method of setting out, and each end of the gauge must remain in contact with the sides as the gauge is moved along the spar taper. The illustration conveys the idea. A draw knife is an excellent tool for removing wood quickly, and is ideal for rough shaping the octagonal section, which is finished with a jack or trying plane. Next remove the corners to make sixteen sides and carefully continue removing the arrises until a satisfactory surface has been obtained. A spar-maker uses their hollow sole planes to finish with. A good rub with glasspaper (using a shaped rubber), starting with middle 2 and working through the grades to 0 should produce a good surface for varnishing.

The making and gluing up of a hollow mast is shown opposite. This type of mast is very light and strong. It is hollowed out and tested with templates for correct shape before gluing. Note cramping-up technique.

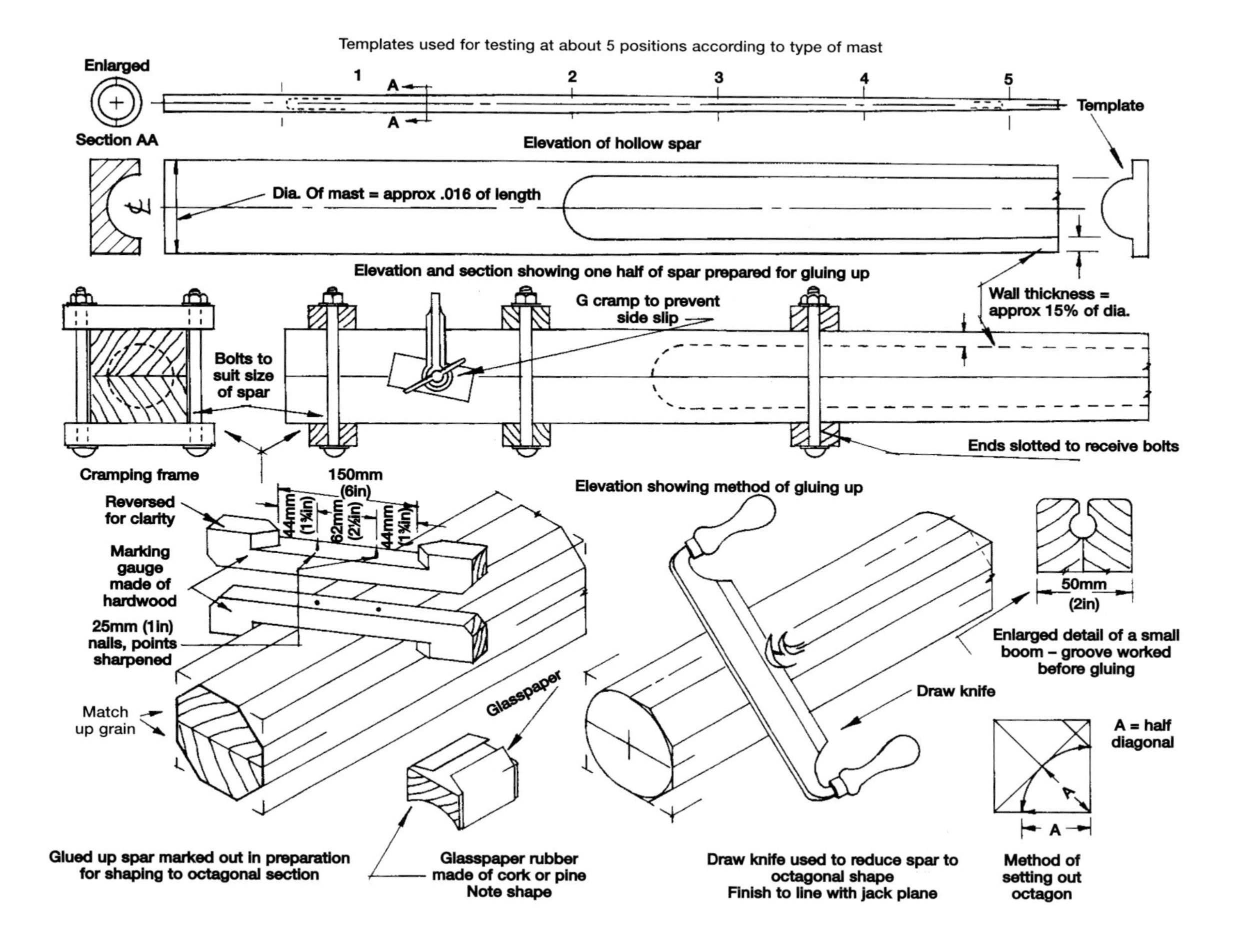
Templates used for testing at about 5 positions according to type of mast
Enlarged
Section AA
1
2
3
4
5
A
A
Template
Elevation of hollow spar
Dia. Of mast = approx .016 of length
Elevation and section showing one half of spar prepared for gluing up
Wall thickness = approx 15% of dia.
G cramp to prevent side slip
Bolts to suit size of spar
Ends slotted to receive bolts
Cramping frame
150mm (6in)
Elevation showing method of gluing up
Reversed for clarity
44mm (1¾in)
62mm (2½in)
44mm (1¾in)
Marking gauge made of hardwood
25mm (1in) nails, points sharpened
Match up grain
Glasspaper
50mm (2in)
Enlarged detail of a small boom – groove worked before gluing
Draw knife
A = half diagonal
A
A
Glued up spar marked out in preparation for shaping to octagonal section
Glasspaper rubber made of cork or pine Note shape
Draw knife used to reduce spar to octagonal shape Finish to line with jack plane
Method of setting out octagon

Boatbuilding

Boatbuilding is a rewarding craft and a celebration of our maritime heritage. The introduction of materials such as resin glues, marine quality plywood and fibre glass, widened the scope of boat designers and builders, who adapted new techniques to meet this challenge. One example, the 'hot-moulded' hull, consists of several layers of thin and narrow laminations glued on a former or mould which is the same shape as the hull. The mould surface is treated to prevent the glue adhering. The hull is then placed in a large rubber bag, and wheeled into an autoclave. It is then subjected to heat and pressure, which 'sets' the glue and laminations to form a shell which is the same shape as the former. This process gives a strong, light, homogeneous and waterproof hull. The introduction of waterproof plywood and the popularity of sailing has encouraged qualified designers to design special classes of boats with mainly the amateur boatbuilder in mind. They have simplified the construction so that large sheets of plywood can be used. The hard-chine method of construction is particularly suitable for this technique. The large majority of these small craft have been proved safe and reliable.

A sailing or rowing boat would make a stimulating project and could well be the beginning of a sailing or rowing club. The building of a canoe can provide a pleasant and useful introduction to boatbuilding. Information on suitable designs can be obtained from yachting magazines, to be found in most public libraries. Plans are available at a reasonable cost, and they generally give full-size details, and full particulars for making.

An elementary knowledge of boat geometry makes one more aware of the graceful lines that are part of a sailing boat or dinghy. A careful study of the drawings opposite should reveal the basic principles of lofting. *The buttock lines* are the shape given by the intersection through the hull, of vertical planes, which are parallel to the longitudinal central vertical plane. A water-line is a horizontal fore-and-aft plane. *Diagonals* are inclined planes passing through the fore-and-aft centre line and are often dispensed with in vee-bottom construction. The boatbuilder – loftsman – enlarges their plans to full size on the mould loft. This is a large floor usually painted black, on which he chalks the lines. Using a chalk line and battens, the loftsman commences by laying down all the straight lines, water-lines above base, buttocks in half breadth plan, diagonals and buttocks in body plan. For curved lines, long pine battens about 32mm (1¼in) square are required. For the *body plan* a thinner batten is necessary, depending on the sharpness of the curves. A separate drawing shows the method of marking-out frames using copper tacks. The use of a batten for marking out, and two useful methods for constructing beam curves are also given.

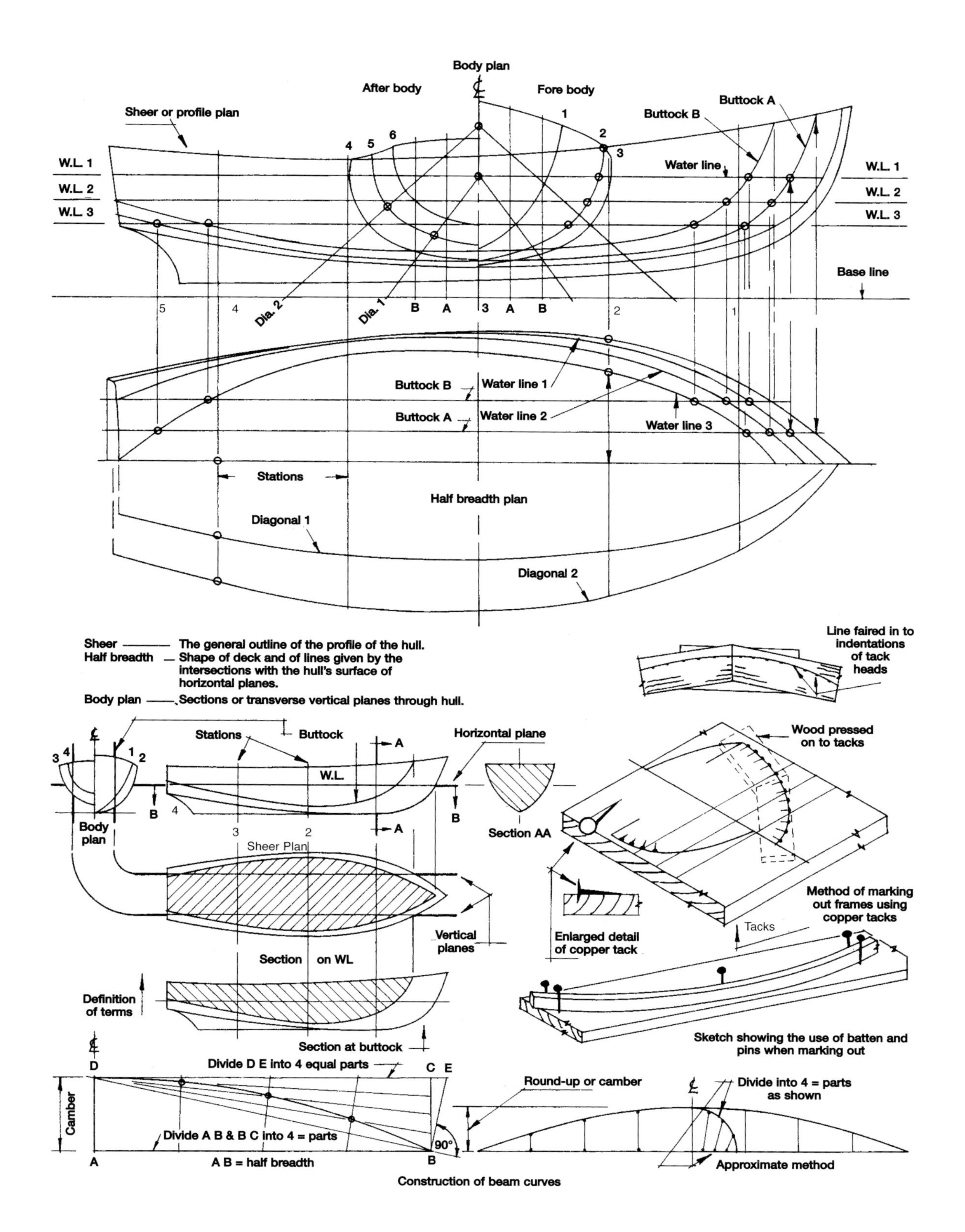
Body plan
After body
Fore body
Sheer or profile plan
Buttock A
Buttock B
Water line
W.L. 1
W.L. 2
W.L. 3
Base line
Dia. 2
Dia. 1
Buttock B
Water line 1
Buttock A
Water line 2
Water line 3
Stations
Half breadth plan
Diagonal 1
Diagonal 2
Sheer — The general outline of the profile of the hull.
Half breadth — Shape of deck and of lines given by the intersections with the hull's surface of horizontal planes.
Body plan — Sections or transverse vertical planes through hull.
Line faired in to indentations of tack heads
Stations
Buttock
Horizontal plane
W.L.
Body plan
Sheer Plan
Section AA
Wood pressed on to tacks
Vertical planes
Section on WL
Enlarged detail of copper tack
Tacks
Method of marking out frames using copper tacks
Definition of terms
Section at buttock
Sketch showing the use of batten and pins when marking out
Divide D E into 4 equal parts
Camber
Divide A B & B C into 4 = parts
A B = half breadth
Round-up or camber
Divide into 4 = parts as shown
Approximate method
Construction of beam curves

Boatbuilding Methods

The three principle methods of construction are: (1) Clinker, (2) Carvel, and (3) Vee-bottom or Hard-chine.

Clinker

This construction is easily distinguished by the overlapping planks or strakes, which are carefully bevelled to fit. It is an extremely skilful operation to fit the planks to the stem and transom. There is no projection at the intersection between stem and planks at these points. The planks must fit flush and snugly in the rebate at stem or transom. This is achieved by rebating and bevelling the top edge of the plank, commencing about 300mm (12in), according to the thickness of planking, from the end and bevelling the bottom edge of the adjacent plank to fit. All surfaces in contact must be treated with varnish or marine glue. Timbers are steamed and bent into position. The planks are fastened to the timbers by means of copper nails, which pass through the centre of the lap and timber. The nails are clenched – or riveted – on the inside. The landings are fastened every 50mm (2in) approximately between timbers. The plank adjacent to the keel, known as the garboard, is usually caulked.

Carvel, or Round-Bilge, Construction

The planks are fixed to timbers or frames, and butt against each other forming a flush surface. The planks are bevelled on their edges to form a seam in which caulking cotton is worked. A separate detail (figure 1) shows nailing technique. Copper boat nails are square in section and the wood must be drilled before driving in the nail. Nails are specified by the gauge, e.g. a No 10 is approximately 3mm (⅛in) square, and a No 16 is approximately 1.6mm (1/16in) square. Rooves are classified by their diameter and bought to suit the nails. After driving the nail through the drilled timber, a roove is punched on the projecting end, an assistant holds a 'dolly' hold-on or large hammer head to hold the nail in place. The end is cut off leaving about the thickness of the nail above the roove. The end is then carefully hammered to spread over the metal and draw up the nail. The completed rivet should be neat and cleanly rounded.

An enlarged detail shows a wedge fitted under the timbers to give a fixing to the garboard plank. Water-ways should always be cut as these are necessary to allow the bilge water to run freely along the hog and facilitates pumping out.

Vee-bottom, or Hard-chine, Construction

This type of craft is extremely light and easier to build than the previously mentioned types. The frames are positioned at approximately 600mm (24in) stations. When planking is used the seam battens run from stem to transom and are housed in flush with the outside of the frames. The planks are butted on the seam battens and nailed. The nails are turned on the inside (see separate detail; figure 2 shows a good method of constructing frames). The frames are halved at the chine and reinforced with plywood gussets. The method of fixing the plywood is also shown. Figure 3 shows a double skin construction. An inner skin, laid diagonally, is covered with fine cotton lawn and the outer skin laid longitudinally. The cotton is oiled, and the inside surfaces of the planks are painted with white lead. The two skins are also clench-nailed making a first class hull.

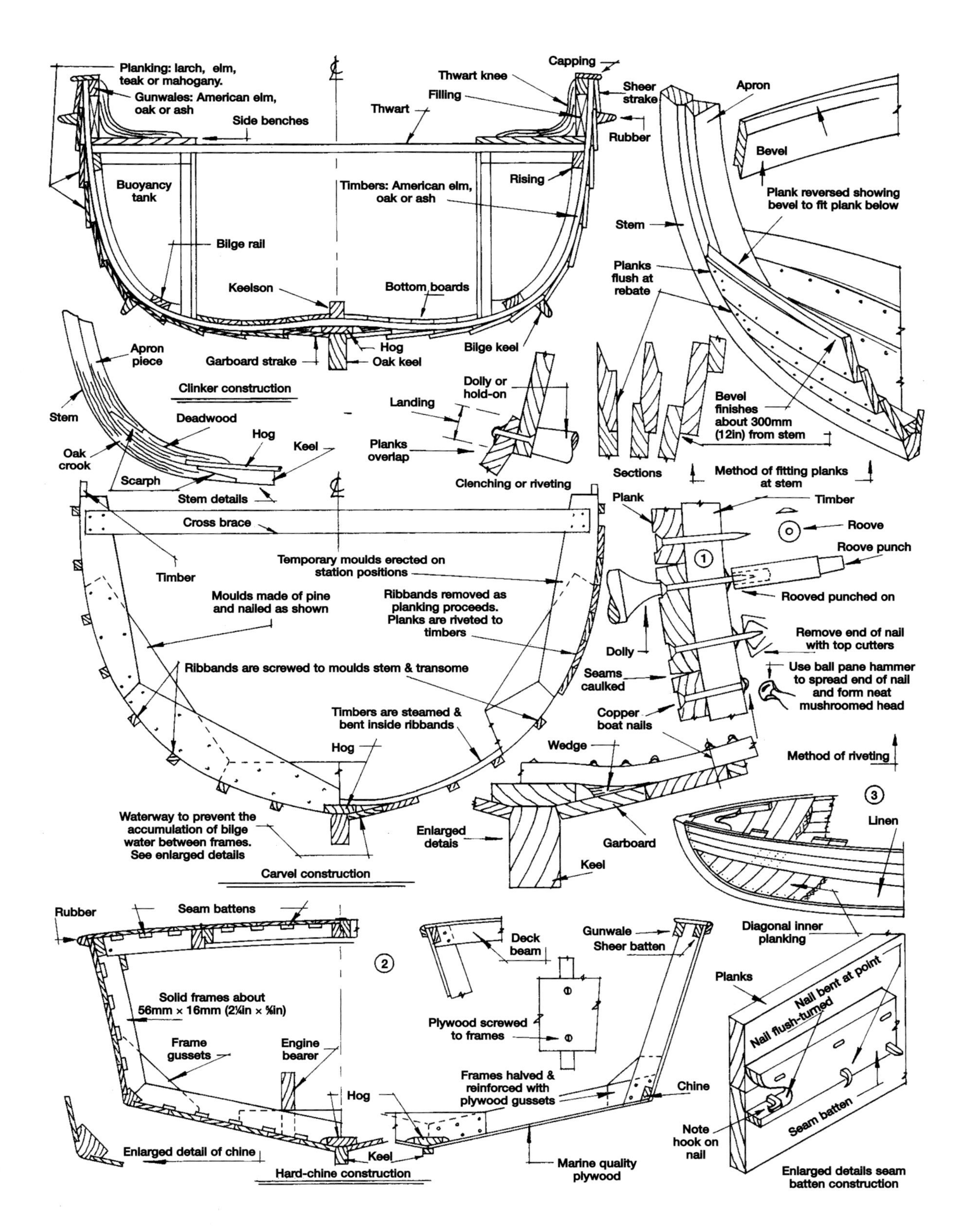
Planking: larch, elm, teak or mahogany.
Gunwales: American elm, oak or ash
Side benches
Thwart
Filling
Thwart knee
Capping
Sheer strake
Rubber
Rising
Buoyancy tank
Timbers: American elm, oak or ash
Bilge rail
Keelson
Bottom boards
Hog
Oak keel
Garboard strake
Bilge keel
Clinker construction
Apron piece
Stem
Deadwood
Hog
Keel
Oak crook
Scarph
Stem details
Landing
Dolly or hold-on
Planks overlap
Clenching or riveting
Apron
Bevel
Plank reversed showing bevel to fit plank below
Stem
Planks flush at rebate
Bevel finishes about 300mm (12in) from stem
Sections
Method of fitting planks at stem
Cross brace
Timber
Temporary moulds erected on station positions
Moulds made of pine and nailed as shown
Ribbands removed as planking proceeds. Planks are riveted to timbers
Ribbands are screwed to moulds stem & transome
Timbers are steamed & bent inside ribbands
Hog
Waterway to prevent the accumulation of bilge water between frames. See enlarged details
Carvel construction
Plank
Timber
Roove
Roove punch
Rooved punched on
Dolly
Remove end of nail with top cutters
Seams caulked
Use ball pane hammer to spread end of nail and form neat mushroomed head
Copper boat nails
Method of riveting
Wedge
Enlarged details
Garboard
Keel
Linen
Diagonal inner planking
Rubber
Seam battens
Solid frames about 56mm × 16mm (2¼in × ⅝in)
Frame gussets
Engine bearer
Hog
Keel
Hard-chine construction
Enlarged detail of chine
Deck beam
Plywood screwed to frames
Gunwale
Sheer batten
Frames halved & reinforced with plywood gussets
Chine
Marine quality plywood
Planks
Nail bent at point
Nail flush-turned
Seam batten
Note hook on nail
Enlarged details seam batten construction

Setting up a Boat

On completion of the lofting, the professional boatbuilder prepares the frames or moulds from the body plan, after deducting the plank thickness. This is necessary as all offsets – measurements giving ordinates of the various curves when lofting – are taken to the outside of the planking. Patterns are made of the keel, stem and apron piece, and most of the preparation and assembly of these members can be completed on the bench. Stocks are set up to fit the underside of the keel, the whole assembly being lifted into position, and securely braced so that the stem is plumb. Stations are set out on the hog and the frames erected in their correct position. The frames are checked for plumb and squareness, and are well braced to ensure rigidity. The boatbuilder often braces the frames to the workshop rafters.

Boats can also be built keel uppermost. The hard-chine type, with planking of waterproof plywood, is easily adaptable to this method. It facilitates planking and this method is particularly suitable for school and club workshops. The drawings opposite show the main features of building, and setting up, but practically all the designs available for small craft give full particulars.

Layout Board

Make full-size drawings of each frame on a piece of plywood. This simplifies the frame making.

Making the Frames

Some frames are halved together and stiffened up with plywood gussets. The frame assembly shown on the layout board is butted at the chine and on the centre line. It is reinforced with solid wood gussets and provides a good fixing for the chines. The frames are temporarily tacked in position, while the gussets are glued and screwed to the frames. Fix a cross band on the frame, mark out centre lines and cut out for hog, chines and gunwales. The marked side of each frame is called the moulded face. Where the design specifies extended frames for fixing, mark out centre line and frame position on the floor. Small locating blocks are fixed to the floor, and the frames are secured to these. Check frames for alignment and for plumb before fixing, and when correct, brace the frames with temporary battens. Fit stem and transom. Mark out and cut the forward end of the gunwale and fit to stem. Screw up temporarily. Bend carefully and 'G' cramp gunwale to frame cut-outs. For a sharp bend cover the timber with clean rags or sacking and pour on boiling water. Leave for approximately 10 minutes before bending. Should the timber not respond to this treatment, steam the end in a steam box. Mark length and bevel at transom, cut and fit in. When dry glue and complete screwing, use the same technique for fitting the chines and risers (see figures 1 and 2). To equalise the pull when fitting gunwales, chines and planking it is important to fix port and starboard members alternately.

Fairing-up the Framework

A batten about 1350mm × 25mm × 6mm (4ft 6in × 1in × ¼in) held and sprung along the frames will indicate which ones need planing. (See separate drawing showing how the frames are faired in.)

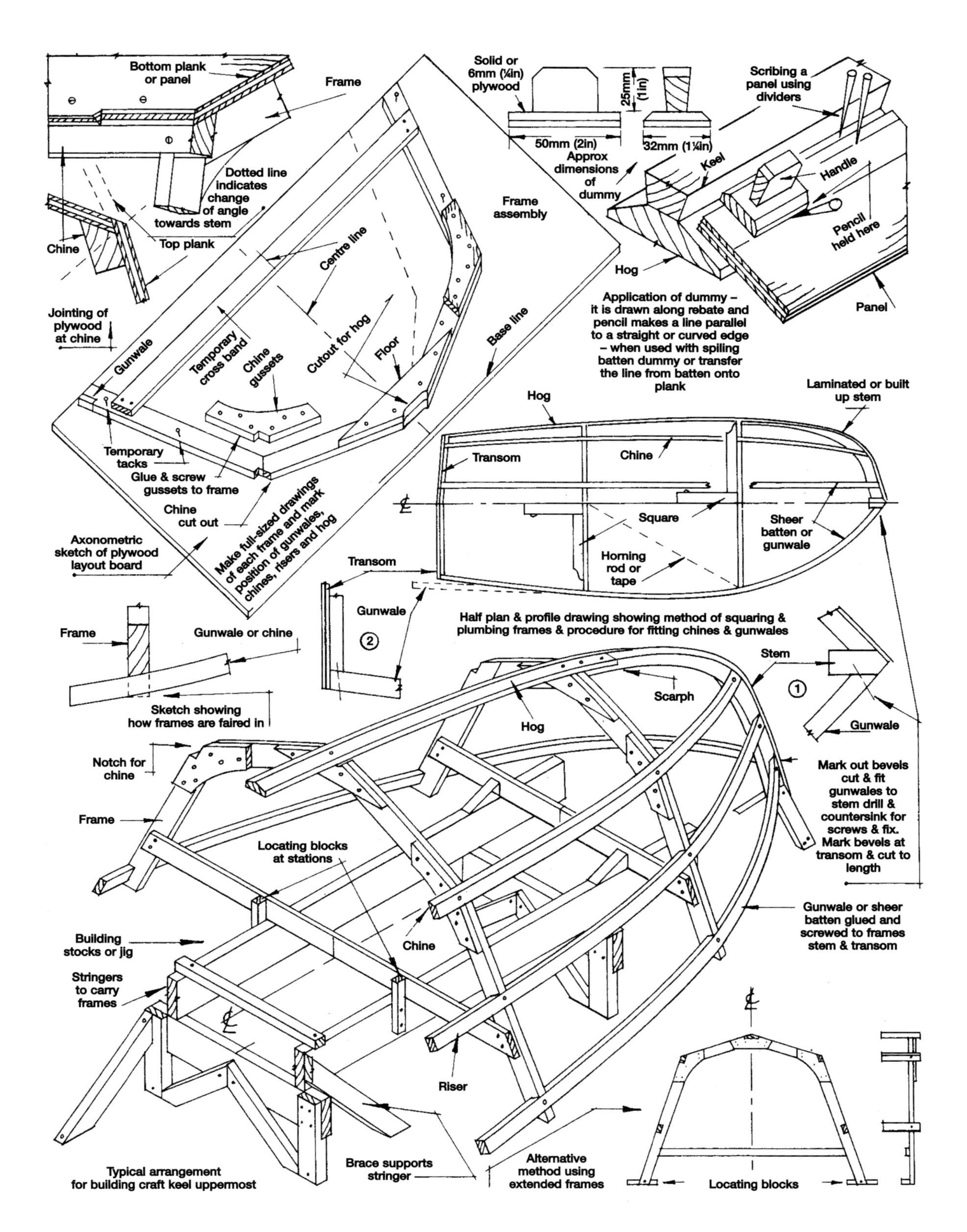
Bottom plank or panel
Frame
Dotted line indicates change of angle towards stem
Chine
Top plank
Jointing of plywood at chine
Frame assembly
Centre line
Gunwale
Temporary cross band
Chine gussets
Cutout for hog
Floor
Base line
Temporary tacks
Glue & screw gussets to frame
Chine cut out
Axonometric sketch of plywood layout board
Make full-sized drawings of each frame and mark position of gunwales, chines, risers and hog
Solid or 6mm (¼in) plywood
25mm (1in)
50mm (2in)
32mm (1¼in)
Approx dimensions of dummy
Keel
Scribing a panel using dividers
Handle
Pencil held here
Hog
Panel
Application of dummy – it is drawn along rebate and pencil makes a line parallel to a straight or curved edge – when used with spiling batten dummy or transfer the line from batten onto plank
Hog
Laminated or built up stem
Transom
Chine
Square
Sheer batten or gunwale
Horning rod or tape
Transom
Gunwale
2
Half plan & profile drawing showing method of squaring & plumbing frames & procedure for fitting chines & gunwales
Frame
Gunwale or chine
Sketch showing how frames are faired in
Stem
Scarph
Hog
1
Gunwale
Notch for chine
Frame
Locating blocks at stations
Mark out bevels cut & fit gunwales to stem drill & countersink for screws & fix. Mark bevels at transom & cut to length
Building stocks or jig
Chine
Gunwale or sheer batten glued and screwed to frames stem & transom
Stringers to carry frames
Riser
Typical arrangement for building craft keel uppermost
Brace supports stringer
Alternative method using extended frames
Locating blocks

Separate drawings give details of marking out and fixing of plywood planks. Fit the bottom planks first. A good quality building paper placed, without wrinkles, over the frames and marked out to locate the chine and keel positions provides a good pattern for awkward shapes.

Useful Tools for Boatbuilding

Jack plane, metal
Smoothing plane, metal, 50mm (2in) cutter
Draw knife
Paring chisels
Spokeshave, flat, 54mm (2⅛in)
Panel saw
Coping saw
Wheelbrace and set of drills
Boat bevel
Boat level 225mm (9in)
Adjustable try square
Screwdrivers
Light hammer with ball pane
Dolly or hold-on
Pair of top cutting pliers
Roove punch
Wood rasp, 200mm (8in)
Flat metal file
Straight edge
Several light battens for bending
Chalk line
'G' cramps

Index